THE VULGAR QUESTION OF MONEY

THE VULGAR QUESTION OF
MONEY

HEIRESSES, MATERIALISM, AND THE NOVEL OF MANNERS FROM JANE AUSTEN TO HENRY JAMES

ELSIE B. MICHIE

THE JOHNS HOPKINS UNIVERSITY PRESS
BALTIMORE

The Johns Hopkins University Press
2715 North Charles Street
Baltimore, Maryland 21218-4363
www.press.jhu.edu

Library of Congress Cataloging-in-Publication Data
Michie, Elsie B. (Elsie Browning), 1948–
    The vulgar question of money : heiresses, materialism, and the novel of
manners from Jane Austen to Henry James / Elsie B. Michie.
        p. cm.
    Includes bibliographical references and index.
    ISBN-13: 978-1-4214-0186-7 (hardcover : alk. paper)
    ISBN-10: 1-4214-0186-x (hardcover : alk. paper)
    1. English fiction—19th century—History and criticism. 2. Material
culture in literature. 3. Money in literature. 4. Material culture—Great
Britain—History—19th century. 5. Great Britain—Social life and
customs—19th century. I. Title.
    PR878.M38M53 2011
    823′.8093553—dc22   2010050251

A catalog record for this book is available from the British Library.

*Special discounts are available for bulk purchases of this book. For more
information, please contact Special Sales at 410-516-6936 or specialsales@
press.jhu.edu.*

The Johns Hopkins University Press uses environmentally friendly book
materials, including recycled text paper that is composed of at least 30 per-
cent post-consumer waste, whenever possible.

For Emily, Sarah, and Molly,
who grew up while this book was being written

CONTENTS

VULGARITY, WEALTH, AND GENDER

When I began working on this book it had become the fashion to introduce academic papers by telling personal anecdotes—a custom initiated, I think, by the epilogue to *Renaissance Self-Fashioning*, in which Stephen Greenblatt tells the story of sitting next to a man on a plane who is going to visit his hospitalized son who has lost the ability to speak and the will to live. I used to begin the papers that eventually formed this book by explaining that I became interested in the rich woman in the nineteenth-century novel after my mother died and left me money she had inherited from her mother and kept in her own name even after she was married. Jokingly, I called that money my matrimony since I was unmarried and it was, in effect, my patrimony.

But telling the story of my inheritance did not work as such anecdotes were supposed to do. It did not elicit sympathy or engage the audience's attention. Instead, as I spoke, listeners' eyes stopped meeting mine. My audience became restless and began to cough and shuffle. They looked down at their feet and seemed to be overcome by what Christopher Herbert has called "a panicky dread of indelicate references to money matters" ("Filthy" 199). It was as if they were literally feeling what we call the embarrassment of riches. One should speak of money in the refined, almost inaudible tones associated with the quiet of banks with their marble halls or of investment offices with their deep carpets. One should reveal it only indirectly as in the haute couture clothes that are so understated that only the cognoscenti know how much they cost. When I talked about my inheritance, I was, like the fashions typically chosen by the nouveau riche and the heiresses I write about here, being too loud, too explicit about the possession of wealth. The term the Victorians would have used to describe my behavior was "vulgar," a word that carried such affective force in the period that the narrator of Anthony Trollope's *The Prime Minister* (1876) can exclaim, "Vulgarity! There was no other word in the language so hard to bear as that" (177).

For us in the late modern era vulgarity is more commonly associated with sexuality and the body than with wealth. But, for the Victorians, it was wedded to what the Reverend Edward Irving called, with some distaste, the "visible element of money" that helps "our sordid minds in the estimation of it" (277). We are tempted, I think, to assume that vulgarity in this sense has lost its power. It is the Victorian era with its heavy furniture and obsession with material objects that was the acme of vulgarity. As Gilbert Osmond tells Caspar Goodwood toward the end of Henry James's *The Portrait of a Lady* (1881), "I don't find vulgarity, at all, before the present century. You see a faint menace of it here and there in the last, but today the air has grown so dense that delicate things are literally not recognized" (444). Coming from the mouth of a peculiarly unpleasant aesthete, this comment shows how easy it is to condemn the Victorians not just for their vulgarity but also for their excessive sensibility over what constitutes vulgar as opposed to refined behavior.

The reaction of my audience when I described my inheritance suggests, however, that we may not be so different from our Victorian predecessors as we might like to think. The distaste for explicit references to money persists even into the twenty-first century; we continue to feel revulsion for what Max Weber calls in *The Protestant Ethic and the Spirit of Capitalism* "that activity directed to acquisition for its own sake [which] was at bottom a *pudendum* which was to be tolerated only because of the unalterable necessities of life in this world" (35). The point, I take it, of Weber's comment is that, while the act of making money can be represented as an expression of the Protestant work ethic, the actual possession and accrual of wealth has something repulsive about it.

Giovanni Arrighi has noted that the fear of accumulation haunts the rhetoric of those writing about nineteenth-century capitalism, providing as two examples Karl Marx's "facetious dictum 'Accumulate, accumulate!'" and Weber's "serious contention that the essence of the capitalist spirit is 'the earning of more and more money . . . so purely as an end in itself, that from the point of view of the happiness of, or utility to, the single individual, it appears entirely transcendental and absolutely irrational'" (229). The term that Jane Austen's contemporaries would have used to describe this position was engrossment. It is this idea of engrossment—of possessing, amassing, and using money for its own sake—that is incarnated in the nineteenth-century novel's rich women or heiresses. In considering the gender of these representations I want to return for a minute to Weber's use of "pudendum" to convey disgust at the acquisition of money. That word marks the shift that takes place as we move from the nineteenth to the twentieth century, when the shame of vulgarity begins to be less linked to class relations than articulated through sexual imagery. But the word is particularly interesting because although in fact it references the genitals of both genders, it is much more commonly used to describe the woman's rather than the man's body. This gender difference reflects what I argue here: that the distaste we feel for indelicate references to wealth and acquisition for their own sakes is more likely to be triggered by female rather than male figures and is most powerfully associated with rich women or heiresses.

In *Outline of a Theory of Practice* Pierre Bourdieu has argued, of men's and women's differing relation to money, that "the urge to calculate, repressed in men, finds more overt expression in women, who are structurally predisposed to be less concerned with the symbolic profits accruing from political unity, and to devote themselves more readily to strictly economic practices" (62). To understand how this gender difference works in fiction, one has only to look at the first novel I discuss, Jane Austen's *Pride and Prejudice* (1813). There Miss Bingley and Lady Catherine de Bourgh are represented as crassly vulgar in a way their male counterparts never are. Mr. Bingley and Mr. Darcy are the novel's romantic heroes, while their female relatives become its scapegoats; they bear the taints associated with the possession of wealth in the stead of their male relatives. The novel's male wealth holders have access to the elevated sphere of ineffable symbolic values Bourdieu describes, while its female wealth holders do not.

This representational difference persists in contemporary culture, in which women of wealth tend not to be depicted in the same way as their male counterparts. As Sally Bingham has argued, "Americans need to transform rich women into witches, evil stepmothers, criminals convicted of no crime except that of using their money (or what they thought was their money before some man claimed it) in a public way" (quoted in Randall 111). This demonization is clearly seen in the differing treatments of Leona Helmsley and Donald Trump in the mid-1980s, when both were in the news as hotel magnates, she taking on the infamous title the "Queen of Mean." I am sure readers can think of other examples, the depictions of Martha Stewart or Teresa Heinz Kerry, for instance, or of the Hilton sisters. The fascinated revulsion audiences feel for the wealthy woman is reflected in television producers' assumption that *The Real Housewives* of almost any American region will be more vulgarly interesting than their wealthy husbands.

I am, however, less interested in a critical enterprise that would rescue such figures from an opprobrium that may or may not be unfair than in thinking about why and how gender is used as an axis or, I might even say, an axe that makes it possible to create the split Bourdieu describes between symbolic and material profits. That split allows readers to feel that in gaining access to the former, they are able to distance themselves from the latter. It inheres in the term "vulgarity" with the association with money it acquired in the Victorian era. It recurs when, as in the newspaper caricatures of Leona Helmsley or Austen's narrative mockery of Miss Bingley or Lady Catherine de Bourgh, we feel what Bourdieu has called "the visceral disgust at vulgarity which defines pure taste as an internalized social relationship, a social relationship made flesh" (*Distinction* 499–500).

But we hear the grinding of that axe of difference even in statements that feel almost emotionally neutral, as when critics distinguish what they call "vulgar" Marxism from other purportedly more nuanced practices. Here, as in the gender dichotomy that Bourdieu describes, one set of critical approaches is defined as overly concerned with material issues, while the other is positioned as being able to transcend those issues by exploring the more rarified field of ideology (surely a version of Bourdieu's symbolic profits). This distinction suggests that, even for those explicitly interested in economic forces, there is an impulse, almost what one would call a knee-jerk reaction, that inclines one to distance oneself from the materialism one is examining by identifying a position that one labels "too close" to those monetary practices. There is in our culture a sense that both money and femininity threaten to slip over into a realm that we view as excessively material, a realm associated with both substance and the body. When money and femininity are brought together in the wealthy woman, cultural anxieties about excessive closeness to materialism are doubled. As a result of this intensification, the heiress became the natural locus of the nineteenth-century novel's exploration of capitalism's loathing of its own propensity to amass wealth.

In his anthropological analyses of village life, Bourdieu found that the women's dealings were "closer to the economic truth of exchange than the men's dealings" (*Outline* 62). In the novel, the rich woman or heiress is closer to the economic truths of nineteenth-century exchange than male characters, who seem more directly connected with economic instruments like the stock market. Through her the novel articulates what its contemporary readers feared about the economic developments that transformed England over the course of the nineteenth century. However, this explicit association with materialism makes fictional depictions of the rich woman particularly difficult to address. As W. H. Auden once jokingly wrote of Jane Austen,

> It makes me most uncomfortable to see
> An English spinster of the middle-class
> Describe the amorous effects of 'brass,'
> Reveal so frankly and with such sobriety
> The economic basis of society. (21)

This is the discomfort my audience experienced when I introduced my work by telling the story of my inheritance. As a woman talking explicitly about money, I placed myself in a narrative tradition that was familiar to them, a tradition that goes back as far as Lady Catherine and Miss Bingley and forward to Lady Bracknell in Oscar Wilde's *The Importance of Being Earnest* (1895), in which rich women talk too loudly about their wealth and become figures we laugh at and disparage.

In telling that story I was violating the underlying principle of such anecdotes, which, as the case of Greenblatt's famous conversation with the passenger with the dying relative indicates, were supposed to be about sympathy. But, as the conclusion of the Greenblatt anecdote also shows, there are moments when we find ourselves incapable of a fully sympathetic act. We can all be moved by the recalcitrance of what Greenblatt calls our "stubborn hold on selfhood" (257). The term "selfhood" makes this quality sound more appealing than it does if we use instead the phrase Percy Shelley employs in "A Defence of Poetry" when he describes "the principle of Self, of which money is the visible incarnation" (531). In the novels I analyze here the rich woman embodies this principle. The problem literary critics have approaching her is that so much of our critical enterprise is based on finding new sites of sympathy.

How do we acknowledge the importance of literary figures that are fundamentally unsympathetic yet also key to the structures the novel uses to articulate sympathy? Linked to materialism through both money and gender, the rich woman seems to be a character whose meaning is so vulgarly explicit and so superficial it is hardly worth paying attention to her. As D. A. Miller has argued in a slightly different context, it feels as if she "matters *because* [she] doesn't signify, and vice versa" ("The Late Jane Austen" 61, emphasis in the original). Instead of accepting the opposition between signification and materialism that is implicit in the dichotomy Bourdieu describes between men's and women's dealings and between high art and vulgarity, I read the materialism that is referenced through fictional portraits of rich women as significant. Examining the details of the heiress's representation in novels from Austen to James, I show how she transforms our readings of the nineteenth-century marriage plot by revealing an interest in and anxiety about economic developments in the place where we least expect or want to find those materialist concerns, at the heart of romantic stories about the triumph of love over money.

ACKNOWLEDGMENTS

In thanking the many people who have helped me bring *The Vulgar Question of Money* to fruition, I have to begin with my colleague Robert Hamm, who has read more drafts of these chapters than anyone should. My other writing groups, which consisted of Daniel Novak, Sharon Weltman, and Pallavi Rastogi and Jacob Berman, Lauren Coats, and Matt Sandler, were also key in helping me finish the book. At an earlier point in time, a writing group that consisted of Rick Moreland, Dana Nelson, and Reggie Young enabled me to formulate the terms of my argument. I am particularly grateful to Dana who asked the hard questions I am still trying to answer. My colleagues Brooke Rollins and Michelle Massé both read parts of the manuscript and gave me useful feedback. I especially want to thank the reader for the Johns Hopkins University Press, John Kucich, who provided an encouraging and insightful report that enabled me to go beyond the place where I thought my argument stopped. The group of people I met through my involvement with INCS (Interdisciplinary Nineteenth-Century Studies) has seen me through both the project and life crises. In particular, I thank Deborah Denenholz Morse for inviting me to air my ideas about Anthony Trollope at Exeter and Mary Jean Corbett for reading chapters at key moments and responding quickly with useful advice. I am grateful to the Dickens Universe and the people associated with it, who have enabled me to present parts of this material in a venue where it received insightful responses. My thanks go particularly to John Jordan, Helena Michie, and Gerhard Joseph, all of whom were intensely encouraging. I also want to thank my associate professor support group, Teresa Mangum, Tricia Lootens, and Carolyn Williams, especially for their virtual toasts to success. The list of people who have read or heard parts of this argument and aided in its development is long and probably not complete. I thank Kathy Psomiades, Sharon Marcus, James Thompson, Devoney Looser, Mary Ann O'Farrell, Harry Shaw, Laurie Langbauer, Beth Newman, Susan David Bernstein, Susan Griffin, Lauren Goodlad, and others for all they have taught me about my project. Andrew Miller proved to be one of the world's superlative editors when he helped me shape material connected to this project for publication in *Victorian Studies*. An ATLAS grant from the Louisiana Board of Regents gave me a year free from teaching to complete the project. My partner, Phil Adams, fussed me when I needed it and believed in me throughout.

Parts of the introduction are taken from my essay "Rich Woman / Poor Woman: Toward an Anthropology of the Nineteenth-Century Marriage Plot," which appeared in *PMLA* 124.2 (2009) and is reprinted by permission of the Modern Language Association. Parts of chapter 1 are taken from "Austen's Powers: Engaging with Adam Smith in Debates about Wealth and Virtue," published in *Novel* 34.1 (2000), reprinted by permission of the publisher, Duke University Press.

RICH WOMAN / POOR WOMAN

AN ANTHROPOLOGY OF THE NINETEENTH-CENTURY
MARRIAGE PLOT

He invests his books . . . with a sort of atmosphere which is not incapable of being
condensed into the moral that people ought to marry for love and not for money.

Review of Anthony Trollope's *Doctor Thorne*

This book explores one of the most common marriage plots in the nineteenth-
century English novel: the story of a hero positioned between a wealthy, materialistic, status-conscious woman who might enhance his social position and a poorer,
more altruistic, and psychologically independent woman who is the antipode of
her rich rival. This bifurcated narrative structure emerges with particular clarity in
those novels that have come down to us as enduringly popular classics of the era. In
Jane Austen's *Pride and Prejudice*, for example, society supposes Fitzwilliam Darcy
will marry either the commercially wealthy Miss Bingley or the daughter of the
landed Lady Catherine de Bourgh, but he chooses instead the genteelly impoverished Elizabeth Bennet. In Charlotte Brontë's *Jane Eyre*, Rochester is married to the
wealthy and big-bodied Bertha Mason and pretends to court the similarly endowed
Blanche Ingram but learns to love the tiny and unpropertied Jane Eyre. And in
Charles Dickens's *Great Expectations*, readers know that Pip would be happier if he
rejected the bejeweled and haughty Estella and married the warm and familiar but
disadvantaged Biddy whose shoes are trodden down at the heels. Such plots insist,
as Frances Trollope explains in *The Life and Adventures of a Clever Woman*, that if
the hero is to be virtuous he must choose a wife "without feeling constrained to
make the vulgar question of money the prominent object" (2.112).[1]

But in order for the ideal marriage to be achieved, the novel must include in its
panorama of characters a rich woman who represents the vulgarity and wealth the
hero must eschew. This rich woman is the subject of my book; she is the vehicle
through which nineteenth-century novelists articulate cultural anxieties about the
changing forms of money and their impact. She is the symbolic lynchpin that

makes it possible for the novel to extol, by negation, the values she does not embody. Bourdieu makes a statement at the end of *Outline of Theory of Practice* that allows us to grasp the rich woman's function in abstract terms. There he argues that the world of art presents itself as "a sacred island systematically and ostentatiously opposed to the profane, everyday world of production, a sanctuary for gratuitous, disinterested activity in a universe given over to money and self-interest" (197). Through a plot structure that positions a hero between two women, one identified with wealth and the other with poverty, the novelist is able to create a romantic narrative in which characters enact in miniature the choice between the pragmatic claims of the material world and the disinterested values that art espouses.

In choosing to focus on the negative figure in this configuration, the woman who represents the economic pressures the novel seeks to rise above, I am both resisting the impulse of the narrative to ignore or deny the importance of such materialist forces and heeding the advice that Bourdieu gives at the end of *Distinction*. In a postscript to this account of the workings of taste in various classes of French society, he advocates what he calls "a 'vulgar' critique of 'pure' critiques" (485). He uses that position to criticize the arguments of writers like Derrida by showing how, even as they make deconstructive moves, they still participate in a centuries-long intellectual pattern in which critics distance themselves from the vulgar in order to establish their own thinking as pure. They insist on presenting their work as "a disinterested activity in a universe given over to money and self-interest." Bourdieu's critical reading suggests that we might find traces of vulgarity at the heart of narratives that seem most focused on the idea of purity. What would happen if we were to bring this vulgar position to the foreground of our critical analyses of the nineteenth-century novel? What do we see if we refuse the critical gesture that establishes our distance from vulgarity? What changes when we focus on the materialist strain that is a necessary component of novels we love because they resist it? How must we rethink the terrain of the novel once we recognize that the rich woman must be present in order to represent the values that are defined against her?

Another way to think about this critical intervention is in terms of the feelings of repulsion and attraction that are mobilized in the contrast between the rich and the poor woman. Sianne Ngai has argued in the afterword to *Ugly Feelings* that

> the striking asymmetry between the careers of disgust and desire in literary and cultural theory raises the broader question of why repulsion has such a long history of being overshadowed by attraction as a theoretical concern, even as we

can plausibly assert that the late capitalist lifeworld is one in which there are at least as many things to turn away from—the strong centripetal pull of consumer culture notwithstanding—as things to be drawn toward. (333)

Both Ngai and Bourdieu insist that our criticism might take a new form if we paid more attention to disgust and vulgarity, but they make that point in the margins or limits of their own texts, in afterwords that function, in Bourdieu's terms, as postscripts to documents that are in some way complete without them. This is, of course, the way readers are invited to view the rich woman in the nineteenth-century novel, as a marginal figure that is exorcised from the novel's main story when it concludes with a hero and heroine who make a marriage based on values other than financial ones.

In this book I put money, vulgarity, and disgust first rather than introducing them as afterthoughts. This gesture transforms the way the relations between gender, property, desire, and exchange have typically been understood to operate in the novel. The model for explaining such relations, the one posited by Gayle Rubin in "The Traffic in Women" and developed by Eve Sedgwick in *Between Men*, involves a singular object of desire, a woman positioned between two men. Once, however, we think of the female object of desire as split between a negative and a positive aspect, a rich and poor woman, the person one should marry and the person one should not, then the space in which property is exchanged ceases to be monolithic. Instead, it is occupied by two antithetical figures and becomes a locus of activity, a space of oscillation between materialist and antimaterialist values. In the model I posit for understanding the link between property and desire in the nineteenth-century novel there are not three but four positions: the two men who are engaged in the exchange and a female position, which is also doubled.[2] If, as one of Anthony Trollope's nineteenth-century critics commented, the novel of manners "is like the attempt of a geometrician to solve by plane geometry a problem which requires geometry of three dimensions" (Smalley 344), we can add in the extra dimension by paying attention to the heiress. She is a figure associated with wealth whose presence in the text makes visible the economic and social arguments that are interwoven into stories of marriage for love rather than money. The rich woman both marks the presence of materialism in the text and has a key function in its symbolic order.

That function can best be understood by conceiving the marriage plot of the nineteenth-century novel as following the patterns of myth as Jacques Lacan explains them in "The Neurotic's Individual Myth."[3] In that essay, Lacan argues that we need to complicate what has traditionally been seen as a triangular model of desire. This model is the one implicit in the Freudian conception of the Oedipus complex, which typically describes a triangle like the one Rubin maps out in "The Traffic in Women" that involves two men and a woman, since the child is generally assumed to be male. But Lacan insists that neurosis is a four- rather than a three-sided structure. In his words, "There is within the neurotic a quartet situation which is endlessly renewed" (416). Appropriately for my argument, Lacan derives this conclusion from rereading Freud's case history of the Ratman, whose neurosis arises because his object of desire is split between a rich and a poor woman. The Ratman's father, as a subordinate officer in the army, chose to marry a woman who was richer and of higher status than he, knowing that her wealth would forward him in his profession. This marriage was, however, distasteful to the Ratman, whose mother mocked his father for having been in love with a woman who was poorer and prettier than she was. The father's dilemma was repeated in the son "when his father urged him to marry a rich woman, and it was then that the neurosis proper had its onset" (411). Here the choice between the rich and the poor woman represents a fracture in the Ratman's psyche, as he is torn between pragmatic material desires and romantic antimaterialist ones and cannot conceive of himself as whole.

For Lacan such fractures are emblematic of the general problem of subject formation: "Each time the subject succeeds, or approaches success in assuming his own role, each time he becomes, as it were, identical with himself and confident that his functioning in his specific social context is well-founded, the object, the sexual partner, is split—here in the form *rich woman or poor woman*" (417, emphasis in the original).[4] This tension is traced in the nineteenth-century marriage plot when the hero is positioned between a rich and a poor woman and his choice of the poor woman is represented as enabling him to prove himself free from the crassness, vulgarity, and improper pride that taint the novel's wealthy women. In the novel, as in the Ratman's case history, this choice necessitates two conceptions of subjectivity, one that is singular and one that is split. As the narrator of Anthony Trollope's *The Eustace Diamonds* puts it,

> Within the figure and frame and clothes and cuticle, within the bones and flesh
> of many of us, there is but one person . . . whose conduct in any emergency may
> be predicted with some assurance of accuracy. . . . Such persons are simple, sin-
> gle, and, perhaps, generally safe. . . . But there are human beings who, though of
> necessity single in body, are dual in character. . . . Such men,—or women,—may

hardly, perhaps, debase themselves with the more vulgar vices. . . . [B]ut ambition, luxury, self-indulgence, pride, and covetousness will get a hold of them, and in various moods will be to them virtues in lieu of vices. (1.163–64)

The typical version of this pattern is one in which a male subject, in being offered two spouses who represent antithetical values, confronts outside himself the division that the selection of a proper love object is supposed to heal.[5] This means that the happy conclusion of the novel of manners is achieved at "the price of a splitting of the sexual object into a rich woman and a poor woman" (Deleuze and Guattari 353).[6]

But this pattern can be reversed, as a woman finds herself confronting two suitors, one of whom courts her for her wealth and the other of whom values her for nonmaterialist reasons. In the nineteenth-century novel, the vulgarity of wealth can, therefore, be evoked through male as well as female figures. One has only to think of Mr. Elton's crass pursuit of Emma in Austen's *Emma* or of the Reverend Mr. Slope's pursuit of Eleanor Bold in *Barchester Towers* or of Ferdinand Lopez's courtship of Emily Wharton in *The Prime Minister*. All of these men are singular in their focus. In contrast, the women they court are, like the male hero of the marriage plot, torn between two options and become fully unified selves only when they choose the man who represents love rather than the love of money.

Yet, there is a gender asymmetry even as the nineteenth-century novel reverses the typical configuration of the marriage plot. For, in the version of courtship in which a man is torn between two women, the woman is vulgar because she possesses the wealth and status the man may himself desire. In contrast when a woman is torn between two men, the one who represents the vulgar option is not a man who has wealth but one who seeks it or presents himself as if he possesses it.[7] Much has been written about Victorian fears of individuals who create the illusion of possessing wealth, fears that are most commonly concentrated in the figure of the male speculator. Criticism that deals with the Victorian novel's relation to economics tends to be concerned with what Jeff Nunokawa calls "the vicissitudes of capital circulation" (13), the dangers of losing rather than having money. The nineteenth-century anxiety critics have not addressed at similar length is the one invoked through the rich woman, a fear of the impact that the possession of wealth has both on the psyche of the possessor and on the society that surrounds her.[8]

In following up on Lacan's observations about the Ratman, Deleuze and Guattari argue that paying attention to the split between the rich and the poor woman would allow critics to read, in stories that seem to be primarily about personal desire, traces of "the libidinal investments of the social field" (353). We can conceive of this link between romance and the social field in historically specific terms by returning to "The Neurotic's Individual Myth," where Lacan insists that the Ratman's obsessive thought patterns are not just a reaction to his own personal, familial drama but an "individual myth." Myth, Lacan argues, "provides a discursive form for something that cannot be transmitted through the definition of truth" (407);[9] it functions as "a certain objectified representation of an epos or as a chronicle expressing in an imaginary way the fundamental relationships characteristic of a certain mode of being human at a specific period[,] . . . the social manifestation— latent or patent, virtual or actual, full or void of meaning—of this mode of being" (408).[10] The marriage plot of the nineteenth-century novel is mythic in this sense. It is an abstract pattern that allows novelists to explore at the level of structure, action, and characterization, the economic demands the story cannot address directly without becoming too crassly materialistic. We might think of the marriage plot as enacting what Bourdieu calls "an imaginary anthropology," which is "obtained by denial of all the negations really brought about by the economy" (*Outline* 197).[11] In the nineteenth-century novel, the rich woman embodies what those narratives must deny in order to achieve their mythic ends, pointing us toward those fictions' engagement with history.[12]

To grasp the marriage plot as a mythic structure that articulates modes of thinking characteristic of life in nineteenth-century England, we need to read the patterns the novel engages through the rich woman in other places in the social network beside fiction. As we look at the Ratman's neurosis in light of novels that were produced in the same period we begin to see his thinking as part of a larger pattern in which the choice between two women becomes a means of articulating nineteenth-century social tensions between the desire for wealth and advancement and the need to regulate one's behavior by another set of values. As we meditate on the structure of the nineteenth-century novel in relation to two other forms of nineteenth-century thinking, its political economy and anthropology, we can come to a fuller understanding of precisely how the fictional choice between the rich and the poor woman allows the novel to articulate an unresolved social dilemma associated with the rise of capitalism in England.

Eighteenth- and nineteenth-century political economy pays consistent attention to wealth and what it represents for the individual. Nineteenth-century anthropology links the questions of property and ownership that were being raised by political economists in the context of nineteenth-century society to the evolution of marriage as a social form. The fictional figure of the heiress brings these two concerns together. She enables us to understand that both Victorian political economy and anthropology are concerned with a tension between wealth and marriage as forms of exchange and as forms of accumulation. Read in light of political economy and anthropology, the heiress emerges as a means by which novelists address anxieties that Victorian thinkers wished to acknowledge and deny, anxieties about the powerful impact of money on nineteenth-century society. The split between the rich and the poor woman allowed novelists to represent, in quasi-allegorical form, the social concern that Raymond Williams argued was central to the nineteenth century, when writers "dramatised, under increasing pressure, . . . the long process of choice between economic advantage and other ideas of value" (*Country* 61).

Debates about this choice harked back to discussions that had been engaged by moral philosophers from the time of the ancient Greeks.[13] Those debates intensified in the eighteenth century as the expansion of commerce and the increasing importance of mobile property made the social impacts of wealth dramatically visible. The ambivalence triggered by these developments is outlined in graphic form in Adam Smith's *The Theory of Moral Sentiments*. Smith argues that in a thriving commercial culture "two different characters are presented to our emulation; the one, of proud ambition and ostentatious avidity; the other, of humble modesty and equitable justice. Two different models, two different pictures, are held out to us, according to which we may fashion our own character and behaviour" (62). This passage identifies the contrast central to the nineteenth-century marriage plot: heroes are offered one set of possible spouses associated with the harmful effects of wealth and another free from those effects and from the money that elicits them. Installed at the heart of the novel, the contrast between the rich and the poor woman opposes self-interest to disinterest. In the process it incarnates in the rich woman the fear that haunted Smith and the nineteenth-century political economists who followed him, including Thomas Robert Malthus, Walter Bagehot, John Stuart Mill, and others—the fear that England's rapid economic development would corrupt the moral sentiments.

In various ways all these political economists argued in favor of the expansion of capitalism, insisting that it was not just inevitable but desirable, creating more wealth, more civilization, more international power, more satisfied consumer desires. But they all also wrote gloomily, in line with Carlyle's characterization of political economy as "the *dismal science*" ("Occasional" 354, emphasis in the original), about the vitiating power of the economic growth they endorsed. In the case of Adam Smith this contradictory combination is typically described as "the Adam

Smith problem." As Istvan Hont and Michael Ignatieff note in their book about wealth and virtue, "It is not an easy task to reconcile his evident distaste for the vulgar materialism of the 'great scramble' of commercial society with his clear endorsement of economic growth" (8–9). One could make a similar point about Malthus, who, though more deeply pessimistic about the psychological drives that fueled the economy than Smith, still endorsed economic expansion while at the same time fearing its effects on both the individual and collective psyche. When Malthus argues that "the substitution of benevolence as the master-spring and moving principle of society, instead of self-love, is a consummation devoutly to be wished" (2004 63), one hears in his wording the dilemma eighteenth- and nine-teenth-century political economists faced. In invoking Hamlet's reference to his own death ("a consummation devoutly to be wished"), Malthus makes clear his fear that altruism would, in effect, kill the commercial economy that had become England's lifeblood.

At the same time, Malthus, like Smith, wanted to imagine a way in which such altruism—what Smith calls sympathy—might be fostered in a rapidly expanding economy that seemed to depend on its opposite. The nineteenth-century English writers who celebrated the substitution of benevolence for self-love were not its political economists but its novelists. It is in fiction that the choice of altruism is made to seem inevitable, desirable, and self-evident, the consummation that we, as readers, devoutly wish for and experience in the nonmercenary marriages that conclude the story. One could, therefore, read political economy and the novel as sister discourses or what Catherine Gallagher calls "fellow travelers" (185).[14] While political economy is primarily concerned with the pursuit of wealth, the novel lauds the pursuit of virtue. Such a reading would dovetail with John Guillory's and Mary Poovey's arguments that political economy split off from aesthetics at the end of the eighteenth century. As Poovey notes, the fracture between virtue and wealth "eventually became a disciplinary split between aesthetics and political economy . . . initiated partly by prizing apart the two models with which Shaftes-bury had figured the relationship between individual interest (or commerce) and social good (or virtue)" ("Aesthetics" 84–85).

But even as the two disciplines separated, they remained haunted by the ghost of the other.[15] Just as eighteenth- and nineteenth-century political economists fre-quently break from their defense of economic expansion to articulate fears about wealth's corruption of what Smith called the moral sentiments, so too nineteenth-century novelists break from their celebrations of virtue to acknowledge the en-grossing impact of wealth. Guillory has argued that, in this period, "the bourgeoisie find it necessary to take up a 'pure' aesthetics supposedly uncontaminated by economic considerations" (316). Though the novel reaches toward such absolute aesthetic purity in its conclusion, traces of economic concerns are present in the figure of the rich woman, who incarnates the negative aspects of capitalism in stories about the triumph of individual choice over crass self-interest.

For a fuller understanding of the symbolic implications of her position within the marriage plot I turn to the writings of nineteenth-century anthropologists. Like the political economists who were their contemporaries, they were interested in thinking through the relation between property, society, and the individual. Lewis H. Morgan exclaimed in the end of *Ancient Society* that "since the advent of civilization, the outgrowth of property has been so immense, its forms so diversified, its uses so expanding and its management so intelligent in the interest of its owners, that it has become, on the part of the people, an unmanageable power"(467). As this comment suggests, Victorian anthropologists linked the development of modern culture to the changing status of property. They were, in particular, interested in the process by which property ceased to be held by a group and passed to individual ownership, a process they linked to changes in the treatment of women. Nineteenth-century social scientists as varied as Sir Henry Sumner Maine, John McLennan, Friedrich Engels, Morgan, and Herbert Spencer attempted, as Kathy Psomiades has argued, "to think through the relations between marriage and capital" (94).[16] All of them insisted that the "development of the conception of property in general" had had "much to do with the development of the marital relation" (Spencer *Principles* 1.645).[17]

They valued modern society for two related freedoms: because a woman could marry whom she wanted and because there was the "complete individualization of ownership [that] is an accompaniment of industrial progress" (Spencer *Evolution* 205).[18] This thinking, as the work of McLennan makes particularly clear, emerged out of the charting of the evolution from a society organized by a tribal structure in which both property and women were held in common to a modern one based around the family, the ownership of private property, and a marital system in which free choice figured.[19] But, for these nineteenth-century social scientists, there was a hitch in that narrative of progression, a hitch marked by the heiress who revealed the unacknowledged limits of both marital exchange and the freedom of material possession.

The social development charted by Victorian anthropologists traced the way, as property began to be located in families rather than tribes, the father could exercise his right to leave his possessions to his descendents. Because this transition from group ownership to patrilineage meant that daughters would inherit if there were no sons, a new class of heiresses emerged that posed a social problem. If those rich women were exchanged outside of the group to which they belonged, the group's property would go with them. As Morgan observes, "Marriage would then transfer their property from their own gens to that of their husband's, unless some restraint, in the case of heiresses, was put on the right" (462). This threat to the group's possessions meant that an exception had to be made. In order to ensure that property remained within the group rather than being transferred outside it, the heiress could not be allowed to exchange herself freely. She must be made to marry within the group. As Engels argued, "After the introduction of father right, the property of a rich heiress would have passed to her husband and thus into another gens on her marriage, but the foundation of all gentile law was now violated and in such a case the girl was not only permitted but *ordered* to marry within the gens, in order that her property by retained for the gens" (132, emphasis in the original).

The terms that nineteenth-century anthropologists used to describe how this tension worked within the system of marital exchange were "exogamy" and "endogamy." McLennan and other Victorian anthropologists insisted that while all other members of the community could be exchanged exogamously, the heiress had to be exchanged endogamously. In the nineteenth-century novel, as in nineteenth-century anthropological accounts of the development of modern culture, the heiress is associated with endogamy. And, in the novel, as in anthropology, this position reflects an implicit acknowledgment that economic and social advancement, which seemed to be extending the possibility of ownership to all, was accompanied by the impulse to prevent circulation by concentrating wealth in the hands of those who already held it.[20]

As I move to think about the nineteenth-century novel in terms of McLennan's concepts of endogamy and exogamy, I want to heed the advice of a number of recent critics about the need for precision in using anthropology to read fiction.[21] On the one hand, Ellen Pollak and Mary Jean Corbett have argued for more nuanced historical readings of the workings of kinship systems in the novel.[22] On the other hand, Ruth Perry has argued for a more detailed understanding of the economic shifts that underlie fictional depictions of kinship exchange.[23] I posit here an intertwining of these two approaches. We can better understand the symbolic function of the fictional heiress if we think of the nineteenth-century novel as depicting a series of kinship exchanges that are as much about property and ownership as about marital relations.[24] This means that in fiction, as in Victorian anthropology, the heiress marks the impulse that political economists feared lurked at the heart of the capitalist enterprise, the impulse not to exchange but to amass property and prevent it from circulating.

The opposition between exogamy and endogamy is very clear in *Pride and Prejudice*, where Darcy's possible marriages to Miss Bingley or Miss De Bourgh are unions that would, either literally or figuratively, leave him marrying close to home, wedding the sister of his best friend or his cousin. In contrast, Elizabeth Bennet is, relatively speaking, not just a stranger but also a woman Darcy finds increasingly attractive the farther she is from her own home, at Netherfield, Rosings, and Pemberley.[25] Critics, however, have observed that while *Pride and Prejudice* seems opposed to endogamy (Elizabeth doesn't wed her cousin Mr. Collins, nor does Darcy his cousin Miss de Bourgh), in Austen's subsequent novel *Mansfield Park* that position is reversed (Edmund Bertram does marry his cousin Fanny Price rather than the outsider Mary Crawford). But if we think of the marriage plot as invoking endogamy and exogamy as economic rather than blood categories, then the patterns of marital exchange within the two novels become consistent.[26] Both endorse marriage between a propertied man and a poorer woman (Darcy and Elizabeth, Edmund and Fanny) as a form of what one might call spiritual, emotional, or psychological exogamy. These marriages bring a set of nonmaterialist values into the heart of a property-owning family group (the Darcys, the Bertrams).

In contrast, marriage to the heiresses in these novels is associated with the attitude toward wealth that eighteenth-century critics like David Hume stigmatized under the rubric of engrossment. In *Pride and Prejudice* Miss Bingley imagines an alliance between her commercial wealth and Darcy's landed estate, while Lady Catherine expects a union between two cousins whose properties will become one.[27] The rich women in Austen's novels endorse the idea of matrimony as endogamous in terms of money; it should consolidate fortunes rather than allowing wealth to pass out of the group to which it has traditionally belonged. The nineteenth-century novel therefore conforms to McLennan's anthropological observation that "the earliest violations of the rule of exogamy would appear to have been called for in the case of female heiresses" (113). This practice is borne out in *Emma*, the only one of Austen's novels to have a rich woman as its protagonist. When Emma marries Mr. Knightley and their estates are joined, that union is represented as a consolidation of property. Her family's land is described as a notch out of his, and the Woodhouses possess the liquid capital that seems to be in slightly short supply at Knightley's estate. Further, the novel's heroine does not move out of her home at the conclusion of the narrative but has her husband move in with her and her father, a domestic arrangement that emphasizes how completely Emma fails to be exchanged on the occasion of her marriage.[28]

The endogamous marriage of the rich woman is reiterated in Margaret Oliphant *Miss Marjoribanks*, a work that has been read as an echo of and tribute to Austen's *Emma*.[29] Oliphant's heroine, a prosperous doctor's daughter, does not marry any of the various suitors presented to her over the course of the novel but ends up with her cousin, the first marital choice offered her. This decision makes the novel seem narratively endogamous in the sense that it circles round to its beginning as if no change in marital options had taken place over the course of the story. That union also emphasizes the nonexchange of its heroine. Lucilla's cousin has the same last name as his bride, so she will marry and still be called Lucilla Marjoribanks (Oliphant herself married her cousin and thereby recovered her mother's maiden name, becoming Margaret Oliphant Wilson Oliphant). Lucilla and her new husband also use the money he has earned in India to buy the landed estate that had been lost to the family, an estate that bears the name of its newly married owners; it is called Marchbanks, which is how "Marjoribanks" is pronounced.[30]

This coming together of persons and property, all of which bear the same name, suggests how fully the story of the rich woman is about the centripetal rather than the centrifugal uses of wealth, a flow that engrosses material goods by pulling them together in a single place rather than disbursing itself outward to a range of locations and persons. In linking the heiress to endogamous exchange, novels like *Miss Marjoribanks* and *Emma* do more than reflect the observations of a nineteenth-century anthropologist like McLennan. These fictions also point to the limits of the symbolic system imagined as balancing exogamy and endogamy. Those limits would not be clearly identified in anthropology until the twentieth century, when Claude Lévi-Strauss used the observations of nineteenth-century precursors like McLennan, Morgan, and Engels to develop an overall model of marital practices, a model that recognizes that "endogamy is merely the expression of a conceptual limit" (47).[31]

As Lévi-Strauss explains, in a system of hypergamy, in which men are expected to marry women of a status inferior to theirs, the problem is how "women of the highest class get married":

> In a system of generalized exchange, the continuity of the link is ensured by a
> single cycle of exchange which connects all constituent elements of the group as

partners. No interruption can occur at any point in the cycle without the total structure, which is the basis of social order and individual security, being in danger of collapse. (474)

These observations make it clear that the heiress represents a potential blockage in the cycle of exogamy that constitutes the fabric of society; she is a knot in the web, an island of endogamy that threatens to stop the movement of property, persons, and names. To solve this problem Lévi-Strauss turns from social practices to the realm of art. He finds in fiction, specifically in fairy tales, a symbolic representation of the overcoming of the barrier that threatens to halt the flow or general exchange when the figures that mark its limits, the woman of the highest status and the man of the lowest, are imagined getting married, as the princess chooses for her husband the poor but virtuous man whose valor has been proved by the tests of the tale.[32]

Though nineteenth-century novels typically emphasize the marriage plot in which the rich man marries or loves a poorer woman, a subset of them feature fairy-tale plots like the ones Lévi-Strauss describes, where a poorer man weds a woman of property. One might think of Arthur Clennam at the end of *Little Dorrit*, Franklin Blake in *The Moonstone*, Frank Wentworth in *The Perpetual Curate*, Gabriel Oak in *Far from the Madding Crowd*, or Louis Moore in *Shirley*. The nineteenth-century British novel typically deals with the tensions raised by such nontraditional unions in two ways. The first is by reducing the property of the woman so that the economic distance between the two spouses is no longer so great. Thus, in *The Woman in White*, Walter Hartright can marry Laura Fairlie only after she has lost her wealth.[33] Similarly in *Little Dorrit*, the Dorrits lose their inheritance before the Clennam marriage. In *The Moonstone*, the diamond that marks Rachel's wealth is taken back to India before the story's end. In *Far from the Madding Crowd*, Bathsheba's wealth is shown to depend on Gabriel Oak, as he keeps her from losing the farm by protecting her crops while her husband sleeps drunkenly by. (By the end of the novel, Oak's status is also elevated, as he becomes the manager not just of Bathsheba's farm but also of Boldwood's.)

The other way novels deal with the problem of the wife's elevated economic status is by introducing a new social category that defines the husband as of a higher class than the wife despite the economic differences of their positions. In George Eliot's *Daniel Deronda*, for example, when the heiress Catherine Arrowpoint, like the princess in a fairy tale, selects the impoverished musician Herr Klesmer as the worthiest of the suitors presented to her, Eliot invokes a category other than property to define the man's position as superior to that of the woman. As an artist, Klesmer is, Arrowpoint tells her parents, "of a caste to which I look up—a caste above mine" (243). Introducing the anthropological term "caste," Eliot resolves the dilemma presented by the rich woman's marriage to someone who is not as wealthy as she is by introducing a hierarchy that privileges the realm of art over that of economics and therefore allows the heiress to define herself as of lesser status than the man she marries. The end of Charlotte Brontë's *Shirley* solves the problem of the poor man's marriage to the rich woman in a similar fashion. The proposal scene between the tutor Louis Moore and the heiress Shirley Keeldar turns on the moment when he calls her "my pupil," and she responds by calling him "my master" (584). This exchange of titles establishes him as of a rank above hers. As her teacher, he provides her with the cultural knowledge she lacks.[34] Both these proposals effectively work around the problem represented by the rich woman's wealth by reinstating the difference that Bourdieu argues is central to the realm of art and gender relations, the hierarchy in which symbolic or cultural capital is elevated over monetary possessions and the former is identified with the masculine position and the latter with the feminine.

But the nineteenth-century novel typically finds it difficult to imagine a conclusion that acknowledges that the woman's wealth does in fact grant her a higher social status than that of the poor man who woos her. At the end of Anne Brontë's *The Tenant of Wildfeld Hall* the novel's hero Gilbert Markham is so paralyzed by his knowledge that Helen Huntingdon is doubly an heiress, having been placed in control of her husband's property at his death and having inherited her uncle's estate, that he almost leaves without seeing her. In the end it is she rather than he who must propose marriage. The same is true in *Far from the Madding Crowd*: when Bathsheba comes to Gabriel to plead with him to stay working for her rather than go to America, she observes that "it seems exactly as if I had come courting you—how dreadful!" (409). In *Tenant* Helen proposes to Gilbert by offering him a Christmas rose, which she thinks of as a representation of herself. This offering suggests the novel's awareness that in this scene of courtship Helen is operating on the basis of natural inclinations rather than social structures. The implications of such a reading are made even clearer in the unequal marriage at the end of Frances Trollope's *The Life and Adventures of Michael Armstrong, the Factory Boy*.

That novel tells the story of a virtuous factory boy exploited by an evil cotton manufacturer, Sir Matthew Dowling. Dowling takes the boy in in order both to prevent strikes and advertise himself as a charitable owner and then sells him to one of the worst factories imaginable, one that works children to their death. This demonic narrative is countered by the parallel story of Mary Brotherton, a cotton heiress, whose sympathetic interest in the adopted boy leads her to uncover the truth about the oppressive conditions in the factories. While the novel repeatedly insists there is nothing its heroine can do on a large scale to ameliorate those conditions (besides fight for the Ten Hours Bill that would limit the amount of time that children were allowed to work), it imagines a fantastic solution to the irresolvable economic problems it has presented by having the wealthiest woman in the novel, Mary Brotherton, marry Edward Armstrong, the brother of its poorest character, the factory boy who has been adopted and abused. Trollope's narrator, however, does not describe this union directly but exclaims instead that "there are some facts which no wise historian will ever venture to dilate upon, lest their strangeness should provoke incredulity; and great wisdom is shown by such forbearance; for it is infinitely better that an enlightened public should be driven to exclaim, '*How very obscure this passage is!*' than '*How very improbable!*'" (386).

Critics have commented on the oddity of this conclusion. Priti Joshi asks, "Why is this marriage . . . [t]he unspeakable event of the novel?" and answers that it is because "Mary and Edward's union violates not only class differences but also assumptions about proper gender roles: Mary is wealthier, older, healthier, and more active than the poor, passive, crippled, sickly Edward" (48, 49). For Rosemarie Bodenheimer, this marriage represents a violation that goes "deeper than class difference; [Trollope's] focus on Edward's anguished sense of social inferiority functions more as a cover for the incest wish than as a serious continuation of the class plot" (31). Though I agree with Bodenheimer that the ending of *Michael Armstrong* feels as if it violates a taboo, I would argue that it is the taboo generated by the nineteenth-century marriage plot, which insists that the heiress should marry endogamously. As I suggested in discussing the workings of endogamy and exogamy in novels like Austen's, the drive of fictional versions of these anthropological patterns is less sexual than it is economic. So, too, the incest wish that critics like Bodenheimer sense in the marriage of Trollope's heiress is not a function of sexuality but property.

In *The Elementary Structures of Kinship* Lévi-Strauss identifies what he calls "social" as distinct from sexual incest. Social incest involves "obtaining by oneself, and for oneself, instead of by another, and for another" (489). This set of phrases aptly describes the heiress's role in the nineteenth-century novel.[35] Often older and potentially infertile, she is engrossed by and identified with her wealth. But, in the novel, as in the systems Lévi-Strauss maps out, the position of nonexchange represented by both the heiress and social incest is necessary in order for the system of exchange to operate; "the laws of kinship and marriage, in their own sphere of interest, laboriously derive" the "world of reciprocity" from "relationships which are otherwise condemned to remain either sterile or immoderate" (Lévi-Strauss 490). This passage describes the opposition between the socially absorbed use of wealth and the altruism of exchange that is established in the nineteenth-century novel through the contrast between the rich and the poor woman that lies at the heart of the marriage plot.

The structure of the novel depends on the heiress remaining an endogamous counterweight to the exogamous relationships depicted elsewhere in the story. Like the incest prohibition, which works to define the sexual gratifications that are closest to home as taboo, therefore driving individuals to find pleasure in more distant exchanges, the prohibition on the exogamous marriage of the heiress works to define the direct enjoyment of one's own wealth as taboo. It drives both the novel's readers and characters to locate pleasure instead in individuals who represent the values of exchange, altruism, and care for others that nineteenth-century political economists feared were vanishing from England's burgeoning commercial economy. One way of reading the marriage plot is as a counterphobic structure. The rich woman embodies those behaviors that individuals feared resulted from the increasing importance of money in the nineteenth century. The novel uses her as a foil to propose the psychological and moral stances necessary to counter such material engrossment.

In a sense the heiress functions as what Lévi-Strauss calls the scandal in the system of marital exchanges. She must be included in order for the novel to establish the values that exclude her.[36] But since, as Derrida has argued in discussing Lévi-Strauss, "there is no scandal except within a system of concepts which accredits the difference between nature and culture" (283), we can transform our readings of the novel by refusing to espouse the logic that insists on the rich woman's eccentric position within its symbolic structure. If we instead acknowledge her pivotal role in the novel's romance plots, we can begin to rethink the nineteenth-century novel's intellectual engagement with England's economic history; we can read its marriage plots as taking an active part in an ongoing discussion about the impact of money on the culture.

This revisionary reading of the nineteenth-century novel may remind readers of Nancy Armstrong's arguments in *Desire and Domestic Fiction*. She, too, insists that the British novel uses the figure of woman not just to inscribe gender relations but also to make arguments about the larger social order. The difference between my work and Armstrong's is that while she is interested in how the nineteenth-century novel uses its female characters to make arguments about class, I am interested in the way the novel uses those same characters to make arguments about money. Figures that might be read in terms of class can also be read as posing arguments about the negative effects of the possession of wealth. Lady Catherine is a perfect example of the aristocratic women Armstrong argues the nineteenth-century novel critiques through its representation of a new form of middle-class virtue encoded in heroines like Elizabeth Bennet. In contrast, Miss Bingley can easily be read in terms of the frequent eighteenth-century critiques of the upwardly mobile commercial classes who have made money in trade and seek to emulate their landed betters. But, when Austen makes these two female figures similar, contrasting the bearing of both to the behavior of Elizabeth Bennet, then it becomes clear that the novel is addressing through these women not just their class position but also the way the possession of property impacts them as it does not their male counterparts, Bingley and Darcy.

Armstrong makes a similar point about the difference of gender in fiction when she insists that

> it is worth noting that the male of the dominant class, though he may bear certain features of the libertine or of the snob, is capable of going either way socially, but his female counterpart is generally not. Such women as Mr. B's sister Lady Davers, or Darcy's aunt Lady Catherine de Bourgh, or Rochester's fiancée Blanche Ingram are hopelessly devoid of feelings and concerned only with displaying their position. They embody the features of a dominant class that, in contrast with a fine pair of eyes or a genteel education, cannot be included among those of the domestic woman. (*Desire* 112–13)[37]

We feel in this passage both the emphasis on class and the distaste that typically make critics turn away from figures like Lady Catherine. However, Armstrong's work is focused not on the figure of the aristocratic woman that novels invite readers to deplore but on the woman whose middle-class virtues make her a counter to such figures. She argues that "we are taught to divide the political world in two and to detach practices that belong to a female domain from those that govern the marketplace" (9–10). This division is inculcated in the novel at the level of its romance plots through the contrast between the poor and the rich woman, with the former representing the mental and spiritual values Armstrong associates with the middle-class woman and the latter the values of the marketplace.

When we read the marriage plot as a symbolic structure, a system in which one character is contrasted to another in order to establish a set of values, then we see that the characteristics that Armstrong associates with the heroine of the novel are presented as countering the social power of money that the nineteenth-novel acknowledges negatively through the figure of the rich woman. I want to press against Armstrong's insistence that in the nineteenth-century novel the domestic realm is a safe enclosure sealed off from the realm of the market. Because the rich woman is a pivotal figure in the romance narratives that celebrate the virtues embodied in the novel's antimaterialist heroine, I read those plots as addressing not simply the domestic sphere but also the history of English society in the era in which money, or what J. G. A. Pocock calls mobile property, played an increasingly powerful role in establishing social roles and relations. The nineteenth-century marriage plot makes arguments that are as much about the social and political realms as they are about the private and personal realms usually associated with them.

To advance this claim I turn to a subset of novels that may seem to be the least historically inflected genre in the canon of Victorian fiction: novels of manners. I do this in part because in novels of manners marital exchange is the central event of the plot and not, as in texts like *Great Expectations* and *Jane Eyre*, part of the deep structure of a story, a vehicle that enables the novelist to address a series of other social issues. But I would also insist that the structures I analyze in novels of manners appear in fictions other than the kinds of texts I have selected for my examples. My hope is that in showing how the marriage plot works in texts where it is plainly visible, I can map out a model that makes it easier to understand the implications of the contrast between the rich and the poor woman in texts where that pattern is not in the foreground of the story.

The novel of manners is also particularly useful because in it the choice between the rich and the poor woman is presented as a matter of taste. That is, the rich woman is defined as an inappropriate marital choice because she behaves in a way that makes her distasteful. One might be inclined to read explorations of taste as relatively superficial in relation to what seem like the more serious social issues raised by works like *Jane Eyre* or *Great Expectations*. In a letter, Charlotte Brontë herself described *Pride and Prejudice* as "an accurate, daguerreotyped portrait of a common-place face; a carefully-fenced, highly cultivated garden with neat borders and delicate flowers" (Barker 180). Yet the cultivation depicted in novels of manners makes them crucial texts for defining what constitutes culture at any given moment in time. As Lionel Trilling has argued in "Manners, Morals, and the Novel," "our attitude toward manners is the expression of particular conception of reality" (207).[38] Through manners we gain access to "a culture's hum and buzz of implication," "that part . . . which is made up of half-uttered or unuttered or unutterable expressions of value" (206). The fictional rich woman is a particularly useful resource for accessing "the whole evanescent context in which [a novel's] explicit statements are made" (Trilling 206).

While the marriage plot allows the novel to make a clear statement about where its values lie, the rich woman evokes the economic context those values are intended to counter. The details of that context are, as Trilling notes, "hinted at by small actions, sometimes by the arts of dress or decoration, sometimes by tone, gesture, emphasis, or rhythm, sometimes by the words that are used with a special frequency or a special meaning" (206–7). So, too, in the novels I analyze, trivial details in the portrayal of the rich woman prove key to tracing her link to contemporary history. In *Pride and Prejudice*, for example, Miss Bingley's talk of her brother buying an estate modeled on Pemberley and the narrator's use of the word "engrossing" to characterize her behavior and that of Lady Catherine de Bourgh would have alerted Austen's contemporaries that the novel was participating in late eighteenth-century and early nineteenth-century discussions of the problem of imitative spending and the link between wealth and engrossment. Anthony Trollope's nineteenth-century readers would have recognized that in making Miss Dunstable an heiress who derives her fortune from the sale of a patent medicine, he was addressing contemporary concerns about the social changes that made his period the era of the commodity millionaires. Through characters like Miss Bingley, Lady Catherine, and Miss Dunstable, novelists of manners allude to what Trilling calls the noise that makes up everyday life, the noise that is available to the modern reader "from letters and diaries, from the remote, unconscious corners of the great works themselves" (206).

But the noise associated with the rich woman is less part of the unconscious corners of the work of art than something so obvious that we, as critics, have failed to pay attention to it because its implications seem transparently clear. In thinking about how little has been written about the rich woman's role in the marriage plot, I have often returned to the passage in Poe's "The Purloined Letter," where Dupin uses the analogy of a map to explain that the most effective hiding place is in plain sight. The part of the map we are least likely to notice is not the names that are writ small, the remote villages and rivers, but those that are writ large, the names of countries that stretch across the entirety of a continent.[39] The contrast between the rich and the poor woman is a pattern whose meaning is written on such a large scale that we have failed to note its import. It is the behaviors of a Miss Bingley, a Lady Catherine, or a Miss Dunstable that grant critics access to what novelists perceive to be the real economic concerns of the era in which they were writing, concerns having to do with money and its impact on nineteenth-century English culture as a whole and the individuals living within it. As Trilling has argued in thinking about manners and the novel, "The novel is born with the appearance of money as a social element—money, the great solvent of the solid fabric of the old society" (209).

The mid-eighteenth century was a period when the heiress was particularly visible in contemporary discourse because of the heated discussions that took place around the passage of Hardwicke's Marriage Act in 1753. That act institutionalized marriage by stipulating that it was "to be performed by ordained Anglican clergymen in the premises of the Church of England, that the banns were "to be called three times or a special license purchased from a bishop," and that "parental consent for those under twenty-one was to be strictly enforced" (Green 69). But the debates about the law's passage were primarily concerned with property. As Erica Harth has argued, "Opponents viewed the bill as endorsing a type of class endogamy that would allow the aristocracy to strengthen its power by monopolizing England's new wealth" (128). They insisted that it was, in the words of Robert Nugent, in England's

> "national interest . . . to prevent the accumulation of wealth, and to disperse it as much as possible through the whole body of the people. . . . Riches is the blood of the body politic; it must be made to circulate." Enactment of the legislation would result in a blockage of the circulation of wealth by what Charles Townshend called "tyrannical power in the father." (Harth 134)

These are the terms in which, as I have shown, the heiress was perceived to function in later nineteenth-century anthropological accounts of the evolution of culture. Those accounts suggest that instead of arguing that one side or the other was correct, we might view the conflict around the passage of the Marriage Act as demonstrating that both endogamy and exogamy are necessary for the system of marital exchange to operate.[40] This means, if we extrapolate from anthropological systems to economic ones, that the discussion of property and the Marriage Act indicates an awareness that the emerging capitalist system depended both on the circulation and noncirculation of property, both on exchange and accumulation.

I argue that the marriage plot that contrasts the rich and the poor woman is born in this moment at the beginning of Samuel Richardson's career and lasts until the end of Henry James's. In Richardson's *Pamela, or; Virtue Rewarded*, the story of a poor woman who marries affluently, we have a narrative that endorses the exchange or circulation of property. In *Clarissa; or, The History of a Young Woman*, an almost identical tale of a rich woman who is persecuted for her possession of wealth, we have a narrative that prevents the exchange of the heiress and therefore implicitly endorses endogamy.[41] However, I begin my analysis not with Richardson but with Austen because she follows up on the implications of what he discovers by telling the story of the rich and the poor woman not in two different novels but in the same one.[42] I would therefore agree with Alex Woloch that *Pride and Prejudice* is an "exemplary narrative[,] . . . a fairy tale, perhaps, about the structure of 'novelness' itself. [It] offers a paradigmatic marriage plot" (45). In that novel Austen writes a narrative that is driven by the contrast between the rich and the poor woman, between Miss Bingley or Lady Catherine's daughter and Elizabeth Bennet. She discovers the shape of the marriage plot that will dominate the novel though to the end of the nineteenth century.

Arrighi identifies the period I associate with this form of the marriage plot, the era that runs from the mid-eighteenth to the early twentieth century, as the span when England was the world's dominant economic power (364).[43] In this book I analyze a series of novelists who provide a fictional counterpart to this economic development. I show how each uses the rich woman to record contemporary reactions to key changes in the sources and perceptions of the wealth that made England a world-dominant power. In chapter 1, I read Austen, who began working on the early versions of her novels in 1796 and first published them in 1811, in relation to Adam Smith's *The Theory of Moral Sentiments*.[44] The overlap between the concerns addressed by aesthetics and political economy was particularly strong in the decades before she began her novels, at the time when the moral philosophers David Hume and Adam Smith were writing about taste as well as commerce. Periodicals like Addison and Steele's *Spectator* and the *Loiterer* (which was edited by Jane Austen's brother James) also moved easily between stories about marriage and essays about the "almost universal depravity of modern times with respect to the extensive and shameful influence of Gold" (*Loiterer* 17). Her novels mark the period when there was a general reaction to the increasing importance of mobile property, which was seen as both fueling the rapid expansion of the English economy and blurring the boundaries of social distinction that had, prior to this period, allowed for clear differentiations between classes.[45]

Chapter 2 turns to Frances Trollope, who was born in 1780 only four years after Austen and grew up in the same region of England. Trollope, however, began her literary career in an era that differed significantly both economically and historically from Austen's. Publishing from 1832 to 1863, Trollope produced her most popular works in the period that Thomas Carlyle famously described as "the Age of Machinery," the moment when England became "the first industrialized nation." This period was associated with the production of an enormous variety of new commodities available for middle-class consumption.[46] That change is reflected in Frances Trollope's novels where wealthy women are not concerned with the status issues that drive them in Austen's novels. Instead of being, as one of Austen's early critics put it of Lady Catherine and Miss Bingley, "purse-proud" (Southam 1.137), they possess what Trollope calls "ever-craving purses" (*Michael Armstrong* 93), an almost insatiable appetite for the things that money provides.[47]

In chapter 3, I turn to Anthony Trollope, whose career his mother helped establish in 1847 and who continued writing until 1883.[48] This was the period when the English economy's sources of wealth shifted from industrial production to the sale and distribution of consumer goods.[49] Published from the 1850s to the 1870s, Trollope's Barsetshire and Palliser series chronicle the period in which English society was invaded by the great commercial millionaires like Cadbury, Guinness, and Lever.[50] This was the moment when the economy began to be associated not with the production of objects, as it was earlier in the century, but with credit and banking and when money began to be seen as an abstract force rather than a concrete entity. While Frances Trollope's novels emphasize the material impacts of wealth and the visceral desires it triggers, Anthony's are concerned with less tangible effects in the form of political influence. That conceptual shift is paralleled by a shift in the representation of the heiress; for the first time she becomes, in Miss Dunstable, Lady Glencora Palliser, and Madame Max Goesler, a positive rather than a negative figure. As it becomes clear that money will inevitably be a mainstay of all forms of modern culture, fiction must find a way to acknowledge mobile wealth's positive sides. This trend continues in the work of Margaret Oliphant, who makes rich women not the villains of the story but its heroines. Oliphant is often seen as a contemporary of Anthony Trollope's, but her career stretched significantly beyond his (she began publishing in 1852 and continued through 1897). Her novels bespeak the moment when capitalism takes on the managerial form we associate with the emergence of the professional classes, a historical development Harold Perkin has identified with the 1880s.

The emergence of the professional as the implicit hero of Oliphant's novels marks a double strain implicit in the novelists I discuss. The writers that are the subjects of chapters 1 and 3—Austen and Anthony Trollope—engage the marriage plot at an elevated social and economic level. Their rich woman are landowners and millionaires, and their novels focus on the estate as an image of ideal, nonmercenary values whose purity is under threat from the increasing social power of other forms of wealth. In contrast, the writers that are the subjects of chapters 2 and 4—Frances Trollope and Oliphant—recount the marriage plot at the level of the middle classes. They tell the stories of prosperous women who are the widows of pharmacists or the daughters of bankers, doctors, and upwardly mobile Dissenting ministers. Moreover, in Frances Trollope's and Oliphant's novels, the rich woman is not introduced simply as a contrasting figure who forwards the romance plot; instead she is the title character of the novels I explore here: Trollope's *The Widow Barnaby*, *The Ward of Thorpe-Combe*, and *The Life and Adventures of a Clever Woman* and Oliphant's *Miss Marjoribanks* and *Phoebe Junior*.

These novels provide an ironic commentary on the mainstream representations of the rich woman, but the question we might ask as critics is whether such an authorial decision contributes to the fact that Frances Trollope and Margaret Oliphant, unlike the other novelists considered here, remain outside the canon of Victorian literature, or what F. R. Leavis calls "the great tradition." Henry James, the novelist with whom I conclude, falls soundly within this tradition and follows the pattern established in the first four chapters of the book by telling the story of heiresses whose wealth seems virtually limitless. In the late James novels I consider here, *The Wings of the Dove* and *The Golden Bowl*, the rich woman bears no trace of the vulgarity that was her signature trait when she was first introduced in Austen's *Pride and Prejudice*. In James, her money comes to be associated with aesthetic rather than crassly commercial values and she becomes an American rather than an English figure.

This representational shift allows us to identify James's novels as written at the moment in the early twentieth century that Arrighi has described as the juncture when the cycle of English economic dominance comes to an end and is replaced by the American cycle. James's novels also signify the end of the period in which the novel uses the contrast between the rich and the poor woman unconsciously as the deep structure of the plot. Writing when he conceives of "anthropology" as "a science born, so to speak, yesterday" (114), James examines the narrative pattern that he has inherited from Austen, the Trollopes, and Oliphant and consciously represents it as a structure that functions like the systems of marital exchange mapped out in nineteenth- and twentieth-century anthropology.[51] His novels complete the process of thinking through the cultural impact of money that I trace on a large scale over the course of my book.

That process of sequentially thinking through the impact of wealth takes place on a smaller scale within each chapter. The portrait of the rich woman never remains static, not even throughout the career of an individual novelist. Representing cultural fears about the possession of wealth, she is a figure the novelist returns to and revises in order to address issues that, at the moment the novel was being written, were associated with the increasing social power of money, the power that good manners and cultivation must counter. Each chapter looks at three novels (or in Anthony Trollope's case three stages in the novelist's career) and analyzes changes in the successive representations of the rich woman. This sequential reading reveals novelists to be engaged in a literary version of the psychological process Freud describes as working through, an attempt to find a way to come to terms with an issue that seems initially to be irresolvable. For the novelists considered here, this process tends to begin with representations of rich woman whose implications seem to be made obvious through comic exaggeration, as for example in the case of Miss Bingley and Lady Catherine de Bourgh in *Pride and Prejudice*. They are figures who are drawn in larger-than-life, almost caricatured terms. The same is true of the versions of the rich woman that appear in Frances Trollope's and Anthony Trollope's early novels, the sublimely vulgar widow Barnaby or the ointment heiress Miss Dunstable, who knows people treat her as if her unfashionable curls are done up in pound notes.

But for all of these novelists the process of thinking through the issues associated with the heiress leads to portraits that are both more serious and more troubling in subsequent work. In Austen's *Mansfield Park* the wealthy Mary Crawford is no longer a caricature but so appealing that the novel's hero almost marries her rather than the object identified for him by the marriage plot, the poor Fanny Price. The later versions of Frances Trollope's and Anthony Trollope's heiresses also have a significantly greater emotional and social impact than their predecessors. This shift in representation reflects the novelists' need to acknowledge the real power of money in a way that their earlier comic renderings of the rich woman did not. This acknowledgment drives the novelists to imagine, in the novels I read as the culmination of a sequential mediation on wealth, an entire philosophical or social system that positions money in relation to the other values the novel invokes. The final texts in each of my chapters deal with money in its most abstract form. We cannot fully grasp the implications of those abstract patterns without reading fiction in relation to nonfictional writings that were being produced in the same moment as the novel. Each chapter therefore brings to the readings of novels the nonfictional writings of those thinking about the societal impact of changing forms of wealth.[52]

The writings I draw on, texts like Adam Smith's *The Theory of Moral Sentiments* or John Stuart Mill's *On Liberty*, might be thought of as what Susan Mizruchi calls "border texts" (15).[53] They were written by writers we think of as political economists, but they address political economy less directly than some of the author's other works. Those border texts help us to identify what Trilling calls noise in the figure of the rich woman, to see how details in her portrait resonate with the observations of those writing about economic developments in a completely different context. The fact that the nonfiction writers address the same concerns as the fiction writers also suggests that contemporary readers of these novels would have recognized the social concerns encoded in the rich woman as we modern readers may not. Immersing the novel of manners in its intellectual context allows us to return to one of the most familiar patterns in the nineteenth-century novel and interpret it in a new light. The complaint voiced in the epigram to my chapter, that such novels are "not incapable of being condensed into the moral that people should marry for love rather than for money" (Smalley 77), can be answered by arguing that their stories are invariably as much about money as they are about love.

Focusing on the way attitudes toward wealth are introduced into the novel through the figure of the rich woman, this book reads stories that insist they have nothing to do with materialism, the romances in which love triumphs over money, as, in fact, narratives about the novel's relation to its social context. The plot that invokes the contrast between the rich and the poor woman is also not, despite the absolute clarity of its central opposition, static. It changes dramatically over the course of the nineteenth century as one moves from Austen to James. Charting those changes, I read the marriage plot as mythic both in the sense that it is unnaturally symmetrical and in the sense that its details register a century-long reaction to the social transformations brought about by the evolution of capitalism in England. In reading romance narratives as making arguments about political economy, I turn Lévi-Strauss's claim that "economic exchanges offer an ideal commentary on marriage transactions" (66) on its head. I argue instead that an informed reading of the novel of manners reveals stories about marriage to be the place where critics can trace fiction's sustained engagement with the economic forces it seeks to resist but that also irrevocably shape the stories it tells.

CHAPTER ONE

SOCIAL DISTINCTION IN JANE AUSTEN

There, not to be vulgar, was distinction.

Jane Austen, *Emma*

Austen's plots intertwine what Walter Benn Michaels has famously called romance and real estate. They tell stories of courtship, but those stories are as much about the psychological stances needed to confront the engrossments of wealth as they are about love. They combine economic and romantic concerns by contrasting a negatively depicted rich woman with the novels' romantic heroines. Through her portraits of those two antithetical figures, Austen represents at the level of fiction the tension that Hume and Smith observed between the problematic effects of the wealth that was enriching English society and the behaviors needed to check the self-interest inevitably triggered by a thriving commercial economy. We need to think of Austen's stories of courtship and marriage as making arguments not just about personal relations but also about the key social issues. In them, Austen uses the contrast between the rich and poor woman to explore, as insistently as the prose writers of her period, "the process by which men living in a commercial society acquire moral ideas and may be taught how to improve them" (Phillipson 182).[1]

The passage from eighteenth-century moral philosophy that most clearly identifies the negative traits Austen associates with her rich women appeared in the version of *The Theory of Moral Sentiments* that Smith completed in 1789, more than thirty years after he had originally published the treatise.[2] By the time he revised that late volume Smith had become deeply pessimistic about the state of his culture and had added in a chapter in which he explained that in modern commercial society the

disposition to admire, and almost to worship, the rich and the powerful, and to despise, or, at least, to neglect persons of poor and mean condition, though necessary both to establish and to maintain the distinction of ranks and the order of society, is, at the same time, the great and most universal cause of the corruption of our moral sentiments. (61)[3]

These are the propensities that Austen captures in Miss Bingley and Lady Catherine de Bourgh in *Pride and Prejudice* (1813).[4] Those early caricatured depictions will be complicated in *Mansfield Park* (1814), whose antagonist, Mary Crawford, is such an appealing figure she attracts the novel's romantic hero, and in *Emma* (1816), where Emma Woodhouse becomes the heroine of her story. Together these three novels engage in a sequential meditation on the impact of wealth on late eighteenth- and early nineteenth-century culture.[5] In them Austen uses the tools of fiction—the structure of the plot, the development of character, the evocation of emotion—to work through the problem key to moral philosophers of the period: the question of what attitudes and values might make it possible to resist the attractions of wealth, attractions that were unavoidable given the expansion of a commercial culture that Smith and his contemporaries endorsed but also feared.[6]

Austen begins to represent wealth's propensity to corrupt the moral sentiments even before she introduces Miss Bingley and Lady Catherine de Bourgh in *Pride and Prejudice*. The thumbnail sketch of Mrs. John Dashwood in the opening pages of *Sense and Sensibility* (1811) allows us to identify the behaviors and attributes Austen will associate with the rich woman in her later novels, behaviors consistently described in terms that echo the writings of contemporary moral philosophers. The first chapter of *Sense and Sensibility* details the economic conditions that underlie its plot, as readers learn that its romantic heroines, Elinor and Marianne Dashwood, are left with little material provision when, on the death of their father, the family estate descends in its entirety to its male heir, their half brother John Dashwood. While Austen's narrator insists, ironically, that Elinor and Marianne's brother is "not an ill-disposed young man, unless to be rather cold hearted, and rather selfish, is to be ill-disposed" (7), the novel reserves the brunt of its satiric critique for his wealthy wife. Readers are told that "had he married a more amiable woman, he might have been made still more respectable. . . . But Mrs. John Dashwood was a strong caricature of himself;—more narrow-minded and selfish" (7). The description of Mrs. John Dashwood as a caricature of her husband underscores the representational slippage that means, as I argued in my preface, that women reveal the negative effects of possessing wealth in more exaggerated or excessive form than men.[7]

Calling attention to her own figurative strategy, Austen stresses that in the caricatured rich woman she is creating a portrait that is the verbal equivalent of the satirical sketches that appeared in *Punch* over the course of the century, drawings whose meaning could be captured in a single phrase or punch line because readers already understood the topical concerns those images addressed. Austen's contemporaries would have described Mrs. John Dashwood by way of reference to "engrossment," a term particularly useful to essayists like Smith and Hume. In the eighteenth century, engrossment was associated with both property and the mind. It referred to "the action of buying up in large quantities, of collecting greedily from all quarters" and was used to describe monopolies and the enclosure of lands.[8] But it was also already used in the sense we know it best today to mean "the state or fact of being engrossed or absorbed in occupations, thoughts, etc." (*OED*). Engrossment therefore marks the way "different modes of" or perhaps different relationships to "property may be seen as generating or encouraging different modes of personality" (Pocock 103). In Mrs. John Dashwood's opening conversations, Austen's readers experience the intertwining of property and psyche as the rich woman reveals the engrossment of her personality by incrementally teaching her husband to think of wealth as something that must be engrossed.

Through a series of interventions she modifies his intentions until finally he is comfortable with contributing no money to the maintenance of his half sisters and their mother. Initially, when he proposes giving his sisters £1000 a piece, his wife argues that since they are only half sisters "it would be better for all parties if the sum were diminished one half"(10). Reminding him of his own interests, she comments that even this smaller bequest would "rob his child, and his only child too, of so large a sum" (9). As she insists, in a phrase that underscores the need to keep wealth consolidated, "when the money is once parted with, it never can return" (10). This impulse toward consolidation leads the couple to view any form of expenditure as negative. As she tells her husband when he proposes to purchase an annuity for his relations, "My mother was clogged with the payment of three to old superannuated servants by my father's will," to which he replies, "It is certainly an unpleasant thing . . . to have those kind of yearly drains on one's income. One's fortune, as your mother justly says, is *not* one's own" (11, emphasis in the original). This conversation shows how engrossment, which purports to be about the pragmatic preservation of wealth, can create a blockage that threatens to do away with the reciprocal social and economic relations that should fuel an active economy.

Hume recognized this danger as inherent in the amassing of wealth that was crucial to the expansion of commerce. In attempting to define the juncture at which acquisitive and consumerist behavior verged on becoming counterproductive, he argued that "no gratification, however sensual, can of itself be esteemed vicious. A gratification is only vicious when it engrosses all a man's expense, and leaves no ability for such acts of duty and generosity as are required by his situation and fortune" (176). The ungenerous behavior described at the opening of *Sense and Sensibility*, as Mrs. John Dashwood leads her husband away from what he initially imagined to be the gesture of duty and generosity required of him by his death-bed promise to his father to take care of his half sisters, constitutes engrossment in the sense Hume means it here, as both an economic and a psychological stance. In Austen's novel this engrossment carries over from Mrs. John Dashwood's attitude toward wealth to her general behavior. She demonstrates, in her deal-ings with her husband's family, "with how little attention to the comfort of other people she could act when occasion required it" (8). When she chooses to move into the Dashwood home immediately after the death of her husband's father, the narrator comments that "no one could dispute her right to come; the house was her husband's from the moment of his father's decease; but the indelicacy of her conduct was so much the greater" (7). Like engrossment, "indelicacy" would have had strong cultural resonances for Austen's readers because of its association with ongoing debates about the impact of wealth on society. As G. J. Barker-Benfield has explained, "'Delicacy' gave particular meaning to the 'moral sense' hypothesized by the Cambridge Platonists and Shaftesbury. When implemented, the code of delicacy mediated a complex power struggle" (299).

The conversations between Mr. and Mrs. John Dashwood that open *Sense and Sensibility* would have allowed Austen's contemporary readers to identify the social issues that underlie the novel's subsequent stories of courtship. The novel is able to work toward the ideals of good taste, good manners, or delicacy represented by the marriages that conclude the story by opening with a rich woman who represents the opposite of the values exemplified in those unions. While the initial chapters of *Sense and Sensibility* may feel like comic set pieces that could be cut without chang-ing the import of the novel's romantic plot, in fact, those scenes provide a baseline that allowed contemporary readers to identify the social and psychological stances that the behavior of Austen's heroines is designed to counter. But though those engrossed values are key to the moral universe of *Sense and Sensibility*, the rich woman who embodies them remains peripheral to the story, appearing only in the novel's first chapters and never reentering the text in significant form after that. It is in *Pride and Prejudice* that the rich woman becomes central to the plot.

Appearing from the story's beginning to its end, Miss Bingley and Lady Cath-erine de Bourgh represent the attitudes toward property that the novel's virtuous characters must reject in order to exemplify the civility the novel celebrates in its climactic scenes at Pemberley. Such refusals work at the level of courtship, as Darcy learns to prefer Elizabeth's behavior to that of either Miss Bingley or Lady Catherine de Bourgh. They also mark the mental growth of the novel's romantic heroines, Jane and Elizabeth Bennet. When the Bennet sisters first meet the Bingleys and Darcy, Jane's optimistic nature leads her to assume that Bingley and his sisters are equally amiable, while Elizabeth's more cynical eye assures her that Darcy and his aunt are equally offensive, both filled with "arrogance . . . and . . . selfish disdain of the feelings of others" (128). By the novel's end these impressions are proved false, as each Bennet sister learns to prefer a wealthy man to his female relatives. Jane asserts, in what Elizabeth describes as "the most unforgiving speech . . . that I ever heard you utter" (228), that Miss Bingley's sisters "were certainly no friends to his acquaintance with me" (227). Soon after Elizabeth asks herself, "How could I ever think [Lady Catherine] like her nephew?" (230). In showing both her heroes and heroines learning to discriminate between the proper and improper uses of wealth, Austen insists, as I argued in my preface, on a difference that runs along gendered lines. Rich women exhibit engrossment, while rich men demonstrate that it is possible to be both wealthy and virtuous, as they choose for their spouses women who embody the resistance to materialist values the novel praises. The marriage between Elizabeth Bennet and Fitzwilliam Darcy that concludes the novel represents the end Deidre Shauna Lynch has argued a number of eighteenth-century texts aim toward; they imagine "a way to be acquisitive and antimaterialist at once" (119).

However, despite the more important role the rich woman plays in *Pride and Prejudice*, Miss Bingley and Lady Catherine de Bourgh remain relatively static figures. Readers know immediately what they represent and how to react to them. Fully identified with the admiration of wealth that corrupts the moral sentiments, they appear in scenes that are isolated from the rest of the narrative, like skits in a burlesque show. These scenes invite readers to laugh at the absurdity of rich women and dismiss them as characters that do not need to be taken seriously.[9] Such portraits suggest, of course, that it is relatively easy for individuals to resist what the rich woman represents: the material appeals that threaten to corrupt the moral sentiments. In *Mansfield Park* we encounter caricatured rich women in the novel's opening chapters, as Thomas Bertram's daughters Maria and Julia are introduced. Those crassly comic figures are, however, quickly superseded by Mary Crawford, a rich woman who is not a caricature but a fully realized individual who attracts the novel's virtuous hero in a way that Miss Bingley and Lady Catherine's daughter never do in *Pride and Prejudice*. Through Mary Crawford, Austen raises the issue that Smith addresses throughout *The Theory of Moral Sentiments* when he shows, at some length, how natural it is for individuals to admire wealth and what it can do.

We feel this attractiveness in the energy and élan Mary Crawford exhibits as she pursues the desires she imagines wealth can satisfy. She is uninterested in the subjects that engross Miss Bingley and Lady Catherine: fashion, taste, and the acquisition of estates. She values not the signs of wealth but money itself. As she tells Edmund Bertram when he asks whether she intends to be very rich, "To be sure. Do not you?—Do not we all?" (146). This is, of course, the problem that troubled both Smith and Hume about the commercial culture that was emerging around them. In her later novel Austen works toward conveying, at the level of plot and desire, the emotional valences of the choice between wealth and virtue in a world where virtue ceases to be conceived as having as much appeal as wealth. The shift between these two novels shows Austen working through a process of thinking one can also trace as one moves from Hume's early to his later work and from Hume's essays to Smith's. In that sequence of texts eighteenth-century moral philosophers gradually cease to imagine that individuals might acquire virtue through the easy admiration depicted in *Pride and Prejudice*. By the moment of Smith's final version of *The Theory of Moral Sentiments*, "The reign of feeling and passion proclaimed in Hume's *Treatise* is over" (Mullan 53). This loss of feeling is reflected in the fact that in *Mansfield Park* Mary Crawford seems to have the wit and exuberance of Elizabeth Bennet and Fanny Price seems to be almost unappealing.[10]

Moving to make the rich woman an attractive figure and acknowledging the universal desire for wealth, Austen transforms the tenor of the world she depicts in *Mansfield Park*. In this novel she paints, as she does later in *Emma*, the world Smith describes in *The Theory of Moral Sentiments*, a place where behavior, even morality, is a social creation, determined by our relation to and perception of others.[11] We feel this emphasis on perception as the novel opens and Sir Thomas Bertram is deciding to adopt his disadvantaged niece Fanny and raise her with his own well-to-do daughters. As he contemplates the problem of providing them with an education that maintains "the distinction proper to be made between the girls as they grow up" (10), we hear echoes of Smith's anxieties about how to "establish and to maintain the distinction of ranks and the order of society" (*Theory of Moral Sentiments* 61). But in *Mansfield Park* those distinctions are established not simply through the possession of wealth but also through the way individuals are taught to think as children. In seeking "to preserve in the minds of my *daughters* the consciousness of what they are, without making them think too lowly of their cousin; and how, without depressing her spirits too far, to make her remember that she is not a *Miss Bertram*" (10), Sir Thomas chooses an education for them that will, as the behavior of his grown-up daughters bears out, produce the self-engrossed and property-conscious individuals Austen's readers were familiar with from her earlier portraits of Mrs. John Dashwood, Miss Bingley, and Lady Catherine de Bourgh.

In *Mansfield Park*, Austen makes a key move from depicting wealthy women as fully formed figures to showing how education and environment might produce such figures. Like the Bertram sisters, Mary Crawford is characterized as someone who might have been virtuous had she not been "vitiated" by the atmosphere in which she was raised. In making this shift from representing the rich woman as a particular kind of being to showing the forces that shaped her, Austen engages in the kind of thinking one finds in the moral philosophies of the era. As Nicholas Phillipson explains, writers like Hume and Smith turned "from the study of ends to the study of means; to the principles which explain how we acquire moral sentiments and ideas of virtue and to the lessons which a virtuously-minded agent could hope to draw from a study of his own moral history and that of mankind in general" (181). Austen completes this process in *Emma*, in which the rich woman is not exorcised from the virtuous community formed at the story's end as the hero chooses to marry her poorer antithesis. Instead, for the first—and last—time in the Austen canon, the rich woman is the story's protagonist, the heroine who marries the novel's propertied and virtuous hero.[12] In this novel, the contrast between the rich and the poor woman is not a large-scale structure that shapes the plot. Instead it is a pattern of thinking that shapes the wealthy heroine's sequential interactions with three women poorer than she: Harriet Smith, Jane Fairfax, and Miss Bates.

In charting the ways in which Emma Woodhouse's happy self-involvement leads to what she finally comes to perceive as an injury to all three women, the novel represents the self-interest triggered by wealth as embedded at a deeper and more psychological level than is true of the rich women in Austen's previous novels. By making Emma a character who internalizes common assumptions about the economic bases of social distinction, Austen invites readers to identify with and critique the pleasures that wealth makes possible at the level not of the possession of objects that we see in *Pride and Prejudice*, nor of thinking that we see in *Mansfield Park*, but of the imagination and unconscious drives.[13] In *Emma*, prosperity leads the individual "to indulge . . . at the expence of other people, the natural preference which every man has for his own happiness above that of other people"

(*Theory of Moral Sentiments* 82). From Smith's point of view, such self-interested behavior is the inevitable consequence of living in a thriving commercial society, but it must also be curbed. He describes that process of curbing in *The Theory of Moral Sentiments*, positing the importance of what he calls sympathy in regulating interpersonal exchange in much the same way that in *The Wealth of Nations* he posits the crucial role the invisible hand plays in regulating market exchanges. Austen will work out the implications of Smith's concept of sympathy in *Emma*, as the problematic attitudes toward wealth that are externalized *Pride and Prejudice* and *Mansfield Park* become part of the heroine's internal makeup, a worldview rather than an external environment.[14]

"Awkward Taste" in *Pride and Prejudice*

Pride and Prejudice works at the level of fiction like the treatises on ethics that Smith describes in the last section of *The Theory of Moral Sentiments*: "Such works present us with agreeable and lively pictures of manners. By the vivacity of their descriptions they inflame our natural love of virtue" (329). The novel's famously lively heroine offers a picture of manners so agreeable one can hardly help loving her and the virtue she represents.[15] This process is enacted within the novel as Elizabeth's behavior brings Fitzwilliam Darcy not simply to love her but to espouse a new form of civility. In *Pride and Prejudice* that ideal of good manners emerges in the late scenes at Pemberley, during which Elizabeth proves, for the first time, to have civil relatives in the persons of the Gardiners, Darcy behaves, for the first time, with "perfect civility" (163), and we encounter, for the first time, in Georgiana Darcy, a wealthy woman whose "manners were perfectly unassuming and gentle" (169).[16] When Darcy is at Pemberley he displays no engrossment but is, instead, properly generous to his subordinates, spending money to fit up a room for his sister and being "just as affable to the poor" (161) as he is to his relatives. As Elizabeth thinks when he finally behaves with what she defines as agreeable manners, "Never, even in the company of his dear friends at Netherfield, or his dignified relations at Rosings, had she seen him so desirous to please" (170–71).

These are the uses of wealth that Hume and Smith praised, uses that enriched those less fortunate. The fact that the encomium that begins to transform Elizabeth's perception of Darcy comes from an underling is proof of his virtuous relation to those below him: "What praise is more valuable than the praise of an intelligent servant? As a brother, a landlord, a master, she considered how many people's happiness were in his guardianship!—How much of pleasure or pain it was in his power to bestow!" (162). The novel has taught readers to understand that, when Elizabeth Bennet finds herself delighted with Pemberley, as she does on two different occasions, her reaction is in no way similar to the delight that Lady Catherine instructs her guest to take in Rosings nor to the fawning admiration that makes Miss Bingley exclaim in the course of her conversations at Netherfield, "What a delightful library you have at Pemberley, Mr. Darcy!" (26). The reader knows that Elizabeth, with her prior experience of her father's library, would also be delighted by the library at Pemberley, but the novel has gone to great lengths to distinguish Miss Bingley's delight from Elizabeth's. Indeed, the function of the three scenes that form the backbone of *Pride and Prejudice*, the scenes at Netherfield, at Rosings, and at Pemberley, is to establish the difference between a proper and improper relation to wealth.

But even in the scenes at Pemberley in which the proper relation is established, still Miss Bingley and Lady Catherine are invoked to mark the negative version of the property values Darcy's estate embodies. Darcy's civil behavior to Elizabeth's middle-class relatives is characterized as something that "would draw down the ridicule and censure of the ladies both of Netherfield and Rosings" (171). Miss Annesley, Georgiana Darcy's paid companion, is described as "a genteel, agreeable-looking woman, whose endeavour to introduce some kind of discourse, proved her to be more truly well bred than either [Miss Bingley or Mrs. Hurst]" (173). The interior of Darcy's house is so impressive because "it was neither gaudy nor uselessly fine; with less of splendor, and more real elegance, than the furniture of Rosings" (159). Even the famous passage in which Elizabeth concludes that "to be mistress of Pemberley might be something!" (159) could be read as alluding to the engrossed rich women who play such a key role in the novel.

The narrator prefaces that comment with a description of the grounds of Darcy's estate, explaining how "a stream of some natural importance was swelled into greater, but without any artificial appearance. Its banks were neither formal, nor falsely adorned. Elizabeth was delighted. She had never seen a place for which nature had done more, or where natural beauty was so little counteracted by an awkward taste" (159). The word "swell" suggests the process by which prosperity swells the consequence of individuals, but there is an uneasy tipping point at which natural importance might become artificial, as the swelling prosperity produces becomes excessive.[17] This is the excess that Austen represents through Miss Bingley and Lady Catherine, characters that exemplify what happens when the natural consequence wealth brings swells into the "awkward taste" that is evoked in this passage to identify what Pemberley is not.[18] In the episodes at Netherfield and Rosings, the rich women display a love of status, distinction, and fashion, the artificiality and false adornment that Austen opposes to the natural beauty evoked at Pemberley.

Those earlier episodes open with conversations in which Miss Bingley expatiates on what kind of estate her brother should buy and what accomplishments a marriageable woman should have and in which Lady Catherine talks about the grandeur of her own estate and the accomplishments that she and her daughter possess by virtue of their social status. Those dialogues, which have a static quality conferred by the rich woman holding forth about values that seem socially self-evident, are followed by interchanges that are much more lively. Elizabeth Bennet engages in a discussion of character, first talking about the differences between the country and the city with Mr. Darcy and Mr. Bingley and later considering Darcy's public coldness as she banters with him and his cousin Colonel Fitzwilliam. The juxtaposition of conversations invites readers to feel the heaviness and pomposity of an engrossed relation to the material world as opposed to the lightness and ease of an attitude that focuses on personality rather than possessions.

Through this difference in behavior Austen allows readers to grasp the concept of manners that was, as J. G. A. Pocock has argued, replacing virtue in this period:

> As the individual moved from the farmer-warrior world of ancient citizenship or Gothic *libertas*, he entered an increasingly transactional universe of "commerce and the arts" . . . [and] was more than compensated for his loss of antique virtue by an indefinite and perhaps infinite enrichment of his personality, the product of the multiplying relationships, with both things and persons, in which he became progressively involved. Since these new relationships were social and not political in character, the capacities which they led the individual to develop were called not "virtues" but "manners." (48–49)

But, as *Pride and Prejudice* demonstrates, the only way to invoke the "manners" that were replacing the older concept of virtue was to depict bad manners or ill breeding, a negative or antisocial relation to persons and things that allows its opposite to emerge as a valued behavior.

In the early scenes in which Elizabeth interacts with Miss Bingley and the Hursts at Netherfield, Austen carefully associates the rich woman's rude behavior with the three factors that were typically identified as the problematic effects of the birth of a consumer society: "social distinction, emulation, and fashion," which combined "to increase production of man-made goods astronomically" (Lubbock 97).[19] William Hazlitt's description of fashion as "the abortive issue of vain ostentation and exclusive egotism," as "haughty, trifling, affected, servile, despotic, mean, and ambitious, precise and fantastical, all in a breath" (150), provides the perfect gloss for the thumbnail sketches of Miss Bingley, her sister, and brother-in-law Mr. Hurst in the early scenes at Netherfield. There they behave as if, in the words of Josiah Wedgwood, "*fashion* is infinitely superior to *merit* in many respects" (quoted in McKendrick 108, emphasis in the original).[20] Insisting on the importance of elegance in all matters of behavior, they exemplify the harmful effects of fashion as detailed in the *Tatler*, which observed that "amongst the Censor's particular targets were women's fashions, their consumption of domestic ornaments and furniture, their grand extravagance and behaviour" (Lubbock 182).[21] The censor also condemned overrefinements in diet, sending out "a patriotic counterblast against the fashion for French fricassés and ragouts and a call for a return 'to the Food of (our) Forefathers'" (Lubbock 184).

Appropriately, given that the novel most extensively explores the impact of wealth on behavior in scenes set at estates, Austen explicitly associates Miss Bingley with what Christopher Kent calls "social emulation" (96–99) and David Spring "positional goods" (60–63) when the conversation turns to the possibility of Mr. Bingley acquiring an estate. As Neil McKendrick notes, by 1763 the *British Magazine* was able to say that "the present rage of imitating the manners of high life hath spread itself so far among the gentlefolks of lower life, that 'in a few years we shall probably have no common folk at all'" (25). These concerns are reflected in the conversation between brother and sister that opens with Miss Bingley exclaiming

> "Charles, when you build *your* house, I wish it may be half as delightful as Pemberley."
>
> "I wish it may."
>
> "But I would really advise you to make your purchase in that neighborhood, and take Pemberley for a kind of model . . ."
>
> "With all my heart; I will buy Pemberley itself if Darcy will sell it."
>
> "I am talking of possibilities, Charles."
>
> "Upon my word, Caroline, I should think it more possible to acquire Pemberley by purchase than by imitation." (26, emphasis in the original)

Though Mr. Bingley is not here explicitly critical of his sister, the word "imitation" in his exclamation identifies Miss Bingley with the desire to emulate the rich that was being increasingly critiqued in the eighteenth century. Miss Bingley's desire to imitate Pemberley is contrasted to her brother's joking offer to buy it.

That offer might at first seem crass, reflecting that the Bingleys' wealth comes from trade, but Austen's novel suggests instead that it is, like the man who makes it, direct and honest and therefore mannerly.[22] In contrast, the more slyly imitative comments of his sister mark her as displaying what the novel will define in the case of Lady Catherine de Bourgh as ill breeding. In this conversation, as I argued in my preface, readers feel the difference not only between Elizabeth and Miss Bingley, or virtue and wealth, but are made aware of differences within the Bingley family, as attitudes toward one's possessions are articulated along a gendered axis in which men display a positive attitude and women a negative one. This difference is reiterated and complicated in the conversation that then follows the one about estates: the interchange about what makes a woman desirable on the marriage market. In the latter exchange Austen makes the problems of Miss Bingley's assumptions more visible by introducing Darcy into the conversational mix.

Through the comments of the paired friends Bingley and Darcy, the novel's two romantic heroes, Austen references the realms Pocock has identified as key to the development of manners in the eighteenth century: commerce and the arts. When Bingley enthuses over how women "paint tables, cover skreens and net purses" (27), he values a series of elegant commodities that ends in a purse, thereby coming close to putting into words what Miss Bingley believes but wishes to avoid articulating directly, that women are like those painted tables and covered screens: decorated objects whose possessions, their purses, are the only things that make them desirable. In contrast, Darcy insists that a woman needs something more to be desirable on the marriage market; her accomplishments must be "more substantial," involving "the improvement of her mind by extensive reading" (27). *Pride and Prejudice* suggests that either of these attitudes is admirable in its own right. The development that was problematic for eighteenth-century moral philosophers was the intermingling of the values of the two, an intermingling represented by Miss Bingley. Positioned between Mr. Bingley and Mr. Darcy, she insists that in order to be desirable on the marriage market "a woman must have a thorough knowledge of music, singing, drawing, dancing, and the modern languages . . . and besides all this, she must possess a certain something in her air and manner of walking, the tone of her voice, her address and expressions" (27). She implicitly conceives of activities that were thought of as arts in the cultural sense—music, singing, drawing, dancing—as arts in the artful sense, external allures that mark a commodity as valuable.[23]

Linking accomplishments that require both talent and training to the purely fashionable attributes of having a stylish walk, voice, and expression, she flattens out any differences between the two arenas. She represents the attitude that was feared during the period, society's propensity to "subordinate the dominion of what would later be called culture to the immediate and ineluctable imperatives of trade" (Agnew *Worlds* 176).[24] While it would be easy to assume that Miss Bingley's problematic tendency to mix commerce and the arts is simply a sign of her family's origins in trade, Austen undercuts this facile association by representing the landed Lady Catherine de Bourgh as displaying attitudes almost identical to those showcased in the moneyed Miss Bingley.[25] Austen's novel suggests that, in a culture where money is becoming a primary value, both those who are upwardly mobile and those who are already established in the upper ranks of society will, in Smith's formulation, be increasingly inclined to assume that the power of wealth should be admired and the effects of poverty disparaged.[26] The difference between Miss Bingley and Lady Catherine is that the former's conversations revolve around fashion and imitative spending, while the latter's reveal an improper relation between social distinction and taste, that category of such importance to eighteenth-century moral philosophers.

Lady Catherine has an enormous confidence in the rightness of her own opinions that leads her to inquire into anything and everything in her inferiors' lives: "Nothing was beneath this great Lady's attention, which could furnish her with an occasion of dictating to others" (109). Her meddling is so intrusive that Elizabeth, who "felt all the impertinence of her questions" (109), must seek an arena where she will be "beyond the reach of Lady Catherine's curiosity" (113). Austen stresses the way this wealth-fueled egoism perverts traditional relations of patronage and deference, transforming concern for others into an occasion to assert one's own superiority. When the narrator tells us that Elizabeth Bennet "had heard nothing of Lady Catherine that spoke her awful from any extraordinary talents or miraculous virtue, and the mere stateliness of money and rank, she thought she could witness without trepidation" (107), we might hear echoes of Hume who seeks to disentangle wealth from taste. He argues that "when a man is possessed of that talent, he . . . receives more enjoyment from a poem, or a piece of reasoning, than the most expensive luxury can afford" (11). In contrast, "when the critic has no delicacy, he judges without distinction, and is only affected by the grosser and more palpable qualities of the object; the finer touches pass unnoticed and disregarded" (147).

Austen works out the tension between these two positions in the scenes in which both Darcy and Lady Catherine comment on Elizabeth's piano playing. While Elizabeth talks about the need for practice to achieve superior execution,

Darcy emphasizes that art has a subtlety that requires a receptive audience, telling her that "we neither of us perform to strangers" (117). Lady Catherine, in contrast, assumes that possessing the externals, wealth and rank, must inevitably mean that one also possesses the ability to perform and discriminate aesthetically.[27] Talking loudly while Elizabeth plays, Lady Catherine then insists that "her taste is not equal to Anne's" and that "Anne would have been a delightful performer, had her health allowed her to learn" (117).[28] Rudely interrupting a conversation between Elizabeth Bennet and her nephew Colonel Fitzwilliam to find out what they are discussing, she exclaims, "Of music! Then pray speak aloud. It is of all subjects my delight. I must have my share in the conversation, if you are speaking of music. There are few people in England, I suppose, who have more true enjoyment of music than myself, or a better natural taste. If I had ever learnt, I should have been a great proficient" (115).[29]

The early description of Elizabeth's piano playing as a "performance [that] was pleasing, though by no means *capital*" (17, emphasis added) is particularly apt since Elizabeth's taste is represented in both the scenes at Rosings and those at Netherfield as an intangible possession, a form of refinement or delicacy that trumps capital. In the looking-glass logic of Austen's world, to have nothing that would make you desirable on the marriage market, to lack fashionable manners and the rank and possessions that accompany them, is, in fact, to have everything, to possess the value or virtue, the good manners, that will protect you from the corruptions of wealth.[30] An emblem of the "immaterialism" Hume celebrated as the epitome of good taste, Elizabeth's behavior is most appealingly evoked in the scenes where she is contrasted to a woman of wealth who assumes that value is established at the level of the grossly material, that her possession of an estate, knowledge of fashion, access to the upper strata of society *must* make her more valuable and tasteful than others.

Miss Bingley and her sister defining Elizabeth Bennet as having "no conversation, no stile, no taste, no beauty[,] . . . nothing, in short, to recommend her" (24), exposes a tension in my argument. I have been describing Elizabeth Bennet and the other women who are contrasted to the rich woman in the novel of manners as "poor." In fact, Elizabeth is a member of the gentry, the daughter of a landowner, a woman who simply stands to inherit little on the occasion of her father's death. The other women who appear in my study are also hardly figures of poverty or social dependence.[31] Nevertheless, the representation of Elizabeth Bennet helps us understand why the heroine of the marriage plot needs to be perceived as poor. The dynamics of a society that values wealth require Miss Bingley and Lady Catherine to define others as lacking in order for themselves to be valued. As they depress the pretentions of others, they also assume those pretentions exist. In Elizabeth Austen creates a character that refuses to emulate or automatically admire those who possess wealth. This refusal is marked, of course, at the ball at the opening of *Pride and Prejudice*, when she does not permit herself to be depressed by Darcy's criticism of her. As she explains to Charlotte Lucas, "He has a very satirical eye, and if I do not begin by being impertinent myself, I shall soon grow afraid of him" (17). Her resistance is reiterated in the scenes at Netherfield and Rosings where she will not perceive herself as lacking in the ways that both Miss Bingley and Lady Catherine insist she is.

The effect of her stance is to reverse the valences of envy, to make the rich woman envious of the intangible attributes the poor woman possesses, as Elizabeth begins to attract the attention of the figure that "engrosses" both Miss Bingley and Lady Catherine (24, 114), the novel's wealthiest character, Fitzwilliam Darcy. This shift is Austen's opening gambit in her attempt to find a way in her fiction to make virtue more attractive than wealth. But it is a strategy that no longer holds in the novels that follow *Pride and Prejudice*. In them, the rich woman becomes more attractive and the appeal of the poor woman less obvious. That representational shift allows Austen to come closer to dramatizing the real fear that informs the writings of both Hume and Smith, the fear that for those living in a thriving commercial culture the pursuit of wealth will feel like such a vital activity that it will be increasingly hard for individuals to discern the attractions of virtue.

Mansfield Park: "Distinctions of a Different Character"

Unlike *Pride and Prejudice*, *Mansfield Park* presents readers with a fully commercial society, which may explain the frequently discussed reference to Sir Thomas Bertram's plantation in Antigua.[32] The person who most clearly voices the values and assumptions of that society is Mary Crawford, whose discussions of wealth reveal the degree to which a new value system has changed both individuals' actions and their consciousnesses. Her comments mark time and again her awareness and acceptance of the extent to which her culture values wealth. For her the marriage market is not about the accomplishments that both Miss Bingley and Lady Catherine mention in *Pride and Prejudice*. It is about expenditure and recompense.[33] She urges Fanny Price to wear the gold chain that Henry Crawford has bought, telling her that he would take pleasure in "seeing round your lovely throat an ornament which his money purchased three years ago" (178). She explains in referring to the pleasure the eldest Miss Bertram will take in hosting a party at her splendid London townhouse, that "she will then feel—to use a vulgar phrase—that she has got her pennyworth for her penny" (268). She tells Fanny to take pleasure in Henry Crawford's courtship; it is delightful "having it in one's power to pay off the debts of one's sex" (246). When she excuses her brother for eloping with the married Maria Bertram, she explains, "I do not mean to defend Henry at your sister's expence" (308). For her, the power that lies in wealth is not of possessing objects that others would envy but of being free to follow one's desires.

She assumes that money and the complex commercial structures it supports allow individuals to control the natural exigencies that have traditionally constrained human freedom. Arriving in Mansfield with "the true London maxim, that every thing is to be got with money" (43), Mary Crawford cannot understand why, if she is willing to pay, she cannot hire a cart to transport her harp. It does not occur to her that at harvest season all such vehicles will be in use bringing in the hay.[34] Later, when her sister Mrs. Grant complains that the swift descent of an early hard frost will destroy her laurel and mean that the turkey must be killed and eaten before the Sunday on which she had planned to serve it, Mary Crawford responds by exclaiming, "The sweets of housekeeping in a country village! . . . Commend me to the nurseryman and the poulterer," to which as Mrs. Grant replies, "We have no such people in Mansfield" (146). Associated with the metropolis as opposed to the countryside, Mary Crawford indulges in the urban tastes that Smith worried would impact rural landowners.[35] "For a pair of diamond buckles perhaps," he observed, "or for something as frivolous and useless, they exchanged the maintenance, or what is the same thing, the price of the maintenance of a thousand men for a year, and with it the whole weight and authority which it could give them" (*Wealth of Nations* 367).[36]

Austen's novel represents the appeal of urban wealth in more intangible terms than this passage suggests. That appeal lies in the energy and freedom such wealth affords and is so strong that it leads the country-bred Edmund Bertram to admire Mary Crawford, despite the differences in their value systems. Those differences are aired over the course of the novel in a series of conversations in which Mary Crawford expresses an admiration of wealth that Smith feared was both an inevitable consequence of commercial society and the factor most likely to cause the corruption of the moral sentiments. As Smith admitted in *The Theory of Moral Sentiments*, "It is scarce agreeable to good morals, or even to good language, perhaps, to say, that mere wealth and greatness, abstracted from merit and virtue, deserve our respect. We must acknowledge, however, that they almost constantly obtain it; and that they may, therefore, be considered as, in some respects, the natural objects of it" (62). His use of the term "natural" here is crucial, since it suggests that the new monetary values have so thoroughly replaced the old that the divorce from nature they entail has in a sense become invisible. Mary Crawford can speak naturally and easily about the value of material success, telling Edmund, "Be honest and poor, by all means—but I shall not envy you; I do not much think I shall even respect you. I have a much greater respect for those that are honest and rich" (147).

This statement confirms, almost echoes, Smith's assertion that "in equal degrees of merit there is scarce any man who does not respect more the rich and the great, than the poor and the humble" (*Theory of Moral Sentiments* 62). As she tells Edmund when he asks her not to look down on his honesty, "I do look down upon it, if it might have been higher. I must look down upon any thing contented with obscurity when it might rise to distinction" (147). Mary Crawford consciously invokes the term "distinction," as both Miss Bingley and Lady Catherine understand it, to mean the acquisition of wealth, power, or social status. Edmund attempts to resist the absolute linkage between distinction and material conditions by arguing for mental and moral rather than monetary criteria, insisting that "there *are* distinctions which I should be miserable if I thought myself without any chance—absolutely without chance or possibility of obtaining—but they are of a different character" (147, emphasis in the original). This passage allows us to identify the shift that takes place between *Pride and Prejudice* and *Mansfield Park* in the values that are contrasted to the materialism represented by the rich woman.

When Edmund and Mary Crawford discuss the differences between legal or military vocations and the church, she asserts that "men love to distinguish themselves, and in either of the other lines, distinction may be gained, but not in the church. A clergyman is nothing" (66). This line echoes Miss Bingley's assertion in *Pride and Prejudice* that Elizabeth Bennet possesses nothing, Miss Bingley assuming that because she has no wealth, she also has no taste, no aesthetic value. In *Mansfield Park* the nothing that is opposed to ambition and the pursuit of wealth is religion. In defending the clergy Edmund argues in favor of morality rather than taste; he insists that "with regard to their influencing public manners, Miss Crawford must not misunderstand me, or suppose I mean to call them the arbiters of good breeding, the regulators of refinement and courtesy, the masters of the ceremonies of life. The *manners* I speak of, might rather be called *conduct*, perhaps, the result of good principles" (67, emphasis in the original).[37] Smith, too, uses the term "conduct," explaining that the *conduct* of all those who are contented to walk in the humble paths of private and peaceable life, derives from the same principle the greater part of the beauty and grace which belong to it; a beauty and grace, which, though much less dazzling, is not always less pleasing than those which accompany the more splendid actions of the hero, the statesman, or the legislator. (*Theory of Moral Sentiments* 242, emphasis added)

The problem of a commercial society as Smith conceives it is how such humble, private, peaceable conduct could be made attractive enough that individuals will choose it rather than the "dazzling" and more obvious pleasures of wealth. This dilemma is played out in *Mansfield Park* as Edmund Bertram is caught between Mary Crawford's sophisticated and excitingly contemporary appeal and the more familiar and less exciting pleasures of Fanny Price, who embraces the puritan values Smith describes when he asserts that "temperance, decency, modesty, and moderation, are always amiable, and can seldom be directed to any bad end. It is from the unremitting steadiness of those gentler exertions of self-command, that the amiable virtue of chastity, that the respectable virtues of industry and frugality, derive all that sober lustre which attends them" (*Theory of Moral Sentiments* 242). The question that both Smith and Austen raise is how one can make the "sober luster" of these stoical virtues visible.[38] In a fully commercial culture, how, as Edmund asks Mary Crawford "may honesty at least rise to any distinction?" (147). This, as Austen's narrator notes, "was not so very easy a question to answer" (147). The problem is not just how honesty and virtue can be granted the rank they deserve but how they can be distinguished at all, made visible in a world where commercial values insistently draw individuals' attentions in other directions.

We come here to the heart of the contrast between the rich and the poor woman as it is depicted in *Mansfield Park*, the question of how the retiring Fanny Price, who seems "almost as fearful of notice and praise as other women were of neglect" (136), can compete with the dashing Mary Crawford, with her flamboyance, her harp playing, her horseback riding, her sophisticated London ways. On watching her wealthy rival flirt with Edmund Bertram, Fanny Price realizes that "*she* could not equal them in their warmth. *Her* spirits sank under the glow of theirs, and she felt herself becoming too nearly nothing to both" (118, emphasis in the original). In the presence of palpable desire, Fanny retires to the blankness of "the little white attic" (105), which is cold because of "there never being a fire in it on Fanny's account" (106). In these scenes virtue is coldness and lack, while wealth is so warm it attracts even the virtuous.[39]

This language of coldness and warmth would, like that of engrossment, delicacy, distinction, and emulation, have been familiar to Austen's contemporaries from the writings of moral philosophers of the period. John Mullan notes that

> Hutcheson wrote to Hume, worrying about the tendency of the *Treatise* to avoid the recommendation of duty or virtue in favour of description and analysis. Hume homed in on this anxiety: "What affected me most in your Remarks is your observing, that there wants a certain Warmth in the Cause of Virtue, which, you think, all Good Men wou'd relish, & cou'd not displease amidst abstract Enquiry." (32)

As the difference between the romantic heroines of *Pride and Prejudice* and *Mansfield Park* suggests, the problem for those writing about the choice between wealth and virtue in the period was that it became increasingly difficult to imagine virtue as warmly attractive in the way that wealth is.

Smith argued in *The Theory of Moral Sentiments* that "the one [is] more gaudy and glittering in its colouring; the other more correct and more exquisitely beautiful in its outline: the one forcing itself upon the notice of every wandering eye; the other, attracting the attention of scarce any body but the most studious and careful observer" (62).[40] In *Mansfield Park* this difference is evoked at the level of the body as well as of behavior. The virtuous Fanny is "delicate and puny" (10), "small of her age, with no glow of complexion[,] . . . exceedingly timid and shy, and shrinking from notice" (11). Her wealthy Bertram cousins note her "inferiority of age and strength" (15) and take pleasure in there being "as striking a difference between [them] in person, as education had given to their address" (11). Fanny's appearance reflects the difficulty of representing the appeals of virtue in a world where, unlike that depicted in *Pride and Prejudice*, wealth is so attractive. We feel that attraction in Mary Crawford who, like the Bertram sisters, is "active and fearless," taking "to the pure genuine pleasure of the exercise" (48). She is first associated with engrossment when she apologizes for "engrossing" the horse that the timid and sickly Fanny needs to use in order to maintain her fragile health.[41]

This emphasis on the body fits with the eighteenth-century use of the term "engrossment" as well as its corollary "avidity," the other word moral philosophers used to condemn the impacts of commerce. As Hont and Ignatieff note, "it was inequality in conditions of economic progress which fueled the particular material 'avidity' of modern commercial men" (9). Like engrossment, avidity linked material desires (hunger) with a mindset focused on the amassing of wealth.[42] In Mary Crawford, too, as in Austen's earlier portraits of wealthy women, bodily engrossment with or in material objects is linked to a form of personal engrossment or egoism. As she explains when she returns Fanny's horse too late for the heroine to use it, "I am come to make my own apologies for keeping you waiting—but I have nothing in the world to say for myself—I knew it was very late, and that I was behaving extremely ill; and therefore, if you please, you must forgive me. Selfishness must always be forgiven you know, because there is no hope of a cure" (49). Mary Crawford's ability to acknowledge and laugh at her flaws, like her ability to admit the power of wealth without being pretentious and overbearing, makes even her engrossment attractive to the novel's romantic hero.

As the novel progresses, Austen increasingly focuses on his point of view, showing how Edmund finds himself not simply drawn to the wealthy Mary Crawford but also unable to distinguish her from the virtuous Fanny Price.[43] This revised version of the marriage plot allows Austen to work through, at the level of characters' behavior, the deep fears articulated by the moral philosophers of her period. In a passage from *The Theory of Moral Sentiments* that makes wealth and virtue sound like the characters they become in Austen's novels, Smith explained that "in some particular features they are, no doubt, different, but, in the general air of the countenance, they seem to be so very nearly the same, that inattentive observers are very apt to mistake the one for the other" (62).[44] In *Mansfield Park*, though the narrative repeatedly emphasizes the absolute difference between Fanny Price and Mary Crawford in terms of body, behavior, and values, it also shows Edmund actively seeking to conflate the two women. Valuing both, he insists that

> I would not have the shadow of a coolness between the two whose intimacy I have been observing with the greatest pleasure, and in whose characters there is so much general resemblance in true generosity and natural delicacy as to make the few slight differences, resulting principally from situation, no reasonable hindrance to a perfect friendship. I would not have the shadow of a coolness arise . . . between the two dearest objects I have on earth. (181)[45]

With this description, which shows how fully even a virtuous individual can confuse the attractions of wealth and virtue Austen's novel reaches a conceptual impasse that it can only resolve spatially: Edmund learns to distinguish the difference only when the women that represent the two positions are physically separated through "a mode that we might call geographical and spatial clarification" (Said 85). This clarification happens when Fanny is sent to Portsmouth, Mary Crawford to London, and Edmund realizes that the two represent antithetical rather than identical values. The distancing gesture Austen makes in her fiction literalizes the figure Smith typically uses to discuss the relation between wealth and virtue. He envisions two paths that lead in opposite directions; "unhappily, the road which leads to the one, and that which leads to the other, lie sometimes in very opposite directions" (*Theory of Moral Sentiments* 64).[46] Austen's novel suggests that this image, which might at first blush seem to represent a dilemma, would, in fact, have been reassuring to eighteenth-century readers. It implies, as does the ending of *Mansfield Park*, that the pursuit of wealth and that of virtue could be absolutely distinguished from one another once the two goals were imagined as set on opposite paths.

As Austen's novel separates Fanny Price from Mary Crawford by moving both away from the country and the estate and into cities, it also reveals the opposition hidden within the apparently clear-cut bifurcation between wealth and virtue that Smith so often invokes. Representing the modern individual caught between money and antimaterialist values, that choice mixes economics with morals. It occludes the fact that the opposite of virtue is vice and of wealth poverty. Late eighteenth-century thinking also gives voice to the reverse antithesis between vice and poverty, as philosophers sought a position, as Dror Wahrman has argued, "not vitiated by luxury on the one hand, and not depressed by poverty on the other" (53). Austen invokes these two positions in the scenes in London and Portsmouth, which show Mary Crawford vitiated by the wealth and Fanny Price depressed by the poverty to which they are exposed when they return to the places where they grew up. In this section of the novel, the two heroines are located in environments literally richer and poorer than anything we have seen so far.

But in evoking Portsmouth and London, Austen also represents wealth and poverty less as physical attributes than as social phenomena. The impact of these conditions is shown to depend on environment and relations with other people. Mary Crawford's behavior is more virtuous in the country, where the uses of money are limited. Her brother Henry Crawford also behaves better at Mansfield when he is courting Fanny Price. When he is there, his manners prove capable of "adapting themselves more and more to the gentleness and delicacy of her character" (159). When both siblings go to London, Henry elopes with a married woman, and Mary Crawford ends up in the society of women who are "cold-hearted [and] vain," "the determined supporter[s] of every thing mercenary and ambitious, provided it be only mercenary and ambitious enough" (285–86). Here we have a group of characters that collectively represent and intensify the negative values associated with the rich woman throughout Austen's work. Though readers never see these women directly, Edmund registers their impact when he writes to

Fanny that "it is the influence of the fashionable world altogether that I am jealous of. It is the habits of wealth that I fear" (286). These are the habits he sees in Mary Crawford when she reacts with sophisticated ease to the news of her brother's elopement with his sister: "To hear the woman whom—no harsher name than folly given!—So voluntarily, so freely, so coolly to canvass it!—No reluctance, no horror, no feminine —shall I say?—no modest loathings!—This is what the world does" (308).[47] Her behavior shows him that she has a "blunted delicacy and a cor-rupted, vitiated mind" (310).

In keeping with Smith's assertion that in modern commercial society "the con-tempt, of which vice and folly are the only proper objects, is most unjustly bestowed upon poverty and weakness" (*Theory of Moral Sentiments* 62), the scenes of Fanny Price in Portsmouth that parallel the ones with Mary Crawford in London show the novel's poor heroine feeling the same kind of disgust at her parents' poverty that Edmund Bertram does at the Crawfords' "vice."[48] Her parents' home causes her "pain upon pain, confusion upon confusion" (273). She feels shame at condi-tions she perceives to be, "in almost every respect, the very reverse of what she could have wished. It was the abode of noise, disorder, and impropriety" (264).[49] That she feels not merely disgust but contempt is clear in the terms used to de-scribe her perception of her mother, whom she judges more harshly than she ever does Mary Crawford, the adulterous Maria Bertram, or even the officious Aunt Norris:

> [Fanny] might scruple to make use of the words, but she must and did feel that
> her mother was a partial, ill-judging parent, a dawdle, a slattern, who neither
> taught nor restrained her children, whose house was the scene of mismanage-
> ment and discomfort from beginning to end, and who had no talent, no conver-
> sation, no affection towards herself. (265)

Ironically, Fanny feels most ashamed of her parents' poverty in the presence of the man who commits the most vicious act in the novel. It is when Henry Crawford comes to visit and Fanny watches him watch her family that she feels the shame of poverty magnified by conceiving of someone else's reactions to it. She is sure that "he must be ashamed and disgusted altogether" (273). Her reaction to his presence confirms Smith's insistence that part of what drives social admiration of wealth is the fact that poverty is something we want to hide: "The poor man . . . is ashamed of his poverty. He feels that it either places him out of the sight of mankind, or, that if they take any notice of him, they have, however, scarce any fellow-feeling with the misery and distress which he suffers" (*Theory of Moral Sentiments* 51).

The complexity of these scenes is underscored by the fact that readers never have access to Henry Crawford's thoughts; we do not know whether he feels the disgust that Fanny imagines him to feel. Her feeling of shame is entirely the product of her imagining his position as a spectator of her condition.

So, too, the scenes where Edmund Bertram uncovers Mary Crawford's nature in London prove to be as much about his perceptions of her as about her nature. That fact is emphasized by Austen's decision not to represent these scenes directly but only through Edmund's letters to and conversations with Fanny. In one letter he tells Fanny of his attempt to convert her erstwhile rival to feel as he thinks she ought to feel, as he assumed she did in Mansfield. He attempts to make Mary Crawford feel contempt at her brother's folly and vice but sees in her instead "a great, though short struggle—half a wish of yielding to truths, half a sense of shame—but habit, habit carried it" (311). She offers him what she has offered throughout *Mansfield Park* "a saucy playful smile, seeming to invite, in order to subdue me" (311). But Edmund prefaces his description of Mary's failure to feel shame by stating that "I imagined I saw a mixture of many feelings" (311). Once this caveat is taken into consideration, we cease to have any certainty about what is going on within Mary Crawford. Her inner life is closed to us and to Edmund. Does she have virtuous feelings? Edmund sees in her the moral struggle he wishes to see, but then, as he eventually acknowledges to Fanny, he always saw Mary Crawford as a reflection of his own desires: "It had been the creature of my own imagination, not Miss Crawford, that I had been too apt to dwell on for many months past" (311).

Such misreadings are, as Smith acknowledged, particularly likely to take place in relation to wealth because the "delusive colors in which the imagination is apt to paint" the condition of the rich make "it seem to be almost the abstract idea of a perfect and happy state" (*Theory of Moral Sentiments* 51).[50] We are misled because "we naturally confound [wealth] in our imagination with the order, the regular and harmonious movement of the system, the machine or oeconomy by means of which it is produced" (183). In *Mansfield Park*, Austen evokes this delusiveness both in Edmund's attraction to Mary Crawford and in Fanny's recollections of Mansfield Park once she has been exiled from it. Immured in poverty, Fanny begins to dwell on that world of comfort in imagination; "she could think of nothing but Mansfield, its beloved inmates, its happy ways. Every thing where she now was was in full contrast to it. The elegance, propriety, regularity, harmony—and perhaps, above all, the peace and tranquility of Mansfield, were brought to her remembrance every hour of the day, by the prevalence of every thing opposite to them *here*" (266, emphasis in the original).[51]

This passage proves that Fanny has learned the lesson Sir Thomas wanted to teach when he sent her to Portsmouth in order to improve "her powers of comparing and judging" (250). She can now value wealth by contrasting her parents' poverty with the comforts and affluence she experienced with the Bertrams. The phrasing Sir Thomas uses to describe his plan—"a medical project upon his niece's understanding" (250)—might remind us of Mary Crawford's assertion that "a large income is the best recipé for happiness I ever heard of" (146). The word "recipe" suggests both cooking and a prescription for health. Sir Thomas wants Fanny to learn the healthy admiration of wealth, the kind of admiration Elizabeth Bennet displays when she recognizes the delights of Pemberley. As Smith argued, "When we visit the palaces of the great, we cannot help conceiving the satisfaction we should enjoy if we ourselves were the masters, and were possessed of so much artful and ingeniously contrived accommodation" (*Theory of Moral Sentiments* 179).[52] But in *Mansfield Park* as opposed to *Pride and Prejudice* the poor woman recognizes the value of properly used wealth not in the presence of the estate but in its absence. Fanny's vision of the delights of Mansfield Park is an imaginative reconstruction fueled by the limits of poverty: "The smallness of the rooms above and below indeed, and the narrowness of the passage and staircase, struck her beyond her imagination. She soon learnt to think with respect of her own little attic at Mansfield Park, in *that* house reckoned too small for anybody's comfort" (263, emphasis in the original).

Here Fanny Price's imagination is at last able to expand itself, as she remembers the prosperous environment that now seems lost to her. Yet, as Smith repeatedly emphasizes, the imaginative confidence fueled by wealth, though almost magically appealing, was also an enormous danger to the social whole. It amplified rather than limited the perceptual mistakes individuals were prone to make, "the natural misrepresentations of self-love" (*Theory of Moral Sentiments* 137). Austen will explore these misrepresentations in the novel that follows *Mansfield Park*. Making the heroine of *Emma* not a genteelly poor woman but one who is "handsome, clever, and rich" and who has "the power of having rather too much her own way, and a disposition to think a little too well of herself" (1), Austen will depict a self-described "imaginist" who is confident that "a very narrow income has a tendency to contract the mind" (56). Telling the story of a heroine who possesses "the real good-will of a mind delighted with its own ideas" (14), *Emma* will show how far the imagination can expand itself when not limited by the constraints of poverty.[53]

Emma: "But One of the Multitude"

Having moved at the end of *Mansfield Park* to represent wealth and virtue through characters' reactions to and perceptions of those states, Austen, in *Emma*, narrates the entire story from the point of view of the rich woman. This strategy means that the contrast between the rich and poor woman is no longer expressed through the marriage plot that had functioned as a deep structure driving the story and allowing it to articulate its values in quasi-allegorical form. Instead that contrast works at the level of a character's consciousness, as Emma, a wealthy woman, repeatedly finds herself in a situation in which she must grasp the impact of her behavior on a poor woman she has injured. This strategy allows Austen to use the three-volume structure of the novel to revisit issues she had raised in the novels that preceded *Emma* and then show how her thinking has developed in the novel that follows them.

In its depictions of Harriet Smith, Mr. Elton, and Emma in volume 1, *Emma* emphasizes class distinctions in their crudest form and tells its story in the broadly comic terms that Austen used to depict Miss Bingley and Lady Catherine in *Pride and Prejudice*. In the marital triangle that emerges in volume 2 of the novel between Jane Fairfax, Emma, and Frank Churchill, Austen returns to the terms of *Mansfield Park*, in which social and sexual interactions have less to do with external distinctions than they do with the psychological effects of wealth and poverty on individuals' perceptions. In volume 3, Austen transforms the traditional opposition between the rich and the poor woman by making the woman Emma injures no longer a romantic rival but the dependent and distinctly unglamorous Miss Bates. Here Austen moves toward acknowledging what I argue throughout this book: that the marriage plot is a way of thinking about social inequities in a general sense. *Emma* shows that those inequities can only be dealt with through a fully internalized stance that checks the self-love fostered by prosperity, the stance Smith characterizes in *The Theory of Moral Sentiments* as sympathy.

The relations between Emma, Harriet, and Robert Martin in volume 1 of *Emma*, as well as those between Emma, Harriet, and Elton, reflect the fact that in this late novel class positions and social distinctions are less fixed than in Austen's earlier novels. *Emma* includes a series of figures that move up and down the social register, this movement being determined by the wealth they possess. Mr. Weston makes a fortune, buys an estate, and becomes a gentleman. Emma's governess becomes the mistress of that estate. In contrast, Jane Fairfax, the daughter of a gentleman, is raised in relative want and may be forced to become a governess. The commercially wealthy Coles invite Emma to dinner, and she goes. Social fluidity makes it particularly difficult to assess people's motives, as we see when Emma's dealings with her protégée Harriet lead her to misread the relative merits of the yeoman farmer Robert Martin and the clergyman Mr. Elton. Though as a character Emma is infinitely more likable than Miss Bingley and Lady Catherine in *Pride and Prejudice*, still, like them, she assumes that those who have a higher social status will have more taste and refinement than those who do not.

She confidently tells Harriet to reject Martin's proposal because he will become "a completely gross, vulgar farmer—totally inattentive to appearances, and thinking of nothing but profit and loss" (20). When Harriet mentions that Martin has not read a novel she loaned him, Emma reinforces her point: "How much his business engrosses him already. . . . He was a great deal too full of the market to think of any thing else—which is just as it should be for a thriving man. What has he to do with books? And I have no doubt that he *will* thrive and be a very rich man in time" (20, emphasis in the original). This comment asserts a distinction between cultural and material capital and assumes that someone who pursues the latter cannot be interested in the former. Yet, in *Emma*, this perception proves false, as it is Martin, rather than the well-to-do Elton, who is the worthier of Harriet's suitors. Martin's behavior confirms Smith's assertion that "in all the middling and inferior professions, real and solid professional abilities, joined to prudent, just, firm, and temperate conduct, can very seldom fail of success."[54] In contrast, "in the superior stations of life . . . the abilities to please are more regarded than the abilities to serve" (*Theory of Moral Sentiments* 63). These statements are borne out by Martin's honest worth as opposed to Elton's fawning flattery.

Austen has already provided an image of the difference between the active valor of the middling classes and the complaisance of their superiors in *Mansfield Park*, where Henry Crawford imagines, enviously, the opportunities open to Fanny's sailor brother:

> He longed to have been at sea, and seen and done and suffered as much. His heart was warmed, his fancy fired, and he felt the highest respect for a lad who, before he was twenty, had gone through such bodily hardships, and given such proofs of mind. The glory of heroism, of usefulness, of exertion, of endurance, made his own habits of selfish indulgence appear in shameful contrast; and he wished he had been a William Price, distinguishing himself and working his way to fortune and consequence with so much self-respect and happy ardour, instead of what he was! (162)[55]

But Martin and Price remain on the margins of Austen's world, men whose virtues are extolled but whose stories are not told. Her novels focus not on these
upwardly mobile figures, though we will get a fuller portrait of such a man in
Persuasion, but on the prejudice that makes it difficult for those with established
social status to recognize the virtues of newcomers.

Though in *Emma* it is Elton rather than Martin who "only wanted to aggrandize
and enrich himself" (88), the novel is less interested in the clergyman's engrossment than in Emma's inability to recognize that fact. As she thinks, when she finally
realizes that Elton is interested in her rather than the poorer Harriet, "If *she* had so
misinterpreted his feelings, she had little right to wonder that *he*, with self-interest
to blind him, should have mistaken her's" (89, emphasis in the original). Here
Austen locates engrossment neither in Martin nor in the self-serving Elton but
in the self-absorption that makes it impossible for Emma to see Martin's virtues.
"Acknowledg[ing] herself grossly mistaken and mis-judging" (92), Emma discovers in herself a failure of taste in the sense that Hume uses that term. Taste requires
"a quick and acute perception of beauty and deformity" (142), which means a man
cannot "be satisfied with himself while he suspects that any excellence or blemish
in a discourse has passed him unobserved" (142–43). Emma's willful blindness to
Martin's excellences and Elton's blemishes reveals the way prejudice and convention cloud taste. As Hume argues, "A very violent effort is requisite to change our
judgment of manners, and excite sentiments of approbation or blame, love or
hatred, different from those to which the mind, from long custom, has been famil-
iarized" (152).

Emma charts a series of these violent efforts, one might call them revolutions,
in which the habits of thinking that rule the heroine's judgment and action are
overthrown and she is compelled to recognize a state of affairs other than the one
she desired. I mention revolution in part because of the charade Mr. Elton writes,
Emma assumes, for Harriet, though it is actually directed to Emma herself. In it
we hear of the "pomp of kings, / Lords of the earth" and of "the monarch of the
seas!" but then of a "reverse" in which "Man's boasted power and freedom, all are
flown; / Lord of the earth and sea, he bends a slave" (46). Though this language is
introduced in the context of a game, it describes the overthrow of what we might
call, following Freud, his majesty the ego. Emma experiences such an overthrow
in each volume of the novel, as she assumes herself to be in control of Harriet's
courtship, able to read the natures of Jane Fairfax and Frank Churchill, and at the
center of affairs at Box Hill. In each case her confidence in her own opinion and
position proves unwarranted.

The imagery used to describe Emma's realization of her mistakes, her discovery of the errors of her perceptions and behavior and the pain they have caused a woman who is poorer than herself, is increasingly associated with violence. She describes her interactions with Harriet as "a blow" (87) and realizes that she, Jane Fairfax, and Frank Churchill "never could have been all three together, without her having stabbed Jane Fairfax's peace in a thousand instances; and on Box Hill, perhaps, it had been the agony of a mind that would bear no more" (276–77). This language reaches its peak after Mr. Knightley chastises her in the wake of her apparently playful mockery of Miss Bates at Box Hill; Emma, "was most forcibly struck. The truth of his representation there was no denying. She felt it at her heart. How could she have been so brutal, so cruel to Miss Bates?" (246). While these images of wounding and injury might make it seem that what teaches Emma to behave with propriety toward the poorer woman, first Harriet Smith, later Jane Fairfax, and finally Miss Bates, is compassion, that is not the case. For as Smith argued, "It is not the soft power of humanity, it is not that feeble spark of benevolence which Nature has lighted up in the human heart, that is thus capable of counteracting the strongest impulses of self-love" (*Theory of Moral Sentiments* 137).

Austen charts the failure of sympathy in its traditional sense most clearly in volume 2 of *Emma*, as she explores the relations between Emma, Jane Fairfax, and Frank Churchill. Here she addresses the limitations of the model of distinction that *Pride and Prejudice* posits as the counter to the emphasis on property asserted by Miss Bingley and Lady Catherine de Bourgh, a model based on talent and taste rather than class and wealth. Austen creates in Jane Fairfax arguably the most accomplished of any of her female characters. But she also insists that Jane would have possessed none of those abilities without the intervention of people with wealth who had the means to foster and develop her talents. If Jane had not been adopted by the Campbells, "there had seemed every probability of her being permanently fixed there [with her aunt and grandmother]; of her being taught only what very limited means could command, and growing up with no advantages of connection or improvement to be engrafted on what nature had given her" (104). Like Fanny Price in *Mansfield Park*, Jane is able to receive the education that develops her sensibilities because she has been adopted into a family that is wealthier than her birth relations. But, like Fanny, she may always be returned to the environment from which she came.

Jane is aware of the precariousness of her situation; she fears, for example, she will have to go out and work as a governess. And as in *Mansfield Park*, so too in *Emma* the vulnerability of the poor woman's situation makes her behave in a manner that is colder and less open or frank than that of her wealthy rival. Growing up in a situation of want, raised by those who have some means but cannot provide for her, Jane Fairfax has learned to guard herself and her feelings carefully. Knowing her vulnerability—that she may at any moment by forced to use her talents, to sell herself in what she describes as the slavery of being a governess—Jane behaves in an opposite manner from that of the gregarious Frank Churchill, whose name signifies his apparent possession of what Smith calls the "frankness and openness [that] conciliate confidence" (*Theory of Moral Sentiments* 337). Like Fanny, Jane exhibits the "reserve and concealment [that], on the contrary, call forth diffidence" (*Theory of Moral Sentiments* 337). But the difference between *Emma* and *Mansfield Park* is that in her later novel Austen does not provide a narrative in which the novel's hero learns to realize that he feels the attractiveness of the diffident woman who represents virtue. Indeed, Austen seems relatively uninterested in the perspective of the male character in the romantic triangles that dominate the plot in volume 2.

Instead she focuses on the relation between the rich and the poor woman, showing that what Emma feels for Jane is less sympathy than envy. Jane's performance as a musician makes Emma "unfeignedly and unequivocally regret the inferiority of her own playing and singing" (150). When Emma eventually looks back on her dealings with Jane, having learned the secret of her engagement to Frank, she feels remorse and "bitterly regretted not having sought a closer acquaintance with her, and blushed for the envious feelings which had certainly been, in some measure, the cause" (276). Such statements make clear the problem posed by the choice between wealth and virtue as they are represented in *Emma*; individuals may recognize virtue but not, in fact, find it appealing. Moral superiority is as likely to trigger envy as sympathetic identification.[56] In showing how easily virtue can become the object of envy, Austen's novel allows readers to feel the emotional undercurrents of Smith's arguments about sympathy, which implicitly acknowledge that goodness is not, in fact, a condition that elicits warm or positive feelings.

As Jean-Pierre Dupuy argues, the shadow of envy haunts *The Theory of Moral Sentiments*:

> In the sphere of moral sentiments, sympathy is the fundamental principle. Envy, its negation, is born out of a deviation of this general principle, when the attention directed at other people goes beyond its proper bounds. . . . In the devalued sphere where the moral sentiments are corrupted and the economic motive emerges, the hierarchy is reversed and envy becomes the dominant principle. (57)

In describing her heroine's interactions with Jane Fairfax, Austen underscores that Emma goes too far in her imaginative speculations about what might have gone on in Jane's private life. What looks like sympathy for the difficulty of Jane's situation becomes a prying curiosity. The difficulty with these scenes is that Emma does not act as if Jane has what George Eliot would call an equivalent center of self. This is what Emma will come to understand at the end of the novel, when she looks back over her dealings with Jane and realizes that "every look and action had shown how deeply [Jane] was suffering from consciousness" (274). Even as she recognizes Jane's consciousness, Emma still fails to feel compassion for her suffering rival; "as far as her mind could disengage itself from the injustice and selfishness of angry feelings, she acknowledged that Jane Fairfax would have neither elevation nor happiness beyond her desert" (264).

What prevents Emma's compassion is the intransigent selfishness that Smith argued cannot be eradicated only curbed. In Austen's novel, we watch this curbing in the scene at Box Hill, which opens with a series of games in which Emma is invited not just to be the center of attention but also to see herself, as Mr. Weston's riddle invites her to do, as an emblem of perfection. With these games, as with the charades and anagrams throughout the novel, Austen illustrates the psychic dynamic between characters, showing how, as Emma's ego is fed, her actions, normally self-involved but also generous to others, become increasingly thoughtless and giddy. As Smith argues,

> When we are about to act, the eagerness of passion will seldom allow us to consider what we are doing, with the candour of an indifferent person. The violent emotions which at that time agitate us, discolour our views of things; even when we are endeavouring to place ourselves in the situation of another, and to regard the objects that interest us in the light in which they will naturally appear to him, the fury of our passions constantly calls us back to our own place, where every thing appears magnified and misrepresented by self-love. (*Theory of Moral Sentiments* 157)

Throughout the novel Emma's dealings with her poorer counterparts have demonstrated how easy it is for views to become discolored. In the interchanges with Harriet and Jane, it is only after she acts out of her self-centered motivations that Emma is able to contemplate her actions in retrospect with the revulsion they deserve.[57]

Smith argues that this new self-critical perspective is engendered through the intervention of an impartial spectator: "It is from him only that we learn the real littleness of ourselves, and of whatever relates to ourselves" (*Theory of Moral Sentiments* 137). He is "a stronger power, a more forcible motive, which exerts itself upon such occasions. It is reason, principle, conscience, the inhabitant of the breast, the man within, the great judge and arbiter of our conduct" (*Theory of Moral Sentiments* 137). Mr. Knightley plays the role of the spectator throughout Austen's novel. He is the person who sees more of the games of anagrams than Emma is aware of, the one who recognizes first that Elton is courting her and not Harriet, the one who grasps the full configuration of the social interactions in which Emma takes part but whose implications remain hidden to her. In Austen's novel, as in Smith's moral philosophy, the individual blinded by self-love makes corrections as the spectator forces him or her to see his or her own acts from the outside. When Mr. Knightley intervenes at Box Hill, teaching Emma to recognize the pain she has caused Miss Bates, he makes her feel what Smith argues the abstract individual feels after the intrusion of the impartial spectator: "The situation of the person, who suffered by his injustice, now calls upon his pity. He is grieved at the thought of it; regrets the unhappy effects of his own conduct" (*Theory of Moral Sentiments* 84).

As in the scenes with Jane Fairfax, where we realize that the individual is not attracted to virtue, here it is clear that Emma does not naturally feel compassion for someone who is poor. She must be brought to recognize the need for sympathy that is implicit in his or her situation. This is the pity that Emma is taught to feel as she is made to acknowledge her cruelty to a poor woman who lacks any of the romantic trappings of the poorer women who are heroines of Austen's earlier novels. In contrast to the Dashwood sisters, Elizabeth Bennet, or Fanny Price, Miss Bates experiences the limitations of poverty, existing on the margins of the Highbury community and struggling to get by. When Mr. Knightley argues that Emma needs to feel compassion for her, he is pointing the way toward the Victorian novels that will follow Austen's, where sympathy for the situation of the poor will become a mainspring of the narrative action.[58] And, appropriately in terms of my own argument, the logic Mr. Knightley uses to chastise Emma reiterates the rationale of the marriage plot. He explains of Miss Bates that "were she a woman of fortune, I would leave every harmless absurdity to take its chance, I would not quarrel with you for any liberties of manner. Were she your equal in situation— but, Emma, consider how far this is from being the case. She is poor; she has sunk from the comforts she was born to; and, if she live to old age, must probably sink more. Her situation should secure your compassion" (246).[59]

This passage articulates the philosophy that is implicit in the courtship plot not just of Austen's earlier novels but of the novel of manners generally: the idea that it is acceptable, even desirable, to laugh at the woman of fortune, while the poorer woman must be carefully protected from such mockery. In this late novel Austen acknowledges how counterintuitive this philosophy is. As Emma explains initially to Harriet, "It is poverty only which makes celibacy contemptible to a generous public! A single woman, with a very narrow income, must be a ridiculous, disagreeable old maid! the proper sport of boys and girls; but a single woman, of good fortune, is always respectable, and may be as sensible and pleasant as anybody else" (55–56). Here Emma describes the world as Smith fears it to be, a place where wealth is admired and poverty denigrated or laughed at. By having Knightley overturn this philosophy, Austen demonstrates her awareness that the plots that dominated her early novels are how fiction attempts to counter worldly assumptions by leading readers to value virtue and poverty over wealth.

In *Emma*, rather than enacting this process of reversal through the dynamics of the courtship, Austen has her heroine experience a revolution in her awareness; Emma is driven to recognize the consciousnesses of others by becoming aware of the suffering she causes them. Exploring the changes that take place within the consciousness of her wealthy heroine at the end of the novel, Austen shows how the workings of her fiction follow the logic of *The Theory of Moral Sentiments*. What Smith added to the moral philosophers who preceded him was the insistence that the impartial spectator was not simply an external figure but someone we internalize in the process of seeking approval for our actions. Hume and Hutcheson also "gave prominence, in their ethical theories, to the approval of 'a spectator' or of 'every spectator,' even of 'a judicious spectator'" (Raphael and Macfie 15). But Smith went further, arguing that once we have conceived of the impartial spectator as watching our actions, he (or she) no longer has to be present for us to check our self-interested behavior: "The judgment of the real spectator depends on the desire for actual praise, that of the imagined impartial spectator on the desire for praiseworthiness" (Raphael and Macfie 16).

Austen stresses this pursuit of praiseworthiness in the last chapters of her novel as Emma seeks to change her behavior toward both Miss Bates and Jane Fairfax by visiting the two women after Box Hill, hoping to make amends for her behavior. Though Jane rejects these overtures, Emma is satisfied with her behavior because she imagines herself being watched and approved of by the spectator who previously criticized her, Mr. Knightley: "She would not be ashamed of the appearance of the penitence, so justly and truly hers. Her eyes were towards Donwell as she walked" (247).[60] As Smith argues, the man who has performed a generous action "looks backward to the motive from which he acted, and surveys it in the light in which the indifferent spectator will survey it . . . and applauds himself by sympathy with the approbation of this supposed impartial judge" (*Theory of Moral Sentiments* 85).[61] This change of perception means that although Emma is unable to make amends for the pain she has caused others, she now knows how to behave even when Mr. Knightley is not present: "She had the consolation of knowing that her intentions were good, and of being able to say to herself, that could Mr. Knightley have been privy to all her attempts of assisting Jane Fairfax, could he even have seen into her heart, he would not, on this occasion, have found any thing to reprove" (257).[62]

But because, as we eventually learn, Mr. Knightley is anything but impartial, since he is in love with Emma, Austen's novel emphasizes what is almost unspoken in Smith's arguments, that to be virtuous is not in fact to be impartial but to feel the pleasure of being able to imagine one's self loved and approved of. The irony of this position is that self-love or egotism is what forces individuals to grant others the status of having egos or selves that are like their own.[63] As Smith explains of the properly regulated man, "This self-approbation, if not the only, is at least the principal object, about which he can or ought to be anxious. The love of it, is the love of virtue" (*Theory of Moral Sentiments* 117). So what makes Emma and individuals generally virtuous is not the love of virtue in others but in themselves:

> It is not the love of our neighbour, it is not the love of mankind, which upon many occasions prompts us to the practice of those divine virtues. It is a stronger love, a more powerful affection, which generally takes place upon such occasions; the love of what is honourable and noble, of the grandeur, and dignity, and superiority of our own characters. (*Theory of Moral Sentiments* 137)[64]

The mental strategy Emma learns at the end of Austen's novel solves the problem that troubled Smith in the final version of *The Theory of Moral Sentiments*, the problem of how to prevent the corruption of the moral sentiments while at the same time maintaining the distinction of ranks and order of society. On the one hand, internalizing the impartial spectator is, at the level of psychology, a radically democratizing gesture. As Smith explains,

> It is he who, whenever we are about to act so as to affect the happiness of others, calls to us, with a voice capable of astonishing the most presumptuous of our passions, that we are but one of the multitude, in no respect better than any other in it; and that when we prefer ourselves so shamefully and so blindly to

others, we become the proper objects of resentment, abhorrence, and execration. (*Theory of Moral Sentiments* 137)[65]

The impulse at the end of Austen's novel is for Emma to behave to those she has wronged as if they are equals. Though Jane Fairfax continues to insist that she is "unequal" to any attentions in a voice of tremulous "inequality" (256), Emma seeks to lavish "every distinction of regard or sympathy" (255) and to engage in "a regular, equal, kindly intercourse" (247) with both her and Miss Bates.[66]

Once, however, the wealthy heroine has been taught to make the mental gesture of acknowledging the equality of others, the story no longer needs to conclude with the equalizing marriages that typically resolve the tension between wealth and virtue at the end of an Austen novel. In *Emma*, the novel does not end with what I have called in my introduction a marriage that is exogamous in terms of property, as a wealthy man weds a poorer woman, thereby bringing the egalitarian values she represents into the traditional realm of landed estates. Instead the marriages that conclude the novel enforce the boundaries that separate the classes. Social distinctions are maintained as Harriet Smith and Robert Martin marry and occupy the lowest social rung, Jane Fairfax and Frank Churchill as well as Mr. and Mrs. Elton the middling territory, and Emma and Mr. Knightley society's upper reaches.

In reviewing Austen's career after the publication of her nephew James Edward Austen-Leigh's memoir of his aunt in 1870, Richard Simpson insisted that "she had no interest for the great social and political problems which were being debated with so much blood in her day. The social combinations which taxed the calculating powers of Adam Smith . . . were above her powers" (Southam 1.250–51). I have argued, in contrast, that Austen's novels engage directly in the debates about wealth and virtue that were of importance to writers like Smith and Hume as they sought to imagine how English society might manage the changes wrought by mobile property, changes whose impacts would be felt even more dramatically over the course of the nineteenth century.

However, by the time Simpson was writing, the terms that would, for Austen's early nineteenth-century readers, have signaled a link to moral philosophy had gone into general parlance. Words like "engrossment," "delicacy," and "distinction" continued to carry general moral valences but no longer bore traces of the specific meanings they held for those concerned about the impact of England's economic development in the late eighteenth and early nineteenth century. It is for this reason that, as we return to Austen's novels from a position even further historically removed than that of Simpson, we can find it easy to read them as explorations of personal rather than social crises. Yet once we see how the terms of the character-izations of rich women like Miss Bingley, Mary Crawford, and Emma Woodhouse intersect with the political and economic debates of the day, we can begin to read those novels as engaging, even in the parts of the story that seem most to have to do with personal preferences, in arguments about the way the influx of money was changing the shape of English society.

Epilogue: Eighteenth-Century Moral Philosophy and the Austen Tradition

One of the effects of Austen's novels is to lift the concept of virtue that she links with manners, conduct, and sympathy out of the context in which those terms were seen as referencing specific historical developments. She refracts contem-porary debates about wealth and virtue but represents them in such a way that they no longer have to be read as necessarily topical or historically specific.[67] The effect of Austen's ability both to invoke and distance herself from the debates being engaged in by the moral philosophers who were her contemporaries is that those terms turn up in critical evaluations of the novelist. There, however, those concepts are taken not as the legacy of a specific historical moment but as markers of the novelist's absolute value.

The tension Jerome Christensen has attributed to Hume between a perception that is crude or gross and one that is so refined its distinctions cannot be grasped by the uninitiated is characteristic of the way critics have valued Austen from the nineteenth century onward. Her novels do not appeal to "the literary taste of the majority [which] is always tinged with coarseness; it loves exaggeration, and slights the modesty of truth" (Southam 1.195). "How," another critic asks, "could people who had once known the simple verity, the refined perfection of Miss Austen, enjoy anything less refined and less perfect?" (Southam 2.203). This position is reiterated throughout the criticism: "Her excellence must be of an unobtrusive kind . . . demanding culture in its admirers" (Southam 2.20–21). As an American critic remarked in 1902, "The appreciation of Miss Austen has come to be one of the marks of literary taste" (Southam 2.7).

These reviews praise Austen in ways that uncannily echo Hume's discussions of taste. Valued for her "minute fidelity of detail" (Southam 1.96), she is deemed to exhibit "the perfection of every sense or faculty, to perceive with exactness its most minute objects" (Hume 142). The famed image of her painting on a tiny piece of ivory reflects Hume's insistence that "the smaller the objects are which become sensible to the eye, the finer is that organ, and the more elaborate its make and composition" (142).[68] Well into the nineteenth and twentieth centuries Austen is described in terms of eighteenth-century discussions of refinement; she is a "singularly gifted woman, of refined, and as would have been said in her day, 'elegant' mind" (Southam 1.200), "a person of exquisite taste, delicate humour, and refined sense" (Southam 1.203). Her writings display what Hume calls "that *delicacy* of imagination which is requisite to convey a sensibility of those finer emotions" (140, emphasis in the original).

In these descriptions delicacy and refinement are often evoked in terms that suggest disembodiment. In 1862 Julia Kavanaugh argued that "wonderful, indeed is the power that out of materials so slender . . . could fashion a story" (Southam 1.195). While such description can turn negative, as when Cardinal Newman exclaims of *Emma* that "there is a want of *body* to the story. The action is frittered away in over-little things" (Southam 1.117, emphasis in the original), they all tend to characterize Austen and her novels in terms that echo her own characterization of the virtuous poor heroines who are opposed to the engrossed rich women who are identified with the gross traits that critics insist are not present in her fiction.

In recent years contemporary critics have intervened in this tradition by insisting that Austen's novels do include representations of engrossed bodily presence. Discussing the depiction of Mrs. Musgrove in *Persuasion*, D. A. Miller argues that a character Austen describes as of "comfortable, substantial size" marks the association of "the fat body" with "materiality" ("The Late Jane Austen" 60, 61). Joseph Litvak refers to such figures, following Patricia Parker, as "literary fat ladies" and argues that in *Pride and Prejudice* "heavy bodies constitute both an affront to the imperative of 'self-discipline' and an obstacle in the way of the smooth course of the marriage plot" (*Strange Gourmets* 23, 15). For both Miller and Litvak such heavy figures are contrasted to a figure less substantially embodied, "the diminutive woman" (Miller "The Late Jane Austen" 62) or the slender Elizabeth Bennet, with her "light and pleasing figure," who, in Litvak's terms, moves sleekly and lightheartedly through the text (*Strange Gourmets* 23). These are the characters that, as Henry Crawford muses when he imagines explaining Fanny to his worldly and materially successful uncle, represent "the very impossibility he would describe—if indeed he has now delicacy of language enough to embody his own ideas" (200).

That Austen herself has been valued in the terms she uses to characterize her slender heroines becomes clear when we set the novelistic portrait of Fanny Price against recent critiques that describe the history of Austen criticism as "impoverished" (Sedgwick "Austen" 836) and "disembodied" (Fraiman 808). These adjectives reiterate what the novel calls Fanny's "disinterestedness and delicacy" (221). The description of Fanny, uncomfortable in "rooms too large for her to move in with ease" (13), should remind us of the images used to enshrine Austen in public memory as a woman who always wrote in the smallest possible physical space. From the publication of Austen-Leigh's *Memoir of Jane Austen* in 1870 onward, Austen's life was renowned for "the narrowness of its sphere of action. . . . There was no large field of view open to her" (Southam 1.227). As Sir Walter Scott once argued, Austen was incapable of "the Big Bow-Wow strain [which] I can do myself like any now going" (Southam 1.106). This is the image of Austen that critics like Sedgwick, Miller, Litvak, and others have sought to counter by showing that Austen was a "contradictory figure neither pretty nor little" (Fraiman 807). But, in using terms like "little," "disembodied," "impoverished," as well as "fatness" and "materiality," modern critics continue to invoke the opposition that lies at the heart of Austen's novels even as they attempt to reverse the valences of the value system those terms implicitly assert. I have argued instead that we need to map out the patterns of that opposition and read it as embedded in the history that was contemporary to Austen's novels. To do so is to realize that Austen does address the historical and economic issues that fascinated Adam Smith through figures, neither pretty nor little, whose embodiment links them to the material engrossment that so troubled political economists of the period, the rich women who are, in the language of contemporary slang, the dogs of the novel, its Big Bow-Wows, spouses its heroes are never supposed to marry. But critics have found it surprisingly difficult to consider the import of these figures, in part because of the way Austen has been enshrined in the critical tradition.

Austen is associated with delicacy not just because readers identify her with her characters but also because they regard her as a detached narrator and author. As one commentator explained, Austen "treats all [her characters] impartially and according to their merits. She seems to look on the world as a curious observer" (Southam 1.213). In the words of Margaret Oliphant, Austen writes with "the soft and silent disbelief of a spectator who has to look at a great many things without showing any outward discomposure"; "she sympathises with sufferers, yet she can scarcely be said to be sorry for them" (Southam 1.216). This perception is reiterated in the twentieth century when Lord David Cecil argues that Austen "surveyed her creatures with too detached an irony for her to identify with them sufficiently to voice their unthinking gushes of feeling" (12). Her merit is "impartiality" (Cecil 28). That is, readers experience reading Austen as a process in which the novelist plays the role of the impartial spectator as it is invoked in *The Theory of Moral Sentiments.*

The gesture Austen makes as an ironic spectator of her characters carries over to readers who imagine the author watching, judging, and, ideally, approving of them. As Katherine Mansfield comments, "Every true admirer of the novels cherishes the happy thought that he alone . . . has become the secret friend of their author" (quoted in Southam 2.126). This idea is most fully worked out by Cecil, who insists that

> if I were in doubt as to the wisdom of one of my actions, I should not consult Flaubert or Dostoievesky. The opinion of Balzac or Dickens would carry little weight with me: were Stendhal to rebuke me, it would only convince me I had done right: even in the judgment of Tolstoy I should not put complete confidence. But I should be seriously upset, I should worry for weeks and weeks, if I incurred the disapproval of Jane Austen. (43)

In narrating his personal reaction to Austen, Cecil uncannily echoes the process Smith describes in *The Theory of Moral Sentiments* when he explains that what checks his behavior is the process of imagining being watched by an impartial spectator who disapproves of his actions. Picking up on the language of the literary critics who preceded him and that will be echoed by those who follow him, Cecil shows that to read Austen is to internalize the stance that her contemporaries would have recognized as part of her engagement with eighteenth-century moral philosophy. Reading Austen has taught the critic to think, without being conscious of it, with Smith's logic.

Passages like Cecil's help explain why it has been so difficult to analyze the role of the rich woman in the novel of manners, a tradition that, I have argued, is established with Austen. The gestures that novels make in imagining the psychological and social stances that would counter the monetary vulgarity the rich woman represents are so powerful they impel critics to view the rich woman and her antithesis not as responses to particular historical moments but as transhistorical assertions of value. Such an interpretation determines subsequent critical responses not just to the novels but also to the novelists in question. In the chapters that follow I trace the process by which immediate reactions to specific economic changes become so internalized that readers fail to recognize the historical origins of their own patterns of thinking. I also show how the economic forces that drive the novel to imagine a form of virtue that can oppose the vulgar effects of wealth are transmuted as the English economy expands and diversifies over the course of the nineteenth century. Fears of the impact of commerce on the culture change shape, as even money is conceived in new ways. New economic practices will lead individuals to experience the acquisition and use of wealth first as a more embodied and then as a disembodied practice. The marriage plot that contrasts the rich and the poor woman persists as we move from Austen to the Trollopes to Oliphant to James, but the forces it represents through its articulation of the contrast between wealth and virtue change dramatically as novelists respond imaginatively to the economic developments that transformed English society over the course of the long nineteenth century.

CHAPTER TWO

FRANCES TROLLOPE AND THE PROBLEM
OF APPETITE

Suspension of the mind's search for significance would somehow make possible an account of the way in which the body inhabits the world.

David Trotter, *Cooking with Mud*

Never can the mind forget that the body is a nasty incumbrance.

Frances Trollope, note for *Domestic Manners of the Americans*

Though Frances Trollope was only four years older than Austen and grew up in an almost identical social environment, the later novelist did not begin her writing career until the 1830s, a period when England's dramatic economic expansion as a result of industrialism was fostering a set of cultural anxieties wholly different from the ones addressed in Austen's novels.[1] In the world as it is represented in Trollope's fiction, wealth is problematic less because it blurs social distinction than because it impacts the body, necessarily arousing appetites or cravings that seem potentially insatiable. Discussions of appetite appeared in a range of discourses in Trollope's period: in psychology, political economy, criticism of the industrial system, discussions of goods, taste, and consumption, and the essays of Romantic poets. All of these writings express fear that England's commercial success in the 1820s and '30s would lead to what Samuel Taylor Coleridge called "the overbalance of the commercial spirit in consequence of the absence or weakness of counterweights" (quoted in Winch 330).[2] Coleridge's term "overbalance" captures the difference between Austen's fictional worlds and Trollope's. While Austen's novels balance the appeals of wealth with those of virtue through mechanisms like Adam Smith's concept of sympathy, Trollope's dwell on the imbalances experienced in an era of extremely rapid growth when terms like "mushrooming," "swelling," and "convulsion" were used to describe the almost violent expansions and contractions of the economy.

All those terms are, in Trollope's fiction, associated with prosperous women whose appetites are so voracious they take over the novels in which they appear, dwarfing the virtues of the poor women, who prove, as Coleridge feared, a weak counterweight to money's vulgar, materialist presence. The decades following the end of Austen's career saw the rise of industrial manufacture, an exponential expansion of the population, the solidification of the British East India Company, an unbridled increase in consumer spending, and "the accumulation of property, extensive beyond all credibility, and . . . rapid in its growth beyond what the most sanguine mind could have conceived" (Colquhoun quoted in Perkin *Origins* 2).[3] England experienced growth "at the material level[,] . . . a rise in human productivity, industrial, agricultural and demographic, *on such a scale* that it raised, as it were, the logarithmic index of society: that is, it increased by a multiple (rather than a fraction) both the number of human beings which a given area of land could support, and their standard of life, or consumption per head of goods and services" (Perkin *Origins* 3, emphasis in the original).[4] The era Thomas Carlyle famously dubbed the "Age of Machinery" led to the enrichment of the country as a whole, as England became the first industrialized nation, and to the material enhancement of the lives of middle-class individuals, who profited from and acquired the new products being manufactured and imported, the "luxury" objects that became available for purchase as more and more wealth became available with which to purchase them.

But the proliferation of what Francis Jeffrey called "'those vulgar comforts and venal luxuries' typical of advanced economies" (cited in Connell 99) necessitated the intensification of desire.[5] In order to stimulate consumers to buy the new range of items, individuals must, as Trollope's narrator comments in *The Widow Barnaby*, be driven to the point "when hunger, but not appetite, has been satisfied" (44).[6] The early nineteenth-century political economist whose writings dealt most explicitly with appetite was Thomas Robert Malthus.[7] One of Malthus's key contributions to the evolution of political economy, as the writings of Malthus's follower, the evangelical economist Thomas Chalmers, made clear, was to link the appetites that now drove the economy—the desire to spend and consume—with the appetites that drove the body—hunger and sexual desire.[8] The word Malthus used to describe the powerful pull of these sensual appetites was "craving":

> The cravings of hunger, the love of liquor, the desire of possessing a beautiful woman will urge men to actions, of the fatal consequences of which, to the general interests of society, they are perfectly well convinced, even at the very

time they commit them. Remove their bodily cravings, and they would not hesitate a moment in determining against such actions. Ask them their opinion of the same conduct in another person, and they would immediately reprobate it. (2004 85–86)

Though Malthus stressed the dangers of such bodily drives by showing how excessive consumption and reproduction could lead to the impoverishment of the economy, he was also convinced that such cravings were not only unavoidable but also made life enjoyable and the economy successful. Insisting on the importance of spending as well as saving, he argued that "if the pleasure arising from the gratification of these propensities were universally diminished in vividness, violations of property would become less frequent; but this advantage would be greatly overbalanced by the narrowing of the sources of enjoyment" (1992 210). This passage reverses the valences of typical early nineteenth-century anxieties about cultural change; it describes a potential overbalance not of the sensual drives but of the rational ones. From Malthus's point of view, such an overbalance would be problematic because it would diminish the "vividness" of experience afforded by the bodily drives, cravings, and appetites whose excesses his contemporaries feared.

Those cravings were also explored in psychological writings of the period, most prominently in George Combe's *The Constitution of Man* (1828).[9] Combe understood himself to be an inheritor of the eighteenth-century moral philosophers: "Dr. Hutcheson, Dr. Adam Smith, Dr. Reid, Mr. Stewart, and Dr. Thomas Brown, have, in succession, produced highly interesting and instructive works on Moral Science; and the present Essay is a humble attempt to pursue the same plan, with the aid of the new lights afforded by phrenology" (ix). His contribution was the insistence that the human brain is divided; one portion "manifests the intellect" or "the moral sentiments, and all the rest the animal sentiments and propensities; and each part acts . . . with a degree of energy corresponding to its size" (143). In a description that meshes with the general perception that English society was more focused on materialist and sensualist needs than on the intellectual and moral principles that were supposed to counter such bodily appetites, he argues that "those parts of the brain which manifest the feelings, constitute by far the largest portion of it[;] . . . the parts which manifest the intellect are smaller" (121). For modern readers such a description would seem to presage a Freudian conception of the mind riven between the forces of the id and the superego. But the key difference between the 1890s and 1830s definition of these drives is that in Combe's formulation there is as yet no conception of the unconscious. Trollope's novels mark the moment at when nineteenth-century culture begins to insist that some drives should be repressed.

In the period when she was writing, fears over the increasing power of materialist drives meant that literature was called on to play a key role in strengthening those parts of the mind that were open to intellectual and imaginative rather than sensual pleasures. As Philip Connell has argued, it became a vehicle for "spiritual values, of 'inward' truth, as opposed to the empiricist philosophy of sensation" (293).[10] But Trollope entered this literary arena in perverse form, as she began her career not by celebrating spiritual values but by exposing the materialist drives literature was supposed to transcend. Her first book, the extremely successful *Domestic Manners of the Americans* (1832), is a send-up of America that concentrates on what happens in a society where "every bee in the hive is actively employed in search of that honey of Hybla, vulgarly called money" (38).[11] This approach dwelt on that portion of the mind that Combe associated with the animal sentiments and propensities, the aspect of the human personality that Trollope's contemporaries perceived as something that should not be written about, particularly in literature. As the critic for the *Athenaeum* put it in 1837, "Her wand (Fiction's, not Mrs. Trollope's), had we the controlling will, should conjure up only 'shadows of beauty, shadows of power,' and leave whatsoever is coarse and squalid, debased and debasing, to sleep out its sodden sleep in the limbo of commonplace reality" (*"The Vicar of Wrexhill"* 708). A virtually identical trope appears in the *Times*, which compares Trollope to Noah's son Ham, "a traitor among the sons of the Patriarch . . . [who] found [his father] drunken and exposed and insulted his fall" (*"The Vicar of Wrexhill"* 2). These images make it clear that, for her contemporaries, Trollope's writing exposed the drives that should remain unconscious, although that term is not yet in use.

Though Trollope explored her society's increasing materialism in a surprising array of fictional genres—anti-Catholic novels, antievangelical novels, an early mystery novel, the story of an abusive marriage, novels of social protest, novels of fashionable life in the silver fork tradition, and novels of courtship and marriage— she was most successful at evoking her era's ambivalence about England's commercial success in novels that depend on but also modify the typical pattern of the marriage plot in which a vulgar rich woman is contrasted to a virtuous poor one. The three novels I examine here, *The Widow Barnaby* (1839), *The Ward of Thorpe-Combe* (1841), and *The Life and Adventures of a Clever Woman, Illustrated with Occasional Extracts from Her Diary* (1854), all feature as their title character a middle-class woman who comes into the possession of wealth that allows her to satisfy her consumerist appetites.[12] They all also contrast that materialist figure to a virtuous and intellectual poor woman who is her opposite. But in Trollope's stories, as we might expect from the comments of both Malthus and Combe, the rich woman is a larger and more vivid presence than her spiritual antithesis.

As the reviewer for the *Times* commented of *The Widow Barnaby*'s romantic heroine Agnes Willoughby,

> The young lady is painted as a strong contrast to her aunt; for whereas the latter may be compared to the gay sunflower or lusty hollyhock, Miss Agnes more resembles the modest violet or gentle bending snowdrop. . . . [N]othing can be bolder or more dazzling than the execution of the widow's portrait, chaster and more delicate than the pretty figure of the niece. ("*The Widow Barnaby*" 5)[13]

When the same critic observes that the niece is "a somewhat insignificant person" (5) as opposed to her aunt, we come to the contemporary fear that Trollope's novels explore through the relation between the rich and the poor woman: the fear that, with the economic advancement of early industrial culture, intellectual virtues may indeed be rendered insignificant in the face of the materialist appetites.

Such fears were articulated with particular vehemence in industrial criticism of the period. As Peter Gaskell put it in his 1836 volume *Artisans and Machinery*,

> Manufactures . . . communicate intelligence and energy to the vulgar mind; they supply . . . ample means of inflaming their passions and depraving their appetites, by sensual indulgences of the lowest kind. Persons not trained up in a moral and religious nurture necessarily become, from the evil heart of human nature, the slaves of prejudice and vice; they see objects only on one side,—that which a sinister selfishness presents to their view. (v–vi)

Writing about the impact on workers of "liberal wages" and "the pecuniary sinews of contention" (vi), Gaskell articulates a general perception of the period: that the rise in manufactured items and the increase in wealth available to people from a variety of classes threatened to inflame appetites, enhance vulgarity, and feed selfishness. Trollope's novels incarnate Gaskell's assertion that "the riches of a great and wealthy nation are pouring into the tide of manufactures, and swelling its ascendancy" (8) in the rich woman whose money makes her feel "as if her power in this life were colossal, and that she might roam the world either for conquest or amusement" (*Widow Barnaby* 66).

Trollope uses words like "swelling," "expansive," "energetic," "industrious," and "vulgar," which appear in the discourse discussing the general impact of wealth in the age of machinery, to describe her wealthy women as they attempt to satisfy the appetites aroused by the possession of wealth. We hear in *The Ward of Thorpe-Combe* that inheritance makes a "hitherto penniless girl feel her new power in every swelling vein" (2.48). As this description suggests, in Trollope's novels money impacts the individual at the level of the body, making its presence felt "at that point of the brain where self-love expands itself into a mesh of ways and means, instinct with will, to catch all it can that may be brought home to glut the craving for enjoyment" (*Widow Barnaby* 69). Using the word "brain" instead of "mind," Trollope echoes Combe, who insists that "the brain is the organ of the mind" (120). Her novels provide a Combean reading of the human personality as they explore "the operation of prosperity on the fine mind" (*Ward of Thorpe-Combe* 2.57) of the protagonists. The characters she creates make readers feel, as the narrator of *The Widow Barnaby* exclaims, in a passage that echoes the title of Combe's work, "how strange is the constitution of the human mind! . . . . And how mutually dependant are its faculties and feelings on each other!" (239).

Trollope captures this dependency through her depiction of the relation be-tween the rich and the poor woman. Though Trollope's novels end, as Austen's do, with the poor heroine marrying the novel's romantic hero, the bulk of the story deals not with the rivalry between the rich and poor woman but with the fact that the poor woman is dependent on her rich antithesis.[14] This dependence means that Trollope's narratives explore at the level of fiction the fear of what would hap-pen if one were "to give the unintellectual power over the intellectual" (Brydges quoted in Williams *Culture* 35). Chalmers had argued that English culture would remain irremediably mired in materialism "so long as the sensual predominates over the reflective part of the human constitution" (quoted in Hilton *Age of Atone-ment* 81). Trollope represents the dominance of sensuality through narratives in which the rich woman's materialist appetites simply take over the story, dwarfing the virtues of the poor woman who is in her charge. Trollope's novels differ from Austen's; in them the rich woman becomes the center of interest for both novelist and reader.

However, Trollope's novels also resemble Austen's in that the rich woman's rela-tion to materialism changes over the course of the novelist's career. In Trollope's case, these representational changes mark her culture's gradual repression of the sensual and materialist drives that fueled an expanding commercial economy. In the title character of *The Widow Barnaby* Trollope evokes those drives in their purist form, creating a woman who revels in the hedonism of possessing and expending her wealth. In *The Ward of Thorpe-Combe* the title character feels the same hedonistic cravings as her precursor but knows she must conceal them if she is to present a properly virtuous image to the world. The heroine of *The Life and Adventures of a Clever Woman* has fully sublimated the sensual pleasures of immediate consumption into the mediated pleasure of achieving long-range social goals. In these sequential portraits Trollope shows that her contemporaries dealt with industrial success's propensity to enhance the sensual drives by articulating what Max Weber was later to identify as the Protestant ethic.

Though Trollope's heroines are consumers, they also display "a spirit of industry" (*Ward of Thorpe-Combe* 3.81). As the heroine of *The Ward* explains, "I have always had the greatest possible dislike to sitting idle, while others do that on which I ought to be employed myself" (2.114–15). Similarly the widow Barnaby "would far rather have obtained any object she aimed at by means of her own maneuvering" (42). Both are aware that "confidence in one's self,—the feeling that there is a power within us of sufficient strength to reach the goal we have in view,—is in general a useful as well as a pleasant state of mind" (*Widow Barnaby* 279). Each takes delight in feeling "her own powers of management swelling within her bosom" (*Widow Barnaby* 21).This is the trait Weber emphasized in *The Protestant Ethic, or the Spirit of Capitalism*. For the middle-class individual, according to Weber, "waste of time is . . . the first and in principle the deadliest of sins" (104). Successful producers, and we might add consumers, aim at "the liberation of energy for private acquisition" (98) so that the individual may "attain . . . self-confidence" in "worldly activity" (67). Trollope elaborates on the spirit of industry most extensively in *The Life and Adventures of a Clever Woman*, whose narrator observes that "no fairy god-mother could have arranged things more completely to the satisfaction of my heroine than she had arranged them for herself" (1.288).

In working to establish herself as "a woman of fashionable consequence and intellectual influence in society" (1.133), Charlotte Morris proves herself able to be "calculating and daring at the same time, above all temperate and reliable, shrewd and completely devoted to . . . business" (Weber *Protestant* 32). The sequence of Trollope's novels reveals the process by which the rapidly expanding industrial society sought to sublimate the physical desires that fueled it success. Weber insisted that the Protestant ethic celebrates "the strict avoidance of all spontaneous enjoyment of life"; it is "above all completely devoid of any eudaemonistic, not to say hedonistic, admixture" (18). Using three different words to signify pleasure—"enjoyment," "eudaemonistic," and "hedonistic"—this passage emphasizes the power of bodily drives that, in the 1830s, were regarded as impulses that had to be harnessed in order for the pursuit of wealth and luxury to be conceived as virtuous.[15] Over the course of her three novels, Trollope will show how these drives are both relegated to the unconscious and redefined as impulses that touch not the pleasure centers of the brain but its rational, calculating half.

The Sublime Vulgarity of *The Widow Barnaby*

What communicates energy and intelligence to the vulgar minds of Trollope's prosperous heroines is the desire to expend or use money rather than produce, save, or amass it. These fictional portraits confirm Colin Campbell's assertion that in the first half of the nineteenth century "that upheaval which went under the title of the Industrial Revolution had to be regarded as centring upon a revolution in consumption as well as production"(8).[16] By the 1830s industrial expansion had forced political economists to acknowledge that spending was as necessary for the economy as saving; "without 'a considerable class of persons who have both the will and power to consume more material wealth than they produce . . . the mercantile classes could not continue profitably to produce so much more than they consume'" (Malthus quoted in Perkin *Origins* 91).[17] This economic shift necessitated a behavioral transformation in the individual consumer, a transformation whose social and psychological consequences Trollope explores in all three of her novels.

In *The Widow Barnaby* she evokes the tension between saving and spending through the two prosperous women who dominate the novel's opening and closing, the parsimonious Betsy Compton and the expending Martha Barnaby. They represent the positions outlined by Adam Smith, who, as Malthus noted, "very justly observed that nations as well as individuals grow rich by parsimony and poor by profusion, and that therefore every frugal man was a friend and every spend-thrift an enemy to his country" (2004 93). But by Trollope's period Malthus had replaced Smith as the political economist whose writings dominated contemporary discourse. Malthus had insisted that "there is a potentially harmful tendency in modern culture to elevate saving and self-denial to the status of absolute virtues" (Herbert *Culture* 117). In *The Widow Barnaby* Trollope creates a Malthusian narrative that demonstrates the necessity of consumption while also stressing that giving expenditure free rein would lead to bankruptcy rather than prosperity.[18]

Betsy Compton represents the old-fashioned values that were praised in the midst of the inconceivably rapid expansion of the 1830s and '40s: "'The old school—slow and sure' was frequently held up in virtuous contrast to the madness of present times, when men thought nothing of spending capital faster than they could recoup it" (Hilton *Age of Atonement* 123). She is a spinster who lives frugally, reinvesting all the income she does not use, thereby building, "as she said to herself (but to nobody else), a sort of nest egg, which, as she should only draw out the interest to lay it in again in the shape of principal, would go on increasing till she might happen to want it" (3). In contrast, Martha Barnaby has been taught to spend as much as possible, having been raised by a mother whose main goal in life was to elevate her daughters, to make the "misses of ten pound a year pin-money look as smart as the squanderer of five hundred" (7).[19]

The two women are opposed not just in terms of how they use money but also at the level of body and appetite. Aunt Betsy is a tiny crippled woman, who inherits half her father's estate and preserves her inheritance by maintaining "her ascetic table" (87), consisting of country food—bread, spring water, and fresh butter made from the milk produced by her own cow.[20] She wears simple, practical, unfashionable, and unadorned clothes that are "always as precisely neat and nice as that of a quaker" (11), a religious reference that would have led contemporary readers to associate her with saving and Puritanism. In contrast the widow Barnaby is a "painted and plumaged giantess" (129) who enjoys the Rabelaisian pleasures of eating. Struggling "between economy and her rather particular love of a comfortable dinner" (102), she invariably gives in to the latter, as when she goes into a cook shop with her niece and orders "one bun for the young lady, and five for me" (100).[21] Though the novel associates Betsy Compton with virtue and Martha Barnaby with the crass desire for wealth, Trollope also underscores the limitations of the ascetic position by showing how the story's virtuous poor woman, the innocent and intellectual Agnes Willoughby, ends up in the care of her vulgar Aunt Barnaby rather than that of her abstemious great-aunt Betsy Compton.

Given their shared values, Aunt Betsy would have been a far more appropriate guardian for the child. As long as Agnes is a child, Betsy loves her because the girl has "one of the fairest and most delicate little faces.... 'It is just such a face as I wanted her to have.... Her father was a gentleman.... She will never have red cheeks, that is quite certain'"(30). This statement sets forth what appear to be the novel's implicit arguments about class and breeding: Aunt Betsy is superior because she is a member of the gentry, the widow Barnaby is inferior because her mother was a member of the commercial middle classes, and Agnes is superior because the widow's sister married a member of the gentry, thereby, at least potentially, counteracting the coarse strain of commercial blood that is part of her makeup. All of these depictions fit with the general perception of Trollope as a conservative writer, who endorsed the Tory values of land and lineage that also play so prominent a role in her son's novels. Yet *The Widow Barnaby* complicates this understanding of Trollope's class sympathies when Agnes returns from school "a short, round, little creature, who though nearly fourteen, did not look more than twelve, with cheeks as red as roses" (58). Convinced that these physical changes "altogether constitute a brilliant specimen of vulgar beauty" (59), Betsy reads the changes in Agnes's appearance as indicating the coarsening of her tastes and abandons her orphaned niece to the care of the vulgar Aunt Barnaby.

What triggers Betsy Compton's aversive reaction is less any indication that Agnes displays the underbreeding of a particular class than the rosiness that marks the presence of bodily appetites that Aunt Betsy associates with expenditure:

> Had Agnes been tall, pale, and slight made, with precisely the same features, her aunt Betsy would have willing devoted the whole of her remaining life to her. . . . But now, now that she saw her, as she fancied, so very nearly approaching in appearance to every thing she most disliked, all the long-indulged habits of frugality that enabled her (as she at this moment delighted to remember) to accumulate a fortune over which she still had entire control, seemed to rise before her, and press round her very heart. (59)[22]

This tension between paleness and rosiness reflects the arguments that both Malthus and Combe made about the balancing of intellectual and bodily drives. The color that Agnes displays is a sign of the vivid presence of visceral drives. As Andrew Combe, George Combe's brother, explained in his treatise on *The Physiology of the Digestion*,

> Whenever any living part is called into vivid action, an increased flow of blood and of nervous energy towards it immediately commences, to enable it to sustain the requisite degree of excitement, and continues till some time after the activity has ceased. In accordance with this law, whenever food is swallowed, the lining membrane of the stomach becomes suffused with blood, and, owing to the greater distension of its vessels, its color changes from a pale pink to a deep red hue. (270)

This autonomic reaction of the body, its excitation in response to physical stimuli, is what Aunt Betsy deplores in the adolescent Agnes whose suffusion of blood reflects the advent not of gastronomic but of sexual appetite.

Agnes is fourteen when she triggers Betsy Compton's disgust, a girl standing on the cusp of sexual maturity, as is the romantic heroine of *The Ward of Thorpe-*

Combe, whose blush is described as "the first symptom of transition from child-ishness to womanhood" (1.265).[23]Anxieties about sexuality, particularly of ado-lescent women, were articulated throughout writings about the age of machinery, which emphasize "the eroticization of industrial production" (Zlotnick 10) in the same way that Malthus's writings emphasized that the "capitalist marketplace" was "strikingly eroticized" (Herbert *Culture* 118). Take, for example, the following pas-sage from *Artisans and Machinery* in which Gaskell describes how

> the stimulus of a heated atmosphere, the contact of opposite sexes, the example of license upon the animal passions—all have conspired to produce a very early development of sexual appetencies. Indeed, in this respect, the female popula-tion engaged in mill labour, approximates very closely to that found in tropical climates; puberty, or at least sexual propensities, being attained almost coeval with girlhood. (103)[24]

The fear articulated in this quasi-anthropological image of a junglelike environ-ment is similar to what Betsy Compton experiences in looking at her red-faced adolescent niece and thinking the girl no longer looks like a gentleman's daugh-ter. It is the fear of a vulgar underclass that is wildly reproductive not just in the sense of producing children but also in the sense of displaying excessive bodily appetite.

Gaskell's word "appetency" is particularly apt for Trollope's novel; it means the "state of longing for, desiring, craving; appetite, passion," an "instinctive inclina-tion or propensity," and is connected to "desire and volition, as distinguished from cognition and feeling" (*OED*). It marks the difference Combe emphasized between the individual ruled by passions and the rational self, between the body and the mind, between the widow Barnaby and the spiritual niece who is left in her care. The widow incarnates the appetencies that Aunt Betsy mistakenly identifies in her niece, appetencies that are in the widow's case, as in her niece's, marked by color, by the fact, that she, like a blushing adolescent, has red cheeks. But the widow's cheeks are red because she rouges, an action that brings together sexual and economic drives, the craving for men and the desire to market herself as a commodity.[25] The commodifying aspect of rouging becomes clear when Agnes, still a child, comments that her aunt's red cheeks make her look like the waxwork dummies used for advertising: "Why, don't I see every time I walk by Mr. Gibbs's shop, his beauties in the window, with their rosy cheeks, and their black eyes, and their quantity of fine ringlets? and you are exactly the very image of one of Mr. Gibbs's beauties, aunt Martha" (33). In the widow Barnaby, this redness is a sign of the sexual appetites that Betsy Compton fears in the niece, but in the older woman the artifice and self-advertising reflect the sexual drives of a middle-aged woman attempting to hold on to her youth rather than those of an adolescent.

As Trollope's narrator stresses, the widow is like a rose about to drop its petals, a "full-blown person" whose "eyes and . . . rouge were as bright as ever" (90). She has "the vigorous maturity of ripened age" that "glowed also with the early brightness of youth"; "like Mrs. Malaprop and the orange-tree, she bore blossom and fruit at once" (301). Trollope's representation of her aging but still sexually active heroine reflects Malthus's uneasiness about his society's propensity to artificially enhance the desire to consume and reproduce that gave life its vividness but also had the potential to exhaust the economy.[26] Trollope works out the implications of the combination of sexual and economic pleasure that troubled contemporaries about Malthus's arguments as the story of the widow Barnaby unfolds.[27] Inheriting a comfortable fortune on the death of her successful pharmacist husband, Martha Barnaby cuts herself loose from the village in which she was born and from the domestic ties that usually bind women to one place and limit their indulgence of their appetites. She sets forth on a journey in which she follows the urgings "of Lust & Hunger both alike Passions of physical Necessity, and the one equally with the other independent of Reason, & the will" (Coleridge quoted in Gigante 61). The novel becomes a tale of "picaresque hedonism" (E. P. Thompson quoted in Laqueur "Sex" 102) as its vulgar heroine moves from watering place to watering place, seeking in each a more intense satisfaction of a desire to consume that is so pleasurable it is equal to and intertwined with sexual desire.

This journey reaches its climax when the widow arrives in Bath, a city known in the period as a center of "unadulterated pleasure" (Barker-Benfield 198) and finds herself at an auction.[28] That venue allows Trollope to show in detail the intertwining of sexual and economic desires that Malthus had emphasized and that was becoming so much a part of modern commercial culture. On display like the objects that are up for bid, the widow advertises herself, as she does throughout the novel, with her rouging and the profusion of her dress. In this case her animated behavior draws attention, as Trollope shows how the possibility of acquisition heightens the individual's energy: "More than one eye-glass was turned towards her, producing that reciprocity of cause and effect which is so interesting to trace; for the more the gentlemen and ladies looked at her, the more Mrs. Barnaby talked and laughed, and the more Mrs. Barnaby talked and laughed, the more the gentlemen and ladies looked at her" (300–301).This interaction becomes explicitly sexual when she attracts the gaze of a nobleman, which causes her heart "to palpitate" (301). In a language of arousal that is almost masturbatory, the narrator tells readers that the widow Barnaby "could not sit still . . . her eyes rose and fell . . . her head turned and twisted . . . her reticule opened and shut" (301–2).[29] Using the image of the purse, Trollope aligns sexual with commercial desire.

The narrative will subsequently link the intense pleasures of this scene of flirtation with the widow's desire to spend money on commodities in order to retain the attention of her high-born suitor. After the auction, Lord Muckleberry, the nobleman engaged in the flirtation, asks his cronies, "Did any of you, gentlemen, ever happen to watch the effect of the sun's rays when thrown upon some soft substance (a pound of butter for example) through the medium of a burning-glass? . . . Such and so great was that produced by the rays of my right eye when sent through my eye-glass upon this charming creature. . . . She warmed, trembled, yea, visibly melted under it" (313). The word "melting" reappears in Trollope's novel after the widow spends so much on clothes and carriages that she is forced to acknowledge "the melting nature of money" (347). Indeed, her insatiable desire to expend eventually lands her in debtors' prison.

Trollope also alludes to the overlay of sexual and economic rhetoric at the conclusion of the auction. As Lord Muckleberry leaves, the widow Barnaby watches until "the last frog on the hinder part of his coat had passed from her eye . . . and then, like the tender convolvulus when the sunbeam that reached it has passed away, she drooped and faded till she looked more like a sleeping picture of Mrs. Barnaby than Mrs. Barnaby herself" (303).[30] The key word in this passage, "convolvulus," with its suggestion of female sexual anatomy and convulsion, binds the erotic and the economic. "Convulsion" was a word used throughout Trollope's era to describe the traumatic effects of excessive economic desires on both individual consumers and society as a whole. Carlyle feared the threat of "English Commerce with its world-wide convulsive fluctuations" (*Chartism* 329). James Kay-Shuttleworth wrote of the "partial ills [that] . . . threaten to convulse the whole social constitution" (18).[31] It is a term that recurs even in modern historians who describe the "necessary analogue to the industrial revolution, the necessary convulsion on the demand side of the equation to match the convulsion on the supply side" (McKendrick "The Consumer Revolution" 17). Trollope incarnates this convulsion of the demand side in the widow Barnaby, whose characterization underscores the tendency of writers of the period to allude to the convulsions of "business crashes in the language of sexual release" (Hilton *Age of Atonement* 148).

Evangelical economists described how "every mercantile activity throbs, and its pulsation is immorality" (quoted in Hilton *Age of Atonement* 142). So, too, the last of the widow Barnaby's suitors takes her hand and puts it on his heart so that she can feel how her presence makes it beat, throb, and flutter (416). Ironically this encounter takes place in debtors' prison where the widow meets Patrick O'Donagough (the illegitimate son of a lord), a handsome, young evangelical minister who eventually becomes her second husband.[32] The widow's confinement for debt is a novelistic working out of the argument Malthus made when he argued that "the dangers to happiness lay not in these impulses themselves"—sexuality and consumer appetite—but "in the 'fatal extravagances' to which they sometimes gave rise" (Winch 264). He also "predicted that financial crises would recur as the country proved unable to consume all the goods and services it produced" (Winch 264). In Trollope's novel this cycle of bankruptcy leads to the reintroduction of Betsy Compton, who rescues her niece when Agnes is left alone after the widow's imprisonment. The narrative moves toward a resolution in which the impulses represented by the two aunts are balanced. Once the excessive consumption of the vulgar aunt is punished, then the abstemious aunt can begin to indulge in expenditure, which she does, spending lavishly to provide her niece with the accoutrements the girl deserves.

The novel then provides an Austenian conclusion: the poor but virtuous niece marries the noble suitor who has loved her all along despite the vulgarity of the aunt who appears to be her only protector. Agnes's gently born father, who was thought to be dead, suddenly reappears and proves on his second marriage to have chosen a member of a noble family, so that he is completely cleansed of any taint of the vulgar commercial strain evoked through his earlier marriage to the sister of the widow Barnaby. All of this is narrated in terms that evoke the Cinderella story, as Aunt Betsy, like a fairy godmother, provides Agnes with a coach with a coat of arms on the side and dresses her in gowns that befit a princess.[33] But these concluding events feel like an eleventh hour return to the romance plot Trollope knows readers expect from the novel of manners. The bulk of *The Widow Barnaby*'s interest lies, as its title and reviews suggest, not in these idealized figures but in the figure of material appetites that is their opposite. Indeed, the extraordinary accomplishment of Trollope's novel, what made it such a success, is the fact that in it Trollope evokes the consumerist desires that were part of her time period so vividly that her contemporary audience was able simultaneously to enjoy them and recognize them as vulgar. The very excesses of the widow's appetites made her appealing.

In its ending, as the widow is imprisoned and eventually forced to emigrate and Aunt Betsy begins to spend, *The Widow Barnaby* constrains its heroine's desires, thereby pointing toward the middle ground that Malthus's follower Chalmers advocated as key to England's ability to continue its economic expansion. Chalmers argued that individuals needed to find a balance "between prudence and moral principle on the one hand, and physical comfort on the other" (quoted in Hilton *Mad* 337). He also insisted that to achieve this balance individuals needed "to elevate their minds above their passionate flesh" (quoted in Hilton *Age of Atonement* 81).[34] Trollope's *The Widow Barnaby* suggests how difficult such an elevation would be by making the desires of the passionate flesh comically, intensely, and pleasurably visible in the vulgar widow who is its title character. The novel tries to end with what Southey called, in the case of Malthus, "an impossible union between stoicism and sensuality" (80), but its evocation of sensuality inevitably exceeds its praise of stoicism.

In the novel that follows, Trollope places the ascetism and consumerism that are embodied in separate characters in *The Widow Barnaby* in a single figure. In the title character of *The Ward of Thorpe-Combe*, she creates a woman who feels the bodily appetites indulged by the widow Barnaby, who "liked comfort exceedingly" (1.111). But, in the face of the emerging world of middle-class values described by Chalmers, she no longer allows herself the freedoms enjoyed by the widow Barnaby. Embodying "the split between feeling and action" (Campbell 74) that Campbell has argued Puritanism makes possible and hedonism requires, Sophia Martin Thorpe presents herself as if she follows the puritan path Chalmers advocates, acting as it she has a mind elevated above the passions of the flesh she also knows she wishes to indulge.[35]

"Little Nice Things" and *The Ward of Thorpe-Combe*

In her later novel Trollope shows the ways 1830s English culture began to sublimate the appetites that were necessary for economic expansion. Like Austen, who began by invoking the rich woman as a caricatured figure in *Pride and Prejudice* and moved to more serious and troubling issues in *Mansfield Park*, so too does Trollope leave the comic valences of *The Widow Barnaby* behind in *The Ward of Thorpe-Combe*. As in Austen's *Mansfield Park*, the anxieties *The Ward of Thorpe-Combe* explores have to do with the problems that arise from confusing wealth and virtue. But while Austen's novel represents the delusive attractions of wealth, Trollope's shows how the materialist individual can mimic virtue. In *The Ward of Thorpe-Combe* the heroine is no longer a giantess who dwarfs her antithesis but a diminutive woman who acts as if she possesses the virtues of a poor woman, thereby convincing her uncle that she is worthy of inheriting his estate. Once the person who desires wealth understands the behaviors her culture reads as unworldly, she can use those behaviors to convey values that may be entirely at odds with her inner tastes. But the novel is as interested in what happens to Sophia after she inherits as it is in the machinations that engender that possession. The story that follows her inheritance shows how the possession of wealth makes it possible for Sophia to indulge the bodily appetites Trollope had emphasized in the widow Barnaby, in particular the pleasures of eating. But in this novel readers experience not the consumer's exuberance but "the corrosive, vainly battled consciousness" (*Ward of Thorpe-Combe* 3.58) of an individual and a society at war with their own cravings.

The Ward of Thorpe-Combe opens as Mr. Thorpe, the possessor of the relatively recently amassed estate of Thorpe-Combe, decides to invite all his living relatives to visit in order to determine who is "the worthiest among [his] kin" (1.17), since his son has, he believes, died in India. As Sir Charles Temple, the financially straitened baronet who is Thorpe's friend and neighbor, tells him, "You have not studied Cinderella for nothing" (1.28). Thorpe is not the only one who understands the Cinderella story. The novel's title character, Sophia Martin, an orphan and the poorest of the relations invited to her uncle's estate, uses the contrast between the rich and the poor woman central to that fairy tale to present herself as the humblest, least materialistic, and most altruistic of his relatives, the one who deserves the reward of her uncle's fortune, which she succeeds in acquiring. In choosing Sophia rather than one of the other candidates, Mr. Thorpe is caught in a misreading; he is unable to see that it his other niece, Florence Heathcote, who in fact embodies the virtues characteristic of the poor woman in the novel of manners. Sophia so effectively camouflages her desire for wealth that she looks as unworldly as her cousin Florence, while Florence's inability to manipulate social signs means that she, though truly a Cinderella, is dismissed as unworthy of being her uncle's heir.

In Trollope's novel, Florence proves her unworldliness the first morning of her stay with her uncle by rising early to explore the beauties of his snow-covered estate and returning home with "the bottom of her dress . . . adorned with a border of icicles, which would make her entering the breakfast-room, without changing it, an act of great indiscretion" (1.152). This image alludes to the scene in *Pride and Prejudice* when Elizabeth Bennet appears at Netherfield and is mocked by Miss Bingley for having let down her skirt to cover the mud on her petticoat. But in *The Ward of Thorpe-Combe* Florence's skirt is marred not by dirt but by ice, an image that conveys the purity Trollope wishes to associate with her heroine and marks the perversion of a society that disapproves of even such uncontaminated evidences of contact with nature. Changing her dress, Florence commits the solecism of being late to breakfast and of having hands that "look of a blood-red hue" (1.164) because she has just come in from the cold. Like the moment in *The Widow Barnaby* when Betsy Compton reacts with aversion to the redness of the adolescent Agnes's cheeks, so too here Mr. Thorpe feels distaste for Florence's hands and her behavior. He prefers instead her cousin Sophia who refuses to go on a walk to see the frozen waterfall because she fears her dress might be dirtied and who wears the simplest and most unostentatious of clothes in order to present an "appearance [that] indicated great care and neatness" (1.51).[36]

The key word in Trollope's description of her heroine is "indicate," a word that recurs when Sophia inherits the objects her uncle once possessed and reads them as "indications of the wealth that surrounded her" (2.140).[37] In the world of *The Ward of Thorpe-Combe* even neatness is an indicator, a sign the heroine can both read and manipulate. In wooing her uncle, Sophia makes her appearance and behavior conform to a pattern she assumes he will recognize and reward. Knowing that a woman will appear virtuous when she is full of care for others rather than for herself, Sophia enacts the part of altruism.[38] Secretly observing her uncle's needs, she makes sure they are met when the other candidates for his fortune seem to be thinking only of satisfying themselves. She shows herself adept at performing actions that, as one of the other characters comments, "inspire us all with respect for her powers of pleasing" (2.28).[39] But this process of pleasing, which can have a positive effect on the person it is aimed at, is experienced by others as having a quasi-repulsive aura, as suggested by the narrator's description of Sophia, who exhibits a "mixture of disclaiming humility and ardent gratitude,—the retiring shyness at one moment, and the creeping cat-like caressingness at another" (1.251).

Sophia's uncle does not feel the distaste her actions should arouse because the novel's heroine makes calculated use not just of general behaviors that signify virtue in the culture but also of specific objects that hold private significance for her uncle. Her campaign to win him over is only fully successful after she has gained access to his bedroom and study, a set of rooms that are the center of both the house and the novel. Those rooms mark Trollope's interest in the increasing privatization of desire, an inward move the novel emphasizes both in its early depictions of Sophia's uncle and in its later depictions of the heiress as she comes to occupy the rooms that once were his. They contain that which is secret, hidden, and inner, the desires that lie behind the public surfaces individuals present to one another in their daily social interactions. When Sophia first enters them, the narrator describes how she "stepped forward into the middle of the room, and looked round about her on all sides with an air of very accurate research, as if reading in the still life with which he was usually surrounded the private history of her uncle's mind" (1.178). For both Sophia and her uncle, as Combe argued in *The Constitution of Man*, "the *highest* interest of human beings is to become acquainted with the constitutions and relations of every object around them, that they may discover its capabilities of ministering to their own advantage" (7, emphasis in the original).[40] In a novel whose title may contain a sly allusion to Combe, Sophia "reads" the objects in her uncle's bedroom as things that, even in the absence of their owner, bear marks of his relation to the world, revealing, as they do, the investments of both his mind and heart.

There is a moment in this scene that echoes Dickens's *Oliver Twist*, when Sophia sees the portrait of her uncle's long lost son hanging on the wall of the bedroom and realizes that she resembles him (as the maid tells her, "I am sure you might be his own sister as far as the hair, and the eyes bean't that much unlike either" [1.180]). In Dickens's novel, Oliver is taken into Mr. Brownlow's home and seen to bear a striking resemblance to the portrait of a woman who turns out to be his mother, and it is the link between Oliver and the painting that explains the strong feelings that almost immediately attach Brownlow to the orphan. In Trollope's world, the orphan Sophia uses such feelings to her own advantage.[41] Retiring to her room and rearranging the details of her appearance, changing her hairstyle and dress so that she looks like her cousin as he is represented in the painting, Sophia appears in the public room that has been transformed into a "mimic grove of mistletoe and holly" (1.228) in celebration of Christmas. She places "herself in an attitude which appeared perfectly natural, where the light fell, as she wished it should do, full upon her, and where she was sure of meeting the eye of Mr. Thorpe" (1.228).[42] In a scene brimful of references to Milton's *Comus*, she makes herself into an image, a virtual mirage, of the heir whose death her uncle mourns and thereby secures for herself both the wealth and emotions her uncle would have given to his son. Sophia "mimics" the feelings and attachments a Dickens novel celebrates in order to sell herself, as one might a commodity, to her uncle as the "natural" choice for his heir.

Because Sophia is aware of how easily feelings can be manipulated, she is careful to keep her own hidden; "Lavater himself could hardly have read emotion of any kind upon her features" (2.37).[43] Even after she is successful and officially informed that she is her uncle's heir, she refuses to display any pleasure at that bequest; "the only feeling she experienced . . . arose from the necessity of not permitting her eyes to wander freely over every part of the room, and every article in it, from the fine Vandyke over the chimney piece to the salt-spoons on the table" (2.140).[44] Though her wealth makes her feel "a sensation of pleasure, too new, and too delicious to be altogether smuggled under the sombre tranquility in which she deemed it proper to veil her features" (2.37–38), she will not show her feelings in public. Her desire for privacy as she enters her uncle's study to contemplate the objects she has just inherited is almost pathological:

> She knew perfectly well that she had locked the door of the room, and that no human eye could share with her own the glory of that sight, unless the door was broken open, or the chimney or the windows invaded. . . . Yet she could not be contented, till she had crept with stealthy step to see that all indeed was safe, and that her deep ecstasy might be indulged without danger that any envious eye should watch it. (2.278–79)[45]

This passage marks Trollope's awareness that, for the culture as a whole, as for Sophia Martin-Thorpe, the newly developed appetites for both possession and consumption that were made possible by wealth were intended to be indulged in private rather than in public.

As a French writer commented of the difference between Paris and London in the 1850s,

> While in France prosperity flaunts itself, here it tries to hide in the general mediocrity. This type of hypocrisy has its maniacs. I am told that there are wealthy bankers who go in person to the butcher's shop every morning to buy the mutton chops, which they carry ostentatiously to some tavern in Fleet Street or Cheapside, where they insist on grilling them themselves. They then buy a threepenny loaf of brown bread and devour this Spartan meal in public. (quoted in Rubinstein *Capitalism* 157–58)[46]

This privatization of appetite allowed consumers to resolve the tension between saving and spending that, as we saw in *The Widow Barnaby*, was key to anxieties about the commercial expansions of the period.

In Sophia's case the tension between these two drives is articulated in a vision:

> On the one side stood firmly, swelling upon its broad base, a glorious money-bag, at whose narrow mouth a few diminutive coins rose in a pyramid, ready for use. . . . But beside it stood a coarse unseemly joint of salted meat, with rude accompaniments, such as the gourmet loves not. On the other side, a like ample

bag lay prostrate, and from its yawning orifice welled forth a stream of glittering gold, while evident collapse reduced its roundness.... But in all directions near it might be seen the very daintiest dishes that appetite ere dreamed of. (3.13–14)[47]

She reconciles the desire for sensual pleasure and for abstemious saving represented by the two bags by choosing to satisfy her palate in private and presenting the appearance of parsimony in public. Indulging in "lonely luncheons" that "became a source of unspeakable comfort to her" (3.14) in the suite of private rooms that once belonged to her uncle, Sophia offers plain joints of salted meat to the relatives who gather at her dining-room table.[48]

In describing her private meals, the novel dwells on the materiality of her desires, as Sophia begins to allow herself small, sensual indulgences. Emphasizing the connection between bodily appetite and psychological engrossment, a connection that, as I have argued, is characteristic of the rich woman in general, the narrator describes how Sophia "hugged herself in an embrace of most fond selfishness" (2.147), as she "sipped with luxurious deliberation" (2.142) the coffee she loves but has previously denied herself because it costs too much, coffee that she will not offer to her guests and family.[49] These appetites, which Trollope associates with the consumption of food, are as omnivorous as the widow Barnaby's, but Sophia does not display them in the excessively large terms of her predecessor. We hear that "the secret consciousness that the general style of her house-keeping, considered *en grand,* was highly economical, prevented all remorse from the costliness of the *very little* morsels" (3.15, emphasis in the original), and she tells her housekeeper, "I want very few dishes on the table; but I am very particular about having nothing but the nicest things, dressed in the nicest manner, and with little nice things, such as mushrooms, you know" (2.178–79).

Having her heroine request mushrooms immediately before one of the servants describes her as a "dirty little, selfish, set-up mushroom" (2.184), Trollope emphasizes that she is depicting through Sophia Martin-Thorpe what in the 1820s and '30s were called the "mushroom" classes, members of the newly enriched middle and lower-middle classes that sprang up over night, like mushrooms, and sought to indulge the tastes that could be both engineered and gratified by the country's economic expansion. Sophia's emphasis on little as opposed to large dishes is characteristic of the way the middle class differentiated its eating habits from those of its aristocratic precursors. The newcomers prided themselves on "the invention and elaboration of an endless variety of ever more refined and delicate dishes" (Mennell 142). This elaboration was a perfect fit for a rapidly expanding consumer economy; "when the possibilities of quantitative consumption for the expression of social superiority had been exhausted, the qualitative possibilities were inexhaustible" (Mennell 142).

But such developments troubled the way the opposition between the rich and the poor woman had traditionally been used in the novel of manners to suggest a contrast between taste or delicacy and engrossment. With the expansion of the economy, the emergence of new classes of consumers, and the explosion of the range of objects available for consumption, the terms of that opposition collapse. Delicacies, refinements, and the niceness of tastes that have been made sensitive to the nuances of small changes are increasingly linked to the material advances that made England financially successful not just as a manufacturer but, as we will see in discussing the works of Anthony Trollope, also as a purveyor of objects for consumption. When its heroine sends to Fordham's in Piccadilly (Trollope's nod to Fortnum and Mason's) for "potted meats, dried meats, hams, tongues, *patés, consommés,* sauces, glazes, fruits dried, preserved, and in jelly, truffles, caviare, laver, pickles[,] . . . these and a thousand other things besides" (2.180), *The Ward of Thorpe-Combe* emphasizes the ways the bodily appetites Sophia displays are inextricably bound up with the expansion of the English economy during this period.

The drives associated with consumption and the body, were, as Gigante has argued, intensified in the early decades of the nineteenth century when Trollope matured and became a writer:

> After Waterloo (1815), as the historian John Burnett writes, many of the greatest French chefs emigrated to England, lured by enormous salaries as "ornaments to the acquisitive society which industrialism had fostered"; as a result, nineteenth-century Britons, "who denounced gluttony almost as vehemently as they did immorality, had their palates educated, and came to be as fond of good food as they were of other sins of the flesh." (167)[50]

But, as the religious language of this passage suggests, the problem for Trollope's contemporaries was that the pleasures of the flesh seemed to be displacing those of the spirit.

Sophia loves the privacy of her uncle's study because it allows her "to enjoy in solitude, silence, and secrecy, the deep, deep, deep, delight of having acquired all that her soul most loved" (2.84). The novel's hyperemphasis on depth and its association of the pleasures of acquisition with the soul, which, as the narrator later comments, "looked forth at her eye" (2.140), marks the boundary that is being crossed as Sophia comes into the possession of wealth—the boundary between material and spiritual desires. She is described as indulging the "savoury meat that her soul loved," "morsels which exhaled their rich but tiny streams, within the small, well-heated silver reservoirs" (3.14, 15). Bringing together the spiritual and the carnal, the soul and the meat, these passages deliberately echo Charles Lamb's famous 1821 essay "Grace before Meat," which describes guests sitting "at rich men's tables, with the savoury soup and messes steaming up the nostrils, and moistening the lips of the guests with desire and a distracted choice" (128). For Lamb, these appetites reveal the materialism of a culture that promotes "the indulgence of the *immoderate* pleasures of the palate" (Gigante 90, emphasis in the original), the pleasures that Sophia is able to experience once she succeeds to her uncle's fortune. In *The Ward of Thorpe-Combe* as opposed to *The Widow Barnaby* those pleasures are associated with eating rather than sexuality, but Lamb's essay makes clear the link between the two bodily appetites when he tells its readers of their pleasure at a meal that they sit "with the ravenous orgasm" on them (128).

Trollope alludes to Lamb's essay earlier in the novel too, when Sophia is cozying up to her uncle in church, using a spiritual venue to promote materialist aims. The narrator then comments, quoting Lamb, that some individuals "praise the gods amiss" (1.251). *The Widow Barnaby* also suggests a link between places of worship and the pleasures individuals can take in material consumption. The novel is most emphatic about the pleasure the widow takes in her appearance when she displays herself in church attired in

> a new dress of light grey gros-de-Naples, with a gay bonnet of *paille de riz*, decorated with poppy-blossoms, both within and without, a "ladylike" profusion of her own embroidery on cuffs, collar, and pocket-handkerchief, her well-oiled ringlets half hiding her large, coarse, handsome face, her eyes set off by a suffusion of carmine, and her whole person redolent of musk. (159)

Citing this passage, the reviewer for the *Times* exclaimed, "The Barnaby is such a heroine as never before has figured in a romance. Her vulgarity is sublime. Imaginary person though she may be, everybody who has read her memoirs must have a real interest in her. We still feel that charming horror which carried us through these volumes" (5).

This combination of sublimity and vulgarity, like Trollope's association of the soul with meat in *The Ward of Thorpe-Combe*, points up the problematic position these prosperous women occupy. As Romantic poetry makes clear, the sublime was, during this period, an aesthetic value that was being posited as the opposite of and the counter to the vulgarity of material engrossment. By creating a figure whose fleshy desires are so intimately entangled with her spiritual ones that her vulgarity can be experienced as sublime, Trollope brings together the two categories that were supposed to be kept completely separate. And, in *The Ward of Thorpe-Combe* as in *The Widow Barnaby*, she suggests that the values represented by the novel's impoverished and virtuous characters are not capable of checking the expansion of the material appetites that drive the novel's title characters. Florence Heathcote's father, an ex-soldier, exclaims of Sophia Martin-Thorpe's appetites that "I am considerably more frightened now than I was at Brussels, when the drums stopped the fiddles just before we took our little trot to Waterloo" (2.128). This comment identifies the shifts in taste and consumption that were taking place in Trollope's period as more unsettling and therefore more socially transforming than dramatically visible historical events like battles.

In *The Ward of Thorpe-Combe* it is not accidental that the impoverished aristocratic hero who eventually marries the unworldly Florence Heathcote is named Temple. Like Florence herself with her reverent response to the beauties of nature, Charles Temple represents religious beliefs untainted by any material component. But these spiritual figures have little power to halt the process by which their materialist antithesis accedes to power. Once Sophia inherits her uncle's fortune, she seems to have absolute control over the characters that espouse alternative values. (Because Sophia is underage, a ward, her uncle and his children, Florence Heathcote and her brother, must remain with her at Thorpe Combe, where they are compelled to live by her rules and eat what she provides.) The only way the novel can limit its heroine's power and appetites is by having Mr. Thorpe's long-lost son turn out to be alive, return from India, inherit the estate, and dispossess Sophia. The irony of this solution is that this is the son Sophia resembles, and she resembles him in more than physical appearance. He was sent off to India in the first place because he could not control his own appetites, in his case the sexual appetites that led him to get involved with a married woman in the village.

The novel suggests that in a man, perhaps especially in a man who is sent to the colonies, appetites like the ones that Sophia exhibits can fuel success; young Thorpe has made himself one of the richest merchants in India and returns to make the estate even wealthier than it was (and, fortuitously, because he is childless, to leave it to Florence Heathcote and her brother). Trollope will invoke a similar relation between male and a female members of the same wealthy family in *The Life and Adventures of a Clever Woman*, where Charlotte Morris never forgot that, whatever we make up our minds to have, we must make up our minds to pay for. It was a truth ever present in her mind, when she had some object in view; and there can be little or no doubt, that this very essential morsel of practical wisdom had been habitually present also to the minds of her commercial and highly respectable ancestors. (1.264)

In Trollope's late novel the sublime and the vulgar are brought together in a heroine who sublimates the materiality of material cravings, as she intertwines economic and self-interested behavior with religious and aesthetic rhetoric.

Bravura in *The Life and Adventures of a Clever Woman*

Trollope's novel allows its self-possessed heroine to tell her own story of the process by which she uses the money and goods her banker father has acquired to establish herself in society. (The novel's full title reads *The Life and Adventures of a Clever Woman, Illustrated with Occasional Extracts from Her Diary.*) The story begins when the widowed Mr. Morris retires, buys a house in an elegant neighborhood in London, and hands the reins of the establishment over to his daughter, who, at seventeen, is only then coming into adulthood. Mr. Morris allows her to use his wealth to satisfy her desires. Focusing not on the father but the daughter, Trollope's novel explores the implications of the Protestant ethic when it is espoused not in the arena where individuals make money but where they spend it and use the objects that money allows them to acquire to enhance the quality of their daily lives.

Such fictional portraits confirm Campbell's assertion that in the early nineteenth-century "the bourgeoisie embraced both the Protestant ethic *and* a consumption ethic" (8, emphasis in the original). Trollope conveys the workings of the consumption ethic as she tells the story of a calculating middle-class heroine who achieves the social position she desires through her manipulation of two families: the aristocratic Knightons and the artistic Richardses. Representing a social milieu different from that of the middle-class Morrises, the Knightons allow Trollope to show first how the middle classes use the Protestant ethic to establish themselves as more virtuous than their aristocratic precursors. In her portrayal of her pragmatic heroine's interactions with a family of artists Trollope goes beyond Weber's theorizing of the implication of the spirit of capitalism; she shows how, for a successful capitalist consumer and social aspirant like Charlotte Morris, the careful use of wealth becomes not merely a religion but a form of artistry.

The opening chapters of *The Life and Adventures of a Clever Woman* depict in some detail how Charlotte Morris succeeds in establishing "a sort of partnership concern in the ball-going and ball-giving line" (1.235) with the Knightons who live across the square from where her prosperous banker father has retired. They are "a family connected with the aristocracy by near relationship to an old title, [who] are not at liberty to spend their money in lace and embroidery" (1.111). Their name indicates their symbolic status as members of the gentry, and their style of life reveals the limitations of their financial resources, a consequence of their having to pour money into maintaining the signs of their elevated status (by keeping a carriage, for example). The two families work well together; the Knightons can offer Charlotte entrée into a social world she could not enter on her own, and she in turn can supply them with the goods they can no longer afford to purchase. When Charlotte Morris and the Knightons interact, neither has to like or even understand the other. Each merely has to perceive how the other can be of use. The daughters of the two families establish a "system of mutual accommodation" that "was greatly improved by the reciprocal frankness with which it was avowed" (2.158).

Charlotte Morris begins teaching the Knighton daughters this philosophy in her very first encounter with the family, when she offers to go with them to a florist shop. Flowers have already been associated with strategic self-presentation in the novel's opening scenes when the title character has "a vase of very choice flowers upon her table," and we are told that "she was herself as advantageously displayed as they were" (1.68). This calculated use of objects persists in the scene where Charlotte and the Knightons go to purchase flowers. At the florist's shop, Charlotte does not, as one might expect she would, buy flowers for the impoverished but genteel Knightons. Instead, proving she knows "the value of flowers" (1.79), she selects the best blooms, "procuring," as the novel aptly puts it, exactly what she wants. Then, refusing to haggle over the price, she pays immediately out of a well-stocked purse. Only later does she send two magnificent bouquets to the Knighton home. Allowing her aristocratic friends to be disappointed, to envy her, and then satisfying their needs, Charlotte teaches them what they can gain through her. As the Knightons come increasingly to recognize, "Miss Morris's '*things*' were really beautiful" (1.69, emphasis in the original), the Morrises are "in fact, exactly the right sort of folks to borrow from, because, . . . all their goods and chattels are in their newest gloss" (1.116).

The difference between the aristocratic household and its middle-class counterpart is here, as would be appropriate in terms of the Protestant ethic, defined in terms of the careful use of money: "Those business people, I believe, always enjoy saving money more than spending it" (1.70). In contrast, the Knightons live in a world of Malthusian overuse; as the eldest daughter complains, "Our things have been growing less and less, as it seems, to me, every party we give" (1.127). Charlotte's father understands that even if one were to try to amend such scarcity, it would inevitably repeat itself. As he explains of the Knightons' perennial indebtedness, "if exactly the number of hundreds or of thousands at which they might state their deficiency were at once added to their income, a very few months would again place them in the same position" (1.109). The difference between the two is like the difference between a healthy and an unhealthy economy; Charlotte can loan her neighbors whatever they need because she knows that even if objects are broken or lost, "her father both could and would repair the loss of such commodities" (1.136).

This material security allows Charlotte to feel superior to the benighted Knightons in terms that fully anticipate Weber's thinking about the Protestant ethic and its association with middle-class values. Charlotte looks down on her upper-class cohorts because

> their object evidently was, to borrow teacups and wine-glasses, and, perhaps, a brooch or a bracelet! Poor people! Their ambition went no further, their imagination reached no higher object!
>
> How great then was the difference, how vast the interval between her motives and theirs! all they hoped for was a trifling and temporary accommodation, or the pitiful gratification of shining for an hour in borrowed gems. But what were her objects? A lifelong enjoyment of admiration, influence, and renown. She certainly was playing the higher game; she felt the superiority, and gloried in it. (1.134–35)

This passage articulates a clear distinction between the pursuit of material goals, the goals that are fueled by literal capital, and the pursuit of symbolic profits, what Bourdieu has taught us to call cultural capital. Emphasizing the importance of cultural capital becomes the means whereby a middle-class character asserts her superiority to the better-born family she has used for entrée into society but whom she now wishes to move beyond.

The implications of transcendence lurking in the phrase "higher object" are made explicit when the novel's heroine, in talking with her father about her ambitions, acknowledges that "I recognized the especial will of providence in it" (1.105). Charlotte's pointing out that their friendship with the Knightons has "opened a way for us" (1.149) and that they need to "profit as much as possible by such a lucky chance" (1.150) reflects her impulse to deploy in the arena of consumption what Weber calls "the providential interpretation of profit-making" (109). In Trollope's novel, the language of religion, including the belief in a providential God, has fully infused the process of establishing oneself as a social success. When Charlotte first attempts to convey to her father the seriousness of her goals in order to enlist his aid in providing financial and emotional support, she is described as approaching her subject "with a degree of gravity which might have befitted Hannah More, when discoursing with her favourite bishops" (1.145). The reference to More, famed for her religious tracts, would have cued contemporary readers to the subtext of the conversation. Charlotte subsequently tells her father, "I believe I think more than most girls of my age; I think of my future existence" (1.145). Mr. Morris assumes that she is referring to life in heaven, responding, in one of Trollope's more wonderfully satirical passages, by telling her that "I should not like to believe that your young thoughts were too unmindful of the world in which we are at present placed" (1.146),

This passage mockingly references the scene in Richardson's *Clarissa* where Lovelace does not realize that Clarissa is, in fact, focused on the next world rather than the present one as she talks about returning to her father's mansion. In an even more ironic echo of Clarissa's reference to her father's house, Charlotte later tells her father how much she admires his mansion:

> What I should like would be always to have just such a nice house as this, just as nicely furnished, and everything about me just as elegant and as comfortable as you have made it here. But even that would not content me, papa, unless I could contrive to make myself in some degree worthy of such a beautiful home; and even if I could do that, it would not content me unless I had a good set of elegant and well-educated people as my friends and acquaintance. My greatest idea of *earthly* happiness, dear papa, is having to preside in such a house as this. (1.148, emphasis in the original)

In *Clever Woman* the heroine will indeed remain in her father's mansion even after she marries because of the material comforts provided there, the objects that allow her to maintain the kind of salon that will make her a woman of note.

In Trollope's novel, however, the religious overtones of the Protestant ethic, the ones that color Charlotte Morris's conversation with her father, have in some sense already become old-fashioned. They represent the perspective of Charlotte's father, reflecting the philosophy associated with the process of earning and saving money that made him a successful banker. In *The Life and Adventures of a*

Clever Woman, this religious perspective is not presented as an absolute value but as merely another ideological stance the heroine can manipulate, as can be seen when her father responds to her assertion about his mansion by exclaiming, "I don't really think you could have said anything more calculated to give me pleasure" (1.149). This comment identifies Trollope's satiric take on her heroine, who uses her father's feelings for her and his belief in a set of higher values as a means to obtain her own ends. In this novel not just objects but also familial feelings have become commodities. The narrator notes that the elder of the two Knighton daughters had "emancipated herself from all those minor matters in the code of filial obedience, which seem, like many other commodities, to wear out by long use, and to be thrown aside like all other worn-out articles" (1.202). Though Charlotte feels herself superior to the Knightons, she, too, treats familial feelings, like the attachment to her father, as commodities that can be used.

For her the Protestant ethic with its emphasis on spirituality has become outmoded, something to be thrown aside and replaced in light of the fact that she is pursuing a different set of goals than her father had pursued, goals associated with the strategic use and expenditure of wealth rather than its acquisition. While in the conversations with her father religion is the subtext that justifies the labor of establishing oneself, in Charlotte's thinking to herself it is art that drives her to pursue the kinds of goals that Weber argued the capitalist would pursue. The question Trollope raises is, once past the initial flush of success, what moves the entrepreneur to continue to work, to engage in the same routines day after day, no matter how painful they become? Trollope's answer is that the individual conceives of her activities as aesthetic. As Charlotte explains of her entertaining, "most entirely did I prefer the tiresome little martyrdom I was undergoing, to any personal enjoyment whatever for which it might have been exchanged. I can only compare this feeling of preference for what was disagreeable, to that which it is easy to imagine a student in music or painting, truly devoted to his art, might feel while studying its elements instead of indulging in some idle amusement" (1.219–20). We learn later that "it was her steadfastness of purpose which so effectively strung her young nerves to concert pitch" (2.4).

Trollope engages the question of the relation between art and rationalist thinking as the second of the two families that Charlotte finds useful enters the novel. Replacing the Knightons and their obsession with plates and cups, are the Richards, a family whose father, a successful painter, gains entrée to society through his scathing caricatures.[51] But the artistic character the narrative dwells on is the Richardses' daughter Zelah, an unworldly figure, who is clearly the novel's avatar of virtue. She embodies the spiritual and intellectual values literature is supposed to convey. When Charlotte first encounters the child,

> she not only saw the sweet face of Zelah, but her light and graceful form also; she saw the elastic movement by which she sprang from the deep recess of the huge arm-chair which was the accustomed scene of all her intellectual pleasures, and assumed the attitude of a good child ready to make an obedient curtsy; and Charlotte, as she looked at her, thought what a pretty toy she would be in a drawing room, amidst a small circle of clever people, who liked to be amused by something a little out of the common way. (1.260–61)

Meeting a character that lacks any form of self-interest, Charlotte finds for "the first time in her life that she had forgotten herself, while contemplating the grace and beauty of another" (1.258). Zelah represents the possibility of feeling in the world of calculation that the characters of Trollope's text inhabit.

And those feelings are associated with Dickens. When Charlotte first sees Zelah, the artist's daughter is oblivious to anything that is happening around her because she is engrossed in *Oliver Twist*. With this reference, Trollope makes explicit what has been implicit in the two novels that preceded *The Life and Adventures of a Clever Woman*: the fact that, in these texts that dwell on the materialism of the prosperous woman's desires, the poor woman has, from her first introduction, been associated with literature. The love of reading is presented as a counter to the values epitomized by the wealthy woman who becomes, for a brief period, her guardian and controller. In *The Widow Barnaby* one of the few things we know about Agnes Willoughby is that she loves her school, "its flowers, its books, and its gentle intellectual inmates" (100). She possesses only one object she values, a complete set of the great works of literature, including "Shakespeare, Milton, Spenser, and Gray," "Racine, Corneille, La Fontaine, and Boileau," and "Dante, Tasso, and Petrarch" (109–10), all neatly fitted into a wooden carrying case, an object given her by the schoolmaster she loved.[52] In *The Ward of Thorpe-Combe* the dependent Florence Heathcote is described as preferring a walk in the snow to see an icicle-adorned waterfall to a comfortable meal inside and as breaking spontaneously into "Hark, hark the lark." These behaviors would have alerted contemporary readers that they were meant to associate her with Romantic poetry, an identification that is underscored when she is called "that wild girl of the woods" (1.163) who is "as hardy as a Cumberland shepherd-boy" (1.193).

Trollope brings this sequence of references to literature up to the moment when she was writing, the 1830s and '40s, by alluding to Dickens, who was her chief rival in the period. But in this late novel Trollope is clearer about the cynical significance of the references to literature, whose implications are only suggested in earlier texts. In *The Widow Barnaby*, the widow contrasts Agnes's love of literature with her own industry, remarking when she sees her niece reading that "I wonder you are not ashamed to sit idle in that way, while you see me hard at work" (140). In *The Ward of Thorpe-Combe*, as we have seen, Florence's Romantic pleasure in nature is what defines her, from her uncle's point of view, as an ineligible heir. In *The Life and Adventures of a Clever Woman* Charlotte uses Dickens's novels as she uses the gift of the flowers to the Knightons; his books enable her to establish a relation with Zelah and the Richardses that will be of material benefit to her. As Trollope's narrator tells us, Charlotte always calculates carefully in "the important matter of *present-making*"(1.246, emphasis in the original). She gives the gift of the novels because she wants to obtain "the undisturbed possession of Zelah" (2.76). She accomplishes this by manipulating the father's self-interest (he is a gambler and happy to have someone else take over the financial care of his daughter) and the daughter's disinterest (she assumes that anyone who loves Dickens as she does must have ideal values). In Trollope's fictional world, unselfishness is not an effective counterforce to the materialism and rationalism that permeate the novel. Instead aesthetic value itself, as embodied, in Zelah, proves to be something the novel's heroine can appropriate and use to further her own ambitions.

As the narrator comments, "In calculating her ways and means for maintaining the reputation of her parties, [Charlotte] was as methodical as a thrifty shopkeeper when 'taking stock.' She knew to an inch the quantity, and she knew to a fraction of its value the quality of the goods she had to offer, and she estimated her possessions accordingly, without the slightest reference to her own private notions of their intrinsic worth" (2.255). The fact that Zelah is an accomplished musician also enters the equation: "Neither was her delicious voice forgotten in Charlotte's business-like estimate of her utility" (2.254).[53] Though Zelah, like the virtuous heroines of Trollope's other novels, ends up marrying its romantic hero, the narrator is less interested in that relation than in showing the inefficacy of the values that Zelah represents in the face of those embodied in Charlotte.[54]

The heroine of *The Life and Adventures of a Clever Woman* is indeed clever, and she uses her cleverness with great skill to obtain the ends she desires. She believes that "when people, having a specific object in view, act rationally in their manner of pursuing it, the chances are greatly in favor of their obtaining it" (1.67). This reference to rationality combined with comments about Charlotte "calculating her ways and means" (2.255) identifies the novel's heroine with the utilitarian philosophy associated with both Bentham and John Stuart Mill's father, James Mill. The narrator earlier notes that Charlotte Morris teaches the daughter of the aristocrat "that very many contingent advantages might be reaped by establishing an intimate friendship with the banker's daughter upon the . . . rational principle of *give* and *take*. She felt to her very fingers' ends the utility of the scheme" (1.241, emphasis in the original). Though there have been some references to utility in Trollope's earlier novels, that pattern of thinking comes to the forefront of *The Life and Adventures of a Clever Woman*, where it is linked to the emergence of the Protestant ethic.[55]

In interpreting this representational shift, it is important to note that while *The Ward of Thorpe-Combe* followed quickly on *The Widow Barnaby*—the first appeared in 1839, the second in 1841—there was a thirteen-year gap between *The Ward of Thorpe-Combe* and *The Life and Adventures of a Clever Woman*. Dickens's *Hard Times* appeared in serial form (from April to August) in the same year *The Life and Adventures of a Clever Woman* was published, and in this period John Stuart Mill was working on his autobiography (the "Early Draft may confidently be dated to 1853–4") (*Autobiography* 18). All three works suggest that in the mid-1850s writers were looking back to the 1830s and '40s, the period of Malthus and Bentham, and redefining it as a period of mechanism and calculation, questioning the idea that Malthus and even Bentham were sensualists.[56]

We might also think of the changes that take place over the course of Trollope's novels in terms of the revisions Malthus made to *An Essay on the Principle of Population*. That text displays a similar draining off of the sensual component of the appetites understood to drive the economy. The language in successive revisions became incrementally less vivid, less likely to move readers at the level of the body. In the original version, Malthus describes passions like sex and hunger as "those deeper seated causes of impurity that corrupt the springs and render turbid the whole stream of human life" (2004 64). When he edits this description, he abandons the words "impurity," "corrupt" "turbid," "springs," and "stream" and calls the passions instead the "deeper seated causes of evil which result from the laws of nature and the passions of mankind" (1992 57). In the later version the language is more explicitly moral ("evil") but also less sensual; it is more clinical and abstract, an analysis rather than an evocation of feelings. As John Maynard Keynes notes,

> The first essay . . . is bold and rhetorical in style with much *bravura* of language and sentiment; whereas in the later editions political philosophy gives way to political economy, general principles are overlaid by the inductive verifications

of a pioneer in sociological history, and the brilliance and high spirits of a young man writing in the last years of the Directory disappear. (117)

We find the same shift from the bold to the sociological in Trollope's prosperous protagonists. That sequence begins, as we saw, with the widow Barnaby who is aptly described in terms that anticipate Keynes's description of Malthus's early style as possessing a "bravura manner" (90). The dictionary definition of "bravura" as "a florid brilliant style" (*Merriam-Webster*) captures what makes the widow such an unforgettable character. She is colorful and brilliant, and she appeals, as the sensual drives do in Malthus's early version of his essay, because she indulges herself so fully in the pleasures of the world. In the ward of Trollope's second novel, these bodily drives continue to be represented in a powerfully sensual form, but the emotional valence of the representation has shifted. Instead of being pleasurable, the heroine of *The Ward of Thorpe-Combe* and the novel itself exude what Trollope's narrator characterizes as "a repulsive power," which is "therefore not greatly to be envied; yet still it *is* power" (2.42, emphasis in the original). In *The Life and Adventures of a Clever Woman* bodily appetite is fully suppressed, and the narrative feels more like sociology than a visceral account of immediate experience. Yet Trollope maintains the idea of bravura in Charlotte Morris.

For "bravura" also means "a passage or piece of music requiring great skill and spirit in its execution, written to task the artist's powers" (*OED*). It is associated with the virtuoso. In *The Life and Adventures of a Clever Woman* Trollope suggests that the pleasures of a sublimated approach to existence in a society that is saturated with commodities resemble not just the pleasures of religion but also those of art. This late novel moves beyond Weber to explore the possibility that, as appetite is harnessed and made increasingly to support the goals of the Protestant ethic, materialist pursuits might subsume both religious and aesthetic values, as the pleasures of virtuosity replace those of virtue. In considering this position Trollope is implicitly criticizing both Dickens and Mill, who stress the opposition between mechanism and the rational pursuit of profit and the values associated with literature. One has only to think of Mill's evocation of Wordsworth in his autobiography and of Dickens's description of Sissy Jump, imagination, and the circus troop in *Hard Times*.

In contrast, in Trollope's novel of the 1850s (and implicitly in the ones that preceded it), the values of literature are represented, through the poor heroines who embody them, as virtually powerless in a world of insatiable and compelling material desires. In *The Ward of Thorpe-Combe* Trollope shows how her heroine can use the emotional ties Dickens praises, like the resemblance between a character and a portrait, to achieve her own ends. In *The Life and Adventures of a Clever Woman*, her heroine literally uses Dickens's novels in the same manner. Trollope's novels suggest that the relentless material desires triggered by an expanding commercial culture are insatiable; they will use everything that is available to them. Nothing stands in their way. Like Austen, Trollope moves from representing the impact of wealth in essentially comic terms to representing it in ways that are more serious, more troubling, and more internalized. Trollope's late novel, like Austen's *Emma*, presents the heroine's relation to wealth in more abstracted and disembodied terms than the earlier texts. In both these late novels the negative appeals of wealth are no longer associated with a particular character who can be exorcized from the text. Instead, in thinking about the vulgar question of money both novelists come to see and represent that materialist presence as inextricably interwoven into general social interactions.

But in Trollope's novel the abstract system that emerges at the end of its meditations on the tension between wealth and virtue is not utopian but dystopian. Given the anxieties about overbalance that I have noted, we should not be surprised to see that her fictions move toward fulfilling her readers' fears by depicting a world in which materialism is dominant. In *History and Class Consciousness*, Georg Lukács argues that the nineteenth-century novel makes us ask "how far is commodity exchange together with its structural consequences able to influence the *total* outer and inner life of society?" (84, emphasis in the original). Trollope's *The Life and Adventures of a Clever Woman* answers that question by showing readers a world in which the commodity dominates all forms of exchange, even those Trollope's contemporaries wanted to believe stood outside the realms of economics. In her final consideration of the impacts of wealth, the material values that underlie the spirit of capitalism are shown capable of co-opting not just social and personal relationships but also the realm of art itself.

Coda: Frances Trollope and Vulgarity

It is no accident that the title of my own book comes from *The Life and Adventures of a Clever Woman*. Characters in that novel are clever enough to understand that the marriage plot depends on one's ability to prove that one is capable of choosing a spouse "without feeling constrained to make the vulgar question of money the prominent object" (2.112). With such comments Trollope shows that she is willing to put into words the crass implications of the novels of manners that preceded hers. Though Trollope is herself frequently compared to Austen in reviews, it is clear that she moves beyond novels like *Pride and Prejudice, Mansfield Park,* and *Emma* in dwelling at much greater length and in visceral detail on what constitutes the engrossment of the rich woman's relation to her property.[57] The effect of this shift in emphasis is that Austen goes down in the critical canon associated with delicacy and Trollope with its opposite. As a contemporary reviewer in the *New Monthly Magazine* commented, "She gives way to a pert, coarse, and prurient style of innuendo and description, which is as inconsistent with delicacy as it is with fairness and candour" (quoted in Heineman 95).

Trollope's novels refuse the gesture typically made by the novel of manners. Instead of celebrating antimaterialist values, they underscore the impact of wealth they are willing to depict in vulgarly explicit terms. The decision to trigger readers' distaste means that Trollope ends up exorcised from the literary canon as surely as the rich woman is exorcised from the virtuous community formed by the happy marriages that typically conclude the novel of manners. As Bourdieu has shown in the postscript to *Distinction*, vulgarity must be excluded in some form or another. Trollope's critical history shows that if it is not excluded within the novels themselves, then the novels' author will be identified with the trait she emphasizes and defined as taboo herself. Austen comes down to us as such a powerful presence within the literary canon in part because she has been critically assessed in terms that place her on the side of virtue as it is represented in her own novels through her portraits of the poor as opposed to the rich woman. In contrast, Trollope was characterized in terms that identify her with the vulgar rich women she depicted.[58] As a result, though Frances Trollope was, as Percy Fitzgerald notes, one of Dickens's chief rivals in the 1830s and '40s, she has now dropped completely out of the literary canon.

Such a critical heritage suggests that to deal directly with or be explicit about the vulgarity that art is supposed to distance itself from is to risk being assessed as a writer who is not capable of maintaining the critical distance that would make it possible for his or her work to be accepted as possessing enduring literary value. In critical evaluations, Trollope and her writing are persistently identified with what Bourdieu has described as the vulgarity of "pleasures that are too immediately accessible" (*Distinction* 486). She is perceived to write novels that both depict and appeal to "those who wallow in pleasure and enjoy enjoyment" (*Distinction* 489). Even her sons represent her as someone to whom pleasure came almost too easily. As Thomas Adolphus Trollope explained in his memoir *What I Remember*, "My mother's disposition . . . was of the most genial, cheerful, happy, *enjoué* nature imaginable. All our happiest hours were spent with her; and to any one of us a *tête-a-tête* with her was preferable to any other disposal of a holiday hour" (41–42).

In his autobiography Anthony similarly associates his mother with joy, asserting that

> of the mixture of joviality and industry which formed her character, it is almost impossible to speak with exaggeration. . . . Even when she was at work, the laughter of those she loved was a pleasure to her. She had much, very much to suffer. Work sometimes came hard to her, so much being required,—for she was extravagant, and liked to have money to spend; but of all people I have known she was the most joyous, or, at any rate, the most capable of joy. (24–25)[59]

Both brothers elevate their diction as they evoke Frances's enjoyment; Thomas Adolphus uses the French word "enjoué," Anthony the Latinate "jovial." Such usages indicate the difficulty of attempting a direct and simple discussion of pleasure; critics need to distance themselves from what they represent. They also reiterate the wording of *The Widow Barnaby* and its contemporary reviews. The novel's narrator stresses the widow's "vivacity, her *enjouement*" (179). The *Times* review of the novel described the widow as a "jovial, handsome, hideous, ogling, bustling monster of a woman" ("*The Widow Barnaby*" 5); the *Athenaeum* called her "an unsympathising ogress in the ranks of her own sex—audacious and experienced in planning—resolute in obtaining[,] . . . calling up the memories of a dead husband as bait to ensnare a living one—loquacious—lynx-eyed—oily tongued[,] . . . a jovial New Year's guest [conjured up] by the busy wand of Mrs. Trollope" ("*The Widow Barnaby*" 9).

The repeated use of "jovial" is particularly interesting, since, through its association with Jove, it suggests that Trollope and her heroine have the power to compel readers to enjoy their excesses. This is the compulsory aspect of vulgarity that Bourdieu argues makes us uneasy. One senses this uneasiness even when critics express their pleasure in Trollope's texts, as when they characterize the widow as unsympathizing or as a monster, terms that define the rich woman's function in the novel of manners. These negative terms reappear in explicitly negative assessments of both Trollope and her work. Writing for *Fraser's*, William Thackeray described Trollope's antievangelical novel *The Vicar of Wrexhill* as a "gross and monstrous libel" (83). The *Times* saw it as "monstrous" ("*The Vicar of Wrexhill*" 2). Henry Chorley argued that such depictions confirmed that Trollope was motivated by "the coarse distortions of a mind which cannot see or sympathise with any of the pure, or good, or kind, or lofty, or spiritual feelings of human nature" (130).

Critics use such comments to distance themselves from Trollope. They note her interest in bodily pleasures but then invoke the category of disgust that Bourdieu has argued is key to understanding the way high art, or what he calls pure critique, deals with vulgarity. The concept of pure taste is, he argues, "nothing other than a refusal, a disgust—a disgust for objects which impose enjoyment and a disgust for the crude, vulgar taste which revels in this imposed enjoyment" (488). Criticism of Trollope insists that the critics are tasteful and the author is not by emphasizing disgust at subject matter they insist Trollope enjoys. As the reviewer for the *Athenaeum* puts it, "She seems, from choice, to delight in subjects which are painful and repulsive. She scents out moral deformities with a sort of professional eagerness, and applies herself to their exposure, regardless of the uncleanness into which her task may lead her, and the soil and foul odours she herself may contract in prosecuting the beloved work" ("*The Vicar of Wrexhill*" 708). When another critic asserts that the same novel is "written with as hearty and thorough-going a *gusto* for what is repulsive and horrible, as if its authoress had drunk of witch broth" (Chorley 115), we sense that the term "gusto" is intended to mark a taste that has become excessive in the taking of pleasure, like the eating habits that Trollope depicts her heroine indulging in in *The Ward of Thorpe-Combe*.[60]

The image of the witch's broth is also, as William Ian Miller has argued, a locus classicus for conveying disgust.[61] Such comments make it clear that contemporary readers responded to Trollope with what Bourdieu has described as "the visceral disgust at vulgarity which defines pure taste as an internalized social relationship, a social relationship made flesh" (499–500). Indeed critics find it almost impossible to avoid visceral language as they accuse Trollope. Her novels involve an "exaggeration of outline and lusciousness of colouring" (Chorley 116); "she seems to luxuriate with a congenial zest" (quoted in Heineman 120). Distancing themselves from the excessive "relish" (quoted in Heineman 96) of the work, critics stress that they, in contrast, feel what Lamb called "disrelish."[62] This visceral disgust at the pleasures of the body is, of course, the reaction that Trollope depicts in *The Widow Barnaby* when she shows Betsy Compton rejecting Agnes Willoughby on the basis of an immediate response to redness of the girl's cheeks.

Interestingly, Aunt Betsy's later realization that "in the bosom of this unrepining solitude it is likely enough that I have nursed opinions into passions, and distastes into hatreds" (78) is echoed in the *Times* review of *The Widow Barnaby*, which opens with the reviewer noting parenthetically of Trollope's novels in general that we fear "that our distaste might have possibly amounted to a prejudice" ("*The Widow Barnaby*" 5). Trollope is accused of being prejudiced throughout the reviews of her novels. The reviewer for the *Literary Examiner* asserts that the idea that "Mrs Trollope is an unprejudiced person no one, we apprehend, imagines within the bounds of probability" (628). Her anti–child labor novel *The Life and Adventures of Michael Armstrong, the Factory Boy* "concentrated every prejudice incidental to the lowest and least educated understandings of the populace" (588). Yet I would argue that peculiarly aversive power of Trollope's novels lies in the fact that she is a diagnostician of prejudice, a writer who accurately and evocatively depicts the behaviors that her contemporaries know trigger in them a distaste that amounts to prejudice.

Such a reading allows us to answer Michael Sadleir's question, "Whence, then, Mrs. Trollope's power, fierce and undeniable, to infuriate contemporaries?" (113). She is irritating because she represented those visceral feelings and reactions the early Victorians knew they had but wanted to deny. She taps into the drives her society wanted to repress, the feelings it consciously sought to keep unconscious. Fanny Kemble noted of the enraged reaction to *Domestic Manners of the Americans* that Trollope "must have spoken the truth, for lies do not rankle so" (quoted in Frazee 108). Mark Twain similarly commented in the section of *Life on the Mississippi* that his publishers initially made him take out because of its sympathy for Trollope that "poor candid Mrs. Trollope was so handsomely cursed and reviled by this nation. Yet she was merely telling the truth, and this indignant nation knew it. She was painting a state of things which did not disappear all at once" (391). It is perhaps because critics recognize this truth that even as they dwell on disgust they also almost invariably acknowledge the effectiveness, accuracy, and power of Trollope's writing. The critic for the *Dublin Review*, for example, after opening with the assertion that "there is perhaps no writer of the day so universally obnoxious as Mrs. Trollope," admits that "few have touched off the 'folly of the day' with a lighter or bolder stroke"; "the quickness and vigour of Mrs. Trollope's own mind are communicated to her writings, and form one great secret of the pleasure they give" ("Modern English Novels" 244, 247).

The word reviewers consistently use to give Trollope a backhanded compliment is "clever." According to the *Times*, her antievangelical novel *The Vicar of Wrexhill* "is dangerous, vulgar, and unjust, but . . . withall singularly clever" ("*The Vicar of Wrexhill*" 2). The review of this same novel in the *Athenaeum* opens with the statement that "Mrs. Trollope is, assuredly, a clever woman: quick of eye, ready of hand, fearless in utterance—not devoid of a taste for what is beautiful, and refined, and luxurious" ("*The Vicar of Wrexhill*" 708). Written more than fifteen years before the publication of *The Life and Adventures of a Clever Woman*, these reviews surely provided Trollope with the word she uses to characterize the heroine of that novel. In the sublimely self-interested Charlotte Morris, she offers back to her reviewers a portrait of herself as they represented her, a woman too practical, too close to earthly aims to rise to the transcendent heights that the novelist should aspire to, someone so pragmatic she was willing to incorporate anything and everything into her novels in order to make them successful. Yet in her fictional portrait of the artist as a clever woman, Trollope also implicitly critiques her critics. By showing how even art can be harnessed to practical ends, Trollope slyly indicts those who insist that her own art fails to be transcendent enough; they, too, are implicitly using the category of the aesthetic for their own practical ends.

The two artists that begin and end the book, Jane Austen and Henry James, are central to the nineteenth-century canon; both have gone down in literary history identified with the absolute refinement of an art that eschews any contact with the contaminations of vulgarity. In contrast, the two artists that are the subjects of chapters 2 and 4, Frances Trollope and Margaret Oliphant, have never made their way into the canon. Both were explicit about the fact that they had to write for money in order to support their families, thereby associating their novels with the mercenary aims that Bourdieu has argued are part of what renders the work of art vulgar rather than transcendently free from the taint of the economic. Both also use the clever woman to poke fun at the pieties that allowed the middle classes to imagine themselves above the realm of material exigency. Described by reviewers as "the clever son of a clever mother" (Smalley 127), Anthony Trollope also admitted he wrote for money, most prominently in the famous section of his autobiography where he listed all the novels he had written and how much he made from them. But he maintained a position within or at least on the margins of the Victorian canon. Trollope accomplishes this balancing act by returning to the patterns of the marriage plot as we found them in Austen and by structuring his narratives around the bifurcation of wealth and virtue as manifested through the choice between the rich and the poor woman. But Trollope added to this narrative a series of clever rich women, through whom he invokes the pleasures of wealth that his mother addressed in her novels. In work written in the 1860s and '70s rather than the 1830s and '40s, however, those pleasures are no longer concentrated in consumption but in the uses to which money could be put at a more advanced stage of capitalist development.

CHAPTER THREE

ANTHONY TROLLOPE'S "SUBTLE MATERIALISM"

It is horrible to think what power money has in these days.

Anthony Trollope, *The Prime Minister*

A new world of ideas is in the air and affects us, though we do not see it.

Walter Bagehot, *Physics and Politics*

As we move from Frances Trollope to her son Anthony, we shift to a world where money has become an abstract force. This representational change reflects the economic developments that took place between the 1830s and '40s when Frances Trollope was writing and the 1860s and '70s when her son's career took off. In that period, England ceased to be primarily a manufacturing economy and became instead one based on marketing and banking, which led to a "profound shift of metaphor from production to circulation" (Mirowski 132). This new perception of money created anxieties that focused less on the engrossment and consumption of wealth that we see in Austen and Frances Trollope than on money's pervasiveness, its ability to mix or commingle with aspects of the culture previously thought to be immune from materialist influences.

Trollope addresses these concerns through heiresses who dominate the Barsetshire and Palliser novels, women who possess the enormous fortunes that made the 1870s and '80s the "age of the millionaires" (Perkin *Rise* 64). In creating these figures, Trollope transforms the traditional form of the marriage plot; in his novels, for the first time, the rich woman is a character that is not only appealing but that represents what the novelist identifies as positive values. Through such portraits Trollope acknowledges the powers and pleasures of possessing wealth, but he also limits money's ability to circulate by not permitting his heiresses to cross certain social barriers. Dwelling on these thresholds allows Trollope to explore the psychological and representational strategies his contemporaries used to imagine ways the enormous power of abstracted cosmopolitan finance could, despite its contributions to England's commercial success, be cordoned off from the rest of the culture.

Though Trollope has generally been read as engaging with England's move from industrial to financial capitalism through the speculators who play key roles in his late novels, *The Way We Live Now* and *The Prime Minister*, in fact he engages questions about fluid rather than landed or manufacturing capital much earlier than this, in the third of the Barsetshire novels, *Doctor Thorne*.[1] There he introduces the ointment heiress Miss Dunstable and begins to explore, with startling explicitness, the economic implications of the marriage plot, implications he will continue to address through the heiresses who dominate the Palliser novels, Lady Glencora Palliser and Madame Max Goesler. The difference between these heiresses and the speculators who have typically been taken to represent the economic changes of Trollope's period is that the former actually possess wealth, whereas the latter, as exemplified by Ferdinand Lopez in *The Prime Minister* and Augustus Melmotte in *The Way We Live Now*, merely manipulate the signs of wealth in the form of promissory notes, bills of exchange, and other forms of credit instruments.

Such speculative figures allow the system of finance capital to be represented as, in some sense, chimerical.[2] In contrast, the heiresses who appear throughout the Barsetshire and Palliser novels are fully identified with enormous fortunes they are readily able to use. As a contemporary reviewer noted, "Deprive . . . Miss Dunstable of her wealth, and [she] cease[s] to be" (Smalley 131–32). The same could be said of Lady Glencora Palliser and Madame Max Goesler, whose fates in the novels in which they appear are determined almost entirely by the money they possess. Writing at the moment when, "for the first time in history, non-landed incomes and wealth had begun to overtake land alone as the main source of economic power" (Perkin *Rise* 64), Trollope evokes through his heiresses the forms of wealth whose fluidity threatened to undermine the economic hegemony of traditional landowning families.[3]

In the ointment heiress Miss Dunstable, he creates a fictional example of the millionaires who were a distinctive feature of the period, men and women who made money not through industrial manufacture but through producing and selling household goods. They were "the new 'shopocracy'" (Wiener 64), whose numbers included the shopkeeper Sir Thomas Lipton, Lord Leverhulme, the soap manufacturer, the brewers, Allsop, Hindlip, Bass, Burton, and Guinness, all of whom made fortunes in "the consumer oriented trades, including large scale retailing" (Rubinstein *Men* 101).[4] The emergence of these commercial millionaires meant that the great English landowners

> ceased to be the wealth élite as the rise of the great international and plutocratic fortunes . . . signified new forms and new amounts of wealth, which were easily and rapidly accumulated, which carried fewer attendant burdens and obligations, and which gradually eclipsed the resources of all but a very few very rich landowners. (Cannadine 88–89)

These economic changes were disruptive at a social and personal as well as a national level as traditional county society was forced to accept the newly wealthy into its midst. The society hostess Lady Dorothy Nevill, daughter of the Earl of Orford, explained in her journals:

> When this incursion first began, English Society, shrewd and far-seeing enough in its way, easily perceived that, unless it swallowed the new millionaires, the millionaires, keen-witted, pushing, clever and energetic, would engulf it in their capacious maw. So everywhere doors were flung open for Croesus to enter; his faults were overlooked, his virtues (and many a one really had virtues) lauded; historic houses passed into his hands, whilst the original possessors besought his good offices for their sons embarking on City careers. (quoted in Perkin *Rise* 69–70)

This passage's references to incursions, swallowing, and engulfment suggest that members of the traditional landowning classes experienced the possessors of the new wealth, and indeed that money itself, as a force that threatened to intrude on provinces from which they had previously been excluded. Trollope traces the dynamics of this intrusion over the course of the Barsetshire novels as he describes county society's initial reaction to and gradual acceptance of Miss Dunstable.

The Palliser novels change the scene from local communities to the nation, as Trollope considers the new wealth as the form of political influence that might challenge the preeminence of land. In making this shift in social focus, Trollope also makes the representational shift that we saw in Austen and Frances Trollope; he transforms the heiress from a largely comic figure into someone who represents a more serious threat to the traditional centers of power. The Barsetshire novels invite readers to enjoy Miss Dunstable's "keen wit, her untold money, and loud laughing voice" (*Framley Parsonage* 222). They amuse us with the idea of an ointment heiress and reassure us when her presence does not change but strengthens the values of county society. The Palliser series raises more serious questions about nonlanded wealth's ability to penetrate not just county society but the highest echelons of political power. This change reflects the shift that Fernand Braudel has described as taking place in advanced capitalist societies when

> we take leave for a time of the noisy and transparent sphere of the market economy, and follow the possessor of money into another hidden abode, where admittance is only on business but which is one floor above, rather than one floor below the marketplace. Here, the possessor of money meets the possessor, not of labor-power, but of political power. (Arrighi 25)

Moving from Miss Dunstable to Lady Glencora, Trollope takes leave of the sphere of the market and turns to politics.

The marriage that lies at the center of the Palliser series, between Plantagenet Palliser, the great Whig landlord and politician and the son of the Duke of Omnium, and Lady Glencora McCluskie, is a union of land and money. Its unsettling political ramifications are underscored, as are the economic ones of Miss Dunstable's story, through Trollope's detailed and historically resonant account of the sources of Glencora's wealth. When she is first introduced, the narrator comments that

> as the only child of the late Lord of the Isles, [she] was the great heiress of the day. It is true that the hereditary possession of Skye, Staffa, Mull, Arran, and Bute went, with the title, to the Marquis of Auldreekie, together with the counties of Caithness and Ross-shire. But the property in Fife, Aberdeen, Perth, and Kincardineshire, comprising the greater part of those counties, and the coal-mines in Lanark, as well as the enormous estate within the city of Glasgow, were unentailed, and went to the Lady Glencora. (*Small House at Allington* 564)

In insisting that Glencora derives a portion of her vast wealth from mines and rental property, Trollope is recording the change that modern historians F. M. L. Thompson, Harold Perkin, Martin Wiener, and David Cannadine have observed taking place from the 1860s onward, as "the greater landlords drew an increasing proportion of their incomes from railways, canals, mines, and urban property, and the growing scale of business organization was producing a new class of big businessmen, wealthier than their predecessors yet less directly involved in management and enterprise" (Wiener 12).[5] While the Palliser marriage might seem reassuring, since it means Lady Glencora's enormous fortune passes to the landed class, the mixed origins of her wealth mark the eroding status of land as the main source of upper-class power.

Trollope's contemporaries knew that England's economic greatness was increasingly made possible not by land, sales, or production but by banking, which provided what Walter Bagehot described as "an unequalled fund of floating money, which will help in a moment any merchant who sees a great prospect of new profit" (*Lombard Street* 15). These funds allowed the English people to be "bolder in dealing with their money than any continental nation" (*Lombard Street* 5). They fueled a market system that "is by far the greatest combination of economical power and economical delicacy that the world has ever seen" (*Lombard Street* 4). Yet this "English" power was both international in scope and identified with those seen as non-English: the Jewish banking fraternity. Trollope evokes the combination of foreignness, power, and delicacy in the last of the three heiresses considered here, Madame Max Goesler.

Though the sources of Madame Max's fortune are not explicitly identified, as are Miss Dunstable's and Lady Glencora's, its associations would have been clear to Victorian readers. By emphasizing Madame Max's Eastern European origins, Jewish traits, and ability to move freely across Europe, Trollope links her to "the peculiar world of the nineteenth-century merchant bank" (Rubinstein *Men* 97), which was most visibly embodied in prominent families like the Rothschilds.[6] As Rubinstein notes, "The merchant banking community in the City of London was overwhelmingly foreign and disproportionately Jewish, especially at the very top levels" (*Men* 92).[7] Thus, as the Palliser series progresses, Trollope acknowledges, at least indirectly, that England's economic power was increasingly based not in national production or even in sales but in its position as a center for international banking.

For the mid-Victorians, banking most clearly evidenced the abstract nature of money, its similarity to force, as it was explained in the physical sciences. As the chemist Stewart Balfour noted in 1874 in describing the difference between potential and kinetic energy, "The former may be compared to money in a bank, or capital, the latter to money which we are in the act of spending" (26). This analogy is part of a general movement that took place in the 1860s and '70s, which Philip Mirowski has traced, when, with the emergence and popularization of James Clerk Maxwell's theories of electricity and fields of force, scientists began to insist that "the world of mechanism is not a manufactory, in which energy is created, but rather a mart, into which we may bring energy of one kind and change or barter it for an equivalent of another kind" (Balfour 34).[8] This observation parallels the economic developments that Trollope's heiresses embody, the developments that meant the English economy ceased to be based on manufacturing and had become instead an international marketplace.

Energy emerged as the key concept in both the economic and physical sciences. As the radiochemist Frederick Soddy put it in the early twentieth century,

> Energy, someone may say, is a mere abstraction, a mere term, not a real thing. As you will. In this as in many other respects, it is like an abstraction no one would deny reality to, and that abstraction is wealth. Wealth is the power of purchasing, as energy is the power of working. I cannot show you energy, only its effects. . . . Abstraction or not, energy is as real as wealth—I am not sure that they are not two aspects of the same thing. (quoted in Mirowski 99)

Wealth, after midcentury, ceased to be defined as a substance and instead began to be regarded as an intangible force. Trollope evokes this force through his rich women, whose money is, as he repeatedly explains, neither good nor bad in and of itself but a power that enables its possessor to be active and energetic, to make things happen. But Soddy's comment also speaks to the problems Trollope confronted as he sought to tell stories that represent wealth as energy; he had to find a way to invoke it as both real and abstract.

Trollope resolves this problem by providing concrete details about the real economic developments of his day and at the same time returning to the pattern of the marriage plot and using it in an almost fully abstract form. The critic confronted with his novels does not have to tease out the historical implications of fictional portraits of rich women, as he or she has to do with Austen's and Frances Trollope's novels. Anthony Trollope has already done that work. He identifies both the forms nonlanded wealth took in the second half of the nineteenth century and the reactions to that wealth articulated by the prose writers who were his contemporaries: Bagehot, Ruskin, and Arnold. Yet at the same time that Trollope densely packs allusions to history in his novels, he also uses the familiar configuration of the marriage plot more frequently and emphatically than his predecessors do. In his novels, that plot becomes a pattern whose outline and implications can easily be traced. As Henry James noted,

> His story is always primarily a love-story, and a love-story constructed on an inveterate system. There is a young lady who has two lovers, or a young man

who has two sweethearts; we are treated to the innumerable forms in which this predicament may present itself and the consequences, sometimes pathetic, sometimes grotesque, which spring from such false situations. (Smalley 532)

Working through, in an almost mathematical sense, the permutations and combinations of the marriage plot, Trollope reveals the way its "false" fictional oppositions can be used to deny or limit the social impact of forms of wealth that seemed, in their very intangibility, to be virtually limitless. In Trollope's novels the tension between the rough shapelessness of reality and the abstract patterns of the marriage plot is concentrated in heiresses who function, I argue, like the real toads Marianne Moore famously described inhabiting the imaginary gardens of poetry. Though these rich women occupy a negative or contrasting position in relation to the novel's romantic heroines, they exceed that familiar binary even as it is invoked. Attractive rather than unappealing, these fictional heiresses reference actual contemporary millionaires Trollope's readers recognized. As with the toads in Moore's gardens, these rich women, who bear traces of real history, effectively make the neat bifurcation of the marriage plot more visible as an imaginary structure. The task I undertake as a critic of Trollope is to map out the relation between self-consciously abstract stories that contrast the rich and the poor woman and the detailed and realistic portraits of heiresses who inhabit that plot. In using the rich woman to acknowledge history directly, Trollope underscores the economic implications of romance plots even as he stresses their romanticism. Moreover, in pointing to historical figures that stand outside the text, his novels allow us to see how even our accounts of history are implicitly shaped by the logic of the fictional marriage plot.

Miss Dunstable: "The Daughter of Plutus"

Trollope's heiresses reflect his era's ambivalent reactions to its own financial successes, an ambivalence whose twin poles were most clearly articulated in the writings of Bagehot, Trollope's friend and contemporary.[9] On the one hand, Bagehot famously argued in *The English Constitution* (1867) that the economic developments of the latter half of the nineteenth century were threatening to make England into a plutocracy. On the other, he insisted in his essays in *Lombard Street*, *Economic Studies*, and *Physics and Politics* that those economic developments were precisely what was making England great: "A place like Lombard Street, where in all but the rarest times money can be always obtained upon good security or upon decent prospects of probable gain, is a luxury which no country has ever enjoyed with even comparable equality before" (*Lombard Street* 8). Trollope evokes both these reactions through Miss Dunstable, the ointment heiress whose story runs as a backdrop throughout three of the Barsetshire novels, *Doctor Thorne* (1858), *Framley Parsonage* (1860), and *The Last Chronicle of Barset* (1867).

He shows, in the opening novel, how easily the appearance of an heiress could trigger the worship of wealth that Trollope's contemporaries deplored. Barsetshire society's reception of Miss Dunstable mirrors the real social receptions of the commercial millionaires. As Beatrice Webb notes of diamond merchant Julius Wehner, "There might just as well have been a Goddess of Gold erected for overt worship—the impression of worship in thought, feeling and action could hardly have been stronger" (quoted in Thompson *English* 300). Conceived of as soon as she appears in Barsetshire society as a "daughter of Plutus" (*Doctor Thorne* 214), Miss Dunstable triggers the fawning behavior that leads the narrator to assert that "mammon, in her person, was receiving worship from the temporalities and spiritualities of the land" (*Doctor Thorne* 186). In these passages Trollope uses rhetorical strategies that would become familiar, particularly in the mid-1860s, as ways of denigrating commercial wealth, those who possessed it, and its impact on the culture.

One strategy is to refer to the millionaires as mythological figures, as when Lady Dorothy Nevill calls them "Croesus." These individuals are so fully identified with the wealth they possess that they simply become it. Another tactic finds the critic invoking images of worship, idolatry, and fetishism, again typically associated with pre-Christian cultures. Ruskin asks his commercial audience in "Traffic" (1864), "What in the name of Plutus is it you want?" (245). Picturing "thousands of gold pieces;—thousands of thousands—millions—mountains, of gold" he asks "where will you keep them? Will you put an Olympus of silver upon a golden Pelion—make Ossa like a wart?" (245). And here we have the final piece of the rhetorical puzzle, the representation of wealth as gold, as something that can be imagined as a literal form of accumulation, a pile, a mass, a mountain. This is the image that Bagehot famously evokes in *The English Constitution* when he condemns the Anglo-Saxon for "always trying to make money; he reckons everything in coin; he bows down before a great heap, and sneers as he passes a little heap. He has a 'natural instinctive admiration of wealth for its own sake'" (69). Such passages convey in an almost hysterically literalized manner the fear that, in an increasingly commercial culture, individuals will become engrossed by the idea of amassing wealth.

By the 1860s, such an engrossment is represented not as peculiar to a few individuals, as it is in Austen's and Frances Trollope's novels, but as the identifying feature of the culture, nation, or race as a whole. There is a fear, in Bagehot's words, of "the rule of wealth—the religion of gold. This is the obvious and natural idol of the Anglo-Saxon. He is always trying to make money" (*English Constitution* 69). Ruskin, again, provides an extreme example of this rhetoric when he describes "this idol of riches; this idol of yours; this golden image, high by measureless cubits, set up where your green fields of England are furnace-burnt into the likeness of the plain of Dura: this idol, forbidden to us, first of all idols, by our own Master and faith" (249).[10] The same imagery appears in more tempered and less vividly pictorial form in *Culture and Anarchy* when Arnold critiques the commercial classes for "this honouring of a false ideal, not of intelligence and strenuous virtue, but of wealth and station, pleasure and ease," a practice he later refers to as "worshipping . . . Hebraistically, as a kind of fetish" (118, 123).[11]

Trollope's evolving portrait of Miss Dunstable suggests that we might read images like those invoked by Bagehot, Ruskin, and Arnold as part of a retrograde attempt to insist that wealth is a substance at the moment when money was beginning to be redefined as an abstraction. Though Miss Dunstable triggers worship in others, she herself views wealth as something to be used; "she well knew the value of her own money, and of her position as dependent on it: . . . she . . . seemed to be no whit absorbed by the titled grandeur of her host's family" (*Doctor Thorne* 220–21). She neither courts nor responds to flattery but instead references her wealth and makes others reference it not as a god, an idol, or gold but simply as money. As Mrs. Smith observes in *Framley Parsonage*, Miss Dunstable forces others "to speak in such a bald, naked way" (297). Her name refers to the long straight road from London to Dunstable and means "direct, straightforward, plain, downright" (*OED*) and also "plain speaking or language" (*OED*).[12] This frankness is characteristic of Miss Dunstable who enters Barsetshire society asserting that her unfashionable curls will "always pass muster . . . when they are done up with bank-notes" (*Doctor Thorne* 187). She bluntly tells the vicar hero of *Framley Parsonage*, "You won't take the money of common, ordinary poor people. You must be paid from land and endowments, from tithe and Church property. You can't bring yourself to work for what you earn, as lawyers and doctors do" (60).[13]

This passage begins to identify the implicit class logic of Trollope's novel, as Miss Dunstable associates the professional middle classes with a neutral rather than an admiring attitude toward wealth. That attitude is evoked in the opening of *Doctor Thorne* when its title character, who represents a new breed of doctors who refuse to work on the patronage system, enters the novel announcing that "his rate of pay was to be seven-and-sixpence a visit within a circuit of five miles, with a proportionally increased charge at proportionally increased distances" (31). In Trollope's novel, this newly emerging professional class is positioned as a buffer that will allow the new wealth to pass from the commercial to the landowning classes without the latter being tainted by the potential vulgarity of the former. There is a strong impulse in Trollope to preserve the conservative image of an untainted traditional English upper class. These sentiments are articulated clearly in the opening chapter of *Doctor Thorne* when the narrator exclaims, "England a commercial country! Yes; as Venice was. She may excel other nations in commerce, but yet it is not that in which she most prides herself, in which she most excels. . . . Buying and selling is good and necessary; . . . but it cannot be the noblest work of man; and let us hope that it may not in our time be esteemed the noblest work of an Englishman" (15).

Despite this protest, Trollope uses the configuration of the marriage plot to chart the way in which commercial wealth does enter traditional county society. The story opens with the heir of a financially strapped country landowning family, Frank Gresham, attaining his majority and being told that he needs to marry money in order to reinvigorate the family estate. He is already in love with the niece of the novel's title character, Mary Thorne, a woman of charm and intellect but no substantial capital. When the ointment heiress Miss Dunstable is brought down to Barsetshire as the financially expedient wife for Frank, the novel sets up a configuration of the marriage plot that is so explicit the narrator can observe that "it was a matter of moment to every farmer, and every farmer's wife, which bride Frank should marry of those two bespoken for him; Mary, namely, or Money" (365). But the very terms of this opposition tell readers that it will play out until Frank finally chooses, as we know he should, the woman who represents virtue rather than wealth. Through this marital dynamic, Trollope creates a symbolic barrier in which commercial wealth is defined as not able to penetrate into what Max Weber called the status order.

That barrier is bridged by the professional middle classes, which stand between the two halves of the upper class, the half that possesses liquid wealth and the half whose wealth comes from land.[14] This positioning is worked out in the double resolution of the love triangle that involves Frank Gresham, Miss Dunstable, and Mary Thorne. For, while it is not appropriate for Frank to marry Miss Dunstable, it is appropriate for Miss Dunstable to marry Doctor Thorne because the middle class's professional attitude toward money means this marriage can be represented as for love rather than money. The disinterestedness that makes Dr. Thorne a fit spouse for Miss Dunstable also makes his niece Mary Thorne a fit mate for Frank

Gresham. As Dr. Thorne is not in pursuit of Miss Dunstable's wealth, so Mary is not in pursuit of Frank's title and status. The heir to a squire can marry the niece of a doctor and prove that he too is not in pursuit of wealth. However, once Frank chooses her, Mary inherits a fortune from Scatcherd, the railway magnate. The Gresham estate is thereby financially reinvigorated as it would have been had Frank chosen Miss Dunstable.

This complex marital exchange enacts a form of symbolic money laundering as the commercial wealth of both Scatcherd and Miss Dunstable becomes socially acceptable once it passes through the hands/possession of the middle-class Thornes.[15] But there is a crucial difference between Scatcherd and Miss Dunstable. The former has acquired his wealth in railway construction and is exemplary of the economic developments associated with the manufacturing boom of the first half of the century. Though he has been granted a knighthood and runs for political office, he neither wishes to be included in county society nor knows how to enjoy the wealth he has amassed. In contrast, Miss Dunstable, like the commercial millionaires of the second half of the century, takes her place with relative ease in county society and finds ways to enjoy and share with others the pleasures of possessing an enormous fortune.

At the end of *Framley Parsonage*, she purchases a country estate from an old landed family who can no longer afford to maintain it, proving herself capable of "indulging the taste, frequently shown by wealthy City men over the centuries, for the pleasure and comforts of life in a large house in the country without the responsibilities of the ownership and management of broad acres, a life which could be led without any real changes in business and social habits of a great financier" (Thompson "Business" 156–57). As the narrator of *Last Chronicle of Barset* explains of Dr. Thorne and his wife, the former Miss Dunstable, "When first Chaldicotes, a very old country seat, had by the chances of war fallen in their hands and been newly furnished, and newly decorated, and newly gardened, and newly green-housed and hot-watered by them, many of the county people had turned up their noses at them" (22). However, eventually, the old families start to visit: "No one saw so much company as the Thornes, or spent money in so pleasant a way. The great county families . . . were no doubt grander, and some of them were perhaps richer. . . ; but none of these people were so pleasant in their ways, so free in their hospitality, or so easy in their modes of living" (22).

The issues Trollope raises here are addressed in a number of historical accounts of the period, which stress that the landowning and aristocratic classes gradually changed their habits and behavior in the second half of the nineteenth century as they became more attuned to the pleasures or hedonism indulged by the possess-ors of the great commercial fortunes. As Thompson observes, "the old aristocracy might have absorbed and dominated the new wealthy elements and imposed the pattern of their standards of behaviour on the plutocrats, had it not been for the fact that these standards themselves were shifting towards a greater preoccupation with pleasure and money" (*English* 300). The point, as Trollope emphasizes, is that fortunes like Miss Dunstable's could be used more freely than those that were en-cumbered by land: "She had enormous wealth at her command, and had but few of those all-absorbing drains upon wealth which in this country make so many rich men poor. She had no family property,—no place to keep up in which she did not live. She had no retainers to be maintained because they were retainers. She had neither sons nor daughters" (*Last Chronicle of Barset* 551).

Through Miss Dunstable Trollope evokes an image of wealth as fully liquid, no longer a discrete substance but something that flows through a system of in-terconnected relations. The landowning Squire Dale discovers when he wants to reimburse her for what she has expended on his niece Lily that there is no way for him to identify how much he owes: "He could not take out his purse and put down the cost of the horse on the table" (*Last Chronicle of Barset* 560). When he confronts her, Mrs. Thorne talks of debts and payments running between her and the squire's son Bernard and of how impossible it is to identify one specific debt. Lily tells her uncle that "when people are so rich and good-natured . . . it is no good inquiring where things come from" (*Last Chronicle of Barset* 552). When the nar-rator comments that "all these things seemed to flow naturally into Mrs. Thorne's establishment, like air through the windows" (*Last Chronicle of Barset* 552), it be-comes clear that Trollope is using his heiress to evoke the economic universe that Simmel describes in *The Philosophy of Money*, where "all things . . . float with the same specific gravity in the constantly moving current of money" (392). Money flows like air, and objects themselves seem disembodied in the ease with which they come and go.[16]

But the novelist faces a peculiarly difficult task in evoking money in its dis-embodied form. To reference it directly would make Trollope as crassly vulgar as Miss Dunstable seems to be when she is explicit about her money. It would also allow the terms of the financial world to penetrate into the fictional world of the novel. Trollope's solution to this problem is to use figurative rather than literal language to reference the institutions that make possible the amassing of enor-mous fortunes. Even Miss Dunstable engages in such allusiveness; she "habitually used strong language; and those who knew her well, generally understood when she was to be taken as expressing her thoughts by figures of speech" (*Framley Parsonage* 336). Like his character, Trollope, too, references the instruments that were driving England's enormous economic development indirectly, through figurative language.[17] In explaining Miss Dunstable's ability to help others, "to be lavish in her generosity" (*Last Chronicle of Barset* 551), he tells readers that

> it was a way with [her] that they who came within the influence of her immediate sphere should be made to feel that the comforts and luxuries arising from her wealth belonged to a *common stock*, and were the *joint property* of them all. Things were not offered and taken and talked about, but they made their appearance, and were used as a matter of course. (551, emphasis added)

The language of this passage identifies Miss Dunstable's personal munificence with the joint-stock banks that were funding the commercial expansions of Trollope's day.[18]

Through these figurative references Trollope associates Miss Dunstable with what Bagehot sought to convey in his economic writings: the energy that economic funds brought to English commerce and to the nation as a whole. As Poovey has argued, "By the second half of the 1850s and early 1860s, England's joint-stock companies and corporations provided an extremely important source of monies for commercial expansion and capital improvements" (*Making* 157).[19] These are the commercial instruments that Bagehot praises in his explanation of the international money market in *Lombard Street*. But as he writes about these funds, Bagehot verges over into territory typically occupied by a novelist like Trollope. As Herbert observes, in Bagehot's essays "the hypothetical actors of political economy are homologous with themes of literary imagination" (*Culture* 133). Bagehot defends English banking by arguing that "a buoyant cheerfulness overflows the mercantile world" (*Lombard Street* 151); there is "no sluggish capital" (*Lombard Street* 125); "The whole machine of industry is stimulated to its maximum of energy" (*Lombard Street* 128).

Trollope captures these energies in Miss Dunstable. Bagehot's insistence that "no country of great hereditary trade, no European country at least, was ever so little 'sleepy,' to use the only fit word, as England" (*Lombard Street* 10) is echoed when Miss Dunstable makes her first appearance in the Barsetshire novels refusing to take a nap after her long journey. She insists that she is never fatigued and describes how she traveled all the way from Rome to Paris without sleeping in order to sell the ointment business. Like the economic funds that bring in new capital, she "is a strong, eager, and rushing force, [that] rarely stops exactly where it should" (Bagehot, *Economic Studies* 29). Like England's speculative fund, she is "so large, so daring, and indeed often so reckless . . . that some persons have imagined that there is nothing which would seem absurd to it" (*Economic Studies* 92). The link between Miss Dunstable and these contemporary economic developments is heightened when Trollope alludes through her to one of the real commercial millionaires of his day, the patent medicine baron Thomas Holloway, whose pills and ointment were so well known in Trollope's era that in 1876, "Gladstone, then in opposition, had made a speech . . . in which he compared the efficacy of his own politics to the purifying powers of the famous pills" (Harrison-Barbet, 76).[20]

What Miss Dunstable says about herself in *Framley Parsonage*, that she possesses "half a dozen millions of money—as I believe some people think" (447), was said of Holloway, who was described at his death in 1883 as having "left an enormous property valued, perhaps with some exaggeration, at some five million sterling" (quoted in "The Victorians and the Pill" 43). This exaggeration is born of his extraordinary success. Holloway himself commented that "as regards my business I have certainly done very well, but it is ridiculous to see what the papers say about my wealth" (quoted in Harrison-Barbet 74). The son of a baker and publican in Penzance, he began making pills and ointments in his kitchen in 1837. Realizing that the key to his success would be promoting his product, Holloway committed himself to producing a series of advertisements that became icons of Victorian commercial culture; his "annual advertising expenditure rose from £5,000 in 1842, to £10,000 in 1845, £20,000 in 1851, and £40,000 in 1863" (Elliot 3).[21] "In 1883, the year of his death, he invested a staggering £50,000, which resulted in the return of an equal sum as clear profit. This would be equivalent to over a million pounds today" (Harrison-Barbet 28).[22] His marketing generated an amount of wealth so enormous that it seemed as if Holloway were virtually minting money, which he literally did in 1857 (the year before Trollope's ointment heiress made her first appearance in *Doctor Thorne*), issuing currency tokens the size of old penny and halfpenny pieces that bore his profile and the legend "Professor Holloway, London" (Bingham 27).

He was, as the writer of his obituary in the *Times* put it, "one of that remarkable class who seemed destined to become rich, who roll wealth together in a way which ordinary men fail either to follow or understand" (quoted in "The Victorians and the Pill" 43).[23] His career showed quite clearly how "money is a sort of creation, and gives the acquirer, even more than the possessor, an imagination of his own power" (Newman 335). Holloway himself consciously realized this power in global terms, explaining of the early part of his career that "in the end [I] succeeded in creating for my preparations a limited reputation throughout the British Isles. This might have satisfied me at one time, but, as our desires increase with our success, I made up my mind to be content with nothing less than girdling the Globe with depots of my remedies" (quoted in Bingham 20). As Trollope's narrator comments in *Doctor Thorne*, "We all know, from the lessons of our early youth, how the love of money increases and gains strength by its own success" (218). In Holloway's case, that restless desire led him to paper the world with advertisements for his product in "a multitude of languages, including Arabic, Chinese, Armenian, Turkish, Sanskrit, and 'most of the vernaculars of India'" (Harrison-Barbet 31).[24]

Depicting Chinese emperors and Arabian chieftains enjoying the benefits of his pills and ointments, Holloway engendered the admiring relation between foreigner and English product that his images evoked.[25] As he proudly explained, "Among my correspondents I number Kings and Princes equally with other distinguished foreigners of all nations" (quoted in Harrison-Barbet 31). "Indeed, King Mongkut of Siam (of 'The King and I' fame) was so pleased," Anthony Harrison-Barbet notes, "with 'the man who had been as it were the saviour of his country' that when an Embassy was sent to Queen Victoria Thomas was presented with an autographed letter from the King as a token of his esteem" (31). His contemporaries understood that Holloway's advertisements invited consumers to worship not just his product but also the man himself. In the words of the *Stockport Advertiser*, "In the Wilds of Tartary, the Siberian Desert, the celestial empire, yea the very mountains of the moon, are the praises of the great pilular deity Holloway sung, and his name blessed in every known and unknown tongue as the 'mighty healer'" (quoted in Harrison-Barbet 75). This tongue-in-cheek reference to Holloway as a "pilular deity" also suggests that Victorian writers consciously and satirically invoked the images of worship that pervaded discussions of the impact of wealth on English society in the latter half of the nineteenth century. The story of Holloway's life also makes clear how little the amassing and worship of gold actually had to do with a success that depended on the circulation of more abstract forms of value.

Though the demonized image of the capitalist as an accumulator appeared in the prose writings of Bagehot, Ruskin, and Arnold, the idea that wealth depended on accumulation or engrossment was already outdated by the 1860s. The case of Holloway makes it clear that the enormous success of the millionaires who were characteristic of the period depended not on the amassing of wealth or the purchasing of objects but on its endless circulation. At this juncture, money began to be conceived as energy rather than substance; it was this energy that made financial success both possible and enjoyable. Trollope makes readers feel the pleasure of that energy in the Barsetshire novels. We enjoy the "vitality and appeal of [Miss Dunstable's] fast-paced life" (Kucich 72), the force that makes her willing to say and do whatever comes into her mind once she has decided to become a partisan of some individuals and not others. She could be criticized, as Arnold criticizes what he calls the Hebraistic attitude in *Culture and Anarchy*, for overvaluing doing (26), driven as she is by what Bagehot calls "a mere love of activity" (quoted in Herbert *Culture* 214). Yet both Trollope and Bagehot find strength in such restlessness, which was characteristic of the individuals who built up the great commercial fortunes of the era. It is not until Trollope turns to the political world of the Palliser novels that he begins to use the heiress to articulate the fears generated by the forms of disembodied wealth that were emerging in the latter half of the nineteenth century, fears not of accumulation or expenditure but of penetration, invasion, or what the Victorians called "commingling."

Lady Glencora Palliser: "The Mixing up of Politics with Trade"

The issue that Trollope raises through the heiress who dominates the Palliser series, Lady Glencora Palliser, is the question of money's relation to political influence. In the second half of the nineteenth century, influence was becoming a subject of special concern. Justin McCarthy commented in an 1870 article for the *Lady's Own Paper* that "social influence is a tremendous power in English politics. The drawing-room often settles the fate of the division in the House of Commons. The smile or the salute of the peeress has already bought the votes which are necessary to secure her husband's triumph" (quoted in Reynolds 153). The problem of influence was addressed with particular vehemence after "the passing of the Second Reform Act," which "had broadened the political base" (Reynolds 163). The "concurrent redistribution of power" diminished "the authority of aristocratic political culture" (Reynolds 163).[26] The Palliser series, which begins in the shadow of debates about the passage of that act, contains a sustained meditation on the increasing power of money as a form of influence.

As Richard Holt Hutton commented of Trollope's career in 1882, "Natural selection had brought speculating stockbrokers, American senators, and American heiresses into the foreground of Mr. Trollope's pictures before he left us, and the advance of both plutocratic and democratic ideas might have been steadily traced in the vivid social pictures with which he so liberally supplied us" (Smalley 504). Hutton's allusion to Darwin is key, since the model that Trollope's contemporaries used to both describe and defend the development of England's economy was that of natural selection.[27] In Bagehot's words, "The rough and vulgar structure of English commerce is the secret of its life; for it contains 'the propensity to variation,' which, in the social as in the animal kingdom, is the principle of progress" (*Lombard Street* 11).[28] For Bagehot this narrative of social development was as anthropological as it was biological. This anthropological interest becomes clear in *Physics and Politics*, where he cites Maine, Lubbock, Tylor, and McLennan to chart an evolutionary history that moves from "early times [when] Providence 'set apart the nations'" to modern times in which "commerce brings [the] mingling of ideas, this breaking down of old creeds. . . . It is nowadays its greatest good that it does so; the change is what we call 'enlargement of mind'" (38).

Here we have the narrative of progress characteristic of Victorian anthropology, which charts the movement of civilization from a period when social groups (families, clans, tribes) insisted on remaining separate to the period associated with modernism when the larger structures of nations evolved through the mingling and interaction of various groups. But, as I argued in my introduction, for the Victorians, the heiress represented an exception to this general rule of progress. Since her exogamous marriage would entail the movement of property outside the group to which she belonged, she was required to marry endogamously. Such marriages marked the continued separation between social groups at the juncture when society was apparently moving toward the mixture Bagehot traces. In the Palliser novels this contradictory perception of the evolution of modern society is evoked through a double narrative. On the one hand, Plantagenet Palliser's marriage to Lady Glencora Trollope provides readers with an image of the mixing Bagehot describes. At the same time, in the romantic plots that parallel this story of economic and political union, Trollope extols endogamous marriages that suggest that such social mixing is not actually taking place.

In the novels in which Glencora plays her biggest role, *Can You Forgive Her?* (1864–65) and *The Prime Minister* (1876), Trollope tells the story of a romantic heroine who is caught between two men, one who desires her for her fortune, the other who does not. In both novels, he deploys a version of the marriage plot, which is slightly modified, since the central figure who must choose is a woman rather than a man. In the story of Alice Vavasor choosing between George Vavasor and John Grey and of Emily Wharton choosing between Ferdinand Lopez and John Fletcher, Trollope works out the anthropological implications of the marriage plot. Both these novels conclude with the heiress being rescued from her impulse to marry exogamously; both therefore reinforce the idea that society is made up of separate groups between which money will not pass. But set against the story of the novel's romantic heroine is the story of Lady Glencora's marriage to Plantagenet Palliser, which manifests the commingling that Bagehot advocated but that mid-Victorian audiences found particularly unsettling.

Trollope embodies this idea of mixture in a fictional heiress whose wealth comes from mixed sources, both land and commerce, and who, in marrying a Whig lord, also commingles her wealth with a traditional landed fortune. Glencora is described as incomprehensible to her more traditional husband because "she so mixes up her mirth and woe together" (*Prime Minister* 2.319). Her attempts to use her wealth to further her husband's career as prime minister threaten, as the narrator tells us quite explicitly, to bring about "the utter corruption which must come from the mixing up of politics with trade" (*Prime Minister* 2.15). What balances this narrative of social mingling is a version of the marriage plot told in explicitly anthropological terms in which a woman of property, who seems initially to be eager for exogamous exchange, is eventually happily and endogamously married.

The image of social groups as tribes permeates both *Can You Forgive Her?* and *The Prime Minister*. In the former, when Glencora Palliser, née McCluskie, is initially drawn to the impoverished Burgo Fitzgerald, the women anxious to promote the marriage are described as "a whole tribe of his female relatives" (325). In the latter Emily's father, Mr. Wharton, insists that "like should marry like" (1.26). The country landowning families of "the Whartons and the Fletchers" are described "as a class . . . more impregnable, more closely guarded by their feelings and prejudices against strangers than any other. None keep their daughters to themselves with greater care, or are less willing to see their rules of life changed or abolished" (2.352–53). When Arthur Fletcher has been rejected by Emily Wharton, his brother insists that he must keep his head up, because "between us, if we both do our duty, the Fletchers may still thrive in the land. My house shall be your house, and my wife your wife, and my children your children. And then the honour you win shall be my honour" (1.310). At the end of the novel, Emily Wharton is told, "You are one of us, and should do as all of us wish you" (2.377).

In both *Can Your Forgive Her?* and *The Prime Minister* this world of clans is threatened by a woman who possesses a fortune. The protagonist's father tells himself in *Can You Forgive Her?* that "Alice was unlike other girls, and that she required no protection. Her fortune was her own, and at her own disposal" (366). Though Emily Wharton does not control her fortune, she is, like Alice, desirable in part because she is an heiress. In a world conceived in quasi-biblical terms as a network of tribes, a woman who possesses a fortune presents a problem. If she chooses to marry outside the clan, then her wealth is lost to it. Though the man Alice desires is her cousin George, Trollope's novel makes it clear that to choose him would be to violate what her other relatives want for her. In *Can You Forgive Her?* the group to which one belongs is defined in terms of practices and values rather than blood relations. As Arabella Greenow puts it, in explaining why she will not give money to her nephew George, "I don't care much about what you call 'blood.' I like those who like me, and whom I know" (441). *The Prime Minister* invokes the logic of blood that *Can You Forgive Her?* avoids via Emily's marriage to a character assumed to be a Portuguese Jew.

In both novels the heroine's attraction to an outsider figure is represented as a desire to cross the boundaries that establish the differences between social groups. Such a crossing is peculiarly emphasized in *The Prime Minister*, as Emily realizes that, in choosing to marry Ferdinand Lopez, "she had divided herself from her own people" (1.281). She compares being married to passing through the grave to another life and tells her new husband that "I have left all my old friends, Ferdinand, and have given myself heart and soul to you" (1.355). However, in both novels, though the heroine seems to choose the most exogamous of exchanges, the bulk of her wealth never passes out of her clan and into the hands of her husband. Trollope's romantic narratives therefore follow the pattern spelled out in the biblical passage from Numbers that Victorian anthropologists most frequently cited to explain why the heiress necessitated an exception to the laws of general exchange:

> And every daughter who possesses an inheritance in any tribe of the people of Israel shall be wife to one of the clan of the tribe of her father, so that every one of the people of Israel may possess the inheritance of his fathers. So no inheritance shall be transferred from one tribe to another, for each of the tribes of Israel shall hold onto its own inheritance. (Numbers 36:8–9)

In Alice's case, the fortune she controls never passes directly to George Vavasor. Her other suitor John Grey intervenes covertly; George thinks he is receiving money from his fiancée, but it is actually coming from her other suitor. These machinations make little sense unless one reads them symbolically, as marking the fact that it is a taboo for Alice's money to pass to George. In Emily's case, wealth flows not from her but from her father to her husband; she is just the intermediary. And, indeed, though in *The Prime Minister* the exogamous marriage does take place and the lovers live briefly on their own, Emily quickly comes to realize the mistake she has made in not marrying one of her own kind. When the couple returns to live with Emily's father because Lopez does not have enough money to support them, the husband tells his new wife that "you've been in the same boat with your father all your life, and you can't get out of that boat and get into mine" (2.38). Such statements make clear that neither Emily nor Alice is ever fully exchanged. Neither becomes part of the world to which her fiancé or husband belongs. Both novels chart a long arc in which the heroine is finally brought to marry the man her clan approves of, the man who represents endogamy as well as the conservative values embodied in the land in contrast to the radical possibilities associated with the man who believes in liquid wealth and speculation.

Trollope deliberately parallels but also contrasts these narratives to the story of Lady Glencora Palliser as it plays out in *Can You Forgive Her?* and *The Prime Minister.* Like Alice Vavasor and Emily Wharton, Glencora is introduced poised between two suitors, one who courts her for her fortune and the other who does not. Like Alice and Emily, Glencora is drawn to the more reckless of the two, the one who desires her money, the spendthrift Burgo Fitzgerald. Like Alice and Emily, Glencora ends up marrying instead the man who owns land and therefore represents the more conservative of the two choices. (Though Palliser, in contrast to both Grey and Fletcher, is a political liberal rather than a conservative.) The difference, however, between Glencora's story and those of the novels' romantic heroines is that the man she marries is not in love with her nor she with him. The marriage between Plantagenet Palliser and Lady Glencora McCluskie is a matter of economics, a union of fortunes rather than hearts.[29]

But though this marriage seems to be about the consolidation of wealth, in some senses Glencora's marriage to Palliser, like the marriage of Emily Wharton to Ferdinand Lopez or the engagement of Alice Vavasor to George Vavasor, proves to be a bond in which property does not change hands. Late in *The Prime Minister*, when political enemies besiege him in part because of his wife's attempts to get Ferdinand Lopez elected to the political seat the Pallisers have traditionally controlled, Palliser begs Glencora not to disjoin or separate herself from him. However, Trollope has from the beginning made it clear that theirs is a fractured joining: "This judicious arrangement as to properties, this well-ordered alliance between families, had not perhaps suited her as well as it had suited him" (*Can You Forgive Her?* 270). Within this bringing together of families and fortunes there is a split or division, since, even after the marriage, "her own property was separated from his" (*Prime Minister* 1.51). This statement suggests not just that a woman who possesses wealth must have her property protected but also that Glencora's wealth must be shut out and not allowed to mix with her husband's.

The dangers of that mixture are most vividly evoked in *The Prime Minister* as the novel's stories about women and money shift from the arena of marriage to that of politics. When Lady Glencora begins to use her personal wealth as a form of influence, spending her money to "improve" her husband's estate, she begins to modify the place where, as we saw in Austen's representations of Pemberley and Mansfield, the value of wealth associated with virtue was most likely to inhere. In Trollope's world modifications to the estate threaten to reveal that money rather than land is the basis of political power. As Palliser realizes when contemplates his wife's expenditures,

> There was creeping upon him the idea that his power of cohesion was sought for, and perhaps found, not in his political capacity, but in his rank and wealth. It might, in fact, be the case that it was his wife the Duchess,—that Lady Glencora of whose wild impulses and general impracticability he had always been in dread,—that she with her dinner parties and receptions, with her crowded saloons, her music, her picnics, and social temptations, was Prime Minister rather than he himself. (1.161)

The anxieties articulated in this passage are intensified by the fact that Palliser's description of his wife's activities fitted, as Trollope's readers knew, a real historical figure, the Lady Frances Waldegrave.[30]

Like the patent medicine baron who lies behind Miss Dunstable and who was said to have "epitomized the finest qualities of his age—an age of which it may be fairly said he was as much an architect as a product" (Harrison-Barbet 9), the figure that lies behind Trollope's portraits of Lady Glencora used her wealth to shape Victorian history. The premier political hostess of the Liberal Party in the latter half of the nineteenth century, Frances Waldegrave was so famous for her salons and political activities that Disraeli is reputed to have said she would have made a brilliant prime minister.[31] Yet, like her fictional counterpart, Lady Glencora, Lady Frances was troubling because part of what enabled her to be so successful as a hostess was the fortune she amassed that allowed her to expend an enormous amount on renovating her estate, Strawberry Hill, to make it the venue for her famous political parties that ran from Friday through Monday.[32]

And like Trollope's heiress, Lady Frances derived a large portion of that wealth not from landowning but from rental properties and mining. The writer for the *Church Rambler* explained that

> Frances, Countess Waldegrave, is a name very familiar to railway travelers who often see it up on coal trucks, for the lady almost set the fashion by which the peerage now owns without shame when it is connected by trade. Being the

owner of coal-pits she trades in her own name, and is no less known in trade than she is conspicuous in the artistic circles of the metropolis. (quoted in Carroll 19)

Such observations reflect the anxieties that Bagehot expressed in *The English Constitution* about traditional sources of wealth and power being overwhelmed by commercial money: "Every day our companies, our railways, our debentures, and our shares, tend more and more to multiply these *surroundings* of the aristocracy, and in time they will hide it. And while this undergrowth has come up, the aristocracy have come down. They have less means of standing out than they used to have" (71, emphasis in the original). Prominent individuals like Lady Frances made visible the uneasy alliance between commerce and the aristocracy that was developing in the latter half of the nineteenth century, an alliance that in history, as in Trollope's novels, was associated with political as well as economic mixture.[33]

While in the first half of the century politics was carried out primarily along party and class lines, those patterns began to shift in Trollope's period. Writing for the *Saturday Review* at the end of the century, Mary Lady Jeune commented that Lady Frances's "reception rooms were open to Whigs, Tories, and Radicals, as well as to representatives of art, science, and literature. She broke away the last barriers of exclusiveness, and socially helped more than anyone to destroy the lines of cleavage" (quoted in Reynolds 163–64).[34] Such a mixture is evoked in *The Prime Minister*; Plantagenet Palliser becomes prime minister because a ministry has been formed by a coalition of the Liberal and Conservative parties that requires a leader.[35] Trollope had linked mixed social gatherings with his fictional heiresses as early as *Framley Parsonage*. There Miss Dunstable begins to hold receptions that she calls *conversaziones* that include individuals with differing political convictions and from different social strata. As the narrator comments, "An effort was to be made to bring together people of all classes, gods and giants, saints and sinners, those rabid through the strength of their morality . . . and those who were rabid in the opposite direction" (*Framley Parsonage* 337).[36] This description reflects the fact, represented by both the real Lady Frances and the fictional Lady Glencora, that, increasingly, "the function of the political hostesses was 'to serve as catalysts for the ongoing fusion of the old nobility . . . with the new magnates . . . on terms favourable to the aristocratic element'" (Mayer quoted in Reynolds 163). Politics necessitated social and political mixing at an unprecedented level.

As is clear in the portraits of both Lady Frances and Lady Glencora, to be successful at bringing about this kind of political mingling, one could not be fully part of the traditional status order; rather one had to be someone who, as Bagehot put it in his description of the evolution of society, was able to bring in the vulgar elements that might lead to the enlargement of social structures and of minds that were otherwise doomed to remain bound to old patterns of thinking. Both Lady Glencora and Lady Frances are evoked as exhibiting what Meredith Townsend calls in his review of *The Prime Minister*, "the vulgarity of a nature too truthful, too daring, too irreverent for an ancient society" (Smalley 421). This irreverence pervades the descriptions of Trollope's fictional heroine and her real-life counterpart. Both are figures of energy that flaunt convention. Like Glencora, whom Trollope introduces as "a fair girl, with bright blue eyes and short wavy flaxen hair, very soft to the eye," who "would dance, and talk, and follow up every amusement that was offered her" with "intense interest" (*Small House at Allington* 564), Lady Frances was famous for her blonde beauty, which made her "absurdly childlike" (Hewett *Strawberry* 58), and for "her youth, her spontaneous gaiety, her amazing vitality": "In the privacy of her dressing-room she danced from sheer exuberance because the sky was blue" (Hewett *Strawberry* 64). Of Lady Glencora we hear that "in the old days, before her marriage, [she] had been passionately fond of dancing" (*Can You Forgive Her?* 533). Lady Frances had an "immense fortune, beauty, accomplishments, whims without end, gigantic animal spirits . . . with every denomination of admirer flitting about her" (Hewett *Strawberry* 77). She entertained with "a minimum of protocol and a maximum of charm" (Hewett *Strawberry* 76), doing outrageous things, like learning poker from an American guest and then insisting that the royal personages who attended her soirées play it.

The stories of both Lady Glencora and Lady Frances counterbalance the potential disruptiveness of the heiress's behavior with a conventional husband, a staid figure, who grants his wife respectability and manages money well but who is eager to uphold traditional political and social values and therefore is anxious to make his irrepressible wife conform to acceptable norms. Trollope emphasizes the refusal to conform to etiquette in Lady Glencora, who tells her cousin Alice Vavasor, "I do so try to be proper,—and it is such trouble. . . . Oh dear!—what fun it would be to be sitting somewhere in Asia, eating chicken with one's fingers, and lighting a big fire outside one's tent to keep off the lions and tigers" (*Can You Forgive Her?* 255). He is also explicit that such spontaneous behavior would be critiqued because it was understood to be inappropriate to the class of the great landowners: "Lady Glencora Palliser had been so conspicuous for a wild disregard of social rules as to be looked upon by many as an enemy of her own class" (*Prime Minister* 1.70). In both the historical and fictional marriage, the husband represents traditional class values. While Lady Frances "was full of fun, & stood up to Gladstone," her third husband, the stodgy William Harcourt, "did not half like the want of *reverence*" (Hewett *Diaries* 90, emphasis in the original) she displayed. He disapproved of his wife's penchant for mimicry, her inclination to find those who were formal and stiff-necked "an irresistible butt" (Hewett *Strawberry* 156). Lady Glencora also mocks the woman held up to her as a model of propriety, the Duchess of St. Bungay, whose complaint about the heating of her own castle Glencora echoes when she exclaims, "'We've got no pipes, Duchess, at any rate,' . . . and Alice, as she sat listening, thought she discerned in Lady Glencora's pronunciation of the word pipes an almost hidden imitation of the Duchess's whistle" (*Can You Forgive Her?* 256).

Palliser gives his wife "almost unlimited power of enjoying her money, and interfered but little in her way of life. Sometimes he would say a word of caution to her with reference to those childish ways which hardly became the dull dignity of his position; and his words then would have in them something of unintentional severity" (*Can You Forgive Her?* 270). Lady Frances's third husband, who helped his wife amass her enormous fortune, exhibited the same repressive attitude: "His passion for detail, the complacent pleasure with which he proved her wrong in front of her guests, and the wearisome prosiness of his lectures on her misdeeds drove her to desperation" (Hewett *Strawberry* 97). Appropriately, in light of Bagehot's description of vulgar elements, we hear that "'vulgar' . . . [is] a favourite word of [Harcourt's] when he wants to torment [his wife]. I never saw such a damp as he threw upon any enjoyment, his powers in that line are indescribable" (Hewett *Diaries* 165). But here we reach the difference between the historical woman and her fictional counterpart. Though Lady Frances Waldegrave was accused of vulgarity, she seems to have been entirely unimpeded by such criticisms. She became what an American newspaper described in 1870 as one of "the three notable women of our time" (quoted in Reynolds 158).[37] In contrast, in Trollope's fictional universe, once Lady Glencora is accused of vulgarity, that accusation prevents her from becoming the influential political hostess that Lady Frances was.

Ironically, but aptly, this accusation is leveled immediately after Plantagenet Palliser recognizes that his wife might be the prime minister rather than himself. He then goes down to his estate and reasserts the power of the landowning order by characterizing the "improvements" his wife's money has made as entailing "an assumed and preposterous grandeur that was as much within the reach of some rich swindler or of some prosperous haberdasher as of himself" (*Prime Minister* 1.175).[38] In condemning Lady Glencora's expenditures as tasteless, Palliser emphasizes his own, or his order's, possession of what Bagehot calls "the *style* of society" (*English Constitution* 69, emphasis in the original). By exhibiting this style, "the order of nobility is of great use, too, not only in what it creates, but in what it prevents. It prevents the rule of wealth" (*English Constitution* 69). And, as Trollope makes clear, the rule of wealth is prevented when the new money is defined as vulgar rather than refined. After Palliser calls Glencora's expenditures vulgar, she wonders, "Was she so weak that a single word should knock her over?" (*Prime Minister* 1.179). The answer to that question, fictively rather than historically speaking, is an unqualified "yes." Through the scene in which Palliser condemns Glencora's use of her money, Trollope shows the strategy by which, in late nineteenth-century culture, even as a fusion was taking place between the aristocracy and the new wealth, that wealth was at the same time being represented in a way that allowed it to be seen as incapable of being fully merged into the status order.

The word that does that work of exclusion is "vulgarity," the term that I argue throughout this book identifies the rich woman's attitude toward her wealth as necessitating her exclusion from the virtuous society formed at the novel's end. In Trollope's novels, the uses and implications of the word "vulgar" become explicit. It works to associate wealth with its material or engrossing form at precisely the moment when wealth is beginning to be acknowledged as abstract. It is when Palliser sees Glencora's wealth in the physical form of improvements like archery grounds that its vulgarity becomes visible. This reincarnation of money as vulgar wealth eliminates the problem that is raised by enormously rich individuals like the commercial millionaires or plutocrats who came to prominence in the period when Trollope was writing. As Weber notes of such figures, "If . . . economic acquisition and power gave the agent any honor at all, his wealth would result in his attaining more honor than those who successfully claim honor by virtue of style of life" ("Class" 192). That is, if status and wealth, no matter what their sources, represented value that was additive, then figures like Lady Glencora who have both a title and commercial wealth would have more power and social cachet than those whose wealth came from traditional sources who possess simply the title.[39] If such mixed forms of wealth were combined with forms of wealth like landowning, their possessors would wield a form of political power that was, as the case of Lady Frances Waldegrave demonstrates, almost unlimited.

Weber argues that this possibility leads to a backlash against wealth coming from sources other than land: "All groups having interests in the status order react with special sharpness precisely against the pretensions of purely economic acquisition. In most cases they react the more vigorously the more they feel themselves threatened" ("Class" 192). Trollope represents this backlash when Glencora's wealth is condemned for its vulgarity and becomes an instance of what Weber calls "naked economic power still bearing the stigma of its extra-status origin" ("Class" 192).[40] Trollope had evoked such naked power in Miss Dunstable. Few fictional images could more effectively convey the stigma of commercial wealth than an heiress whose fortune comes from the sale of an "ointment," a substance easily imagined as smearing the money it generates.[41] As the land agent of the Duke of Omnium puts it, Miss Dunstable is "a gallipot wench whose money still smells of bad drugs" (*Framley Parsonage* 488).

Appropriately, as we have seen, in the Barsetshire novels Miss Dunstable is given a certain amount of economic power and freedom but does not become part of the status order through marriage. In Lady Glencora we have a fictional figure whose wealth is less visibly tainted by its commercial origins and who does marry into the status order. But even she is symbolically redefined in *The Prime Minister* as someone whose wealth is not allowed to penetrate that order and grant its possessor political power. It is in Madame Max Goesler, the last of the great heiresses Trollope introduces into his Palliser series, that Trollope gives readers the portrait of an heiress whose wealth and behavior are not marked by the potential vulgarity that hovers around the edges of his generally sympathetic portraits of Miss Dunstable and Lady Glencora. But even with the story of Madame Max, Trollope continues to invoke a narrative pattern that quarantines nonlanded wealth, representing it as symbolically separate from the forms of wealth and power that govern the status order.

Madame Max Goesler: "Money *pur et simple*"

The novels that feature Madame Max Goesler address the national and racial anxieties triggered by the idea that commerce brings about the propensity to variation or commingling that Bagehot praises. For him, this development involves a "subtle materialism . . . playing upon the nerves of men, and, age after age, making nicer music from finer chords" (*Physics and Politics* 10). Trollope traces the development by which money becomes an increasingly subtle social force through the evolving portraits of his heiresses. Alluding through Miss Dunstable to the freedom of money unencumbered by land, he still links that wealth to a specific source, which is viscerally invoked: the ointment of Lebanon. Lady Glencora's wealth is more abstract, coming as it does from multiple sources. Nevertheless, when she begins to spend it, her money is transmuted in the material objects that Palliser can critique for their vulgarity. It is through Madame Max that Trollope evokes wealth that is fully intangible, that has no identifiable source, and that can flow everywhere in the social field, exercising its power not simply within England but internationally.

But, as soon as money is conceived in a fully abstract form associated with "the unconscious grace of life" (Bagehot *English Constitution* 69), a counternarrative emerges that represents the social mixture brought about by the new wealth in terms of images of racial intermingling or miscegenation.[42] Though Bagehot argued that the hatred of variation was a characteristic of the "pre-economic age" (*Physics and Politics* 12), before commerce had brought about the loosening of the barriers between races and nations, Trollope's novel show that this hatred was characteristic also of the modern period. In the Victorian era, fears of the social variation brought about by the admixture of commerce into the general community were projected onto the Jews. Defined as both within and outside mainstream English culture, the Jews were associated with money particularly in the abstract form it took in international finance.

Trollope introduces Madame Max in terms that link her with Victorian images of Jews. He describes her in the novel in which she first appears, *Phineas Finn*, as having

> thick black hair, which she wore in curls ... which hung down low beneath her face, covering, and perhaps intended to cover, a certain thinness in her cheeks. . . . Her eyes were large, of a dark blue colour, and very bright. . . . She seemed to intend that you should know that she employed them to conquer you. . . . Her forehead was broad and somewhat low. Her nose was not classically beautiful, being broader at the nostrils than beauty required, and, moreover, not perfectly straight in its line. Her lips were thin. Her teeth, which she endeavored to show as little as possible, were perfect in form and colour. (2.25)

But the ethnic implications of this description are undercut, or at least complicated, when Trollope describes Lizzie Eustace, the protagonist of the Palliser novel that appeared between the two novels that tell the story of Madame Max Goesler, in almost identical terms. In *The Eustace Diamonds* an explicitly English and Anglican heiress wears her black hair in long ringlets and has "lips [that] were too thin," "teeth . . . without flaw or blemish" and eyes that "were too expressive, too loud in their demands for tenderness" (1.18). In making Lizzie Eustace a body double for

Madame Max, Trollope can unmoor the set of tropes associated with Jewishness and identify them as signifying not racial difference per se but the attitudes toward wealth the Victorians linked to the Jew.

Indeed, Trollope invokes those associations so powerfully in Lizzie that Madame Max comes by contrast to represent their opposite or their absence. Both women have an intimate physical relation to objects; their bodies drip with jewels and their lodgings are crammed with ornaments. Paul Delany has argued of Madame Max that "there are two set-piece descriptions of [her] possessions[,] . . . one of her dress and jewelry, the other of the drawing-room of her cottage on Park Lane. Exquisite as her appurtenances are, they are unequivocally a bait, designed to tempt Phineas away from the simple, true-hearted Irish girl to whom he is betrothed" (40). Lizzie Eustace, too, uses her wealth as bait in her attempts to lure Frank Greystock away from his truehearted fiancée, Lucy Morris. But Trollope also establishes a difference between the two women by defining Lizzie as someone who is interested in wealth in its objective forms and Madame Max as someone who scorns the materiality of money.[43] As the narrator of *Phineas Finn* tells us of the latter, "though she prized wealth, and knew that her money was her only rock of strength, she could be lavish with it, as though it were dirt" (2.170). Directly countering the fears of money worship that pervade the prose of the period, Madame Max tells Phineas that "money is neither god nor devil, that it should make one noble and another vile. It is an accident, and, if honestly possessed, may pass from you to me, or from me to you, without a stain" (2.318).[44]

Trollope emphasizes the contrast between the two heroines by opening the novel in which Madame Max reappears with her being bequeathed a collection of valuable diamonds on the death of the Duke of Omnium. In a playful reference to *The Eustace Diamonds*, she tells Plantagenet Palliser, "I have written the lawyer to renounce the legacy, and, if your Grace persists, I must employ a lawyer of my own to renounce them after some legal form. Pray do not let the case be sent to me, or there will be so much trouble, and we shall have another great jewel robbery" (*Phineas Redux* 1.263–64). With this gesture she establishes herself as someone who does not care for wealth in its objective forms. And in this novel, *Phineas Redux*, a work whose title indicates that it is a return to, a post-*Eustace Diamonds* rewriting of, *Phineas Finn*, Trollope is clearest about how Madame Max's wealth differs from Lizzie's and from that of the other heiresses in the Barsetshire and Palliser novels. She tells Phineas the second time she proposes to him that with respect to her money "there must be no question between you and me of whence it came" (2.355). Her wealth has no identifiable source or roots. It is a version of the *credit mobilier*, which has no location because it is not fixed but fluid, not English but international.

Like "the cosmopolitan loan fund [that] runs everywhere as it is wanted, and as the rate of interest tempts it" (Bagehot *Economic Studies* 89), Madame Max in *Phineas Redux* is able to do what the English woman Laura Standish cannot, travel across Europe to free Phineas from a false accusation of murder, "spending her wealth, employing her wits, bearing fatigue, openly before the world on this man's behalf" (2.224). That wealth, which comes from Austria and Prague, Eastern Europe, and the Levant and is inherited from a Jewish banker husband, would, as I have suggested, have been identified with the world of merchant banking, where commerce is no longer perceived as having to do with objects or substances. The image typically used to convey the complexity of finance capitalism is that of a network. It was composed of "a million filaments of politics and finance" (Chesterton quoted in Cheyette 185) and was a perceived as a "vast web of international connections" (Rubinstein *Men* 97), which allowed intangible, abstracted wealth to flow easily from place to place as it was needed. As Bagehot exclaimed admiringly, "How mobile this sort of money is, and how it runs from country to country like beads of quicksilver" (*Economic Studies* 92).

Trollope provides a visual image of such a valuable and mercurial network in his uncharacteristically lengthy description of Madame Max's dress when she first appears in the Palliser novels. It has "traceries of yellow and ruby silk which went in and out through the black lace, across her bosom, and round her neck, and over her shoulders, and along her arms, and down to the very ground at her feet, robbing the black stuff of its sombre solemnity, and producing a brightness in which there was nothing gaudy" (*Phineas Finn* 2.26).[45] This description conveys what Madame Max represents in the Palliser series: she is bright without being gaudy, wealthy without being vulgar, powerful without being loud, and she possesses and stands for the kind of money that enabled England to achieve its late nineteenth-century economic hegemony. It is money that has been purified, made abstract or disembodied, by having passed through the international money market, what Bagehot described as "the 'commerce of imperceptibles'" for which the Jews had shown a marked facility; they "excel on every Bourse in Europe" (*Economic Studies* 199).

But, as this comment suggests, the definition of wealth in its most abstract form as fully intangible triggered in the Victorians a need to reembody commerce by associating it with a specific race, the Jews. As Bryan Cheyette has argued, this strategy allows novels like Trollope's to link "the Hebraized 'commercialism' of

England as a whole" with "the racial degeneration (through inter-marriage) of the aristocracy" (41). In the novels in which Lady Glencora figures, fears of the intermixture of nonlanded wealth into the dominant culture are managed through accusations of vulgarity or bad taste. In the novels in which Madame Max appears, those fears are rewritten in terms of racial difference.[46] Appropriately, given Lady Glencora's association with vulgarity in *The Prime Minister*, she is the mouthpiece in the Phineas Finn novels for the vulgar thoughts that others have but will not speak, in this case the vulgarity of explicit racism.

When her husband's father, the Duke of Omnium courts Madame Max, Glencora imagines the progeny of a such a marriage as "some wizened-cheeked half-monkey baby, with black brows, and yellow skin, [to] be brought forward and shown to her some day as the heir!" (*Phineas Finn* 2.176). Such racial images reassured in the same way that images of the worship of wealth as gold did by making the economic forces that were influencing the development of society visible (as Bagehot noted, "a new world of ideas is in the air and affects us, though we do not see it" [*Physics and Politics* 3]). They allowed intangible capital to be reimagined and associated with a concrete, hyperembodied image. Money is reincarnated in the absoluteness of gold and idols. Those who deal with money are presumed to have racially marked bodies of the Jews. These narratives allow money, at the moment when its abstract form seems to make it more socially pervasive than ever, to be defined as something that can be localized and therefore excluded from mainstream culture.

Both Simmel and Weber wrote at length about the link between the social exclusion of Jews and the development of international financial markets in which money was seen as abstracted and therefore pure. Simmel argued that "the importance of money as a means, independent of all specific ends, results in the fact that money becomes the centre of interest and the proper domain of individuals and classes, who, because of their social position, are excluded from many kinds of personal and specific goals" (*Philosophy of Money* 221).[47] Defining the people associated with wealth as absolutely, physically unwilling to merge with the dominant population solves the problem of mixture, since it makes them a separate class, what Weber calls a caste, that functions within the culture without ever fully becoming part of it.[48] What is invoked here is a narrative that, like the anthropological narratives about the heiress, uses endogamy to mark social barriers that cannot be crossed. Weber notes that the Jews are the most striking example of such closed castes; they are defined as "ethnic communities [that] believe in blood relationship and exclude exogamous marriage" ("Class" 189).[49]

While the Phineas Finn novels appear to violate the implicit logic of the marriage plot by allowing the rich woman to marry a man significantly poorer than she, they do so by invoking, at the level of racial mixture, a narrative that insists on the value of endogamy even as endogamy seems to be disrupted by a narrative of exogamy. Madame Max ceases to be seen in racist terms as soon as it becomes clear that she will not enter the English aristocracy through marriage. Once Glencora knows that the exogamous marriage between the duke and a foreigner will not take place, she no longer sees Madame Max as

> a thin, black-browed, yellow-visaged woman with ringlets and devil's eyes, and a beard on her upper lip,—a Jewess,—a creature of whose habits of life and manners of thought they were all absolutely ignorant; who drank, possibly; who might have been a forger, for what any one knew; an adventuress who had found her way into society by her art and perseverance,—and who did not even pretend to have a relation in the world! (*Phineas Finn* 2.216)

Instead, the two women become the closest of friends.

Such narratives suggest that the assertion that the Jews chose to define themselves as endogamous commonly found in Victorian writings about the Jews was useful to the dominant culture because it could then claim that the Jews sought to remain a separate social group. This image of groups perceived as not fully mixed into the social mainstream is doubly emphasized with Madame Max who is associated with Jewishness and who chooses in the end to marry not an English duke but an Irish MP.[50] Corbett has noted the subtlety of Trollope's representation of Finn, who, like Madame Max, is marked as ethnically different while at the same time washed clean of any of the negative associations typically linked to that racial stereotype.[51] In the case of Trollope's hero, stereotypical Irish traits are incarnated in his colleague Lawrence Fitzgibbon rather than Phineas. Similarly, as a number of critics have argued, in the series of novels that includes *The Eustace Diamonds*, stereotypical Jewish traits are incarnated in Josef Emilius rather than Madame Max.[52] And, as I have argued, stereotypical images of the worship of wealth associated with the Jews have been exorcised through the portrait of Lizzie Eustace. Such representational strategies mean that both Madame Max and Phineas Finn are curiously hybrid figures, racially other yet not racially marked.[53]

The term the Victorians used to describe such figures was "cosmopolitan," a term that also typically described "abstracted cosmopolitan finance directed by a handful" (Belloc quoted in Wiener 85).[54] As Bagehot explains, "In the beginning of things there was no cosmopolitan race like the Jews; each race was a sort of 'parish race,' narrow in thought and bounded in range, and it wanted mixing accordingly" (*Physics and Politics* 66). Here, following the evolutionary logic of Victorian anthropologists, Bagehot imagines an earlier period in history, when society was broken up into separate groups, tribes, clans, or races that maintained clear boundaries with one another. For him, commerce helps to overcome these boundaries, bringing about the mixture that will allow society to progress. But, as I have been suggesting, this idea of mixing provoked as much anxiety as it did anticipation. There were, therefore, for the Victorians, figures that also represented resistance to or refusal of such mixing through their association with endogamy. The heiress was one, the Jew another. For, as Bagehot explains, "it is said, in answer to the Jewish boast that 'their race still prospers, though it is scattered and breeds in-and-in': 'You prosper *because* you are so scattered; by acclimatization in various regions your nation has acquired singular elements of variety; it contains within itself the principle of variability which other nations must seek by intermarriage'" (*Physics and Politics* 66, emphasis in the original).

The Jews can achieve the effect of variation brought about by progress and exogamy because, while they are endogamous, they have no fixed roots. They have lived all over the world. So, too, in the case of Madame Max, the heiress's wealth is defined as both endogamous (when she does not marry an English duke) and purified (because it is international). Her original, unsuccessful offer of herself to Phineas Finn is graceful in a way that Lizzie Eustace's is not, because Madame Max does not propose in English. Instead, "in French, blushing and laughing as she spoke,—almost stammering in spite of her usual self confidence,—she told him that accident had made her rich, full of money. Money was a drug with her. . . . Would he not understand her, and come to her, and learn from her how faithful a woman could be?" (*Phineas Finn* 2.98). A similar linguistic shift occurs in *The English Constitution*, when Bagehot, after criticizing his countrymen for their inclination to worship wealth, suddenly insists that "money alone—money *pur et simple*—will not buy 'London Society'" (69). Repeating the word "money" as he denies its power, Bagehot attaches French qualifiers to it, as if those words elevate the term, purifying money of its grossness by making it non-English, as Trollope is able in Madame Max to purify the rich woman of the vulgarity typically associated with her in the marriage plot, making it suitable, even romantic for her to marry a poor man at the end of *Phineas Redux*.

The gesture of purification we find in both Bagehot and Trollope occurs also in contemporary accounts of Lady Frances Waldegrave, whose life Trollope's Victorian readers understood to underlie the story of Madame Max as well as of Lady

Glencora Palliser. As Osbert Wyndham Hewett notes in his biography, in 1873 and 1874 when "Trollope's *Phineas Redux* had been appearing in the *Graphic*[,] ... everyone was trying to recognize the characters." Although "some people had previously thought Lady Glencora was based on Frances, they now felt the possibility that Madame Max Goesler was taken from her" (*Strawberry* 236). If, through Lady Glencora, Trollope alluded to Lady Frances's role as a political hostess, through Madame Max, and perhaps also Lizzie Eustace, he references Lady Frances's complex marital career and initial social status as an outsider.[55] As Leonore Davidoff explains, Frances Waldegrave's "social background should have disqualified her from even entering 'Society' on at least four criteria. Her father was Jewish, he had made his fortune as a concert singer and he had an acknowledged illegitimate son by his mistress before marrying her very middle-class mother from Manchester" (105n24).[56]

Though Davidoff does not mention them, Lady Frances's first two marriages would also have marked her as a social outsider. She wed first the illegitimate elder son of the sixth Earl of Waldegrave, who was "remarkably good-looking[,] ... but he was an epileptic and spent his life drinking with grooms and stable boys" (Hewett *Strawberry* 17). After he died of delirium tremens within a year of the wedding, Frances married his legitimate younger brother who subsequently died "of dissipation, leaving her a title and a fine income—in fact, everything he had" (quoted in Carroll 18).[57] Trollope may allude to these unions in *The Eustace Diamonds* when he describes Lizzie Eustace gaining her wealth and title through Sir Florian, a man mortally ill when she marries him because he had "denied himself no pleasure, let the cost be what it might in health, pocket, or morals" (*Eustace Diamonds* 1.6). Like Lizzie, Lady Frances was accused of being mercenary: "A number of people openly said that she had married the dying John Waldegrave for his money, and had then made an incestuous marriage to gain a coronet" (Hewett *Strawberry* 59).[58] Like Lizzie, she claimed the legality of her inheritance in part by associating it with Scotland.[59] But, unlike Lizzie, who is never able to use the wealth she acquires through marriage to establish a legitimate place in society, Lady Frances used the title and estate she inherited from the Waldegraves to become one of the great social figures of her day.

After the death of her second husband, "the twenty-six- year-old dowager ... married George Granville Harcourt, a staid pompous, pedantic man of sixty-one" (Hewett *Diaries* 4), whose family held a powerful position in the Whig party. This position enabled Frances to indulge in the political entertaining that is referenced in Trollope's descriptions of Lady Glencora in the Palliser novels. The Phineas Finn novels allude to Lady Frances's fourth and final marriage. When Harcourt died in 1862, Lady Frances was, like Madame Max, courted by an English duke.[60] She chose instead to marry Chichester Fortescue, an Irish MP, who had been her close friend for eleven years during her marriage to Harcourt and whose political career closely parallels Phineas Finn's.[61] The sequential narrative of Lady Frances's marital career followed the pattern Madame Max describes when she looks back on her life. Thinking of her marriage to a Jewish banker, proposal from a duke, and interest in Phineas Finn, she acknowledges that

> from the former she had, as his widow, taken wealth which she valued greatly; but the wealth alone had given her no happiness. From the latter, and from his family she had accepted a certain position. Some persons, high in repute and fashion, had known her before, but everyone knew her now. And yet what had all this done for her? Dukes and duchesses, dinner-parties and drawing-rooms,— what did they amount to? What was it that she wanted?
>
> She was ashamed to tell herself that it was love. (*Phineas Redux* 1.266)

Implicitly articulating the logic of the marriage plot not as an either/or choice between wealth and virtue but as a narrative arc, this statement suggests that, if, in the end, individuals choose love, they can be represented as untainted by any admixture of vulgar money that seemed to shadow their earlier unions.[62]

Lady Frances's life was retrospectively reconceived in just such a linear fashion by Trollope's contemporaries. Though it is clear that the wealth she acquired in her first three marriages was key to allowing her to become the successful political figure she was, that influence is denied or made invisible in the image of her, at the height of her career, as a kind of political god.[63] Insisting that she was "worldlywise without being worldly" (quoted in Hewett *Strawberry* 234), the reporter for the *Graphic* reminisced about her power on the occasion of her death in 1879:

> It was at Strawberry Hill, in those days, that political programmes were discussed and decided upon; that differences were patched up which otherwise might have switched history on other lines; that promising converts were received; that promising postulants were examined, and were accepted or rejected according to the judgment passed upon them by Lady Waldegrave and her experienced friends. This one craved for place, Lady Waldegrave procured it for him; that one was eager to obtain a title, Lady Waldegrave obtained it for him; another yearned for social recognition, in an instant every door in Mayfair flew open to receive him and his. (quoted in Hewett *Strawberry* 235)[64]

This passage evokes an image of Lady Frances that conforms to what Arnold calls "our best self, which is not manifold, and vulgar, and unstable, and contentious, and ever varying, but one, and noble, and secure, and peaceful" (136).

But the life of Lady Frances was, as we have seen, more vulgar, contentious and unstable than this final image of her suggests. In his fictional portraits of heiresses Trollope touches on the vulgarity that is occluded in the historical portrait of Lady Frances Waldegrave, but he does so in order to show how the ideas of mixture and variation that, for Bagehot, enabled the emergence of modern culture elicited extraordinarily powerful anxieties. Those anxieties are articulated with particular clarity in a passage from Simmel's *The Philosophy of Money* (1900) that rehearses the logic of the marriage plot in the Darwinian terms that we hear also in Bagehot's references to variation. In the midst of a treatise that praises the grace and abstractness of wealth, in much the same way that Trollope does in his descriptions of Madame Max and the *Graphic* does in its description of Lady Frances, Simmel suddenly breaks from the general calmness of his tone to assert, in the language of visceral disgust that might surprise readers, that

> love is decidedly superior to money as a factor of selection. In fact, in this respect, it is the only right and proper thing. Marriage for money directly creates a situation of panmixia—the indiscriminate pairing regardless of individual qualities—a condition that biology has demonstrated to be the cause of the most direct and detrimental degeneration of the human species. In the case of marriage for money, the union of a couple is determined by a factor that has nothing to do with racial appropriateness—just as the regard for money often keeps apart a couple who really belong together. (381)[65]

Love must be elevated over money, because to admit money as a factor in the selection of a marriage partner, as in selection of a political candidate, would lead to racial and national degeneration. Symbolically, it would open the door to panmixia, the possibility that money is able to cross all boundaries, to mix with everything. The possibility of panmixia is denied in the *Graphic*'s final portrait of Lady Frances. She is all-powerful, but that power does not come from her wealth. Indeed, she is a gatekeeper preventing wealth from mixing into the dominant culture, keeping it pure.[66] Trollope's novels associate these fears of panmixia with heiresses who trigger disgust in others—repulsion at the worship of Miss Dunstable's wealth, distaste at what Palliser calls Glencora's vulgar expenditures, the racist stereotyping of Madame Max. But they do not represent these rich women as disgusting. Trollope understands, as his oblique references to Thomas Holloway and Lady Frances Waldegrave make clear, that money was penetrating to the heart of the culture even as his contemporaries sought to deny that fact. The difference between Trollope and the novelists who precede him is that while they use the marriage plot to police the boundary between wealth and virtue, he exposes and explores that boundary. He depicts the dynamics of interchanges in which wealth is deemed vulgar and excluded from the mainstream culture rather than insisting that wealth should be excluded in this way.

But although he is extraordinarily sensitive to the psychological and rhetorical strategies mid-Victorians used to resist the mixture of wealth into the dominant culture, he also never allows the boundary crossing his contemporaries feared to take place in his fiction. His novels reveal the ideological implications of the marriage plot, yet they also continue to dwell on "socially taboo heiresses" (Herbert 273). Miss Dunstable does not marry Frank Gresham; Lady Glencora does not become a powerfully successful political hostess; Madame Max remains ethnically outside mainstream culture. The potential social boundary crossings that are denied in these fictional heiresses were, as I have argued, enacted in the lives of the real historical persons Trollope references. In alluding to such figures, Trollope underscores his awareness that the marriage plot works to deny the socially transformative impacts of economic change. But he never quite gives us a narrative that works against that denial. It is in the novels of Margaret Oliphant that we will find stories in which the apparently impermeable social boundary between the commercial and the status order is crossed, as the rich woman becomes not just, as she is in Trollope, a positive and entertaining character, but the novel's moral center.

Coda: Anthony Trollope and History Redux

Interested in the moment when characters, and, as I have argued, the wealth they represent, seem to be about to cross invisible social boundaries and are condemned for their vulgarity, Trollope was himself seen as treading on just such a boundary. He was critically perceived as at first able to distance himself from and then imbued with the vulgarity he wrote about. While the critical portraits of Austen associate her with the forces that would limit the engrossment of wealth and those of Frances Trollope with all that is negative about the possession of money, Anthony Trollope walked the tightrope between these two positions. Though frequently compared to Austen, he was also seen as more crassly direct than she was. As John Vernon puts it, he is "a kind of vulgar Jane Austen" who "defines the terms that lie embedded in Austen so that we can perhaps see them more clearly: in fact he points them out explicitly, with less subtlety and with obsessive repetition" (44). For nineteenth-century reviewers, this explicitness had to do with money. As Hutton explained of the difference between Austen and Trollope, "The former is, above all things, mild and unobtrusive, not reflecting the greater world at all[,] . . . while the latter is, above all things, possessed with the sense of the aggressiveness of the outer world, . . . of the rush of commercial activity" (Smalley 509).

But Trollope was also seen, at least in the first part of his career, as being able to represent these commercial activities without having his prose tainted by the vulgarity of what he described. In the words of a truism that recurs throughout his fictions, he was able to touch pitch and not be defiled. Noting the similarities between his novels and those of his mother, critics argued that Anthony Trollope's ability to walk the line that separates the vulgar from the nonvulgar was his greatest strength; "a novelist who can paint vulgarity of this sort while he manages to inspire a constant conviction that he himself is not in the least vulgar, can do what very few people could do" (Smalley 186). The terms critics use to praise Trollope remain remarkably consistent throughout the Barsetshire series. Then, as he moves into the Palliser novels and becomes more explicit about money as a form of political influence, the tone of the reviews begins to shift. As one reviewer comments, "There is a limit not easy to define, beyond which pictures of human nature distorted by vulgarity, cease to amuse and become simply offensive" (Smalley 231).[67] Trollope and his writing, like the central heiress of the Palliser series, Lady Glencora, threaten to cross a quasi-invisible, unspoken boundary whose transgression will make them vulgar.

For Trollope's contemporaries, with the publication of *The Way We Live Now* and *The Prime Minister*, he crossed over into that vulgar territory. Reviewers condemned *The Way We Live Now* with a visceral disgust that might remind us of reviews of Frances Trollope's novels. He is described as having "surrounded his characters with an atmosphere of sordid baseness which prevents enjoyment like an effluvium" (Smalley 397). The terms of this review are reiterated in reviews of *The Prime Minister*, which is condemned because it reveals that Trollope has "the disposition to attribute to the majority of mankind an inherent vulgarity of thought" (Smalley 419). Like his mother, he is vulgar because of his propensity to represent vulgarity in others. The reviewer, Meredith Townsend for *The Spectator*, finds that even the novel's romantic heroine, Emily Wharton, bears "a trace of vulgarity" (Smalley 420), since she is attracted to Ferdinand Lopez. Townsend saves his vitriol for Lady Glencora, whose "vulgarization is perhaps more natural, for Mr. Trollope, whenever he has presented her, has suggested that her charming qualities covered some faint tinge of vulgarity inherent in her nature" (Smalley 421). But "Lady Glencora in *The Prime Minister* pushes like any parvenue who wants to become a personage. . . . [S]he . . . perspires with effort in the vulgar crowd till she is utterly unrecognizable" (Smalley 421–22).

Ironically, this critique is anticipated by and replays the scene within the novel in which Plantagenet Palliser condemns his wife for her vulgarity, a scene that demonstrates Trollope's interest in exploring the ideological work that the gesture of labeling someone else vulgar accomplishes. By including this dynamic in his fiction, in a chapter whose running title, outrageously enough, is "Vulgarity," Trollope shows that he is willing to address vulgarity directly. In making such a gesture he is implicitly following the advice Bagehot gave in his literary criticism when he argued that "too much conviction of what constitutes decorum prevents an author from acknowledging the existence of vulgarity in a universe that, after all, inextricably commingles low and high elements" (quoted in Orel 42). Bagehot is here identifying as a necessary component of literature the intermixture that he also saw as an inevitable consequence of the expansion of commerce. But Townsend's review suggests that it is almost impossible to halt and examine the work of exclusion performed by the social concept of vulgarity without the writer having his reputation be informed by the quality he analyzes.

Indeed, the work of exclusion, so crucial to the Victorian reaction to the economic changes taking place in the latter half of the nineteenth century, is perpetuated not just in contemporary reviews and assessments of Trollope but also in twentieth-century accounts of Trollope's historical period. As I have argued in my analysis of the function of the heiress in Trollope's novels, what is being condemned in the scene where Lady Glencora is accused of vulgarity is nonlanded or commercial wealth in the forms in which it was making itself felt in late nineteenth-century English culture. For the Victorians the term "vulgarity" created a fracture in the concept of money between funds that came from traditional sources and funds that came from other sources. That fracture or difference persists in modern historical accounts of the period. Thompson notes the "air of rich vulgarity and indeed opulence [that] was beginning to permeate society" (*English* 300). Rubenstein describes commercial millionaires as a "vulgar and ignorant . . . *nouveau-riche*" (*Men* 45). Cannadine argues that "in London high society was diluted (or, as some claimed, polluted) by the advent of vulgar international plutocrats, American born millionaires, and Jewish adventurers, who brutally and brashly bought their way in" (28). Cannadine refers to what he calls "the vulgar wealthy," "vulgar wealth," "vulgar new wealth," and "the arrival of 'mere wealth'" (30, 183, 298, 202).

In putting quotation marks around "mere wealth," Cannadine underscores the irony of using that term to designate the enormous fortunes of social arrivals like Thomas Holloway, Lady Frances Waldegrave, or the Rothschilds. But modern historians' continued, if self-conscious, use of such descriptors for wealth reiterates the logic of the Victorians. We might think here of the *Graphic*'s posthumous evocation of Lady Frances, which also uses the word "mere," asserting that "the mere possession of money, if it influenced her at all, did so to the disadvantage of the candidate" (quoted in Hewett *Strawberry* 235). The condemnation of wealth as vulgar that allowed the mid-Victorians to reassure themselves of money's inability to penetrate to the heart of the culture has entered our discourse to such an extent that the word "vulgar" is now used as if it no longer carries the emotional force it had in Trollope's day, a force marked in both his novels and the reviews of them. In the language of historians "vulgar" comes across simply as describing the difference between one kind of wealth and another.

Ironically, as I have argued in this chapter, that descriptor begins to be used with particular force at the moment when money ceases to be perceived as having a vulgar material form and comes instead to be grasped as ineffable, a form of energy or abstraction. With such a shift in definition, it becomes clear that, in fact, all forms of money are the same. As Madame Max points out, it does not matter where wealth comes from. But, as Trollope's novels show, the idea of money as an entity that can flow anywhere in the social sphere is particularly unsettling. So, at that moment when money becomes most abstract, a need arises to insist that it still bears a vulgar material form. This need creates a fracture not just between wealth and virtue but within wealth itself, between good money and bad. This split continues to pervade critical thinking, particularly thinking about the economic strains in literary and cultural texts.[68] It is the split I note in my preface that marks the difference between what we call "vulgar" Marxism and other forms of critical approaches that deal with the impact of money in less crudely materialist forms. This critical tradition demonstrates how fully we have internalized the gesture Palliser makes when he condemns Glencora's expenditures as vulgar. We know the impropriety and effects of making wealth a vulgarly explicit category in our analyses.

CHAPTER FOUR

Margaret Oliphant and the Professional Ideal

There's also a difference between good vulgarity and bad vulgarity. That's what we're trying to sort out.

New York Times, 26 November 2000

With the novels of Margaret Oliphant, the marriage plot ceases to work as a deep structure that drives the novel's romances. Oliphant's characters, as well as her narrators, prove ironically conscious of their involvement in plots whose ideological implications are not only clear to them but also capable of being reversed. We see the beginning of this ironic awareness in Anthony Trollope's novels and in reviews of his work.[1] When, for example, the hero of *Doctor Thorne* is offered the choice between Mary and money, Trollope moves halfway to identifying the implications of the marriage plot by acknowledging that in it the rich woman represents wealth. But he refuses, as we have seen, to give up the marriage plot's romantic allure. That refusal is marked by the fact that he continues to allude to the poor woman as a person rather than a property or quality; she represents a locus of value that cannot be crassly identified without the novel's moral valences being undermined.

For Oliphant this kind of logic depends on what she calls in her early fiction "modern sentimental ethics" (*Doctor's Family* 164). In her later novels she moves beyond the sentimentality inherent in the marriage plot by representing the choice of spouses as a matter of rational calculation rather than emotional impulse. In *Miss Marjoribanks* and *Phoebe Junior* the heroines "look upon the matter as a superior mind, trained in sound principles of political economy, might be expected to look upon the possible vicissitudes of fortune, with an enlightened regard to the uses of all things, and to the comparative values on either side" (*Miss Marjoribanks* 93).[2] Oliphant consciously addresses the overlap I have been tracing throughout this book between economic self-interest and marital choice, and she does so by engaging with the thinking of John Stuart Mill.

Perhaps remembering the etymological roots of the word "economy" in the Greek *oikos*, the home, and *nomos*, rules or customs, Oliphant explained in her 1869 review of Mill's *The Subjection of Women* that family hierarchies reiterate "the official superiority of man in the economy of the world" (*"The Subjection of Women"* 578). A husband and wife are "the typical pair . . . who are to found all human economies, all domestic relations" (583). Man buys "his economic post of superiority dearly enough" (587). The position of women "is not a matter of individual right, but of social necessity and policy, and what we may call the economics of humanity" (589). Such comments have typically been read as signs of Oliphant's conservatism with respect to gender relations. Yet they also indicate her interest in thinking about how gender relations reiterate the terms of individuals' relation to the larger economy. In both *Miss Marjoribanks* and *Phoebe Junior* she explores that relation by intertwining stories about life in the rural English town of Carlingford with references to Mill's philosophies. But the Millian arguments that interest her most are not those of *Subjection* but of *On Liberty* (1859), "Utilitarianism" (1861), and *Dissertations and Discussions* (1859–75), arguably the writings of Mill's that had the most immediate impact on Victorian culture. As Oliphant herself commented when she submitted the first of her reviews of *Subjection* to Blackwood, "I send you a little paper I have just finished about Stuart Mill and his mad notion of the franchise for women. . . . Probably you will think it too respectful to Mr Mill, but I can't for my part find any satisfaction in simply jeering at a man who may do a foolish thing in his life but yet is a great philosopher" (quoted in Mouton 235n4).[3]

In Oliphant's case we have a writer who identified herself with the Tory position and the Tory periodical with which she worked her entire professional life, *Blackwood's Edinburgh Magazine*, but who also actively engaged with Mill's liberal arguments. This intervention confirms Mill's own assertion in the essay on Coleridge that "a Tory philosopher cannot be wholly a Tory, but must often be a better Liberal than Liberals themselves" (*Dissertations and Discussions* 381). We know that Oliphant engaged in contemporary discussions of Mill through her friendship with John Tulloch, the headmaster of St. Andrews School, who dedicated his 1885 *Movements of Religious Thought in Britain during the Nineteenth Century* to Oliphant.[4] In that volume Tulloch argued that theirs was an age that confronted "the fundamental antithesis between the materialistic and the spiritualistic schools" (233) and located himself, and presumably Oliphant as well, in the spiritual as opposed to the material camp.[5] Certainly Oliphant seems directly critical of Mill in the fiction that has to do with the spiritual realm, the ghost stories and tales about the Little Pilgrim's adventures in the afterlife.[6]

But this stance is modulated in her domestic novels, which take what I would describe as a more playfully satiric attitude toward what Mill, Tulloch, and others saw as the influx of materialist values in the 1860s and '70s. Evoking such values through her heroines, Oliphant mocks them while at the same time exploring what it would mean, for both society and the form of the novel, to follow out the implications of Mill's arguments. In *Miss Marjoribanks* she addresses the issues raised in *On Liberty*, arguably the Millian text that had the most general impact in the period.[7] In *Phoebe Junior* she addresses those raised in *Dissertations and Discussions*, a collection of essays that appeared first in book form in 1859 and was reissued in 1875, a year before the appearance of Oliphant's novel. Introducing the heroine of that text with "a book in her hand. . . . It was, I think, one of the volumes of Mr. Stuart Mill's 'Dissertations'" (76), Oliphant makes it clear that, in the period in which she was writing, Mill's works were impacting not just specialists but also the general reading public. Though Oliphant goes on to make fun of fiction by arguing that "Phoebe was not above reading novels or other light literature, but this only in moments dedicated to amusement, and the present hour was morning, a time not for amusement, but for work" (76), her own novel represents a systematic engagement with the arguments presented in *Disserations and Discussions*.

Oliphant opens *Phoebe Junior* by addressing the topic of the first essay, "The Right and Wrong of State Interference with Corporate and Church Property." The novel then takes up a fictional exploration of the issues raised in the paired essays that conclude Mill's volume, the analyses of Bentham and Coleridge that F. R. Leavis has argued counterpoise the values key to mid-Victorians' conceptions of themselves as social beings.[8] In these two pieces Mill argues that Bentham's vision of society as "a collection of persons pursuing each his separate interest or pleasure" (*Dissertations and Discussions* 296) can be counteracted by Coleridge's philosophy, which fosters "a principle of sympathy, not of hostility; of union, not of separation," such that "one part of the community do not consider themselves as foreigners with regard to another part" (*Dissertations and Discussions* 343).[9] Here Mill unites his advocacy of self-interest with a concern for the community that would balance or soften the materialism of the utilitarian approach. As the marginal economist William Stanley Jevons was later to explain, "No small part of the favour with which these Essays have always been received by the general public is due to the happy way in which Mill has combined the bitter and the sweet. The uncompromising rigidity of the Benthamist formulas is softened and toned down" (523). This is the combination of feelings that Oliphant represents through her heroines, particularly as she moves from the more individually focused *Miss Marjoribanks* to the more socially focused *Phoebe Junior*.

Concluding the series of fictions Oliphant called the Chronicles of Carlingford, these two novels show how Mill's explorations of the tensions between enlightened self-interest, individual liberty, and communal responsibility underwrote the ideal of professional behavior that emerged in England in the last decades of the nineteenth century.[10] As a whole, the Carlingford series can be divided into two parts, each of which deals with one of the two key social positions Ann Douglas identifies with the emergence of professionalism: "the minister and the lady" (8).[11] Written at the end of the era Douglas analyzes, Oliphant's novels mark the juncture at which a clergyman and a lady ceased to be conceived in sentimental terms and became instead positions that were, either explicitly or implicitly, professional.[12] In the clergy stories in the Carlingford series—the short story "The Rector" (1863) and the novels *Salem Chapel* (1863) and *The Perpetual Curate* (1864)—Oliphant depicts disinterested professionals who struggle with their relation to a larger group that employs them and attempts to regulate their standards of behavior.[13] In the marriage stories that parallel the clerical ones—the short story "The Executor," the novella "The Doctor's Family," and the novels *Miss Marjoribanks* and *Phoebe Junior*, Oliphant explores the professional not as a member of a group but as an exemplar of Mill's idea of the cultivated individual who displays a set of talents through which he or she can achieve a position of distance or detachment enabling a form of social action that those who are less distanced and more involved in the immediacy of daily affairs cannot achieve.[14]

In order to understand how Oliphant links Mill's thinking to the emergent ideal of professional behavior, I want to look briefly at two novels she wrote after the Carlingford series, *Hester* (1883) and *Kirsteen* (1890), both of which include heroines who are full-fledged professionals.[15] Her descriptions of these heroines' actions and attitudes provide models of professional behavior. In *Kirsteen*, for example, the dressmaker heroine is

delighted with the beautiful materials, which were thrown about in the workroom, the ordinary mantua-maker having little feeling for them except in view of their cost at so much a yard. But Kirsteen, quite unused to beautiful manufactured things, admired them all, and found a pleasure in heaping them together and contrasting with each other the soft silken stuffs. (164–65)[16]

Oliphant depicts a similar combinatory activity in *Miss Marjoribanks* and *Phoebe Junior*, whose heroines use their personal energy and cultivation to bring about a form of social coherence in which disparate community members are brought together as the pieces of cloth are for the dressmaker. As the narrator of *Miss Marjoribanks* explains, its heroine confronts "that chaos which was then called society" (19) and succeeds in "making a harmonious whole out of [its] scraps and fragments" (21).

For Mill, the ability to unite the community resided with the genius whose extraordinary individualism meant that he or she simply could not conform to societal expectations.[17] As Oliphant explains, "Kirsteen tried her active young powers upon everything, being impatient of sameness and monotony, and bent upon securing a difference, an individual touch in every different variety of costume" (164).[18] In her late novels, Oliphant wrenches originality and genius out of the context of high art and intellectual culture and resituates them in a new more explicitly material environment. Mill argues that "people think genius a fine thing if it enables a man to write an exciting poem, or paint a picture" (*On Liberty* 74). Oliphant, too, tells readers that Kirsteen plays with fabrics "as a painter likes to arrange and study the more subtle harmonies of light and shade" (165). But possessing "a true genius for her craft" may, as the narrator comments, "not be thought a very high quality in a heroine" (164). In using genius and originality to describe a practical activity that leads to financial success, Oliphant violates the barrier that Barbara Herrnstein Smith has argued enforces "the double discourse of value," the barrier between "money, commerce, technology, industry, production and consumption, workers and consumers" and "culture, art, genius, creation and appreciation, artists and connoisseurs" (127).[19]

When Mill redefines the concept of genius by insisting that "in its true sense" it means "originality in thought and action" (*On Liberty* 74), he makes it possible to associate genius with business as well as the arts. Oliphant makes such associations explicit in *Hester* when she describes her banker heroine as possessing a "genius for business, as distinct as genius in poetry, which makes everything succeed" (22). In *Phoebe Junior* the millionaire railway entrepreneur has "that kind of faculty which is in practical work what genius is in literature, and, indeed, in its kind is genius too, though it neither refines nor even (oddly enough) enlarges the mind to which it belongs" (44). In that same novel, Oliphant argues that "if a squire looks fondly at his land, and a sailor at his ship (when ships were worth looking at), why should not a shopkeeper regard his shop with the same affectionate feelings?" (140).[20] This statement marks the perceptual shift that takes place between Anthony Trollope's novels and Margaret Oliphant's. In his fictions, the boundary between the estate and the shop or between landed and commercial wealth is, in the end, maintained. In hers it is crossed at the conceptual level, as her heroines are represented as both materially interested and high-minded, and at the level of class relations, as members of the commercial factions of English society intermingle with those who possess more traditional forms of social status (land, an Oxford education, preferment in the Anglican Church).

These changes in the form of the novel reflect social changes in English society, changes associated with the rise of the professional classes in the 1880s and the emergence of managerial capitalism at the end of the nineteenth century. *Miss Marjoribanks* points to the boundary crossings such developments entailed, as its heroine exhibits "that singular genius which made itself so fully felt to the farthest limits of society, and which even indeed extended those limits miraculously beyond the magic circle of Grange Lane" (105). Lucilla Marjoribanks extends her entertaining from the place where the professionals—bankers, doctors, retired Indian civil servants—live, embracing both the landowning county families and the commercial side of town. In *Phoebe Junior* the heroine, in bringing her cosmopolitan, urban education to the same small town of Carlingford, is able to bridge gaps between Dissenters and Anglicans. The social territories that were, in Trollope's fiction, buffers between commerce and landed wealth, professionalism and cosmopolitanism, become in Oliphant's the locus of potential border crossings.

Looking at the half of the Chronicles of Carlingford that focuses on women, I demonstrate that it is through an exploration and critique of the traditional form of the marriage plot that Oliphant comes to the point where, in the concluding scenes of *Phoebe Junior*, the last novel in the series, she is able to explore the full implications of Millian thinking for the image of professional behavior that emerges in the late Victorian period. Oliphant begins experimenting with the traditional form of the marriage plot in the early "The Executor" and "The Doctor's Family," where she explores its limitations by making her characters conscious of their inability to live up to its romantic expectations. This antiromantic, or in her terms antisentimental approach, leads Oliphant to be more interested in the figures who play a negative role in the marriage plot than in those who are typically its heroes and heroines, the man who marries the poor woman for love rather than money.

Oliphant's turn away from sentimentality is fully realized as she moves from the early short fiction to *Miss Marjoribanks*, a novel in which she chooses, ironically, to make the rich woman not a negative figure but the novel's heroine and point-of-view character. Through this figure and the similarly pragmatic heroine who follows her, the eponymous protagonist of *Phoebe Junior*, Oliphant uses irony to explore the combination of self-interest, altruism, and cultivation characteristic of the extraordinary individuals who, in the free society Mill imagines in *On Liberty*, would be able to hold communities together while at the same time allowing the individual agents within those communities the freedom to satisfy their own personal ambitions. It would, in some sense, have been impossible for a public intellectual like Oliphant not to have taken notice of writings that formed the thinking of a generation, those written by both Mill's advocates and his opponents. In using her fictional heroines to work through Mill's arguments at the level of everyday life Oliphant shows herself both sympathetic to and critical of the liberal position.

She was particularly interested in the fact that those who endorsed Mill's thinking had not fully worked out the implications of a complex stance that was at once idealistic and materialist, at once in favor of liberty and of constraining it. In allowing her fictions to go down the path that connects the two realms the marriage plot normally keeps separate, Oliphant begins to work through the connection between Mill's thinking and the emerging idea of professional behavior. But here too she underscores the way in which professionalism, in distancing itself from the vulgarity of wealth through detachment and service, proves itself deeply dependent, without wishing to acknowledge it, on money. Oliphant is a Tory novelist who acts as a kind of comic hair shirt for liberal readers, making them laugh at the same time that she makes them uncomfortably aware of the limitations and contradictions in their thinking, the seams that Slavoj Žižek has argued ideology is always seeking to sew up.

"The Prose Concerns of Life": "The Executor" and "The Doctor's Family"

Oliphant's early shorter works in the Chronicles of Carlingford function as trial balloons that make it possible for the novelist to develop the ironic form and voice of her later novels. "The Executor" (1861), "The Doctor's Family" (1863), and *Miss Marjoribanks* (1866) all allude to the traditional pattern of the marriage plot in which a man is defined as virtuous if he can choose a woman out of love rather than more practical or mercenary motives. But Oliphant's impulse is to tell that story from the point of view of the character that readers would see as the least sympathetic figure in the preceding story. We might think of this revisionary process as a version of what Žižek has called, in the title of one of his most well-known books, *Tarrying with the Negative*. There Žižek advocates dwelling on figures socially coded as the objects of dislike or disgust because that gesture allows critics to identify the splits that ideologies cover over. In the short story and novella that precede *Miss Marjoribanks*, Oliphant undertakes a systematic critical exploration of the contours of the marriage plot that culminates, in the conclusion of "The Doctor's Family," with her identifying the wealthy woman as the negative figure that anchors, by antithesis, the novel's romantic stories and therefore marks the fractures in the ideology they set forth.[21]

Once Oliphant isolates the rich woman's function, she is freed up not just to write a novel from the rich woman's perspective but to reverse the polarities of that representation, as the previously maligned figure becomes the positive rather than the negative choice for the novel's hero.[22] Oliphant can introduce these innovations because she was writing at the moment when the general reader of the Victorian novel was beginning to resist the implications of the marriage plot. This resistance is articulated with particular vehemence in a review of Anthony Trollope's *Doctor Thorne* that appeared in the *Spectator* in 1858, just three years before Oliphant began her Carlingford series. The incisiveness of the position taken in that review may be attributed to its likely having been written by the noted jurist Sir Henry Sumner Maine, who was an active participant in anthropological debates about the relation between gender and property.[23] In reacting to Trollope, Maine argues that the novelist's use of the marriage plot is too obvious, that he "invests his books . . . with a sort of atmosphere which is not incapable of being condensed into the moral that people ought to marry for love and not for money" (Smalley 77). Chafing against the absolute bifurcations of such plots, Maine imagines a narrative that would make it less easy to accept the virtuous poor woman as the obvious choice for the novel's hero. What would happen, he asks, if the poor woman had a father who is "a drunken hypocrite," a mother who is "a disreputable vixen," and siblings who are "each more profligate, vicious, mean, and idle than the other"? (78).

Would the novelist then be able to insist on the happiness of a marriage based solely on love? Maine's answer is emphatically no:

> Neither [Trollope] nor any other novelist ever has the courage to teach such a
> lesson. . . . The fact is, that in his heart every man knows and feels that society

has real claims which no man has a right to deny. Of course it is infinitely mean to marry for money a person who is the object of dislike or contempt; but it does not follow that no marriage can be wise or happy unless those who contract it feel for each other an overwhelming passion. The mass of marriages are, no doubt, determined chiefly by feeling, but by feeling of a much more manageable kind than that which novelists describe. (Smalley 78)

The limiting circumstances and manageable feelings that Maine wishes for emerge in Oliphant's early short fictions, where characters are conscious of the plots that confine them and of their own failure to conform to the expectations embedded in those narratives.

The first of these stories, "The Executor," begins when an elderly woman, Mrs. Thomson, dies and leaves her estate in trust to a John Brown, a lawyer who will inherit £20,000 if he fails to find the dead woman's long-lost daughter, instead of the relatives who were anticipating it. Because her mother fails to receive the inheritance she expected, the pretty young woman at the center of the story, Bessie Christian has "before her—nothing but this dark, monotonous, aching present moment" (10). Adding in the circumstantial detail that Maine desires, Oliphant underscores that her poor heroine needs to care for parents who cannot support themselves. Bessie's father is a paralytic and her mother a hysteric, who has destroyed the family's only source of income, the school Bessie ran, by boasting about the money the family was to inherit. As Maine predicted, Bessie's suitor, Doctor Rider, finds that although Bessie is the classic heroine of the marriage plot—pretty, blonde, and dutifully trying to bear the burdens placed on her—he cannot live up to the expectations of marrying her under those circumstances. When he thought Bessie's family was about to inherit, "in imagination, he had helped his Bessie to minister to the comfort of the poor old sick parents in Mrs. Thomson's house" (14–15).

But now that Bessie has no money, his imagination works in the opposite direction. Thinking about the burden of Bessie's parents, he sees "one moment a pretty young wife, all the new house wanted to make it fully tenable; but he had scarcely brought her across the threshold when a ghastly figure in a chair was carried over it after her" (14). Though Rider loves Bessie, he cannot propose to her; as the narrator comments, "Nothing could change those intolerable circumstances" (14). With its insistence on circumstances, "The Executor" reflects the philosophical shift that took place in the late 1850s and '60s, when, instead of assuming that social behavior was guided by absolute principles, writers like Mill were increasingly calling for a greater attention to social circumstances.[24] In the conclusion of Oliphant's story, we hear the skepticism that emerges when fiction follows this philosophical shift. The lawyer, who eventually inherits the old woman's money because he is unable to find the long-lost daughter, marries Bessie, who therefore finally comes into the wealth her mother had initially hoped to inherit. The poor heroine marries a prosperous man, but, in Oliphant's world, this is a union shorn of romantic trappings. The forty-six-year-old lawyer is "not a highly attractive or interesting figure" (15). His marriage to Bessie fits neither the morally good nor morally bad categories we expect from the end of a Victorian narrative: "To have called them lovers would have been absurd—to have supposed that here was a marriage of convenience about to be arranged would have been more ridiculous still. What was it?" (32). Their union is, in some senses, simply a matter of circumstances.

Though the novella that follows "The Executor," "The Doctor's Family," ends with a more emotionally satisfying romantic union, in it Oliphant engages in a more trenchant and more systematically worked out critique of the marriage plot. It takes for its hero the character who is least able to conform to the dictates of the marriage plot in "The Executor," the doctor who cannot marry the woman he loves because he fears the financial burdens she will bring with her. "The Doctor's Family" opens with an odd recursive moment in which the narrator details the hero's consciousness of how others must have viewed his actions in "The Executor": "You don't suppose that he did not know in his secret heart, and feel tingling through every vein, those words which nobody ever said to his face?" (68). Such passages mark Rider's ability to comment consciously on the plot in which he plays a role and to note, ironically, his failure to meet its expectations and therefore receive its rewards.[25] He knew that "he was not a hero or a martyr; men made of that stuff have large compensations" (68), compensations that are, in the nineteenth-century novel, both moral and material. As Maine notes, in Trollope's novels heroes "make desperate efforts to marry beggary and infamy; but when they try to do so, the desert blossoms as the rose" (78). Oliphant, however, selects for her tale a hero whose decisions have already proven him to be "an ordinary individual, with no sublimity in him, and no compensation to speak of for his sufferings—no consciousness of lofty right-doing, or of a course of action superior to the world" (68).

In "The Doctor's Family," Rider once again falls in love with a poor woman he cannot marry. This time the object of his affections is an Australian woman, Nettie Underwood, who has come to reunite her sister and her sister's children with the husband and father of their family, Dr. Rider's alcoholic brother. In describing the relations between Nettie and Rider, "The Doctor's Family" seems almost deliberately to follow the exaggerated suggestions Maine makes when he speculates on a novel that would make the marriage plot impossible. Dr. Rider must support his financially and emotionally parasitical brother. The rational and hard-working Nettie has an equally hopeless and dependent sister, a woman completely guided by her emotions, who has a number of children for whom she provides inadequate care. Nettie must assume the burden of her sister's children, as Rider assumes that of his brother. Dedicating her small savings and all her emotional and physical labor to maintaining her sister's family, Nettie is in some senses a reiteration of the Bessie Christian figure from "The Executor." It is as if Oliphant insists on putting her hero in the same situation and tracing out at greater length the implications of his inability to surmount the power of circumstances. This repetition reveals Oliphant's awareness of the marriage plot as a template that can be adapted to a variety of circumstances. In substituting Nettie, a dark woman whose name marks her as coming from the colonial underworld, for Bessie, whose "Saxon" blondness and revealing surname make her seem like a character out of *Ivanhoe*, Oliphant emphasizes that Rider, can be serially attracted to different kinds of virtues, all of which can be inculcated in the figure of the desirable poor woman. (One might read the repetitive structure of Oliphant's narratives as making a sardonic comment on England as a country that, like the heroes of her novels, is attracted to a set of values that can shift over time.)

Though "The Doctor's Family" reiterates the patterns of "The Executor," it also expands that story's focus by dwelling on the impact not just of circumstances but also of what we might call character—the novella calls it human nature—on the evolution of the plot. The very terms "hero" and "heroine" seem inappropriate for Rider and Nettie, since both perceive themselves as by nature incapable of conforming to such categories. Rider can no more propose to Nettie than he could to Bessie: "Some people are compelled to take the prose concerns of life in full consideration even when they are in love" (119). The narrator again emphasizes the character's ironic self-awareness: "Dr. Rider, eager as love and youth could make him, was yet incapable of shutting his eyes to the precipice at his feet. That he despised himself for doing so, did not make the matter easier. These were the limits of his nature and beyond them he could not pass" (120). Nettie, too, knows that while she might look like a type of the virtuous heroine, she, in fact, deviates from that pattern. When someone asks her why she labors so hard to maintain her ungrateful sister's family, she replies, "If I were to say it was my duty and all that sort of stuff, you would understand me" (98).

But Nettie insists that one can only describe as duty something one does not enjoy, and she likes doing what she does. The narrator marks the story's failure to conform to Victorian norms by observing that "to fancy this wilful imperious creature a meek self-sacrificing heroine was equally absurd and impossible. Was there any virtue at all in that dauntless enterprise of hers? Or was it simple determination to have her own way?" (117). Such comments make it impossible to read Oliphant's novella in the simple bifurcated terms that Maine deplores in the Victorian novel. The hero cannot choose Nettie, not because he doesn't value her but because he must take circumstances into account. But she likewise cannot be read as an emblem of virtue. Both are caught up in psychological and social patterns that they know drive them to behave as they do. While in a novel like Trollope's *Doctor Thorne*, such confusions are resolved once the hero declares his love for the novel's heroine despite her financial impediments, in "The Doctor's Family," this clarification never takes place.

When Rider is at last driven to break from the prudence that typically governs him and avow his love for Nettie, that confession does not resolve the problem. Instead of reacting by admitting her love for him, the response the hero's turn to the poor heroine typically elicits, she reacts with confusion:

> In former days, when she scornfully denied it to be self-sacrifice, and laboured on, always indomitable, unconscious that what she did was anything more than the simplest duty and necessity, all was well within the dauntless, all-enterprising soul; but growing knowledge of her own heart, of other hearts, cast dark and perplexing shades upon Nettie, as upon all other wayfarers on these complex paths. (163–64)

At this moment, as the story deviates from the typical plot of the Victorian novel, Oliphant's narrator insists that "the effect upon her mind was different from the effect to be expected according to modern sentimental ethics" (164).[26] This comment identifies the patterns that had previously governed the nineteenth-century novel's depictions of heroes and heroines, patterns that Maine associated with the choice between love and money, as based on "sentimental ethics."[27]

Mill's discussion of sentimentality in the essay on Bentham provides a useful gloss on this phrase. There Mill argues that "every human action has three aspects: its *moral* aspect, in that of its *right* and *wrong*: its *aesthetic aspect*, or that of its *beauty*; its *sympathetic* aspect, or that of its *loveableness*. The first addresses itself to our reason and conscience; the second to our imagination; the third to our human fellow-feeling" (*Dissertations and Discussions* 316, emphasis in the original). "Sentimentality," he concludes, "consists in setting the last two of the three above the first" (*Dissertations and Discussions* 317).[28] The pattern typical of the nineteenth-century novel, the contrast between the rich and the poor woman, appears to offer a moral choice, the opposition between wealth and virtue. But the reader is invited to respond to that choice in sentimental rather than rational terms, as the virtue the poor woman represents is made desirable when she is rendered both aesthetically pleasing and sympathetic, both beautiful and loveable. At the same time the commercial values associated with rich woman are experienced as negative as she is represented as distasteful and unsympathetic. Oliphant underscores this linkage between values and image in "The Doctor's Family" when she eventually introduces the familiar contrast between the rich and the poor woman.

In a fit of pique after Nettie has refused to marry him, Rider decides he will court a woman of practical use, the daughter of the town's established physician. Contemplating the uses of money rather than love, Rider asks himself "savagely why he should not make an advantageous marriage now, when the chance offered. Old Marjoribanks's practice and savings, with a not unagreeable, rather clever, middle-aged wife—why should he not take it into consideration?"(128). But the novella insists, as is typical of the marriage plot, that the rich woman is never really attractive to the story's romantic hero. It describes how, passing Miss Marjoribanks on the street,

> the guilty doctor took off his hat to that stout and sensible wayfarer, with a pang of self-disgust which avenged Nettie. Along the very road where that little Titania, eager and rapid, had gone upon her dauntless way so often, to see that comely, well-dressed figure, handsome, sprightly, clever—but with such a world of bright youth, tenderness, loveliness, everything that touches the heart of man, between the two! No harm to Miss Marjoribanks; only shame to the doctor, who, out of angry love, pique, and mortification, to vex Nettie, had pretended to transfer homage due to the fairy princess to that handsome and judicious woman. (147–48)

The difference between Miss Marjoribanks and Nettie is the difference between wealth and virtue as it is typically represented in the marriage plot, a difference between material and immaterial values that is inscribed at the level of the woman's body, a difference between being stout and sensible and a tiny, elfin sprite, a featherweight who can be described as Titania.[29] Once this paradigmatic contrast is invoked, "The Doctor's Family" begins to follow the sentimental logic of the marriage plot. The marriage between the novel's hero and the poor woman is made possible when, through a chain of improbable events, the circumstances that have constrained them evaporate. Fortuitously, the doctor's dissolute brother drowns on his way home from a drunken evening out. Once he is out of the picture, an Australian farmer magically appears and avows that he has always loved the drunkard's widow, Nettie's sister. Marrying her, he takes all but one of the unruly children Nettie has been caring for back to the other side of the world, where he and his new wife will set up housekeeping. Oliphant underscores the improbability of these events when one of the novel's minor characters comments of Nettie's sister's Australian suitor that "to think he should have come in such a sweet way and married Mrs Fred! just what we all were wishing for, if we could have ventured to think it possible" (203).

Through such observations, which are placed in the mouths of characters that play little or no active role in the novella, Oliphant invokes readerly expectations regarding the endings of nineteenth-century novels, which depend on mysterious returns and secret inheritances. When Dr. Rider learns that Nettie is free to marry him, he looks so happy that his serving girl "carried down-stairs with her a vivid impression that somebody had left her master a fortune" (195). Though Oliphant does not enrich the doctor, she does mark her awareness of such familiar patterns by having one of her characters think "if Miss Marjoribanks had only been Nettie, or Nettie Miss Marjoribanks! If not only love and happiness, but the doctor's old practice and savings, could have been brought to heap up the measure of the young doctor's good fortune! What a pity it is that one cannot have everything!" (204–5). In *Miss Marjoribanks*, the novel that follows "The Doctor's Family," Oliphant will imagine a way to have everything, not by offering the typical ending of the Victorian novel in which, as Maine argued, disinterestedness is rewarded with wealth but rather by conceiving of a wealthy heroine who is also an emblem of virtue.[30] The movement from short story to novella to novel suggests that as Oliphant turned to the apparently negative aspects of the triangle that traditionally structures the marriage plot, she found herself with more and more to say.[31]

"The Raw Material of Human Nature": *Miss Marjoribanks*

In *Miss Marjoribanks*, Oliphant discovers a way not just to include narrative commentary on how her writing fails to follow traditional paradigms but to refuse and rewrite those paradigms by making the undesirable rich woman, the stout and sensible Miss Marjoribanks who triggers disgust in Dr. Rider, the heroine of the story. Oliphant even playfully exaggerates her heroine's apparently unappealing traits, describing Lucilla as "large in all particulars, full and well-developed, with somewhat large features" and "a mass of hair" in "ponderous locks" (4–5); "her gloves were half a number larger, and her shoes a hairbreadth broader, than those of any of her companions" (4–5). Using a mock heroic-tone that deflates any celebration of romantic excess and inventing a pragmatic heroine who delights because of her unflappably rational response to everything that happens to her, Oliphant creates in *Miss Marjoribanks* a novel that insists it is not sentimental.[32]

In its opening paragraph, the narrator tells readers that "Dr. Marjoribanks was too busy a man to waste his feelings on a mere sentiment" (3). Though his daughter initially imagines herself, in typical Victorian fashion, dutifully bound to her father on the occasion of her mother's death, those expectations are disrupted when he sends her back to school, where she persuades the headmistresses to "let me learn all about political economy and things, to help me manage everything" (11). This education sets the tone for the rest of the novel, as Lucilla returns to Carlingford determined to follow the precept she has been "taught at Mount Pleasant, that feelings had nothing to do with an abstract subject" (223). The narrator's insistence, for example, that "she took it all in the way of business" (18) highlights Oliphant's decision to create in Lucilla Marjoribanks an antisentimental heroine who appeals not to readers' sense of beauty or what is loveable, not to aesthetic and sympathetic responses or imagination and feeling, but to reason, consciousness, and irony. In describing her heroine's actions as she sets out "for the good of society" to create "a revolution in taste"(33), Oliphant engages in a mock-serious consideration of the arguments that Mill makes in *On Liberty*. She does so through a trio of characters who conform to the traditional shape of the marriage plot: the wealthy Lucilla Marjoribanks, the poorer drawing-master's daughter, Barbara Lake, whom Lucilla invites to sing at her parties, and the suitor who is torn between the two women, Mr. Cavendish.

Using these figures Oliphant makes the center of the novel of manners, the English drawing room, a comic environment in which she explores in quasi-allegorical fashion the thinking of both Mill and the associationist psychologist Alexander Bain, who helped shape Mill's arguments about how to manage a modern commercial society in which individuals must be left free to follow their own desires without that social freedom leading to the anarchy that writers like Arnold feared. The pleasure of Oliphant's novel lies in the tension between its humorous tone and the trivial actions it describes and the care with which it references terms key to the moral philosophy of the period. In the contrast between the rich and the poor woman, Oliphant sets forth the different aspects of the human personality as Bain understood them. This psychological grounding allows her in her portrait of Lucilla to depict the detached stance that Mill argued was necessary for the extraordinary individual to rise above the pull of personal passion, a stance that would, in the latter part of the century, be increasingly identified with professional behavior. In this dynamic Cavendish represents the ordinary individual. Drawn to both the rich and the poor woman, he feels the pull of the two contradictory halves of the psyche they represent. Tracing the story of his dealings with Lucilla throughout the three volumes of her novel, Oliphant works out in an ironic format the implications for the community of the process by which, as Mill argued, the extraordinary individual could prevent the desires of the ordinary person from wreaking social havoc.

From the perspective of the poor woman, Barbara Lake, the interactions between the three characters promise to take a form familiar from novels like *Pride and Prejudice.* When she first attends Lucilla's evening parties, whose other guests are of a high social status, Barbara is immediately drawn to her hostess's wealthy suitor, Mr. Cavendish. She regards him "with a certain fierce interest, and remember[s] . . . how often in books it is the humble heroine, behind backs, whom all the young ladies snub, who wins the hero at the last" (85). But in *Miss Marjoribanks* this pattern does not play out in its usual form, since the story is told from the perspective not of the poor but the rich woman. From Lucilla's position, the poor woman is less an emblem of virtue than of the emotions or sentimentality that Oliphant had critiqued in her earlier Carlingford stories. She describes Barbara satirically as having "no intellect to speak of," although she did have "what she called a heart—that is to say, a vital center, of inclinations and passions" (108). The language of this passage is both pointedly antisentimental and echoes the thinking of Bain, the titles of whose books—*The Senses and the Intellect* and *The Emotions and the Will*— reflect his insistence that the human personality is made up of layers: the "higher" abilities of the intellect and the will, associated with enlightened self-interest, and the lower powers of the senses and the emotions.[33] As Bain argued, "There is a real difference in the constitution of human beings, founded on the unequal predominance of the three great leading functions of the mind—Emotion, Volition, Intellect" (35).

Bain taught Mill to see that the "feelings, passions, actions, are the raw materials out of which character is to be wrought by aiming at a balance" (Shairp 15). In

Oliphant's novel, Barbara Lake represents such raw material. As Cavendish tells Lucilla when she first brings Barbara to sing at her Thursday evening social gatherings, "that contralto of yours is charming raw material; but if I were you I would put her through an elementary course. She knows how to sing, but she does not know how to move; and as for talking, she seems to expect to be insulted. If you can make a pretty-behaved young lady out of that, you will beat Adam Smith" (90–91).[34] The problem Lucilla confronts dealing with the raw material of feelings is that they are so powerful they can grant the individual a will that rivals the force of the intellect. As Oliphant's narrator explains of Barbara, "The inclination towards another and determination to have her own way, which in such a mind calls itself passion, . . . sometimes, by sheer force of will, succeeds better than either genius or calculation" (178).[35] From Mill's point of view, this is the emotional power that necessitates the cultivation of rationality, for that cultivation enhances the intellectual side of the self, allowing it to control and develop "the raw material of human nature" (*On Liberty* 69), which might otherwise run wild.

The novel associates such rationality with Lucilla, who, unlike her rival, proves repeatedly that she can set her feelings aside. Though attracted to Cavendish, Lucilla sends him down to have tea with Barbara because that is the only way to stop the public flirtation that threatens to destroy the social harmony of the evening. In a comment that echoes Mill's insistence that the greatest good "is not the agent's own greatest happiness, but the greatest amount of happiness altogether" (*Utilitarianism* 282), Lucilla is described as having "proved herself capable of preferring her great work to her personal sentiments" (100). In contrast to George Combe, who also insisted on a difference between the lower and higher aspects of the human personality but who saw those layers as standing in a clear relationship in which the higher dominates the lower, Bain does not present the aspects of the personality in a strictly hierarchical relation: "Bain's underlying conception is that intelligence, will, and the other higher faculties are born from, and find their principle of growth and change in, turbulent difficulty. They grow by materially dialectical, and not by ideally teleological, activity" (Rylance 197). Oliphant's novel traces this dialectical process, as Lucilla's rationality is strengthened when it is brought into conflict with and refuses to be moved by Barbara's powerful emotions.[36]

The encounters between the two are represented as a battle in which Miss Marjoribanks bests her less well-armed opponent.[37] She is described raising her standard, carrying a buckler, and "piercing through and through the thin armour of her incapable assailant" (250).[38] The confrontations between the women allow Lucilla's and Barbara's stances to be represented as a difference between high-minded,

self-sacrificing self-interest and the pure selfishness of personal desire.[39] The heroine's unselfishness is underscored when the narrator comments that "it was the
Lamp of sacrifice which Lucilla had now to employ" (100). This is an allusion to
Ruskin, who in *The Seven Lamps of Architecture* argued that the ability to sacrifice
immediate gratification in service of a higher goal was the strongest counter to the
materialism of contemporary society.[40] This ability means that Lucilla retires from
the fray a victor because she has not allowed her emotions to be disturbed. She
thinks to herself when she decides not to snub Barbara that "there is . . . a sweet-
ness in sacrificing such impulses to the sacred sense of duty and the high aims of
genius which is still more attractive to the regulated mind" (117). Refusing to be
drawn into the competition, Lucilla displays what Mill calls

> the conscious ability to do without happiness . . . [that] can raise a person above
> the chances of life, by making him feel that, let fate and fortune do their worst,
> they have not power to subdue him: which, once felt, frees him from excess of
> anxiety concerning the evils of life, and enables him, like many a Stoic in the
> worst times of the Roman Empire, to cultivate in tranquility the sources of sat-
> isfactions accessible to him. (*Utilitarianism* 288)

This passage allows us to identify the difference between Oliphant's short stories and her novel. In her earlier texts, characters feel overwhelmed by the power of
circumstances; in *Miss Marjoribanks* the heroine's tranquil self-possession is able
to counter them.[41] But in Oliphant's fiction as in Mill's essays, temperament and
circumstances present two slightly different problems. While circumstances are
relatively easy to overcome, or at least resist, through a distanced professional perspective, temperament or what we might call human nature proves more difficult
to control. We see this in *Miss Marjoribanks* less through Barbara Lake, who seems
merely to represent the raw material of the passions, than through Mr. Cavendish,
who, in being offered the choice of Lucilla or Barbara, is effectively, like the ordinary rather than the extraordinary individual, torn between appeals to the higher
and the lower parts of himself, drawn to both the emotions and the intellect.

In using the contrast between the rich and the poor woman to evoke this fracture within human nature, Oliphant emphasizes that the marriage plot itself depends on the act of discrimination that was crucially important to thinkers like
Mill and Bain. Both argued that the act of comparison was a fundamental human
activity: "We are accustomed to scrutinize the actions and conduct of those about
us, to set a higher *value* upon one man than upon another, by comparing the two"
(Bain 203, emphasis in the original).[42] This emphasis helps explain the importance

of the cultivated individual, for, as Mill argued, "human beings owe to each other help to distinguish the better from the worse, and encouragement to choose the former and avoid the latter" (*On Liberty* 86). We might think of the general history of the marriage plot as following this pattern: it is how novelists help readers to distinguish between the higher and lower choice, between wealth and virtue, allowing them to prefer the latter and avoid the former.

The question Mill raises is how far ordinary individuals can be enlightened. Can their taste be cultivated enough that they can make the higher rather than lower choice? The figure that marks the limits of such efforts is Mr. Cavendish, whom Lucilla conceives, from the first moment she meets him, as someone she can improve: she "had the consciousness that she could indeed make a great deal of Mr. Cavendish. Nobody had ever crossed her path of whom so much could be made" (320). Theoretically, as Mill argued, "these developed human beings are of some use to the undeveloped" (*On Liberty* 73). But the limits of Cavendish's character render Lucilla's attempts futile. No matter what she does, Cavendish's actions are directed by the emotional drives that pull him toward Barbara rather than the rational interests that tell him he should prefer Lucilla. Such behavior confirms Bain's and Mill's observations that because individuals are, by nature, invariably made up of a combination of higher and lower elements, of intellect and emotions, their choices will not necessarily follow the best course: "Many who are capable of the higher pleasures, occasionally, under the influence of temptation, postpone them to the lower" (*Utilitarianism* 281).[43] The demands of a liberal society require, however, that individuals be allowed the freedom to satisfy their desires, even if those desires are of the lower rather than the higher nature. As Mill argues of the ordinary individual, "Considerations to aid his judgment, exhortations to strengthen his will, may be offered to him, even obtruded on him by others; but he, himself, is the final judge" (*On Liberty* 87).

Oliphant traces this process as Cavendish repeatedly proves himself unable to make the choices that will be beneficial to himself, Lucilla, and the community, despite Lucilla's help. Her novel implicitly asks the question that also troubled Mill: what use is the enlightened individual if she cannot raise others to the level of her awareness because of the limitations of the raw material of human nature with which she has to work? Oliphant's answer is that while the enlightened individual cannot prevent others from making the selfish choices that arise from relying on emotion rather than intellect, he or she can act to prevent those choices from having a detrimental impact on the community as a whole. Lucilla undertakes just such a course of action in volume 2 of *Miss Marjoribanks* when she learns that Mr. Cavendish is not, as he pretended to be, one of *the* Cavendishes but rather a former stable boy who was able to pass himself off as a gentleman because of money he inherited from his employer. Knowing that the revelation of this secret "would be a dreadful blow to the community, and destroy public confidence for ever in the social leaders" (152), Oliphant's heroine works to prevent a fracture of the social union her presence has catalyzed.[44]

Realizing that in dealing with Cavendish's secret, "she had never yet had any piece of social business on so important a scale to manage" (213), Lucilla decides not, as we would expect from the Victorian novel, to reveal Cavendish's past and ensure his return to his rightful social place. Instead she chooses to keep the knowledge of his origins hidden from the general community, explaining to herself that "so far as the adventurer himself was concerned, no doubt he deserved anything that might come upon him; but the judgment which might overtake the careless shepherds who had admitted the wolf into the fold was much more in Miss Marjoribank's mind than any question of abstract justice" (153). Mill, too, argued against an abstract justice, insisting that unless an individual commits a crime that harms others directly, he should be left alone since he "already bears, or will bear, the whole penalty of his error" (*On Liberty* 90). In Oliphant's novel, Cavendish is effectively left in such a position, as Lucilla forces the man who has knowledge of his past to come to terms with Cavendish directly rather than revealing the secret publicly. Brokering a private interchange between the two that allows them to work through their personal differences, Lucilla makes sure that society remains undisturbed by troubling facts she as an enlightened individual decides it does not need to know.[45]

Through her depictions of Lucilla's behavior during this interaction Oliphant points forward to the ideal of professional behavior as it would be articulated by Emile Durkheim at the turn into the twentieth century. In language that might remind us of Bain's discussions of the intellect and the emotions, Durkheim argues that the professional must show detachment because "men's passions are only stayed by a moral presence they respect" (xxxii–xxxiii). The professional detachment Lucilla exhibits in these scenes is peculiarly necessary in modern commercial society because of

the continually recurring conflicts and disorders of every kind of which the economic world affords so sorry a spectacle. For, since nothing restrains the forces present from reacting together, or prescribes limits for them that they are obliged to respect, they tend to grow beyond all bounds, each clashing with the other, each warding off and weakening the other. (Durkheim xxxii)

In *Miss Marjoribanks*, Cavendish is, from almost his first introduction, associated with money. In the community of people from whom Lucilla draws her support, he is the only one who has not gained his wealth through work. As Dr. Marjoribanks querulously comments when he thinks his daughter is about to marry Cavendish, that his wealth does not come from any identifiable source, not from land, or earnings, or the funds. The secret the heroine hides from the community is that Cavendish acquired wealth not by earning it or inheriting it through normal family ties but by cozening an elderly man out of his possessions and defrauding the woman who would otherwise have been the legitimate heir. This easy acquisition has, as the novel emphasizes, made Cavendish charming but also selfish and relatively uninterested in the community; he enjoys "that luxury of comfort which a man who has . . . 'only himself to look to,' can afford to collect around him" (267). This taste for luxury undermines his propensity to choose the higher over the lower good. As the narrator comments when Cavendish returns from Europe somewhat the worse for wear in the last volume of *Miss Marjoribanks*, "He might . . . have asked whose fault it was that he was getting stout and red in the face, and had not the same grace of figure nor ease of mind as he used to have. . . . He had been living fast, and spending a great deal of money, and this, after all, was the only real ambition he had ever had" (384).[46]

In a commercial society, as Mill recognized, the necessities of a market meant such inferior choices had to be tolerated: "Almost every article which is bought and sold may be used in excess, and the sellers have a pecuniary interest in encouraging that excess; but no argument can be founded on this" (*On Liberty* 113). In a liberal society, such economic practices are part of the freedom individuals enjoy. Therefore "their choice of pleasures, and their mode of expending their income, after satisfying their legal and moral obligations to the State and to individuals, are their own concern, and must rest with their own judgment" (*On Liberty* 113).[47] Oliphant is quite specific about the choices offered the individual in a free society as she describes Cavendish once again feeling the appeals of Barbara Lake:

Pleasure, in a magnificent gush of song wooed him on one side, while Duty, with still small voice, called him at the other. He stood still, he wavered—for fifty seconds perhaps the issue was uncertain, and the victim still within reach of salvation; but the result in such a case depends very much upon whether a man really likes doing his duty, which is by no means an invariable necessity. Mr. Cavendish had in the abstract no sort of desire to do his unless when he could not help it, and consequently his resistance to temptation was very feeble. (439)[48]

Oliphant's image of Cavendish's wavering looks forward to the developments that were to take place in political economy in the era that followed Mill's, when marginal economists like Jevons would argue that a nation's economic health depended not on the actions of enlightened individuals but on an accurate calculation of the emotional vacillations of consumers: "We may estimate the equality or inequality of feelings by the decisions of the human mind. The will is our pendulum, and its oscillations are minutely registered in the price lists of the market" (11–12). In *Miss Marjoribanks* we remain in the Millian world where ordinary individuals are free to follow these vagrant desires because extraordinary ones prevent those decisions from having a harmful impact on the community. This logic is worked out to its limit case in the last volume of *Miss Marjoribanks* when Mr. Cavendish returns from Europe to run for parliament. Here we see that the individual who makes the lower choice need not be punished by the community because he effectively punishes himself.

Having presented himself as electable because he is a reformed individual who has given up pleasure, Cavendish undermines his own credibility when he is seen publicly making the choice of Barbara Lake. In negotiating the tensions of the election of someone who once was her friend but who is clearly now an improper candidate for public office, Lucilla again acts as Mill argues the enlightened individual should. In volume 2 of the novel, she kept Cavendish included in the social whole that is Carlingford. In volume 3 she adopts as her candidate not Cavendish but another man, the landowner Ashburton, who is eventually elected. Lucilla's actions underscore that, while Mill's liberal community includes all individuals no matter what their choices, its leaders must come from the enlightened professional realm rather than from the level of ordinary individuals, who are more likely to make lower or selfish choices than to make the higher, self-denying ones required of the cultivated individual.[49] Of course, all of this is ironically presented in Oliphant's novel, since the community the novel endorses is itself extremely limited, and it is Lucilla who conceives of herself as the higher of the two choices offered to members of that community.

As she thinks, looking back over the novel's courtship plot, "Poor men! They had had two ways set before them, and they had not chosen the best" (333), "all the Cavendishes . . . and Riders who had once had it in them to distinguish themselves by at least making her an offer, and who had not done it" (465). Reversing the pattern of the marriage plot by allowing Lucilla to identify herself, the rich woman, as the better of the two choices, Oliphant marks the conceptual realignment that took place as Millian thinking began to have an impact on Victorian society. Mill had reconceptualized the opposition between wealth and virtue that had had such a long philosophical and novelistic tradition. In "Utilitarianism," he insists that wealth and virtue are, in fact, not different but similar; both function as means to an end that can be either positive or negative. In his words, "Virtue is not the only thing, originally a means, and which if it were not a means to anything else, would be and remain indifferent, but which by association with what it is a means to, comes to be desired for itself, and that too with the utmost intensity. What, for example, shall we say of the love of money?" (309).

Mill's contemporaries found the logical implications of this argument peculiarly unsettling. As J. C. Shairp noted in the *North British Review* in 1867, a year after *Miss Marjoribanks* first appeared, "Another equally startling position maintained by Mr. Mill, is that virtue is pursued primarily only as a means to an end, namely happiness, just as money is; but that in time it comes to be regarded as part of the end, happiness, and as such is pursued for its own sake, just as misers come to love money for itself, and not for its uses" (23). In working through its revision of the marriage plot, Oliphant's novel comes to the point where it can represent this radically new version of the relationship between wealth and virtue in fictional form. Yet even as *Miss Marjoribanks* seems sardonically to present self-interest as the only rationally justifiable choice, it, too, like novella that precedes it, "The Doctor's Family," concludes by returning to the sentimental logic of the marriage plot, with its emphasis on impractical rather than pragmatic choices.

By the novel's end, Lucilla finally has a suitor who proposes to her, a man "sensible like herself, public-spirited like herself—a man whose pursuits she could enter into fully, who had a perfectly ideal position to offer" (465). But at this juncture Lucilla makes the romantic rather than the practical choice, picking the cousin that she has been attracted to since the novel's opening chapters, a man who fortuitously returns from India in its last pages having amassed just enough money in his colonial pursuits to marry Lucilla, who has discovered on the occasion of her father's death that she has no fortune because it has all been lost in a bank crash.[50] Together the two buy the run-down estate that originally belonged to the Marjoribanks family, and Lucilla ends the novel about to exercise her extraordinary managerial talents on her new tenants. This union has a peculiar double valence. On the one hand, it feels, as I argued in my introduction, like the kind of endogamous union that is typically associated with the rich woman. On the other, it has the emotional feel of marriage for love rather than money that is typically associated with the choice of the poor woman. It is as if Oliphant in concluding *Miss Marjoribanks* wants to have it both ways. It is not till her next Carlingford novel, written ten years later, that she will push the critique of the marriage plot that begins in "The Executor" to its logical conclusion and depict a protagonist who consciously chooses wealth over virtue.

Phoebe Junior and "Mental Property"

In *Phoebe Junior* (1876), Oliphant sets her rationally minded heroine's negotiations against a social backdrop that emphasizes much more fully than *Miss Marjoribanks* the social fracture that became increasingly visible in the latter decades of the nineteenth century, "the division between the business and the professional classes" (Perkin 83). Perkin has described this as "an important vertical barrier, not always conscious or watertight, but in some ways more significant than the division between upper and lower middle class" (*Rise* 83). As Oliphant shows in her depictions of the interactions between the millionaire entrepreneur Copperhead and Sir Robert Dorset, an impoverished baronet who is a distant relative of Copperhead's second wife, this barrier extends from the middle to the upper classes, including the boundary between commercial and landed wealth that is so rigorously enforced in Anthony Trollope's novels.[51] In Oliphant's novel the patterns of thinking that exclude the commercial classes are represented as a form of "class racism" (Bourdieu 338). Sir Robert agrees to attend a ball at the Copperheads' "as a man . . . might consent to go to the Cannibal Islands, to see how the savages comported themselves" (60). Later, the Anglican minister the Reverend Mr. May invites the Dissenting granddaughter of a grocer to tea "out of curiosity, as, being about to be brought in contact with some South Sea Islander or Fijian" (212).[52]

The tension between material and aesthetic values is established early in the novel as Copperhead and Sir Robert Dorset stand in front of a Turner painting that Copperhead has purchased because the entrepreneur "was fond of costly and useless things; he liked them for their cost, with an additional zest in his sense of the huge vulgar use and profit of most things in his own life. . . . It swelled his personal importance to think he was able to hang up thousands of pounds, so to speak, on his walls" (47).[53] To counteract the preeminence of wealth, Dorset boasts of his own more modest possession, "a bit of vague Italian scenery, mellow and tranquil, . . . a true 'Wilson,' bought by an uncle of Sir Robert's, who had been a connoisseur, from the Master himself, in the very country where it was painted" (348).[54] *Phoebe Junior* marks a crossover between these two realms by identifying its heroine, who comes from the commercial classes, as a connoisseur who can recognize the beauty of an embroidered shawl, "an Indian rarity which . . . no one had used or thought of till Phoebe's artistic eye fell upon it" (172).

The novel then asks what power her cultivated taste might have to overcome the class barriers described in its opening chapters, a prejudice she herself feels when she returns to the small town where her mother was born and is disgusted, as she places her arm gingerly on what she conceives of as the "greasy" sleeve (129) of her grocer grandfather.[55] As Phoebe explains to Horace Northcote, the Dissenting minister newly hired by the Carlingford congregation, "To be educated in another sphere and brought down to this, is hard. One cannot feel the same for one's relations; and yet one's poor little bit of education, one's petty manners, what are these to interfere with blood relationships? And to keep everybody down to the condition in which they were born, why, that is the old way" (166).[56] Going down to Carlingford, Phoebe is for the first time outside the world in which she was raised, experiencing the moment when, as Mill argued, "we cease to be merely members of our own families, and begin to have intercourse with the world; that is, when the teaching has continued longest in one direction, and has not commenced in any other direction" (*Dissertations and Discussions* 113). This transition is crucial to the formation of the liberal self, which requires the individual to have sympathies wider that those that connect him to "his party, his sect, his church, his class of society" (*On Liberty* 24).

In Oliphant's novel, Phoebe both experiences such sympathies and engenders them in others, as she forces Northcote to confront the Anglican Reginald May, a man Northcote publicly attacked at a chapel prayer meeting. Described as like a child who puts two stag beetles face to face to watch them fight, Phoebe invites both Northcote and May to tea at her grandfather's house. Here the novel emphasizes Phoebe's cultivation as she displays her interest in a quarterly review essay she offers Northcote and in her grandmother's antique Wedgwood tea service, whose beauty she praises to Reginald. She turns out to have gotten it wrong; the Anglican is a connoisseur of reviews, the Dissenter of china. But she knows the pleasures of both kinds of appreciation, a talent she displays by playing the most complex of Beethoven sonatas, a piece that Reginald recognizes is beyond his comprehension.[57] Her intervention leads not just to a polite social interaction between the two men but to Northcote visiting Reginald at the college living

Northcote himself had decried as a sinecure in a public prayer meeting at the Dissenting chapel.

In these scenes Oliphant works out the implications of Mill's insistence that "opposing views must . . . be brought 'into real contact with [one's] own mind,' and this can occur only if one '[hears] them from persons who actually believe them'" (Anderson 17). As Northcote hears Reginald explain the source of his own faith, the Dissenter for the first time experiences the appeal of a fifteenth-century chapel.[58] For a moment the two "stood together . . . under the vaulted roof, both young, in the glory of their days, both with vague noble meanings in them, which they knew so poorly how to carry out. They meant everything that was fine and great" (256). The position that Reginald holds, as warden for a college founded by a medieval corporation is the kind of endowment that Mill, somewhat surprisingly, endorses in the first essay in *Dissertations and Discussions*: "These endowments . . . should be sacredly preserved for the purposes of spiritual culture; using that expression in its primitive meaning, to denote the culture of the inward man—his moral and intellectual well-being, as distinguished from the mere supply of his bodily wants" (30). We can, perhaps, better understand the implications of Mill's argument if we link it to the assertion that Durkheim made more than thirty years after the publication of Mill's essay, when he described the medieval corporation as the perfect model for a professional society: "The corporation was a collegiate religious body" in which "a commonality of interest replaced ties of blood" (xl).

So, too, in Oliphant's novel, the mutual appreciation of the spiritual culture represented by the chapel surmounts social differences that seem grounded in blood, the ones that make Anglicans and Dissenters see one another as of a different race. The novel proceeds to show how easily Dissenters and Anglicans can interact, as the Mays begin to entertain Phoebe in their home, and a hybrid society forms round her, which includes Reginald and his sister Ursula and the Dissenters Horace Northcote and Clarence Copperhead. Phoebe brings an urban sophistication to Carlingford.[59] For Mill, the function of such cultivation is to foster a community that ignores the fractures that normally separate social sects: "The 'others' with whom we have to identify have, ideally, to be seen as coextensive with humanity at large . . . , and not with any of those smaller units of kinship or locality to which the feelings more naturally attach themselves" (Collini 72). In Oliphant's novel, under Phoebe's influence, "the Parsonage became gradually the centre of a little society. . . . They came together, fortuitously, blown to one centre by the merest winds of circumstance, out of circles totally different and unlike" (281).[60] The characters feel briefly that "their little atoms of individual life had all united for the moment into one sunshiny and broad foundation, on which everything seemed to rest with that strange sense of stability and continuance" (294).[61]

Yet Oliphant qualifies the idealism of these moments by insisting that the aims of the extraordinary individual who brings about such social unions are both altruistic and self-interested. That dual motivation is introduced through the marriage plot, as both Reginald and Clarence are drawn to Phoebe, offering her the choice between virtue and wealth, which here corresponds to a choice between the noncommercial and commercial halves of the middle or upper classes. Caught between a suitor who possess what Bourdieu calls "cultural capital" and his philistine opposite who possesses vulgar wealth, Phoebe understands the implications of her position. She recognizes that in Reginald "perhaps she had never touched so close upon a higher kind of existence, and perhaps never again might have the opportunity" (343), but she still opts for the wealthy Clarence. This choice was particularly offensive to contemporary reviewers; the *Athenaeum*, for example, argued that "a perfect lady would hardly have gone in for the prize"; "Phoebe is not of a high moral type" ("*Phoebe Junior*" 851).

Phoebe herself understands that she does not conform to the expectations of marriage plot. Imagining Clarence Copperhead's family reacting to the possibility that he might marry her, she thinks

> even his mother, who was a romantic woman, would not see any romance in it, if it was she, Phoebe, who was the poor girl whom he wanted to marry. Ursula might have been different, who was a clergyman's daughter, and consequently a lady by prescriptive right. But herself, Tozer's granddaughter, Tom Tozer's niece, fresh from the butter-chop, as it were, and redolent of that petty trade, which big trade ignores, as much as the greatest aristocrat does. (302)[62]

Oliphant's reviewers argued that Phoebe's choice of Copperhead might have been redeemable if Oliphant had represented it in more sentimental terms. The *Spectator* observed that

> a trace of liking for young Copperhead, or of respect, or even of bedazzlement at his position, would so have redeemed the over-judicious young woman who, neither blind nor beguiled, but only true to her own narrow theory of life, accepts him against her better nature, and in accepting him succeeds in all her objects, and lives and dies unrepentant and content. ("*Phoebe Junior*" 770)

As the critic for the *Saturday Review* commented, "Phoebe . . . set[s] not her heart, but the mammon within her head, upon a lout of a lover" (*"Phoebe Junior"*113). But Oliphant's point is that Phoebe's choice of Clarence is rational. Deciding she has "nothing to appeal to heaven about, or to seek counsel from Nature upon" (300), she takes "counsel with herself, the person most interested" (300).[63]

In Oliphant's novel, though individuals have emerged into a world of socially relative choices, there remains a version of the differentiation that is enacted by the marriage plot when it separates virtue from wealth. That separation is represented not as an opposition between materialism and something outside it but as a forking within the material realm. Phoebe chooses Clarence because he meant "wealth (which she dismissed in its superficial aspect as something meaningless and vulgar, but accepted in its higher aspect as an almost necessary condition of influence)" (300). Mill effects a similar bifurcation in defending utilitarianism against the accusation of worldliness. He asks whether "worldly" implies "what is commonly meant when the world is used as a reproach—an undue regard to interest in the vulgar sense, our wealth, power, social position, and the like, our command over agreeable outward objects, and over the opinion and good offices of other people?" (*Dissertations and Discussions* 123). This passage identifies the attributes of vulgarity that are typically associated with the rich woman in the novel and, as in the marriage plot, Mill seeks to create a split between good and bad or higher and lower. Defending an elevated version of worldliness, he argues "that our actions take place in the world; that their consequences are produced in the world; that we have been placed in the world; and that there, if anywhere, we must earn a place in heaven" (124).[64]

We might remember Anthony Trollope and the eulogizers of Lady Frances Waldegrave making a distinction between being worldly and worldly-wise. The difference between Trollope and Oliphant is that while Trollope attempts to underscore two similar but slightly different concepts and words, Oliphant wants readers to feel the axis of difference within the word that has typically been used in the pejorative sense to indicate something vulgar. Her narrator asks of Phoebe's decision to marry Clarence, "Was she mercenary or worldly-minded in her choice?" and then answers, "it would be hard to say so" (406), arguing elsewhere that "other feelings mingled in Phoebe's worldliness. . . . And yet while it was not pure worldliness, much less was it actual love which moved her" (337). Phoebe is worldly, but that worldliness could, Oliphant's novel suggests, be cleansed of the taint of vulgarity. To Phoebe, Clarence represents money in its higher aspect because of what he will enable her to accomplish: "Yes; she could put him into parliament, and keep him there. She could thrust him forward (she believed) to the front of affairs. He would be as good as a profession, a position, a great work to Phoebe" (300). In this moment professionalism emerges as an explicit category in Oliphant's novel, a social category that, as I argued initially, she will explore in more detail in *Hester* and *Kirsteen*.

In both *Phoebe Junior* and *Miss Marjoribanks*, she is less interested in the concrete particulars of professional behavior than in the ideological crossover it makes possible between the two courses that have been represented as polar opposites in the traditional marriage plot: wealth and virtue. Oliphant stresses that through the image of the professional it becomes possible to imagine a way in which, as Magali Sarfatti Larson has argued, one might make "virtue pay"(59). This professional stance is the means by which money can be imagined as purified of the taint of vulgarity that had dogged it since at least the period of Adam Smith and Jane Austen. In *Phoebe Junior* Oliphant makes her most incisive points about professionalism not through direct descriptions of her heroine but through the parallels between that self-interested figure and a character who seems to espouse a set of values absolutely opposed to hers, the Anglican curate Reginald May, who represents the choice of virtue that Phoebe does not make when she chooses Clarence Copperhead. Like Phoebe, Reginald is offered the choice between an abstract ideal of virtue and the reality of wealth when he is pressured not to accept the job of being warden of a college because it is a sinecure. And, like Phoebe, he makes the pragmatic choice and accepts the position he is offered.[65]

Though almost 150 pages separate Reginald's acceptance of his job and Phoebe's choice of a husband, readers might, if only subliminally, recognize the similarities in the way Oliphant characterizes the two decisions. Phoebe chooses Clarence because he "would be a career. . . . She did not think of it humbly like this, but with a big capital—a Career" (300). Reginald chooses the position at the college because it offers "'a nice old-fashioned house all ready for you to step into, and an income,' cried Ursula, her tone deepening to mark the capital letter; 'an Income quite sure and steady'" (160). While Phoebe seems to have made the worldly choice by marrying the wealthy Copperhead and Reginald the unworldly one by dedicating himself to his parishioners, Reginald chooses an income and Phoebe a career. He needs money in order to be able to work; she needs work in order to redeem the Copperheads' money from its vulgarity.[66] This combination of career and income is what constitutes professionalism. As Reginald's case makes clear, payment in these circumstances is acceptable because the professional voluntarily follows the calling made possible by his salary.[67]

Perkin has argued that the concept of the professional that crystallized in the 1880s depended on a "belief in what we call contingent as opposed to absolute property, that is in property rights contingent upon the performance of some justifying service" (*Rise* 123). In Oliphant's novel the key term in this description, "service," is critical not just to the way Reginald's choice of a sinecure is made acceptable but also to the way the novel invites us to read the action Phoebe takes at the story's climax. In scenes that parallel the ones in *Miss Marjoribanks* where Lucilla brings together Mr. Cavendish and his accuser, Phoebe intervenes in the angry confrontation between her grandfather and the Reverend Mr. May. Like Lucilla, Phoebe acts professionally at this juncture, relying entirely on her own judgment in deciding whether a secret should be revealed or concealed.[68]

In *Phoebe Junior* the stakes are considerably higher than in *Miss Marjoribanks* since the secret in question is actually a crime, the fact that May, in want of money because of his inability to live within his means, has forged Tozer's name to a bill of exchange, thinking that he would be able to repay it before the grocer ever knew. The bill has fallen due and May, in a rush of insane fear at the thought of his guilt, is confronted by Tozer in the full flush of his anger at the misuse of what is most valuable to him, his professionally honorable name. But in *Phoebe Junior*, as in *Miss Marjoribanks*, the rationally distanced heroine views the errant action of a single character as not worthy of official punishment. As the narrator comments, Phoebe sees the forged bill and recognizes May's handwriting, but "The copy of her grandfather's signature did not wound her moral sense" (372).[69] This freedom from moral outrage allows Phoebe to protect May, by seizing the note, the only proof of his crime, and negotiating to keep his actions hidden.[70] As she makes this decision, Phoebe feels the freedom Reginald experiences when he accepts the job as warden of the college and thinks of himself as "independent! and with an income, without which independence is a mockery—free to go where he pleased, buy what he liked, spend his time as best seemed to him, with a 'position' of his own" (188). Phoebe

> felt like a man who has been out all night, who has his own future all in his hands, nobody having any right to explanation or information about what he may choose to do, or to expect from him anything beyond what he himself may please to give. Very few people are in this absolutely free, position, but this was how Phoebe represented it to herself, having, like other girls, unbounded belief in the independence and freedom possessed by men. (375–76)

This freedom allows her to remain unmoved by her grandfather's rage and to force him to confront rather than to punish May. As Mill argued, "it is not on the impassioned partisan, it is on the calmer and more disinterested bystander, that this collision of opinions works it salutary effect" (quoted in Anderson 18). This argument revives Adam Smith's concept of the impartial spectator; in Mill, however, that figure is no longer part of the psyche but a social being, the cultivated self that actively intervenes, forcing the participants to restrain the self-interest that makes them opponents rather than coparticipants in a social whole. In Mill, as in Smith, the growth of commercial society necessitates such disinterested action: "One of the effects of a high state of civilization . . . is . . . the concentration of [energy] within the narrow sphere of an individual's money-getting pursuits" (*Dissertations and Discussions* 143). In the scene where Tozer confronts May, Phoebe intervenes to force an individual whose whole life has been devoted to money to acknowledge the suffering of another: "The sight of this superior being, thus humbled, maddened, gazing at him with wild terror and agony, more eloquent than any supplication, struck poor old Tozer to the very soul" (400).

Refusing to act on the desire for financial and judicial recompense, Tozer burns the forged note, thereby freeing May from prosecution. Phoebe's actions make her grandfather's self-interest dissolve, as she teaches him to act in accordance with "the professional view that the rights of persons and the welfare of the community came before the rights of property" (Perkin *Rise* 140). Tozer never fully grasps the precise sequence of events that led to the burning of the note; he "got hazy about it after a while[,] . . . though he knew that he had done Mr. May a wonderful service" (418). Phoebe thinks of her actions as a service not just to May but also to Reginald, a means of recompensing "him a little, poor fellow, for the heart he had given her, which she could not accept, yet could not be ungrateful for" (401). And, as this language suggests, professionalism links virtue and wealth because the professional performs a service and teaches others higher values but also understands that such acts merit compensation.

Phoebe receives her compensation in the scenes that parallel the ones in which Tozer forgives May in which she confronts the novel's other avatar of the single-minded pursuit of wealth, Clarence Copperhead's father, who threatens to cast off his son if Clarence proceeds to marry Phoebe. In the interchange between the two, Phoebe proves herself, like a true professional, both interested in financial reward and unwilling to abandon her values in pursuit of that goal. While she consciously chose Clarence for pragmatic reasons, because his wealth offered her a career, she insists that she will stick by him whether he is wealthy or not. In this scene, as in the one with Tozer, Phoebe's professional detachment forces the figure that embodies wealth to allay his passion and behave in a manner that acknowledges values other than pure materialism.

In accepting Clarence's marriage to Phoebe, Copperhead recognizes that he will acquire something equivalent to if not better than wealth: the "human capital" (M. Cohen 40) that professionals offer. As he tells his friends,

> Money is money . . . but brains is brains, all the same—we can't get on without 'em—and when you want to make a figure in the world, Sir, buy a few brains if they fall in your way—that's my style. I've done with stupid ones up till now; but when I see there's a want of a clever one, I ain't such a fool as to shut my eyes to it. They cost dear, but I'm thankful to say I can afford that, ay, and a good deal more. (413)

This passage brings together the two elements Mill defines as "of importance and influence among mankind: the one is property; the other, powers and acquirements of the mind" (*Dissertations and Discussions* 132). Making the intellectual half of this pair all the more materialist by using the word "brain" instead of "mind," Oliphant has the character nineteenth-century readers found to be the most vulgar in her novel articulate the logic that underwrites professional self-justification.[71] For, as Perkin has argued, "The professional concept rests as much on a scarce resource as the landed or capitalist, but instead of controlling land or capital it sets out to control the supply of expertise" (*Rise* 378). This is the expertise Phoebe possesses and for which she is recompensed, through her approved marriage to Clarence once his father explicitly identifies her skills as having a monetary value.

This marriage also marks the novel's generational solution to the problem of the differences between the commercial and intellectual factions of both the middle and the upper classes. For the Tozer/Beecham and Copperhead families exemplify the *Buddenbrooks* model of social advancement in which "the first generation sought money; the second, born to money, sought civic position; the third, born to comfort and status, sought the life of music" (Gagnier *Insatiability* 114). In the case of Tozer and Copperhead Senior, Oliphant represents even the first generation, the one that made money, as possessing what she calls "the hunger of wealth for that something above wealth" (58). While neither Copperhead nor Tozer can satisfy this need directly, later generations are able to access the intellectual realm from which the commercial entrepreneur is excluded in his own person.[72] The Tozers move from a grandfather who is grocer to a son-in-law who is a Dissenting minister who leaves his congregation in a country town to establish a parish in London where he can provide his daughter the education her mother lacked.[73] Oliphant charts a similar pattern in the Copperhead family when Mr. Copperhead selects for his second wife an impoverished member of the gentry classes, the governess of the children from his first marriage. The son of this second marriage, Clarence, differs from the children of his first marriage in that he is sent to Oxford and is not expected to work.

This treatment reflects the family's movement away from "the capitalist ideal of active property" (380) that Perkin has identified as characteristic of the shifts in thinking associated with the rise of professional ideals in the latter half of the nineteenth century. That process will be completed in Clarence's and Phoebe's children who will, presumably, bear no traces of either of their parent's commercial origins three generations back. This movement toward collapsing the distance between what have been traditionally defined as distinctly separated classes is how Anthony Trollope has Plantagenet Palliser define liberalism in *The Prime Minister*: "The Liberal, if he have any fixed idea at all, must, I think, have conceived the idea of lessening distances,—of bringing the coachman and the duke nearer together,—nearer and nearer, till a millennium shall be reached" (2.265).[74] But we might note here how much easier it is for Palliser to imagine the collapse of the distance between himself and those lower on the social ladder than it is to imagine collapsing the vertical barrier that separates him from the vulgarity of the grocer and the entrepreneur.

Mill is a little more explicit about the class movements of the period, arguing in *Dissertations and Discussions* that "with respect to knowledge and intelligence, it is the truism of the age, that the masses, both of the middle and even of the working classes, are treading upon the heels of their superiors" (137–38).[75] This is the process of assimilation that Oliphant's novel charts, but it was a process her contemporary critics deplored. As the reviewer for the *Saturday Review* put it,

> She finds an easy amusement in bringing together by their ears men of different religious creeds and professions, and subduing them to uniformity by their weaknesses. A sort of unity indeed is established by this means; if people do not think all alike, at the end of the book they are all alike, which comes to much the same thing. And it is the triumph of woman to bring about this practical unanimity. ("*Phoebe Junior*" 112)

By creating a narrative that represents the implications of Mill's thinking at the level of fiction, Oliphant could and did trigger readers' indignation at what her characters do and choose; she points to the aspects of Mill's philosophy that Victorian readers were least comfortable with (and that modern readers perhaps find troubling as well), in particular the wedding of materialism and the mind that was critical to his thinking.

Coda: Reviving "Disinterested Culture and Intellectual Liberty"

In order to see the effect of this negative critique on contemporaries or near contemporaries I want to look briefly at the role Oliphant plays in Virginia Woolf's *Three Guineas* (1938). Woolf's essay seems like a modernist continuation of the arguments made in Oliphant's novels; it considers the relation between women and the professions and is explicit that in order to understand that relation one must address the question of money. Writing between the two world wars, Woolf is more aware than her Victorian precursors of the penetration of economic values into every aspect of society. As she comments midway through *Three Guineas*, "'Here we go round the mulberry tree, the mulberry tree, the mulberry tree,' and if we add, 'of property, of property, of property,' we shall fill in the rhyme without doing violence to the facts" (100). Nevertheless, despite Woolf's apparent openness, Oliphant enters Woolf's argument not as a fellow traveler, a colleague in the world of female professionals seeking to earn a salary, but as someone who pollutes art by writing for money. In a series of comments that echo *Phoebe Junior*, Woolf castigates Oliphant for selling her brain. This critical gesture allows Woolf to use Oliphant as a scapegoat in the process of "strip[ping]" art, literature, and education of the "money motive" (146) in order to reassert "disinterested culture and intellectual liberty" (140). Though *Three Guineas* seems comfortable addressing the vulgar question of money, in the end the essay works, almost violently, to disentangle the link between mind and property that Oliphant's novels had revealed at the heart of Mill's idea of the liberal subject.

Initially, Woolf seems to engage in an enterprise almost identical to the one undertaken in Oliphant's fictions, particularly if we read Oliphant's novels in relation to Anthony Trollope's. Woolf begins her consideration of women and property by acknowledging the influence exercised by figures like the fictional Lady Glencora Palliser or the real Lady Frances Waldegrave. The great political hostesses at the end of the nineteenth century were powerful: "Their famous houses and the parties that met in them play so large a part in the political memoirs of the time that we can hardly deny that English politics, even perhaps English wars, would have been different had those houses and those parties never existed" (19). But Woolf, like Oliphant, shifts the discussion of women's influence to the level of the middle rather than the upper classes. Traditionally, "the influential are the daughters of noblemen, not the daughters of educated men" (21). The question her essay raises is how and whether middle-class women might exercise social influence. This is, of course, the terrain of Oliphant's novels, whose heroines come, not like Trollope's, from the upper reaches of society, but from the middle classes. They are the daughters of doctors and Dissenting ministers, which is how Woolf identifies Oliphant herself; she is "an educated man's daughter, who earned her living by reading and writing. . . . With the proceeds she earned her living and educated her children" (139).

Both Oliphant and Woolf therefore have a stake in the influence that education or cultivation grants middle-class women within the domestic sphere of marriage and family and in the larger public sphere. Like Oliphant, Woolf acknowledges that the domestic activities women undertake are both implicitly professional and often entail some form of financial recompense. She explains, in terms that might remind us of the conclusion of *Phoebe Junior* that "the profession of marriage in the educated class is a highly paid one, since she has a right, a spiritual right, to half her husband's salary" (83). Shifting from the private to the public sphere, Woolf, like Oliphant, is extremely sensitive to the difference between men's and women's relations to professional salaries. Imagining that the male barrister with whom she is in dialogue might "object that to depend upon a profession is only another form of slavery" (23), she asks him to "recall the joy with which you received your first guinea for your first brief, and the deep breath of freedom that you drew when you realized that your days of dependence . . . were over" (23).

Here Woolf makes the same point as Oliphant when she describes Reginald May exulting in the freedom he feels at the idea of a salary. And, like Oliphant, Woolf works to deflate the male intellectual's sense that his educational accomplishments grant him a cultural status that is in some way different from the status granted by material possessions and accomplishments. As she tells her imagined interlocutor of his attire,

> If you will excuse the humble illustration, your dress fulfills the same function as the tickets in a grocer's shop. But, here, instead of saying, "This is margarine; this is pure butter; this is the finest butter in the market," it says "This man is a clever man—he is a Master of Arts; this man is a very clever man—he is a Doctor of Letters; this man is a most clever man—he is a Member of the Order of Merit." (29)

This reference to a grocer, and even to butter, almost deliberately echoes Oliphant's novel, in which the grocer Tozer is repeatedly characterized as a butter man. And in Woolf's essay, as in Oliphant's fiction, the aim of such invocations seems to be to collapse the distinction between the commercial and intellectual sides of English society, to recognize that the pursuit of commerce is not all that different from the pursuit of an education. As Woolf notes, "There can be no doubt of the enormous value that human beings place on education" (36).

Like Oliphant, she insists on linking the professions to money, arguing that "the professions are the only way in which we can earn money. Money is the only means by which we can achieve objects that are immensely desirable" (104). However, once Woolf acknowledges the potential link between money and desire, the tone of her writing shifts from the pragmatically ironic to highly moralistic, as she asks "the question we put to you, lives of the dead, is how can we enter the professions and yet remain civilized human beings?" (114). Having posed this question, Woolf turns to Oliphant as an example of how we enter professions and become vulgar. Asking her readers to browse a selection of Oliphant's voluminous work, the "novels, biographies, histories, handbooks of Florence and Rome, reviews, newspaper articles innumerable [that] came from her pen" (139), Woolf exclaims

> when you have done, examine the state of your mind, and ask yourself whether the reading has led you to respect disinterested culture and intellectual liberty. Has it not on the contrary, smeared your mind and dejected your imagination, and led you to despise the fact that Mrs. Oliphant sold her brain, her very admirable brain, prostituted her culture and enslaved her intellectual liberty in order that she might earn her living and educate her children? (139)

The image of selling one's brain, which may have come to Woolf from *Phoebe Junior*, was so powerful she returns to it later in the essay, arguing that "to sell a brain is worse than to sell a body, for when the body seller has sold her momentary pleasure she takes good care that the matter should end there. But when a brain seller has sold her brain, its anaemic, vicious, and diseased progeny are let loose upon the world to infect and corrupt and sow the seeds of disease in others" (142).[76] Elaine Hadley has pointed out that "mid-Victorians generally were loathe" to reference "mental property" ("The Past Is a Foreign Country" 11). Woolf's comments convey the loathing implicit in the word "loathe," the visceral disgust that makes Oliphant and those like her who sell their minds into something very close to the image of Error in Spenser's *The Fairie Queene* spewing forth books as diseased progeny. The disgust Woolf articulates here is concentrated in the act of selling one's brain, an act that Oliphant's novel has identified as central to professional activity. Spewing Oliphant out with the disgust Julia Kristeva associates with impulse to vomit, Woolf rescues the values that Oliphant's text ironically but intentionally locates in the granddaughter of a butcher who represents to an Oxford-educated clergyman the "still higher world of culture and knowledge, where genius, and art, and intellect stood instead of rank and riches" (275).[77]

When Woolf opens her essay by telling her barrister interlocutor that "we both come of what, in this hybrid age when, though birth is mixed, classes still remain fixed, it is convenient to call the educated class" (4), she acknowledges the hybridity and mixed origins that Oliphant's *Phoebe Junior* also addresses, but in the end Woolf insists that the educated classes remain inviolately separate from that mixture. When she addresses the professions and talks about their inevitable relation to money, she seeks to distinguish one realm by asserting that "the profession of literature differs, it would seem, from all the other professions" (136). The problem with Oliphant's work is that it refuses such differences. Her novels insist that the educated classes do sell themselves for a salary. Oliphant's autobiography, which was the immediate trigger for Woolf's disgust, insists that literature is, in fact, a profession like any other. When Woolf argues that these texts "smear" the reader's "mind," she is presenting another version of the image of Oliphant selling her brains. In both cases the mind is imagined as coming in contact with a form of matter or materialism that contaminates or pollutes its intellectual status. Oliphant's novels moved toward acknowledging the material rewards of intellectual labor, but Woolf's modernist text works to purify the intellectual realm and even money of grosser aspects. Simmel argues in *The Philosophy of Money* that in the advanced stages of capitalism's development money, "after having made the purely intellectual professions possible" succeeds "in supporting . . . the production of purely intellectual values" (312). While Oliphant acknowledges the importance of money in enabling professionalism, modernists like Woolf and, as we will see in the next chapter, Henry James seek a fictional form that allows money to be represented as a purely intellectual value.

CHAPTER FIVE

HENRY JAMES AND THE END(S) OF THE MARRIAGE PLOT

The more it is really money in its essential significance, the less need there is for it to be money in a material sense.

Georg Simmel, *The Philosophy of Money*

In the middle of the preface to *The Golden Bowl* James describes the anxiety he felt about having to revise his own work when he was preparing the New York edition, explaining that he came to terms with that process by thinking about the meaning of the word "revise." He reminded himself that "to revise is to see, or to look over, again—which means in the case of a written thing neither more nor less than to re-read. I had attached to it, in a brooding spirit, the idea of re-writing" (xvi).[1] This comment sums up, I would argue, James's relation to his literary precursors as well as to his own earlier work; his novels prove him to be a brilliant rereader of the fiction that preceded his, particularly of the novel of manners. Aiming to rewrite a narrative pattern that had structured courtship narratives throughout the nineteenth century would, as James's comments suggest, have burdened him with a creative task it was almost impossible to bear. Conceiving of himself instead as reseeing or rereading the tradition that preceded his eases James's mind; it allows him to write simultaneously as a literary critic and a novelist. In *The Spoils of Poynton*, *The Wings of the Dove*, and *The Golden Bowl* James undertakes a sequential rethinking or rereading of the marriage plot he had inherited from Austen and Trollope.[2] Focusing on the contrast between the rich and the poor woman, James looks back in order to rethink the implications of an opposition of values his own novels prove is central both to the moral universe of the Victorian novel and to the drive that binds plots together into coherent wholes.

In the preface to *The Golden Bowl* James represents the author who revises or resees old material as resembling someone looking at a field of snow who sees the path that has already been made and finds himself "naturally falling into another, which might sometimes indeed more or less agree with the original tracks, but might most often, or very nearly, break the surface in other places" (xiv). In rethinking the patterns of the marriage plot, James starts out in *The Spoils of Poynton* following the path set out by his precursors, with its easy contrast between the rich and the poor woman. But as he writes his way through that plot in the novels that follow, James begins to fall into other patterns that break the surface of the literary tradition he engages and allow him to explore the subtexts of a structure whose implications had seemed obvious. When James asks how we can be in touch with "our richest and hugest inheritance of imaginative prose" (xx–xxi) and answers that "our relation" to the past "is essentially traceable, and in that fact abides, we feel, the incomparable luxury of the artist" (xxv), he is presenting his own novels as reading or tracking traces of the past.

For the artist, it is crucial "not to *be* disconnected, for the tradition of behaviour, he has but to feel that he is not; by his lightest touch the whole chain of relation and responsibility is reconstituted" (xxv, emphasis in the original). Seeking connection with the traditions that preceded him, James turns to the familiar form of the marriage plot. But, as the terms "chain" and "relation" suggest, he invokes it as a structure, a set of elements linked together. The sequence of *The Spoils of Poynton*, *The Wings of the Dove*, and *The Golden Bowl* charts the "responsibility" various characters bear for the unfolding of that structure. But in the end, responsibility lies not with the actors but with the structure itself. In these novels, "it's as if the geometry of human relations *implied* what we call human feelings into existence" (Bersani 148, emphasis in the original). In the opening pages of the preface to *The Spoils of Poynton*, James argues that "life being all inclusion and confusion, and art being all discrimination and selection, the latter, in search of the hard latent *value* with which it alone is concerned, sniffs round the mass as instinctively and unerringly as a dog suspicious of some buried bone" (xxxix–xl, emphasis in the original). The difference, James's comments imply, between art and life is that the former must exclude something in order to create the semblance of order.

This is, of course, the way anthropologists understand the rules that govern marital exchange; those rules impose cultural order on what would otherwise be an undifferentiated mass of natural material. They do so by defining some individuals as excluded from the range of possible spouses available for marriage. For James, life "is capable . . . of nothing but splendid waste," while art "saves and hoards and 'banks,'" shaping its materials into a "sublime economy" (*Spoils of Poynton* xl). Defining art, like kinship, as a method of discrimination and selection, James asks, "What are the signs for our guidance, what the primary laws for a saving selection?" (xl). I have argued throughout this book that in the nineteenth-century novel the marriage plot functions as just such a saving law of selection. It teaches readers and characters to discriminate between desirable and undesirable marriage partners and creates a structure that seems to allow us to dig up the latent aesthetic value that is buried, hidden by the more manifest material values presented by a commercial culture.

But in his late novels James will demonstrate that the capacity that allows the reader to appreciate aesthetic value, taste, is itself formed by the structure of the stories that validate it. He argues at the end of the preface to *The Golden Bowl* that in his own work "'old' matter is . . . re-accepted, re-tasted, exquisitely re-assimilated and re-enjoyed" (xvii). As a result there is a "re-assertion of value" that allows one "to retrace the growth of one's 'taste,' as our fathers used to say" (xvii). In attaching the prefix "re" to the verbs "accept," "taste," "assimilate," "enjoy" and "trace" and setting the word "taste" off in quotation marks, James marks the fact these concepts are not unthinkingly part of his narrative; they are consciously engaged and rethought. In the novels I consider here, James returns to the marriage plot in order to retrace the ways his literary forefathers (and foremothers) used that pattern to inculcate models of taste.

In *The Spoils of Poynton* he is particularly interested in the links between the rich and the poor woman and bad and good taste, arguing in his notes to the novel that "there would be a particular type and taste of the wife the son would have chosen—a wife out of a Philistine, a tasteless, a hideous house" (*Notebooks* 79). Evoking the negative qualities of the wealthy woman, he imagines "the mother having fixed on a girl after her own heart for the son to marry," a girl "with the same exquisite tastes that *she* has" (*Notebooks* 80, emphasis in the original), a girl "who hadn't a penny in the world . . . whose only treasure was her subtle mind" (*Spoils of Poynton* 8). Fleda Vetch, the poor woman, then "discovers a community of taste—of passion, of sensibility and suffering" (*Notebooks* 80) with the mother of the man she would wish to marry. But in *The Spoils of Poynton* the contrast between the rich and the poor woman is not a deep structure that orders the narrative but a pattern imposed by one character on others. It is the hero's mother who insists on defining Fleda as the opposite of her wealthy rival and on teaching her son to value the poor rather than the rich woman.

The difference between *The Spoils of Poynton* and the novels that follow it shows that once James has acknowledged the extrinsic or imposed nature of the contrast between the rich and the poor woman, he is able to reverse the moral and aesthetic polarities typically inscribed through that opposition. In *The Wings of the Dove* he creates a rich woman who is associated with immateriality, the wealthy Milly Theale, who is an "heiress in moral principle no less than in material fact" (Rahv 229), and a poor woman who is associated with the grasping materialism typically invoked through the rich woman.[3] These characterizations shift the marriage plot 180 degrees from what it was at the beginning of the nineteenth century, when Jane Austen associated the rich woman with the crassness, materiality, and vulgarity of wealth and the poor woman with the aesthetic values that oppose those material- ist drives. James's reversal was peculiarly unsettling because it threatened to reveal how counterintuitive the original configuration was. Why would the rich woman be associated with avidity or the desire for wealth and the poor woman with an op- posite set of values? Surely it makes more sense, as James shows in *The Wings of the Dove*, for an unpropertied woman to feel the attraction of money and a proper- tied one to find herself above its exigencies? Read in light of James's late novel, the scapegoating of the rich woman in earlier versions of the marriage plot looks like a form of wishful thinking, a way of imaginatively limiting the impact of wealth by associating money's negative influence with those who already possess it.

To refuse this easy linkage and associate the desire for wealth with the novel's romantic heroine and aesthetic purity with her rich rival was to undo the comfort- able ethical certainty of the novel of manners, to create what readers experienced as "a diabolical world, determined by values, but with the signs reversed" (Simmel *Philosophy of Money* 59). As Henry's brother William commented after first read- ing *The Wings of the Dove*,

> What shall I say of a book constructed on a method which so belies everything that *I* acknowledge as law? You've reversed every traditional canon of story telling . . . and have created a new *genre littéraire* which I can't help think- ing perverse, but in which you nevertheless *succeed* for I read with interest to the end . . . and all with unflagging curiosity to know what the upshot might become. (Gard 317, emphasis in the original)

William's reaction suggests how fully readers had come to experience the structure of the marriage plot as providing a set of laws that needed to be followed in order for the novel to make moral and aesthetic sense. In reversing the valences of those laws by making the rich woman a center of moral value and her poor antithesis the locus of vulgar desires, James's novel overturns the structure that gave meaning to the novelistic world as nineteenth-century readers knew it.

Such a representation is perverse because it reveals that the familiar traits that readers would recognize as traditionally associated with the rich and the poor woman are not inherent, or what James calls in the preface to *The Golden Bowl* "value intrinsic" (vii). They are positions in a conceptual system in which it is their opposition that allows one to be elevated over the other.[4] In representing the values endorsed by the marriage plot as relative, James's novels reflect the conceptual changes that were taking place in the moment he was writing, when economic value was itself no longer experienced as absolute.[5] The contemporary writer who wrote most extensively about this changed perception was Georg Simmel, the writer who described modern society as a diabolical world where values have their signs reversed. But, for Simmel, the key development of modern culture is not the reversal but the relativity of value. As he explains in *The Philosophy of Money*, the process of economic exchange means that value inheres not in objects or subjects but in the relation between them: "Both elements presuppose each other in their existence: neither would have any objective meaning or intellectual interest if the other did not stand in opposition to it" (111). In modern culture, "the essence of objects are transposed into regulative principles which are only points of view in the progress of knowledge" (110).[6]

James's late novels explore the developments Simmel traces, as wealth is experienced as so detached from substance and the material world of objects that it becomes entirely disembodied.[7] In Simmel's words, "Money is involved in the general development which in every domain of life and in every sense strives to dissolve substance into free-floating processes" (168).[8] Though the abstractness of late Jamesian style has typically been read as detaching his novels from their economic and historical contexts, that abstraction, in fact, reflects the gradual change in the perception of money that I have been tracing over the course of this book. The peculiar fluidity of James's late novels marks the end point of that narrative of increasing abstraction and the novel's entrance into the modern world described by Simmel. Ironically, then, in associating the heiresses with immateriality rather than engrossment, James is both reconfiguring the marriage plot and conforming to it. Even in his late novels the rich woman continues to function as she has from Austen onward: as an index of the changing contemporaneous perception of money.

James uses the opposition between the rich and the poor woman to contrast the appeal of money as an abstraction to the sensuality of material objects.[9] While the heiress who possesses enormous amounts of wealth is a disembodied figure, the poor woman who is her rival both feels and embodies the quasi-sexual appeal of things.[10] When Kate Croy moves in with her wealthy Aunt Maud, she sees as she had never seen before how material things spoke to her. She saw, and she blushed to see, that if, in contrast with some of its old aspects, life now affected her as a dress successfully "done up," this was exactly by reason of the trimmings and lace, was a matter of ribbons and silk and velvet. She had a dire accessibility to pleasure from such sources. She liked the charming quarters her aunt had assigned her—liked them literally more than she had in all her other days liked anything. (19)

In using the contrast between the poor and the rich woman to evoke the tension between objects and the abstraction of money, James was working along the same lines as Simmel, whose version of Adam Smith's choice between wealth and virtue is a "choice between the totality of material goods and the totality of ideal goods" (*Philosophy of Money* 216).

But Simmel complicates this choice in two ways. First, he insists that, given such a choice, individuals would have to opt for the material over the ideal: "We should probably be obliged to choose the first, because to renounce it would be to negate life" (216). Second, he insists that in this opposition there is no realm of virtue separate from wealth. Equating the totality of ideal goods with the abstraction of money, he argues that individuals are faced with a choice between "money and concrete objects of value; a choice between the objects as a whole and money as a whole" (216).[11] Presenting this choice in *The Portrait of a Lady* (1881), James experimented with the plot structure that he would develop at greater length in *The Wings of the Dove* and *The Golden Bowl*. All three novels tell the story of a man positioned between a former lover with no money and an American heiress who possesses incalculable wealth. In the famous first meeting between the impoverished Madame Merle and the soon-to-be wealthy Isabel Archer, James begins to establish the difference between the appeal of material objects and the abstractness of wealth.

Madame Merle tells Isabel that

there's no such thing as an isolated man or woman; we're each of us made up of some cluster of appurtenances. What shall we call our "self"? Where does it begin? where does it end? It overflows into everything that belongs to us—and then it flows back again. I know a large part of myself is in the clothes I choose to wear. I have a great respect for *things*! One's self—for other people—is one's expression of one's self. (175, emphasis in the original)[12]

Here the novel invokes an idea of "embeddedness," through which individuals experience themselves as surrounded by, anchored in, and defined by a set of objects. Anthony Giddens has contrasted such embeddedness to the idea of disembedding, "the 'lifting out' of social relations from local contexts of interaction and their restructuring across indefinite spans of time-space" (21). Such disembedding is characteristic of the experience of modern life as described by Simmel. In James's novels, it is a condition associated with American heiresses who resemble Isabel Archer when she insists that "nothing that belongs to me is any measure of me; everything's on the contrary a limit, a barrier, and a perfectly arbitrary one" (175).[13]

Another way to think of this contrast is in terms of the difference between the individual's relation to fashion, on the one hand, and art, on the other. James invokes this difference in elucidating the relation between the wealthy Milly Theale and the poor Kate Croy in *The Wings of the Dove*. Describing the two women together, the narrator explains that they explore "the London of shops and streets and suburbs oddly interesting to Milly, as well as of museums, monuments, 'sights,' oddly unfamiliar to Kate" (119). They find themselves "in the presence alike of old masters passive in their glory and of thoroughly new ones, the newest, who bristled restlessly with pins and brandished snipping shears" (120). The contrast James evokes here was integral to Simmel's thinking about the individual's relation to money and objects in modern culture. As Simmel argued, in fashion "we encounter . . . a close connection between the consciousness of personality and that of the material forms of life" ("Fashion" 545). In contrast, "the purity of art requires a distance, a release from emotion. This is the essential meaning of art, for the artist as well as for those who enjoy it, namely, that it raises us above the immediacy of its relation to ourselves and to the world" (*Philosophy of Money* 154).[14]

From Simmel's point of view, art, in detaching the viewer from the vulgar visceral immediacy of material world, functions like money as it is experienced in the modern world:

> The pure potentiality of money as a means is distilled in a general conception of power and significance which becomes effective as real power and significance for the owner of money. It is like the attraction of a work of art, which is produced not only by its content and the associated psychological reactions, but by all the accidental, individual and indirect complexes of feeling that it makes possible. (*Philosophy of Money* 218)

The implications of this contrast are perhaps clearest in *The Golden Bowl*, which opposes the concreteness and materiality of Charlotte Stant to the abstract conception of wealth espoused by the American art collector Adam Verver and his daughter Maggie. In that novel the poor woman is associated not just with the materiality of objects but also with money as a material object. When Charlotte Stant makes her first appearance in *The Golden Bowl*, Prince Amerigo, her former lover, sees in her "a likeness also to some long, loose silk purse, well filled with gold pieces, but having been passed, empty, through a finger-ring that held it together. It was as if, before she turned to him, he had weighed the whole thing in his open palm and even heard a little the chink of the metal" (35).[15]

In contrast, Maggie Verver and her father consciously think of their wealth as a disembodied mediator in the sense Simmel conceives it in *The Philosophy of Money*. Adam Verver knows worth is measured "not by mass or weight or vulgar immediate quantity" (125) but in "the comparison of fine object with fine object" (138). From his point of view, "There is a *reciprocal* determination of value by the objects" (*Philosophy of Money* 75, emphasis in the original).[16] Maggie knows that she functions as "a value, but as a value only for the clear negation of everything. She was their general sign, precisely, of unimpaired beatitude" (451). She is aware that as a rich woman, she is equivalent to that sign of general value, money itself. *The Golden Bowl* is the perfect novel with which to end my book. In it the moral and aesthetic implications of the contrast between the rich and the poor woman are consciously addressed, as the rich woman thinks through the implications of her position in the marriage plot in which she knows herself to be embedded.

"The Romantic Taste That Is in Us All": *The Spoils of Poynton*

In *The Spoils of Poynton* (1895) James returns to and rethinks the implications of the marriage plot before he plunges into reconfiguring its positions in *The Wings of the Dove* (1902) and *The Golden Bowl* (1904).[17] The rethinking he undertakes in *Spoils* amounts to representing the marriage plot not as an inherent structure but as an organizing principle that is imposed in order to achieve a particular end. He undermines that pattern's apparently neutral status as a revealer of virtue by showing instead how those who follow or believe in it have objects to gain as much as those who are condemned within it for their pursuit of wealth rather than virtue. Having insisted on the self-interested nature of the plot that seems to be about the overcoming of self-interest, James then moves to depict his characters consciously thinking about the implications of their positions within its structure. Indeed, that consciousness will in some sense prevent them from enacting the roles expected of them, precisely because they see the implications of the part they must play all too clearly. In particular, *Spoils* makes readers conscious of the point of view of Fleda Vetch, whose meditations on her own position anticipate the opening of *Wings of the Dove*, where Kate Croy thinks intensely about her fate in terms that echo the typical presentation of the poor heroine in the novel of manners. James must explore the consciousness of the poor woman before he can, in the middle of *Wings* and the second half of *The Golden Bowl*, turn to the consciousness of the rich one.

Through the opposition between the rich and the poor woman, *Spoils* contrasts two forms of taste that are conceived, as they were by the nineteenth-century novelists who preceded James, as based on the individual's negative or positive relation to engrossment and avidity. Mona Brigstock, the rich woman who is initially engaged to the novel's hero, is described as "the massive maiden at Waterbath," and "a magnificent dead weight" (137), who "expand[s] in the wrong place" (17) and whose "thick outline never wavered an inch" (137). Mona might remind us of the large-bodied heroine of Margaret Oliphant's *Miss Marjoribanks*, a novel James would probably have known, since he references Oliphant in his *Notes on Novelists*. But James's novel has none of the playfulness, comedy, and affection one feels in Oliphant's. Mona is relentlessly derided for her materialism; as one of the characters comments early on, "I hardly see Mona as the 'soul' of anything" (52).[18] These characterizations become particularly vicious as James associates the wealthy parvenu Brigstocks with the philistinism that Matthew Arnold decried in *Culture and Anarchy*.

This failure of taste is made visible in the objects collected in the family home, its stuffed birds in glass cases, shellacked furniture, and ponderous ornamental décor. Those objects are deliberately contrasted to the spoils of the novel's title, the objects the Gereths have collected that are on display at Poynton. The Victorian furnishings displayed at Waterbath underscore the Brigstocks' attempt to "pass off a gross avidity as a sense of the beautiful" (18), while the art objects at Poynton reveal "how little vulgar avidity had to do with [it]. It was not the crude love of possession; it was the need to be faithful to a trust and loyal to an idea" (30). It is Fleda's "submission to [the] perfect beauty" (13) of the objects at Poynton that makes her Mona's opposite. As Mrs. Gereth explains, "You feel as I do myself, what's good and true and pure" (21). But this statement also marks what differentiates *The Spoils of Poynton* from the novels of manners that precede it: the presence of Mrs. Gereth, a character that consciously articulates the plot's moral and aesthetic values.

As the novel opens, she is a guest at Waterbath because of her son's interest in Mona Brigstock. Conceiving of herself as "the only person in the house incapable of wearing in her preparation the horrible stamp of the same exceptional smartness that would be conspicuous in a grocer's wife" (1), Mrs. Gereth looks for someone to support her sense of her own exceptionalism and settles on Fleda.[19] In these scenes, Fleda effectively plays the same role as the various objects that Mrs. Gereth and her husband have collected in their travels across Europe: she vindicates the chooser's sense of her own extraordinarily subtle taste. Fleda lacks immediate appeal; she has none of the glossy surface that makes Mona resemble an expensive object, newly made, sitting in the brilliantly lit window of a London shop. Fleda is rather like a dusty object sitting in a secondhand shop whose value only a connoisseur might appreciate. Once, however, Mrs. Gereth has appropriated her and polished her apparently unpromising exterior, Fleda ceases to see herself, as she does initially, as possessing "no beauty," while "Mona's beauty figured powerfully" (73). Instead Fleda realizes that she "was not only a brilliant creature, but she heard herself commended in these days for attractions new and strange: she figured suddenly . . . as a distinguished, almost as a dangerous beauty" (96).

Echoing Shakespeare's *The Tempest*, the description of Fleda as "new and strange" suggests that she undergoes a sea change in which she is reborn as the heroine of the novel of manners. When the narrator of *Spoils* comments that "no one in the world was less superficial than Fleda" (62), we know she represents the depth that nineteenth-century fiction traditionally endorses through the poor woman. Yet, in James's novel, Fleda comes to occupy this valued position only after Mrs. Gereth intervenes. It is Mrs. Gereth who teaches Fleda to see herself as desirable. This intervention amounts to more than what Sharon Cameron has described as James's tendency to depict "one consciousness dictating to another how the latter thinks of itself" (123). For Mrs. Gereth also presents Fleda to others as valuable; the heroine has "the impression . . . of being advertised and offered" (96). The description of Mrs. Gereth circulating a "handsome published puff of Fleda Vetch" (94) with its literary tone thus seems particularly apt. Mrs. Gereth is promoting not just Fleda but the traditional plot of the Victorian novel in which the propertied man proves his virtue by learning to perceive and value the discriminating poor and to reject the crass rich woman.

The man in question is Mrs. Gereth's son Owen, who, despite the echoes between his name and the word "own," displays "no natural avidity" (64). Engaged to Mona as the story opens, he learns the distinction by being taught to contrast his fiancée's behavior to that of the poor rival his mother advertises. As he tells Fleda, "When I got into this I didn't know you, and now that I know you how can I tell you the difference? And *she's* so different, so ugly and vulgar, in the light of this squabble" (67, emphasis in the original). Just as Darcy comes to see Elizabeth Bennet as the most beautiful woman of his acquaintance in *Pride and Prejudice*, so, too, in *Spoils*, Owen tells Fleda that "as I saw you and noticed you more, as I knew you better and better, I felt less and less—I couldn't help it—about anything or anyone else" (113). James is quite conscious that in telling the story of Owen's attraction to Fleda, he is trespassing on the territory of the nineteenth-century marriage plot. In the section of the novel where he describes Owen's attempting to find a gift for Fleda, the imagery marks *Spoils*'s relation to the novels that precede it by echoing them.

Meeting Fleda in London and realizing his attraction to her, Owen thinks that "what he would really have liked, as he saw them tumbled about, was one of the splendid stuffs for a gown" (43). This passage echoes the moment in *Jane Eyre* when the wealthy Rochester wants to buy Jane opulent fabrics for her wedding dress but cannot because, as she makes clear, her poverty would make such gifts impossibly patronizing. Fleda's teasing Owen about "his exaggeration of her deserts" (43) and her insistence that she will only accept "a small pin-cushion, costing a sixpence" (43) reiterates a moment in Anthony Trollope's *Can You Forgive Her?* when Alice Vavasor accepts "a small steel paperknife[,] . . . a thing of no great value, of which the price may have been five shillings" (493), from the man who is not interested in her wealth. Like Jane Eyre, who refuses Rochester's rich gift, Alice will not accept diamonds from the man who courts her for her money.[20] These references mark how fully James's novel is commenting on the logic of the nineteenth-century works that preceded his.

But in James's novel the difference between the rich and the poor woman, which is represented through the gift of valuable or cheap objects, is not something that Owen knows instinctively, as Alice Vavasor's worthy lover does. Nor is it something that he learns through punishment and deprivation, as Rochester does in *Jane Eyre*. In *Spoils*, the difference between wealth and virtue is something that Owen is taught by his mother, who makes him see the value Fleda possesses. As James comments in his notes for the novel, "What must be thrown up to the surface is the coming back, through Owen of Mrs. Gereth's OFFER of Fleda at Poynton. Owen has understood it since—*lived* on it—and it all is *in* him now" (*Notebooks* 159, emphasis in the original). I would emphasize the italicized preposition "in" in this phrase, a preposition that recurs in critics' responses to the novel. *Spoils* is a tale where one character implants values *in* another by means of the familiar configuration that teaches heroes and readers to prefer the poor to the rich woman.

Having taught Fleda to think of herself as a beauty, Mrs. Gereth induces Owen to desire her protégée.[21] Explaining Mrs. Gereth's manipulations in his notes to the novel, James explains that "*she sets the girl on him*—cynically, almost, or indecently (making her feel AGAIN how little account—in the way of fine respect she makes of her. . . .) She presses Fleda—yes—upon him: would ALMOST like her, in London, to give herself up to him. She has a vision of a day with him there as 'fetching' him" (*Notebooks* 155–56, emphasis in the original). Though Thomas Otten associates Fleda's name with vetch, "a plant that takes its form from another plant, adapting its structure to something outside itself" (*Superficial* 48), we should surely also hear echoes in Fleda's surname of the word "fetch." Her function in *The Spoils of Poynton* is to fetch something for Mrs. Gereth and become fetching to Owen. Mrs. Gereth is perfectly aware of what she is doing, telling Fleda very early on in *Spoils* that "I contrasted you—told him *you* were the one" (78, emphasis in the original).[22] Like the author of a novel of manners, Mrs. Gereth deliberately contrasts the rich and the poor woman so that the novel's hero, her son, will be taught to perceive the aesthetic values that lie with the poor rather than the rich heroine. But, in thinking about this process, James insists that it is not morally neutral. Describing Mrs. Gereth initially in his notebooks as an emblem of "exquisite tastes" (80), he ends up emphasizing also her "unconscious brutality and immorality" (156).

Creating a character that consciously works to make the novel follow the form of the nineteenth-century marriage plot, James effectively asks what the stakes are of that plot. What are its ends? Why is it imposed? Who gains by it and what do they gain? He observes in both the notes and preface to *Spoils* that what drew him to the story in the first place was the fact that in the original anecdote from which the novel was taken, the property that the mother and her husband collected, would pass to her son on the occasion of his marriage.[23] It is the relation between women and property that interests James in writing *Spoils*. In his portrait of Mrs. Gereth's strategies to retain control of her property, he exposes the unspoken logic of the traditional configuration of the marriage plot. For *Spoils* makes it clear that if Owen marries Mona, control of the objects at Poynton will pass out of Mrs. Gereth's hands into those of her son's wealthy wife instead. In contrast, if he marries Fleda, control and possession will remain with Mrs. Gereth. As Mrs. Gereth's protégée all Fleda can imagine doing, if she were to marry Owen, is becoming an in-house appreciator, a guide or cicerone, who points out the beauties of the objects that would still belong in a deep sense to her mother-in-law.

James's novel shows that the whole system of hypergamy, the system enforced in the nineteenth-century marriage plot, is less the opposite of endogamy than its mirror image. Making the romantic heroine poor and of a lower social ranking than the hero allows the control of property to be retained by the hero's family.[24] It, too, is a means of concentrating wealth or goods within a family rather than allowing them to pass into another line. We might call this, remembering the term William James used in his reaction to *The Wings of the Dove*, a perverse reading of the marriage plot, a perversion that is concentrated in the term "spoils," which is used in the novel's title to refer to the art objects at Poynton, the objects that mark the epitome of good taste. We should read those spoils both literally and figuratively. They represent what Mrs. Gereth stands to gain, or retain, if she can orchestrate a relation between her son and Fleda that follows the pattern of the nineteenth-century marriage plot in which the propertied man marries the poorer woman. But they are also a fictional incarnation of the aesthetic rewards the nineteenth-century novel typically offers its readers when the hero and heroine make the right rather than the wrong marriages, the ones based on taste and love rather than wealth and ambition.

James's novel offers an objective correlative to those values in the art objects at Poynton, objects that are, as Bill Brown and Otten have argued, both curiously disembodied and at the same time suggestively linked to the image of the novel.[25] Through these objects and the marriage plot that is orchestrated around them, James's novel seemed to provide what one contemporary critic described as "material enough and to spare for the sentimental novelist." Yet in the end the story "allows nothing for the romantic taste that is in us all" (Gargano 29) because it refuses to satisfy the desires its plot structure elicits in readers. It shows the characters that have been characterized as possessing taste rather than avidity as unable either to make the right marriages or to hold onto the objects that have been the touchstone of taste, as Mrs. Gereth loses control of the objects at Poynton, which pass to the vulgar Mona Brigstock. One could read *The Spoils of Poynton* as narrating Mrs. Gereth's desperate attempts to retain the spoils. She seeks first simply to hold onto them, then to transfer them to a new venue, and finally to imagine that, through realizing a marriage between Owen and Fleda, she will maintain control of them. But none of these impositions work. Owen marries Mona, and the spoils pass into the hands of the vulgar rich woman, as they should not in the novel of manners.

This transfer seems to represent a victory for the crass or philistine taste represented by the Brigstocks. As Mrs. Gereth tells Fleda, "Mona Brigstock isn't weak. She's stronger than you!" (155). In Nancy Bentley's words, "To all appearances, the Waterbath barbarians win the game" (155). Yet this is not a full reading of the novel. For the spoils do not remain in Mona's hands. They are consumed in a mysterious fire before Owen can complete the last romantic gesture he hopes to make, of giving Fleda the most valuable object from the collection, presumably the Maltese cross, as a token of his appreciation of her. This intention marks his impulse to do something that would identify his love as associated with the economy of the gift rather than of commerce. His desire therefore reflects the implicit undercurrent of the nineteenth-century marriage plot, which insists on asserting that certain generous acts and desires can remain outside the realm of exchange. But in James's world those acts are never completed. The spoils are destroyed, and Mrs. Gereth is last glimpsed among a new set of things, the ones she inherited from an old aunt at Ricks, the objects that are truly hers, because they come to her through the maternal line and are not the possessions of her son.[26]

Those new objects are described as giving "the impression somehow of something dreamed and missed, something reduced, relinquished, resigned: the poetry, as it were, of something sensibly *gone*" (172, emphasis in the original). I read this as James's description of the state of the marriage plot as he experiences it at the end of the nineteenth century. The aesthetic values offered to readers by that pattern can no longer be recovered. It is a pattern whose remains we may lament but whose collapse makes way for what James calls in *Spoils* "a new version of the old story" (94). James will tell this story in *The Wings of the Dove* and *The Golden Bowl*, but he anticipates it at the end of *The Spoils of Poynton* as he explores why, in that novel, the marriage plot cannot come to the traditional conclusion that the romantic taste of James's readers would surely have desired. That novel cannot end with the marriage between the poor woman and the rich man and the recovery of the spoils and all they represent because Fleda Vetch finds herself incapable of doing anything to bring that conclusion about. Though the novel's romantic hero does fall in love with her, she does not act so as to force him to commit himself to her. As she explains to herself, "She could never lift a finger against Mona. . . . It would seem intolerably vulgar to her to have 'ousted' the daughter of the Brigstocks" (72). Indeed the only thing that Fleda can do to stay virtuous is to be unrewarded.

The "fineness of Fleda" (*Notebooks* 133), the demonstration of which James described in his notebooks as the goal of the novel, is a fineness of inaction. Contemporary reviewers became frustrated with James's "finer heroine," who fails to act as her lover "is about to marry an arch-Philistine"; "we almost lose patience for a subtle virtue that is so much beyond the needs of the case" (Gard 267). But "virtue" is the attribute that James questions in his portrait of Fleda and will question in the poor woman who follows her, Kate Croy of *The Wings of the Dove*. As Fleda's comments suggest, the poor heroine of the marriage plot can no longer easily be represented as a center of virtue if she is rewarded with marriage to the novel's propertied hero. That ending taints her with the vulgarity that is, in the traditional novel of manners, imagined to be safely contained in her antithesis, the rich woman. In *The Wings of the Dove*, Kate Croy's exclamation that she does not want to be "a hypocrite of virtue" (24) conveys James's sardonic reading of the position of the poor woman in the marriage plot. That plot makes her a hypocrite by rewarding her materially for behavior that it defines as virtuous because she eschews materialism.

Fleda refers to the narrative in which she would marry the wealthy Owen Gereth and settle down at Poynton as "the old story of being kicked upstairs" (94). Kate says similarly of her relatives' desire that she achieve a great marriage that "it's a perpetual sound in my ears. It makes me ask myself if I've any right to personal happiness, any right to anything but to be as rich and overflowing, as smart and shining, as I can be made" (50). In *Wings*, Kate tells her lover Merton Densher that "that's all my virtue—a narrow little family feeling" (50), by which she alludes to her offer to move in with her father after her mother's death. Such a statement marks virtue as a desire not to be exchanged, to remain with one's family rather than moving out into the marriage market. But, in both *Spoils* and *Wings*, it is impossible for the poor heroine not to become an object of exchange. Indeed she feels herself pressured by others to become such an object, and, when she does, she comes to regard herself as an emblem not of virtue but of what James calls value. Kate acknowledges to Densher that she cannot stay at home and must marry well because she represents "a sensible value" (6) for her impecunious father and sister: "My position's a value, a great value, for them both. . . . It's *the* value—the only one they have" (50, emphasis in the original).

So, too, Fleda realizes that "her own value" to Poynton and to Mrs. Gareth "was the mere value, as one might say, of a good agent" (24). The adjective "mere" suggests the problem that both Fleda and Kate recognize; they are caught in a narrative system that gives them, as poor women, a particular value that is expected by readers. But in the modern world that James's novels depict that value is no longer fixed or absolute; the heroine is no longer an emblem of virtue to which the hero aspires. Instead in James's narrative, as in modern culture generally, "the value of things has become detached from the objects and has acquired an independent existence in a specific substance": value "attaches to any object, person, relationship or happening" (Simmel *Philosophy of Money* 165, 68). In the preface to *The Spoils of Poynton* James twice indicates that the term "value" is of special interest to him. On the first page, he italicizes it when he characterizes art, as opposed to life, as "in search of the hard, latent *value*" (xxxix, emphasis in the original). The phrase "latent value" is important enough that he will return to it in his preface to *The Golden Bowl*. Near the end of the preface to *Spoils*, he puts "value" in quotation marks as he describes "the 'value' represented by Fleda" (xlix). The shift from thinking in terms wealth and virtue to value makes it possible for James, in the novels that follow *Spoils*, to shift the terms of the marriage plot, as both the poor and the rich woman come to understand that each represents a value in relation to the other.

"The Question of Money": *The Wings of the Dove*

At both the end of *The Spoils of Poynton* and the opening of *The Wings of the Dove* James is interested in representing the poor woman's consciousness of how the expectations of the traditional marriage plot work to attach value to her. And in *Wings* as in *Spoils*, that awareness is linked to the presence of an older, propertied woman who seeks to impose the structure of the marriage plot on the other characters. In *Wings*, that figure is Maude Lowder, the wealthy aunt who agrees to adopt Kate Croy so long as Kate is willing to make the kind of marriage expected of the novel's poor heroine. Kate's decision to accept her aunt's offer, to be the value her father and sister wish her to be, means, as her unacceptable poor lover, Merton Densher, comments toward the end of *Wings*, that Kate "was always, for her beneficent dragon, under arms; living up, every hour, but especially at festal hours, to the 'value' Mrs. Lowder had attached to her." The narrator concludes that "our young man now recognized in it something like the artistic idea, the plastic substance, imposed by tradition, by genius, by criticism, in respect to a given character, on a distinguished actress" (233). The references to art, tradition, genius, and criticism link the values imposed on Kate to the literary tradition that makes her into a particular kind of character.

And in this novel, as in *Spoils*, that tradition is the one that expects the beautiful, unpropertied woman to marry someone of status. Maud Lowder seeks to orchestrate this fate for her niece once she takes Kate into her home. It is the story that, Fleda comes to see, Mrs. Gereth hopes to make real in *Spoils*. But *The Wings of the Dove* opens with James reconfiguring the position of the poor woman, a reconfiguration he had already begun in *The Spoils of Poynton*. In that earlier novel, James had, as he indicates in his notebooks, intended for Fleda, "having grown up surrounded with lovely things," to have "exquisite tastes" (80). But in the end he gives her the seediest of backgrounds, describing both her father's and her sister's London lodgings in terms that he will pick up in the opening chapters of *The Wings of the Dove* as Kate Croy contemplates the sordidness of the places where her father and sister live. In *Spoils*, Fleda's father is deliberately contrasted to the world of taste, evoked in the novel through the objects at Poynton. He is a collector of "old brandy-flasks and match-boxes, old calendars and hand-books, intermixed with an assortment of pen-wipers and ash-trays, a harvest gathered in from penny bazaars" (99).[27] In *Wings*, Kate's father's apartment is epitomized by an "armchair upholstered in a glazed cloth" that exuded a "sense of the slippery and of the sticky" (1).[28]

In both novels this tawdriness extends to the heroine's sister, whose home is marked by the remnants of food. In *Spoils*, Fleda "pick[s] her way with [her sister] Maggie through the local puddles, diving with her into smelly cottages and supporting her, at smellier shops, in firmness over the weight of joints and the taste of cheese"; "at the evening meal, her brother-in-law invited her attention to a diagram, drawn with a fork on too soiled a tablecloth, of the scandalous drains of the Convalescent Home" (123). In *Wings*, Kate and her sister have their most serious discussion "in the presence of the crumpled table-cloth, the dispersed pinafores, the scraped dishes, the lingering odour of boiled food" (25). This culinary debris marks the abrupt intrusion of naturalist details of daily life into the world of the heroine who has been evoked from Austen onward as poor but with a poverty that is genteel rather than pressingly actual.[29] In James, in contrast, we feel the pressure of the intransigently real even at the moments where the narrative seems most romantic. In *Spoils*, half-eaten food is vividly evoked in the scene that most explicitly echoes *Pride and Prejudice*: the episode in which Mona's mother breaks in on Owen and Fleda during their brief rendezvous at Fleda's father's home in London.

That scene, which James acknowledged in his notebooks he found particularly interesting (158), was patterned on the scene in Austen's novel in which Lady Catherine de Bourgh visits Elizabeth Bennet. In both episodes an imperious older, wealthy woman intrudes on the novel's poor heroine in an attempt to disrupt the threat of her marriage to the novel's hero. In each case these dowagers behave, as Mrs. Brigstock comments in *Spoils*, "as if I had come here to be rude to you!"

(120). And in both cases this intrusion of vulgar self-interest triggers an implicit admission of the love that is its opposite. Elizabeth refuses to give up Darcy, and Owen defends Fleda to Mrs. Brigstock, explaining later that "I told her you were the noblest and straightest of women" (126). In Austen's novel, this scene triggers the story's final romantic resolution. In James, too, it leads to a kiss between Fleda and Owen that seems to promise their future union. Yet in *Spoils* this potentially romantic scene is also marked by the sordid details of everyday life. As Mrs. Brigstock intrudes into the apartment, her "eyes attach themselves to a small object that had lain hitherto unnoticed on the carpet. This was the biscuit of which, on giving Owen his tea, Fleda had taken a perfunctory nibble: she had immediately laid it on the table, and that subsequently, in some precipitate movement, she should have brushed it off was doubtless a sign of the agitation that possessed her" (115).

This detail prefigures what proves true in *The Wings of the Dove*, that the environment that surrounds the poor woman is vulgarly material. In this novel, Kate's father lives on "a vulgar little street [that] ... offered scant relief from the vulgar little room" (1); her sister makes Kate behave in ways "more vulgar than it had seemed written that any Croy could possibly become" (26); and her aunt is "colossally vulgar," with "her massive, florid furniture, the immense expression of her signs and symbols" (53).[30] James's point here, I take it, is that the traditional configuration of the marriage plot, with its story of a virtuous heroine who marries magnificently, is less a counter to vulgarity than something that arises out of it. Indeed one way to read Kate Croy's father and sister would be as readers of the marriage plot, readers who sit in the midst of their slippery armchairs and food-littered tablecloths and imagine something finer as they think about the magnificent marriage Kate can make. Yet Kate experiences herself as like the hero rather than the heroine of the marriage plot. She finds herself torn between a love she describes as "not a bit vulgar" (51) and the fate her family desires for her.

It is this nonvulgar man, Merton Densher, rather than a woman, Kate Croy, who represents genteel, intellectual poverty, the disembodiment typically associated with the heroine of the marriage plot. He "hasn't money" and "he'll never get it" (28), but he has none of the vulgar seediness of Kate's father and sister. Instead he represents what Kate calls "all the high, dim things she lumped together as of the mind. It was on the side of the mind that Densher was rich for her, and mysterious and strong; and he had rendered her in especial the sovereign service of making that element real" (34–35). Acknowledging, in terms that echo the traditional bifurcation of the marriage plot, that the only thing vulgar would be to "chuck" him, Kate insists that "I cling to some saving romance in things" (51). Ironically,

Merton Densher fully grasps the significance of the world that is opposed to him, the world represented by Kate's wealthy Aunt Maud, whom Densher describes in terms that make her a virtual compendium of the rich women that have preceded her in the novel of manners.

We hear echoes of Austen when he explains to Kate that Aunt Maud is confident she will win the battle with her niece because Kate's "pride and prejudice" (63) will eventually lead her to reject Densher and marry Lord Mark, the suitor her aunt has selected. In commenting that he enjoys Aunt Maud because she is "vulgar with freshness, almost with beauty, since there was beauty, to a degree, in the play of so big and bold a temperament" (54), Densher suggests a version of the "sublime vulgarity" that Frances Trollope evoked through the widow Barnaby. The surname "Lowder" associates Aunt Maud with the loudness that in Anthony Trollope's novels defined the heiress's possession and display of commercial wealth as vulgar, traits that linked the rich woman to the loud vulgarians of the period.[31] When Densher asserts that Aunt Maud "doesn't disparage intellect and culture" (62) but "wants them to adorn her board and be named in her programme" (62), we should be reminded of Oliphant's novels, which represent intellectual accomplishments as something that can be acquired through money. Like Oliphant's prosperous heroines, Maud exudes "the general attestation of morality and money, a good conscience and a big balance" (55), and has "ambitions, that would figure as large, as honourably unselfish" (137). But in *The Wings of the Dove*, James invokes this familiar image of the rich woman only to replace it with a new version of wealth, just as he replaces the reader's traditional image of the poor woman with a new version of poverty in Kate Croy.

The American heiress Milly Theale possesses a form of wealth defined as completely opposite to that represented by Maud Lowder. As Milly's companion and Maud's school friend Susan Stringer explains, "Aunt Maud sat somehow in the midst of her money, founded on it and surrounded by it," while "Milly, about hers, had no manner at all" (136). Here we have an explicit reference to the difference between embedding and disembedding that is key to James's reconception of the relation between the rich and the poor woman. Maude is embedded in and defined by her wealth as it is emblematized in the objects at Lancaster Gate, which are both vulgarly tasteless and powerfully appealing. In contrast, Milly has no fixed milieu. She appears first in the Alps, later in London society, and finally in Venice, where she inhabits a palace surrounded by possessions that are not hers.[32] As Susan Stringer again explains of the difference between the two rich women,

Mrs. Lowder was keeping her wealth as for purposes . . . on the day they should take effect. She would impose her will, but her will would be only that a person or two shouldn't lose a benefit by not submitting if they could be made to submit. To Milly, as so much younger, such far views couldn't be imputed: there was nobody she was supposable as interested for. It was too soon, since she wasn't interested for herself. Even the richest woman, at her age, lacked motive, and Milly's motive doubtless had plenty of time to arrive. (137)

This passage evokes the differences between England and America. America, a young country, lacks the history of its European counterpart, a history that has marked English wealth as coming from particular sources and being directed toward particular aims. American wealth is, on the contrary, from the English perspective, simply an abstraction. It has no particular origin, aim, or history.[33] As a result of both her American origins and the enormous size of her fortune, Milly represents wealth in a completely abstract form. As Susan notes, "It came back of course to the question of money. . . . A less vulgarly, a less obviously purchasing and parading person she couldn't have imagined; but . . . the girl couldn't get away from her wealth. . . . That was what it was to be really rich. It had to be *the* thing you were" (84–85, emphasis in the original). She is, like the other rich women I have been examining, identified with and defined by her wealth. Yet she has no vulgarity about her. Her presence raises the question of money, but in this novel it is not a *vulgar* question.[34] Milly represents the potentiality of money, a possibility vividly grasped by Kate Croy, the poor woman who is her opposite.

As the novel begins to dwell, as James notes in the preface, on "the more or less associated consciousness of the two women" (15), it is Kate who allows Milly to see herself in a new light: "Milly actually began to borrow from the handsome girl a sort of view of her state; the handsome girl's impression of it was clearly so sincere. This impression was a tribute, a tribute positively to power, power the source of which was the last thing Kate treated as a mystery " (121). If Kate teaches Milly to realize that the possession of wealth makes her a potentially powerful figure, Milly also sees that Kate's poverty makes her potentially "the heroine of a strong story" (119). Visiting Kate's sister, Milly hears "a mixed wandering echo of Trollope, of Thackeray, perhaps mostly of Dickens" (133). She recognizes Kate as the heroine of a traditional English novel, the heroine of the marriage plot. The problem James's novel faces and cannot quite resolve is how to connect the story of the old heroine represented by Kate Croy to the story of the new one represented by Milly Theale.

In the preface to the New York edition of *The Wings of the Dove* James notes the difficulties he had with the novel's structure, explaining that it "happens to offer perhaps the most striking example I may cite . . . of my regular failure to keep the appointed halves of my whole equal" (13). The opening sections that describe the relations between Kate Croy and her family and between Maud, Kate, Densher, and Milly take up more room than they should. As a result the novel has a "make-shift middle" (13), and its ending half, the "false and deformed half" (13), is not equal to its opening. It falters after "Book Fourth, where all the offered life centres, to intensity, in the disclosure of Milly's single throbbing consciousness" (12). But Milly's "situation ceases at a given moment to be 'renderable' in terms closer than those supplied by Kate's intelligence, or, in a richer degree, by Densher's" (12). As J. Hillis Miller has noted, Milly's consciousness disappears almost entirely from the closing sections of the novel (*Literature* 160).[35] James links this problem to the novel's overall structure, which involves "solid *blocks* of wrought material, squared to the sharp edge, as to have weight and mass and carrying power" (8, emphasis in the original). These blocks represent the consciousnesses of various characters that James allows to structure the narrative of *The Wings of the Dove*.

But, as he experiments with this form, James also worries about "the gaps and the lapses" (9) between those blocks, explaining that "I mourn for them all . . . the absent values, the palpable voids, the missing links, the mocking shadows, that reflect, taken together, the early bloom of one's good faith" (9). Here James notes the absence of a set of values that would make the narrative feel coherent. Those missing values can be identified with the traditional form of the marriage plot that has begun to collapse in *The Wings of the Dove*. We saw in *The Spoils of Poynton* that James understands the values upheld by that plot to depend on our assumption that its heroes and heroines are, in fact, acting in good faith as they espouse virtue over wealth or aesthetic over material desire. But, as he also showed in that novel, and shows more fully in *Wings*, it is possible to look as if one is choosing the less vulgar of two options and yet still be vulgarly self-interested. In *Spoils* Mrs. Gereth endorses the contrast between the rich and the poor woman so that she can profit from it, retaining control of the spoils whose importance is marked by the novel's title. So too in *Wings*, Kate seems to make what the novel of manners would describe as the "right" choice when she remains faithful to Densher rather than abandoning him for the more socially prominent suitor her aunt has chosen for her.

But the moral valences of that choice shift once Kate realizes that Milly is dying and prompts Densher to woo the heiress so that he can inherit her fortune, allowing the novel's lovers, like the hero and heroine of a novel like *Pride and Prejudice*, to end the story possessing both love and wealth. In *Spoils* and *Wings* these subplots skew the moral opposition that seems so clear in the traditional marriage plot, where seeking to marry for money represents a set of materialist drives that can easily be condemned once the novel invokes marriage for love as its opposite. Densher himself wonders when he watches Kate Croy negotiate with her wealthy Aunt Maud whether "marrying for money mightn't after all be a smaller cause of shame than the mere dread of marrying without" (44). Comments like this have tended to lead to critics' debating characters' innocence or guilt, their good or bad intentions. James's decision to break up the narration of *The Wings of the Dove* into blocks has, if anything, reinforced the critical tendency to focus on the consciousnesses of individual characters.

But I want to suggest that we might instead conceive of James dividing his novel into a series of separate blocks in order to give readers the feel of the modern world of relative values. This is the world described by Simmel, where individual subjectivities increasingly experience themselves as separate from one another and from the world of objects in which they live. In Simmel's universe, the breaking up of experience into discrete units is counterbalanced by what floats between them, the element in which they are immersed, the abstract presence of money, which mediates relations between subjects, between objects, and between subjects and objects. James begins to work out a narrative form that features a series of separate blocks in the novel, where, in Milly Theale, he creates his first full fictional instantiation of "the heir of all the ages" (6), an idea that he had been brooding over for a long time. In breaking up his narrative into separate units, James is as interested in the milieu in which they float as he is in the consciousnesses of the individual characters represented by them.

In the conclusion of *The Wings of the Dove* he returns to Kate and Milly, the two characters whose contrasting perspectives were key to the novel's middle section. Here he presents their relationship through the perspective of a third character, Merton Densher, whose observations throughout the conclusion of the novel emphasize the mediated rather than absolute nature of value. The narrator comments early on, when Densher returns from America, that the "abrupt extrusion of Mr. Densher altered all proportions, had an effect on all values" (130). It is he who, at the novel's end, contemplates the implications of the contrasted but interconnecting consciousnesses of Kate Croy and Milly Theale. The novel thus simply parallels its closing scenes to its opening ones. Writing about Kate watching the dying Millie as she entertains her guests during her doctor's visit to Venice,

James explains that "the occasion on which, in the splendid saloon of poor Milly's hired palace, she takes the measure of her friend's festal evening, squares itself to the same synthetic firmness as the compact constructional block inserted by the scene at Lancaster Gate" (12). Acknowledging again the compositional structure that involves dividing the narrative into blocks, James tells his readers that his novel's structure works by giving them a scene that allows them to contemplate again the same set of social relations they have already experienced in an earlier narrative block.

In the case of the scene at the palace, the key relation that is being seen or represented again is the one between Kate and Milly, the contrast between the poor and the rich woman that is central to the novel of manners. But the difference between these late scenes and the earlier ones in which Kate and Milly explore London together is that in the later scenes the relationship between them is mediated by a third figure, whose perspective allows readers to perceive value to be located not in individual figures but in the relation between them. It is Densher, who, at the gathering at Milly's Venetian palace, experiences Kate as "somehow—for Kate—wanting in luster" (362), while he sees Milly as exuding, "the candour of her smile, the lustre of her pearls, the value of her life, the essence of her wealth" (371).[36] This image marks the reversal of values that James's novel enacts, as the poor woman ceases to attract, while the rich woman's wealth becomes completely dematerialized and is represented as a radiance or effulgence. Shortly after this scene, Densher will describe Milly as having "inestimable value" (374), a value that Kate crassly imagines Densher will possess if he marries Milly and the heiress dies leaving him her fortune.

But Densher himself wonders whether one can possess value: "Wasn't it perhaps even rather the value *that* possessed him?" (374, emphasis in the original). He will enforce the mediated nature of value at the novel's end, when he receives the letter from the lawyers detailing Milly's bequest. Handing that document to Kate, he forces her to realize the indirectness of her access to value. When she asks "how can I can touch [the wealth] but *through* you?" he replies, "You can't. Any more . . . than I can renounce it except through you" (490, emphasis in the original). Here James marks his awareness of the way the traditional marriage plot uses the rich and the poor woman as vehicles through which readers (and other characters within the novel) can vicariously experience the sense of touching values, both materialist and antimaterialist, the value of wealth but also of the refusal of wealth. In the earlier scene in the Venetian palace, Densher looks at Kate looking at Milly's pearls and sees the material side of the story: "He knew in a moment that

Kate was just now, for reasons hidden from him, exceptionally under the impression of that element of wealth in her which was a power, which was a great power" (363). And he too is, both here and later in the novel, brought to see Kate as she sees herself in the mirror of Milly's wealth: "She would have been splendid. . . . Milly's royal ornament had—under pressure not now wholly occult—taken on the character of a symbol of differences, differences of which the vision was actually in Kate's face" (363).

This plot of the poor woman's acquisition of the wealth that becomes her is never realized in *Wings*, which ends on an ambiguous note, leaving readers uncertain as to the fate of Milly's fortune. It will come to fruition in *The Golden Bowl* when the penniless Charlotte Stant marries the wealthy Adam Verver and confirms what Densher assumes about Kate in *Wings* when he exclaims, "What a person she would be if they *had* been rich—with what a genius for the so-called great life, what a presence for the so-called great house, what a grace for the so-called great positions!" (485, emphasis in the original). The reference to great houses marks this vision as alluding to the end of the marriage plot in which the poor heroine becomes the mistress of the hero's great house. *Wings* holds up this vision as it is about to withdraw it, the moment when we assume that Milly has left Densher a magnificent bequest on her death that is also the moment in which we learn that he will not accept it. As in *The Spoils of Poynton*, so too in *The Wings of the Dove*, virtue can only reassert itself in the world of multiform material desires through inaction, through refusing to grasp the reward the narrative trajectory typically offers the hero and heroine, though, in James's novels, it is hard to know whether to think of Fleda and Owen or Kate and Densher as hero and heroine.

We might note here James's own anxieties about the endings of his novels, which his editors repeatedly pressed him to make more upbeat. As he commented in his reminiscences to the *Atlantic* publisher James T. Fields, William Dean Howells's advice that he should have made the ending of *The American* more positive was the "first note of warning against not 'ending happily' that was for the rest of my literary career to be sounded in my ear with a good faith of which the terms failed to reach me intelligibly enough to correct my apparent perversity" (quoted in Bell 218). Here we have terms, "good faith" and "perversity," that echo James's own description of the new form of *The Wings of the Dove* and William James's reaction to it.

In not allowing his narratives to come to the expected conclusion of the marriage plot, a happy ending that symbolizes the uniting of love and wealth, James acted in "bad faith," knowing he was creating a narrative readers would experience as perverse. He remarked of his ideas for the conclusion to *The Wings of the Dove* that "I can scarcely imagine any—I doubt if I can—that isn't ugly and vulgar: I mean vulgarly ugly" (*Notebooks* 104–5). This comment underscores why readers were frustrated with this novel as they were also with *The Spoils of Poynton*. It too refuses to provide a narrative that offers an imaginative escape from the vulgarity that, as the opening of *Wings* shows, so permeated modern culture. And yet, despite the apparent cynicism of these comments, James cannot conclude *The Wings of the Dove* without gesturing toward the choice that invariably structured the nineteenth-century marriage plot, the choice that positions the novel's hero or heroine standing at a moral crossroad that marks the divergence of the path to wealth and virtue, or to money and love.

The novel ends with Densher offering Kate a choice; she can either have him or she can have the inheritance but not the combination of the two, the state she has pursued throughout the novel. When he tells Kate that "I make over to you every penny," and she replies, "Precisely—so that I must choose" (492), we hear put into words the imperative that drives the Victorian novel, the insistence that its characters must be forced to choose, often over and over again, between wealth and virtue. That choice creates heroes and villains, heroines and monstrously deformed avatars of wealth. Yet here the choice no longer structures the narrative. It is not the force that reveals the true natures of characters, the choice that, in effect, structures all other choices and is revealed to be the basis of the law that explains how characters behave. Instead here the choice is offered by one character to another at the very last moment of the story, as if, with a gesture, Kate might, if she chose rightly, be redeemed and redeem Densher through renouncing the vulgar material desires that have driven the plot over the course of the novel.

Though such an ending would be perverse in itself, since it would entail the sacrifice of Milly to the lovers' desires, James refuses to end on so definitive a note. The story evokes the idea that Kate's renunciation might return the lovers to the position they see themselves as occupying at the opening of the story, when there is nothing vulgar about their desire for each other. But, in the end, Kate tells Densher that they will never again be as they were. This statement is as much about the form of the novel as about the fate of the lovers. Like the description of the art objects at Ricks at the end of *The Spoils of Poynton*, Kate's statement at the end of *The Wings of the Dove* indicates James's belief that the novel will never again be as it was. It will not again end with rewards granted, the spoils attained, as if the hero and heroine's marital choices could mark virtue in some absolute way. Instead, in *The Golden Bowl*, James will find a new conclusion that allows him to let go of the values celebrated by the marriage plot and show that plot to be a configuration that forces characters to occupy certain positions in relation to one another.

The Golden Bowl: "The Grossness of Avidity"

In the preface to *The Golden Bowl*, James returns to Fleda Vetch, describing her in retrospect as, "the all-noting heroine of 'The Spoils of Poynton,' highly individualised *though* highly intelligent" (vii, emphasis in the original).[37] He reintroduces Fleda in order to insist that "the register" of Maggie Verver's "consciousness is as closely kept" (vii) as Fleda's. In Fleda's case that consciousness involves an awareness of the way she has been used by Mrs. Gereth. She knew that "she had been treated by her friend's act as a conscious prize" (146), and the emphasis on Mrs. Gereth's use of her asks readers to become aware of the dynamic of the marriage plot, to understand that in that configuration the poor woman must become a conscious prize. Thinking through Mrs. Gereth's attempt to force her into that position, Fleda recognizes that she has little inherent value; rather "her value consisted all in the power the act itself imputed to her" (146). In the preface to *The Golden Bowl* James links his heroine's consciousness to a doubled form of value; the register of heightened consciousness that Maggie shares with Fleda "duplicates, as it were, her value." Maggie "becomes a compositional resource, and of the finest order, as well as a value intrinsic" (vii). In *The Spoils of Poynton* James traces the movement from intrinsic value to an awareness of value as generated by one's own and others' relative positions within a structure that governs both narrative and marital relations. By choosing in *The Golden Bowl* to locate this awareness not in the poor but the rich woman, James is able, for the first time, to explore the configuration of the marriage plot from the perspective of the individual who must be excluded in order for it to function.

This exploration means that in *The Golden Bowl* James represents marital exchange in explicitly anthropological terms. *The Spoils of Poynton*, as I have suggested, can be read as implicitly making an anthropological argument about women and property. James suggests his conscious linking of *Spoils* to nineteenth-century anthropological thinking when he explains that what drew him to the historical story that was its basis was the question of "mother right," a term that comes from the work of J. J. Bachofen. Like John McLennan, whose book *Primitive Marriage* James owned, Bachofen posited that civilization developed as patriarchal structures rose out of early matriarchal cultures.[38] In *Wings* James's language sounds most anthropological when he is describing what we might think of as matrilineage, as Maud Lowder attempts to control the destiny of her own fortune by determining who her niece will marry. In these negotiations she "taboos" Densher (136) and indulges in "the cultivation of consanguinity" (23). These anxieties about women and exchange are worked out in *The Golden Bowl* through a narrative that depends on the tension between endogamy and exogamy, the ideas that McLennan introduced into anthropological thinking.

Though James never uses those words, the concepts are key to the marital exchanges depicted in his novel about an heiress whose relation to property and kinship structures means that she has to be prohibited from marrying outside the group to which she belongs. In narrating the marriage of its American heiress to an Italian prince *The Golden Bowl* explores the problems implicitly raised at the end of *The Wings of the Dove*, where Milly Theale is figured, particularly in her relation to Kate Croy, as a princess. In one of the many scenes in the Venetian section of the novel whose descriptions evoke the painterly, the two women are characterized as

> figures so associated and yet so opposed, so mutually watchful: that of the angular, pale princess, ostrich-plumed, black robed, hung about with amulets, reminders, relics, mainly seated, mainly still, and that of the upright, restless, slow-circling lady of her court, who exchanges with her, across the black water streaked with evening gleams, fitful questions and answers. The upright lady, with thin, dark braids down her back, ... makes the whole circuit, and makes it again. (308)

In this image Milly's wealth has a gravitational force that pulls the poorer woman into an orbit around it.[39] The question implicitly raised here—of whether the rich woman can herself be mobile, whether she can, in the language of anthropology, economics, and science, circulate—is explicitly addressed in *The Golden Bowl*.

In various anthropological considerations of kinship, the princess has a particular resonance. Because women must marry upward on the social scale, the woman of the highest social status represents a conceptual problem. The only way to resolve this problem, as Lévi-Strauss explains in *The Elementary Structures of Kinship*, is to imagine, as fairy tales typically do, "a person occupying a high social rank ... giving his daughter in marriage to a man of any status, who has performed some extraordinary feat, or better still, has been chosen by the girl herself. How else could she proceed, since, as a king's daughter in any hypergamous system she would be denied any spouse if the rule were strictly observed?" (475). The possibility of the rich woman giving herself is suggested toward the end of *The Wings of the Dove* where Kate and Densher speculate that Milly "may *offer* marriage" in "the manner of princesses, who do such things?" (371). But the promise is never fulfilled, as Milly dies without marrying. *The Golden Bowl* opens as the rich woman is given in marriage to a poorer spouse and becomes a princess in the process. But *The Golden Bowl* also insists that that woman imagines she can negotiate a marriage that is not exogamous.

That possibility conforms to the fate of the heiress as it was conceived in both nineteenth-century anthropology and earlier biblical criticism. As McLennan explains of heiresses in *Primitive Marriage*, "Such ladies, if they made proper marriages according to the old law . . . must have carried their estates into other tribes or gentes, and so have cut off their own gentiles from the prospect of succeeding them" (113). Writing about the Bible at an earlier historical moment, Jeremy Taylor made the same point in terms that were not yet anthropological, explaining that "if the woman was an heiress she was to pleasure her own family rather than strangers" (quoted in Pollak 52).[40] This is the position Maggie Verver assumes in *The Golden Bowl* when she imagines that in marrying Prince Amerigo she can also please her father:

> She had surrendered herself to her husband without the shadow of a reserve or a condition, and yet she had not, all the while, given up her father by the least little inch. She had compassed the high felicity of seeing the two men beautifully take to each other, and nothing in her marriage had marked it as more happy than this fact of its having practically given the elder, the lonelier, a new friend. (302)

The tie between father and daughter is so strong that it remains undiminished even after Maggie has a child with Amerigo and her father marries Maggie's American friend Charlotte Stant. As the prince tells his new mother-in-law, "It would have taken more than ten children of mine . . . to keep our *sposi* apart" (226); "Maggie and her father had, with every ingenuity, converted the precious creature into a link between a mamma and a grandpappa" (116). The closeness between Maggie and her father is as much about money as it is about love and emotional attachment; "Mr. Verver . . . took care of his relation to Maggie. . . . He relieved [Amerigo] of all anxiety about his married life in the same manner in which relieved him on the score of his bank account" (214). As it intertwines marriage and property owning, this sentence replicates the logic of nineteenth-century social theorists as diverse as Morgan, Engels, and Spencer, all of whom charted the interconnected evolution of the two social institutions. James's narrator insists that Adam Verver's "good understanding with his daughter" had "the same deep intimacy as the commercial, the financial association founded, far down, on a community of interest" (214).[41]

For Victorian anthropologists, this was the community of interests that meant the heiress could not be exchanged outside the group to which she belonged. In *The Golden Bowl*, Amerigo thinks in the quasi-anthropological terms of tribes and gentes; he perceives his wife and her father to be part of a group that defines itself as a whole and excludes him: "Those people—and his free synthesis lumped together capitalists and bankers, retired men of business, illustrious collectors, American fathers-in-law, American fathers, little American daughters, little American wives—those people were of the same large lucky group[;] . . . they hung together" (215).[42] Amerigo understands, as clearly as Maggie does herself, that the marriage between them has not been exogamous.[43] Maggie does not pass out of the group to which she belongs, nor does Amerigo pass into it. Moreover, though the opening of the novel stresses the negotiations that take place on the occasion of the union, subsequent comments make it clear that the marriage does not involve the exchange of property either. Mr. Verver's "easy way with his millions had taxed to such small purpose, in the arrangements, the principle of reciprocity" (4); the marriage between Amerigo and Maggie is not a reciprocal exchange.

In fiction, marital exchanges have typically been read, following the work of Gayle Rubin, in terms of a triangle in which a woman is positioned between two men who exchange her. But we also need, as I have suggested, to conceive of a second triangle in which a man is positioned between two women, one rich and one poor. In *The Golden Bowl* the triangle that features Maggie suspended between her father and her husband is complicated by the addition of another character to the mix, the penniless Charlotte Stant. Once Maggie's father marries Charlotte, Prince Amerigo finds himself positioned within his own family configuration between the American heiress he has married for her wealth and the woman he once loved but could not marry because "she has only twopence in the world" (134). This love triangle, which forms within the triangle of marital exchange, arises, the novel makes clear, from the Ververs' desire to resist the pressures of the market. As Maggie explains to her father of the change that happens once she marries Amerigo, "It was as if you couldn't be in the market when you were married to *me*. Or rather as if I kept people off, innocently, by being married to you. Now that I'm married to someone else, you're, as in consequence, married to nobody. Therefore you may be married to anybody, to everybody. People don't see why you shouldn't be married to *them*" (127–28, emphasis in the original).

In characterizing the women who wish to marry Adam Verver for his money, the novel uses the phrase the "grossness of avidity" (97), which perfectly captures the negative qualities that have, from Austen onward, been associated with rich women. To avoid being touched by this grossness, the Ververs introduce Charlotte Stant into the equation, believing that she will shield them from crassly materialist desires: "They had brought her in . . . to do 'the worldly' for them, and she had done it with such genius that they had themselves in consequence renounced it even more" (234). As Fanny Assingham explains, "Charlotte was a person who *could* keep off ravening women—without being one herself, either, in the vulgar way of the others" (288, emphasis in the original). Here James is providing a cynical reading of the poor woman's use in the marriage plot; her function is to protect not just the novel's virtuous characters but also its readers from contamination by the worldliness of material ends.

The Golden Bowl goes out of its way to insist that there is nothing vulgar about Charlotte or Amerigo. In describing Charlotte's past it provides none of the seedy background details associated with Kate Croy and Fleda Vetch in *The Wings of the Dove* and *The Spoils of Poynton*. Maggie simply tells her father that she "never saw [Charlotte] do anything but laugh at her poverty" (134). The novel also insists in its opening descriptions of Amerigo as he anticipates his marriage to Maggie that he wishes "to resist . . . the temptation toward any vulgar rapacity" (Porter 141). He intends to be a good husband. Even the adultery that eventually takes place between the prince and Charlotte is represented not as an act of avidity or grasping but a moment when the two accept an experience that the prince thinks of, in imagery that echoes the description of Milly Theale in *The Wings of the Dove*, as "rounded and lustrous as some huge precious pearl": "he hadn't struggled nor snatched; he was taking but what had been given him; the pearl dropped itself, with its exquisite quality and rarity, straight into his hand" (265). *The Golden Bowl* therefore differs from its Jamesian predecessors in insisting that it is not avidity or bad faith that generates the complications of the marriage plot; it was Maggie's "feverish little sense of justice" that "had brought the two others together as her grossest misconduct couldn't have" (293).

In imagining innocently that it is possible to refuse to enter the world of marital exchange, Maggie and her father come to represent the very avidity they wish to protect themselves from, the avidity associated with the impulse to amass or engross rather than exchange wealth and the persons who represent it.[44] *The Golden Bowl* makes visible in the barest of terms the quadrangle that implicitly underlies both fictional and anthropological accounts of marital exchange. In it

James explores the dynamics of the marriage plot in their most abstract form, shorn of the clutter of detail that often masks their contours in the nineteenth-century novel of manners. Edith Wharton once asked James, "What was your idea in suspending the four principal characters in 'The Golden Bowl' in the void?" to which James replied, "My dear—I didn't know I had" (Wharton 191). The novel, however, shows both its author and its characters to be quite conscious of the movement from triangular to rectangular structure. As Maggie understands of the relation between herself, her father, and Amerigo, "Having but three, as they might say, it wanted another, and what had Charlotte done from the first but begin to act, on the spot, and ever so smoothly and beautifully as a fourth?" (316).

In the novel's preface James emphasizes that "we see very few persons in 'The Golden Bowl,' but the scheme of the book, to make up for that, is that we shall really see about as much of them as a coherent literary form permits. That was my problem, so to speak, and my *gageure*—to play the small handful of values really for all they were worth" (viii). Through his use of the word "gageure," which means "wager," in which individuals make a bet and agree to render each other reciprocally what they have engaged to pay in the event they lose the bet, James reintroduces the idea of reciprocal exchange into the novel not at the level of what the characters are doing but at the level of the literary form itself.[45] It would be possible to think of that form as emblematized in the golden bowl. For, as the novel repeatedly reminds us, though the bowl looks as if it is gold, a solid symbol of value, it is, in fact, crystal. It is as if, in James's novel, the crystalline structure of the bowl represents the grid-like pattern of the implicitly anthropological laws that structure the characters' marital exchanges.

When Fanny Assingham breaks the bowl, it falls apart into three irregular chunks, which Maggie finds she cannot pick up all at once. She can only lift two of the pieces in her hands, after which, she must return to pick up the third, the bowl's stem, which she then deposits on the mantle together with its other parts. Here we have James's visual image of what *The Golden Bowl* does in its narration. It rives the abstract lattice of the marriage plot, showing how it is made up of a relation between three parts, which are, however, typically grasped in terms of twos, the marital pairs that emerge at the end of the story. The third position in this con-figuration, the rich woman typically represented as the person the hero should not marry, is, I have been arguing, the base on which the whole plot stands. We might also think of the image of the bowl being broken into disparate pieces in terms of James's description in the preface to *The Wings of the Dove* of the new form his novel is beginning to take, a form that involves presenting its material in separate blocks with gaps or holes between them. *The Golden Bowl* is divided into two fully separate sections, entitled "The Prince" and "The Princess."[46] That division allows James to avoid the problem of imbalance that plagued him in *The Wings of the Dove*. Here the second half of the novel must, because of its structure, be equal to the first half. In it James will provide what is absent from both *Spoils* and *Wings*, the rich woman's contemplation of her own problematic position within the marriage plot.

In its second book *The Golden Bowl* both negotiates and examines the passage to exogamy that seems so easy in the novels of manners that precede it. That contemplation begins in the famous passage, in the opening of the second half of the novel, which describes Maggie thinking that "the pagoda in her blooming garden figured the arrangement—how otherwise was it to be named?—by which, so strikingly, she had been able to marry without breaking, as she liked to put it, with her past" (302).[47] The image of the pagoda (an object familiar to the English in the nineteenth century at least from the example in Kew Gardens) with its incrementally decreasing series of roofs provides, I would argue, the perfect visual correlative to the cycles of kinship exchange charted in *The Elementary Structures of Kinship*.[48] Lévi-Strauss represents these exchanges as a set of cycles that invariably involve the woman marrying a man who is of a higher status than she. As Jan Van Baal explains, "The point is that no woman is permitted to marry a man of lower rank" (90). These cycles reach their limit cases, the point of the pagoda, with the woman of the highest social status and the man of the lowest. The question is how they manage to get married.

In the context of thinking through the marital "arrangements" of the novel Maggie comes to acknowledge that her own marriage to Amerigo and her father's to Charlotte have not been "measurably paid for" (303). Realizing that she and her father have been "able at once so to separate and so to keep together" (303), Maggie identifies the endogamous marital exchange that was, in the first half of the novel, the goal she aimed for. Maggie's recognition in this scene and the one that parallels it, when she thinks through the interrelations of the entire quartet of lovers as they play bridge at her father's estate at Fawns, is complicated by the commentaries of Fanny Assingham, who functions in *The Golden Bowl* as Mrs. Gereth and Maud Lowder do in *The Spoils of Poynton* and *The Wings of the Dove*.[49] She is the one who seeks to impose various versions of the marriage plot on the materials of the novel. It is she who brought Maggie and Amerigo together and who later chooses not to reveal Amerigo's relation to Charlotte in order that the impoverished Charlotte may successfully marry the wealthy Adam Verver. Providing what Bersani describes as "a kind of critique *in medias res* in which the dependence of novelistic plot on critical speculation is introduced as a literal possibility within the novel itself" (149), Fanny also functions, as the crass implications of her name might suggest, as a locus of vulgarity.

Her vulgarity does not take the form of the desire for wealth, though the imagery surrounding Fanny links her to both Jews and money. She represents instead the vulgar desire to know, to be explicit about the configuration of the story.[50] As a storyteller, she displays, the "admitted grossness of her avidity" (389) that echoes the avidity Maggie locates in the women who pursue her father for his wealth. It is Fanny who understands that the heiress's innocence introduces grossness into the novel. It was Maggie who drove the others to accept "from the first, so guilelessly—yes, so guilelessly, themselves—her guileless idea of still having her father, of keeping him fast, in her life" (290). Fanny reiterates this idea, almost a hundred pages later, as she again thinks through the implications of the novel's marital exchanges in a scene that prefaces Maggie's fuller, more intimate examination of the same problems. In her second set of meditations, Fanny comments of the adultery between Prince Amerigo and Charlotte Stant that "that's what a creature of pure virtue exposes herself to when she suffers her pure virtue, suffers her sympathy, her disinterestedness, her exquisite sense for the lives of others, to carry her too far" (395). In her reference to virtue, sympathy, and disinterest, Fanny captures the values the poor woman typically incarnates in the nineteenth-century novel.

Playing the role of quizzical respondent, Colonel Assingham observes that his wife has "supplied [the Prince] with the enjoyment of *two* beautiful women" (395, emphasis in the original) by both introducing him to Maggie and making it possible for Charlotte to return to the scene. When Fanny replies that it is "not . . . 'two' of anything. One beautiful woman—and one beautiful fortune" (395), we have James's fullest commentary on the sleight of hand played by the typical configuration of the marriage plot. In placing the hero between two women, one rich and one poor, it looks as if he is being offered two equivalent choices. But the deck is always stacked. The two women are not commensurable but instead embody opposed values, the one aesthetic, the other economic, the values of virtue and wealth. It is this very incommensurability that has made it so hard for critics to see that the rich woman plays an equivalent role in the marriage plot, an equivalence that the structure of James's novel has allowed him to uncover.

James fully articulates the implications of the rich woman's role in the marriage plot in the second scene in which Maggie meditates on her own position within the novel. Here she begins to contemplate the relation between the four major characters of the novel less in terms of her own desires than in terms of an abstract pattern that necessitates that she behave in a particular way. In that scene, she exits the great house in order, as with her imaginative contemplation of the pagoda, to look in at it from the outside. This time she looks through the window to watch her father, her stepmother, and the Assinghams as they play bridge together:

> It all left her, as she wandered off, with the strangest of impressions—the sense, forced upon her as never yet, of an appeal, a positive confidence, from the four pairs of eyes, that was deeper than any negation, and that seemed to speak, on the part of each, of some relation to be contrived by her, a relation with herself, which would spare the individual the danger, the actual present strain, of the relation with others. They thus tacitly put it upon her to be disposed of, the whole complexity of their peril. (469–70)

Bridge is a perfect analogue for the marriage plot because in the game there are four positions, just as I have argued there typically are in fictional and anthropological depictions of marital exchange : the two men who are doing the exchanging and the two women who are contrasted in order to establish the values that will be ratified over the course of the exchange. But in bridge one of the positions is the dummy, a player who possesses cards valuable to a partner but who sits the hand out. The rich woman in the marriage plot typically functions as the dummy in the system. She is present and necessary but not an active player in the game. What Maggie understands about her role is that she is expected to perform it "because she was there, and there just *as* she was, to lift if off them and take it; to charge herself with it as the scapegoat of old" (470, emphasis in the original). Susan Mizruchi has written of James's long-standing fascination with the image and anthropological implications of the scapegoat.[51] In this brief passage, James brings that fascination to bear on the nineteenth-century marriage plot, having his heroine recognize that she functions in that plot as the scapegoat.

The rich woman embodies those impulses that must be abandoned for the hero and heroine to establish their moral merit.[52] She is a scapegoat but not in the traditional sense that involves the killing of the sacrificial animal; it "indeed wasn't *their* design and their interest, that she should sink under hers; it wouldn't be their feeling that she should do anything but live, live on somehow for their benefit[,] . . . to keep proving to them that they had truly escaped and that she was still there to simplify" (470, emphasis in the original). This reference to simplifying echoes the passage at the end of *The Spoils of Poynton* where Fleda Vetch turns to Mrs. Gereth and tells her, "You simplify far too much. You always did and you always will. The tangle of life is much more intricate than you've ever, I think, felt it to be. You slash into it . . . with a great pair of shears; you nip at it as if you were one of the Fates!" (155). In both these passages James represents the plot that contrasts the rich and the poor woman, the plot that Mrs. Gereth attempts to impose and that Maggie Verver finds herself enacting, as a simplification, a violence done to the tangled materials of existence in order to give them a morally and aesthetically clear form, one in which the rich woman absorbs and carries the negative associations of the possession of wealth, thereby freeing the novel's other characters from that taint.

In this sense the rich woman functions as a living scapegoat. She must live in order to head off those distasteful possibilities. Even as it marginalizes and excludes her, this structure also grants the rich woman extraordinary power. Contemplating the individuals engaged in the game of cards, Maggie sees that "they might have been figures rehearsing some play of which she herself was the author; they might even, for the happy appearance they continued to present, have been such figures as would, by the strong note of character in each, fill any author with the certitude of success" (470). We see Maggie represented as a kind of author later when she joins Charlotte in the garden, ostensibly to provide her with the first volume of a Victorian novel because Charlotte has mistakenly been given the second.[53] This confusion suggests that the story itself has become confused, leaping forward to marriages, without having disentangled the kinship strands that need to be separated before such marriages can effect separation. Maggie's impulse at this point could be read as both writing and righting the story, in the sense of making it start where it needs to begin, in the first volume.

The effect of her presence is to make Charlotte exclaim exactly what Maggie thinks after discovering Amerigo's adultery with Charlotte. When Charlotte cries out, "I place my husband first" and "I want . . . to have him at last a little to myself" (528, 529), she articulates the sentiments that drive Maggie in the second half of the novel. At the end of this scene Maggie cries out "You want to take my father *from* me" (529, emphasis in the original). This is, of course, the way Maggie felt in the first volume of the novel, but it is not the way she feels in the second. Maggie now recognizes that the division between herself and her father is necessary. She must be exogamously exchanged.

With an inversion like the one James performs in *The Golden Bowl*, the forces of wealth are revealed to be not marginal but central to the novel's plot. At this point the forces that are opposed to them, the characters moved by love rather than money, the characters that typically function as the novel's hero and heroine, may seem peripheral or, in James's words, decorative. This term appears in the concluding scene of *The Golden Bowl*, the scene in which Amerigo and Charlotte rendezvous for the last time before the Ververs leave for America. The narrator tells us that

> Mrs. Verver and the Prince fairly "placed" themselves, however unwittingly, as high expressions of the kind of human furniture required, aesthetically, by such a scene. The fusion of their presence with the decorative elements, their contribution to the triumph of selection, was complete and admirable; though in a lingering view, a view more penetrating than the occasion really demanded, they also might have figured as concrete attestations of a rare power of purchase. (561–62)

This passage has often been read as a sign of James's general cynicism about early twentieth-century culture, yet it seems to me to also be a statement about the form of the nineteenth-century novel.

For, if you invert the plot of the novel, making visible the way the desire to consolidate wealth works behind the scenes, then the characters that represent the opposite values come to look like so much decorative furniture, the objects that make readers feel better about living with the money they possess but want to imagine does not determine their choices. At the end of the scene at Fawns where Maggie meditates on her own role in the marriage plot, she contemplates "the horror of finding evil seated, all at its ease, where she had only dreamed of good, the horror of the thing hideously *behind*, behind so much trusted, so much pretended, nobleness, cleverness, tenderness" (471). This passage conveys not just Maggie's awareness of her husband and stepmother's adultery but also James's perception that beneath the structure of the nineteenth-century novel, beneath the nobleness, tenderness, and cleverness that are celebrated by the marriage plot, lurk the desires the marriage plot defines as evil. An emblem of those desires, of the wish to retain rather than exchange wealth, the rich woman can be a represented as a demonized or purified figure. But James's last novel insists that the vulgar avidity that is her keynote can never be fully exorcized from narratives of marital exchange.

The novel of manners always tells a story that is as much about the vulgar question of money as it about tenderness and nobleness, reciprocal feelings, that are, of necessity, defined by their opposite. I have been arguing throughout this book that the rich woman is crucial to the plot of the nineteenth-century novel. In writing, the image I have had of the gesture I have been making is of turning something inside out, and since the rich woman is, from Austen onward, so frequently associated with the purse, that image has been specifically of emptying a purse, thereby making visible the money it contains. In much the same way I have shown how the rich woman functions as the vehicle, or what James might call a receptacle or reticule, through which the novel seeks both to represent and contain the monetary interests that press against its romantic stories. In James's late novels, these forces are no longer circumscribed, as money is acknowledged to mediate all forms of cultural interaction. With that gesture James brings the marriage plot to its close, as he places the figure that had been marginalized at the center of the story and allows her to contemplate the ends to which that narrative has been directed. The wonder, as Maggie exclaims of her fellow characters in *The Golden Bowl*, is that "they thought of everything but that I might think" (540). But perhaps the wonder of the marriage plot is that it takes the nineteenth-century novel almost a century to become fully conscious of the rich woman's implication in the novel of manners.

FROM PEMBERLEY TO MANDERLEY

The idea that the pattern I have been tracing here comes to an end with the late novels of Henry James makes sense if, as I posit in the introduction, we read the marriage plot as a literary structure that parallels the rise and fall of British economic dominance. In James's late novels, the heiresses are typically Americans. That representational shift reflects the fact that in James's period America was replacing England as a world-dominant economic power, beginning an ascendancy that may be now winding down. Yet the marriage plot did not simply vanish with late Jamesian experimentation and the end of the Victorian novel. It continues to interest readers, as is witnessed by the enduring popularity of *Pride and Prejudice*, *Jane Eyre*, *Great Expectations*, all novels whose plots, as I argued initially, depend on the contrast between the rich and the poor woman. That contrast also continued to shape post-Jamesian narratives like Daphne du Maurier's 1938 *Rebecca* as well as numerous popular culture texts.[1] Though I have written about the marriage plot as a literary device characteristic of a particular period and genre, the nineteenth-century novel, we might also think of it as what Alain Badiou calls a configuration. In his words, "A configuration is not an art form, a genre, or an 'objective' period in the history of art . . . . Rather, it is an identifiable sequence, initiated by an event, comprising a virtually infinite complex of works" (13). Configurations never really come to an end. They cannot be fully exhausted. All a configuration can do is to reach "its point of saturation" (13). The evolution of the marriage plot suggests that once authors become fully conscious of the configuration that structures their plots, that pattern ceases to be associated with a particular historical moment and becomes instead transhistorical, a structure that feels natural or self-evident rather than one that seems pointedly to comment on contemporary events.

This book has charted the process by which, over the course of the nineteenth century, the marriage plot that features the contrast between the rich and the poor woman gradually reaches its saturation point. Finding in it a structural solution to the difference between the rich and poor woman's stories that was introduced into the novel by the early works of Richardson and Burney, Austen initiates the use of that pattern in *Pride and Prejudice*, which introduces the paradigm of the marriage plot in such a clear form that its contours are dramatically visible as the engine that drives the narrative toward its satisfactory conclusion. In explaining the subject of my book to friends, both academic and nonacademic, I found myself time and again coming back to Miss Bingley and Lady Catherine de Bourgh as the quintessential examples of rich women. As soon as I mentioned them, my interlocutors knew what I meant by the vulgar question of money; they knew why I described rich women as the characters we love to hate. *Pride and Prejudice* also instantiates, in its conclusion, the image that incarnates the opposite of what the rich woman represents: the harmonious union of wealth and virtue, of economics and aesthetics, which is associated with land rather than mobile wealth. This ideal is incarnated in the estate, as Elizabeth Bennet sees it when she tours Pemberley and realizes imaginatively, since we never see her in the role, what it might mean to be its mistress. This triumphal conclusion of the first full instance of the marriage plot also marks a peak the configuration will never again reach.

Generations of readers have been drawn to the imaginative plenitude represented by Pemberley, which offers what Fredric Jameson famously described, citing Lévi-Strauss's work on myth, as an "imaginary resolution of a real contradiction" (*Political* 256n42). In that image the pursuit of virtue can be imagined as allied with the pursuit of wealth. But almost as soon as this resolution is imagined it becomes unattainable. In *Mansfield Park*, the Austen novel that follows *Pride and Prejudice*, the wealth of the Bertrams' estate is explicitly identified as coming from the labor of slaves, and the acquisition of that estate does not figure in the marriage between the propertied man and genteelly impoverished woman that resolves the plot.[2] It is a diminished resolution, one that does not, as the reactions of generations of readers prove, allow for the libidinal satisfaction that *Pride and Prejudice* provides.[3] If we move beyond the limits of Austen's career to contemplate the history of the marriage plot not just in the novel of manners but in the nineteenth-century novel in general, we see the image of an estate that gradually disintegrates over the course of the century, as a satisfying ending to the marriage plot begins to be seen as increasingly less achievable. While in *Pride and Prejudice* Pemberley, with its perfectly maintained grounds and collections of paintings and art objects, represents wealth used to achieve aesthetic order, Rochester's estate in *Jane Eyre* is, as its name Thornfield suggests, overgrown and uncultivated; its house is no longer in full use, and the attics are crammed with the furniture of the earlier eras.[4] It is also an estate whose existence is explicitly associated, like the one in Mansfield

Park, with wealth derived from English colonies, and it is a great house that will, in the end, be destroyed by fire.[5]

In *Great Expectations* Miss Havisham's Satis House serves as the estate in the imagination of the novel's hero. However, in Dickens's novel, the estate is no longer a possession of the landed gentry but of a brewer. (This reference echoes Anthony Trollope's novels of the 1860s and '70s, which depict estates purchased by ointment heiresses and made vulgar by money that comes from coal mining and rental properties.) And in Dickens's novel the estate is already in ruins as the novel opens. There is no longer here even what we had in *Jane Eyre*, a moment when the protagonist sees in landed wealth an image of past greatness. And, in *Great Expectations*, as in *Jane Eyre*, that estate is completely destroyed by fire as the novel reaches its climax. Miss Havisham's draperies catch on fire; she is partially burned, and the ruined remnants of her decaying dwelling are consumed. This sequence of novels makes it clear why James chooses, in his tribute to the nineteenth-century marriage plot, *The Spoils of Poynton*, to have the estate and its art objects destroyed at the story's end by a mysterious fire. He is following but also elaborating on the tradition that preceded him. *The Spoils of Poynton* contains no image of the ruined estate that haunts the ends of *Jane Eyre* and *Great Expectations*. In James's novella, the heroine arrives at the train station, learns of the destruction by fire, and simply turns around to take a train back to the place from which she came. The objects that have been the center of the power struggles in the piece simply vanish from its pages as if they never existed.[6] The trajectory of this tradition becomes particularly clear when we add *Rebecca* to the sequence of these nineteenth-century novels.

In *Rebecca*, too, the estate is an emblem of what the poor woman who marries the rich man seems most to desire. But in that novel, the beauties of the estate are evoked only in retrospect. When the story opens, Manderley is already a ruin, having been burned to the ground. Indeed the structure of the story is oddly circular, since it begins and ends with the novel's narrator, the unnamed poor woman who is the wealthy Maxim de Winter's second wife, heading toward the ruins of the estate that represented all she seemed to be gaining by marrying him. As in James's novella, the ruin is never depicted directly. In the novel's ending that narrator and de Winter are returning home, when they see a red glow in the sky and realize that it is not the dawn because it comes from the west rather than the east. That glow, which represents the end rather than the beginning of something, comes from the fire that destroys Manderley. The novel ends before they reach their destination, but that destination has already been evoked in the opening chapter, which begins, as does Hitchcock's famous film version of the novel, with the line "last night I dreamt I went to Manderley again. It seemed to me I stood by the iron gate leading to the drive, and for a while I could not enter, for the way was barred to me . . . . Then, like all dreamers, I was possessed of a sudden with supernatural powers and passed like a spirit through the barrier before me" (1). In a scene that echoes the end of *Jane Eyre* when Jane returns to Thornfield Hall and imagines briefly that it is still intact, the unnamed narrator of *Rebecca* imagines that Manderley is lit and inhabited only to have a shadow pass over the moon as she realizes that it is actually a burnt-out ruin. The chapter ends with her waking and explaining that "Manderley was ours no longer. Manderley was no more" (4).

In du Maurier's novel the estate is doubly removed at the story's opening; the vision the narrator describes is not of the ruin itself but of the protagonist's dream of it. As the unnamed heroine comments in the chapter that follows, "We can never go back again, that much is certain. The past is still too close to us. The things we have tried to forget and put behind us would stir again" (5). That she's trying to forget her old life at Manderley may surprise the reader, since one would think that what she would most desire would be to return to the world as it was before the estate was destroyed. Like Pemberley in Austen's *Pride and Prejudice*, Manderley seems to represent the use of wealth to create an aesthetic perfection in both the natural world of the grounds and the inhabited world of the house. It embodies a timeless perfection. As the narrator comments in one of the last moments when the estate is still depicted as whole: "The peace of Manderley. The quietude and the grace. Whoever lived within its walls, whatever trouble there was and strife, however much uneasiness and pain, no matter what tears were shed, what sorrows born, the peace of Manderley could not be broken or the loveliness destroyed" (357). We know, of course, that this evocation is a denial since the novel has opened with the dream vision of Manderley destroyed. It is a denial of the fact that the heroine has herself experienced there almost nothing but sorrow and unrest. And it is a denial of the fact that this very perfection was brought about not by the novel's hero, or by his marriage to the poor woman he loves, but by the wealthy woman who is the novel's villain. In *Rebecca*'s revelation scene the novel's penniless heroine learns, as is apropos of the marriage plot, that the novel's hero has never, as she had feared, loved the rich woman who was her predecessor. Instead he hated her: "She was vicious, damnable, rotten through and through" (271).

Yet this damnable figure was the source of the beauty that Manderley represents. As de Winter tells his second bride:

Her blasted taste made Manderley the thing it is to-day. The gardens, the shrubs, even the azaleas in the Happy Valley, do you think they existed when my father was alive? God, the place was a wilderness, lovely yes, wild and lonely with a beauty of its own, yes, but crying out for skill and care and the money that he would never give to it, that I would not have though of giving to it—but for Rebecca. Half the stuff you see here in the rooms was never here originally. The drawing-room as it is to-day, the morning-room—that's all Rebecca. . . . The beauty of Manderley that you see to-day, the Manderley that people talk about and photograph and paint, it's all due to her, to Rebecca. (274–75)

This twentieth-century version of the marriage plot undoes the distinction that was central to the nineteenth-century novel. The novels I examine in this book invariably oppose the crassness of the wealth, which is typically associated with the rich woman, to the tastefulness of wealth, which it typically linked to the man who chooses the poor woman rather than her rich antithesis. Even in James's novels where this pattern is inverted, the marriage plot still insists on a contrast between gross avidity and aesthetic purity. Du Maurier's novel collapses this opposition by making the vilified rich woman the source of the aesthetic beauty the novel celebrates in the image of the estate. Good taste is revealed to have nothing to do with virtue; its owner can be vicious but still create perfection because she possesses wealth. In this novel taste does not allow one to distinguish good money from bad.

Written after the end of the historical period that I have associated with the rise of the marriage plot, *Rebecca* no longer uses that configuration to address the economic issues that had been central to it since the era of Richardson and Austen. Instead du Maurier's novel engages the Manichean thinking of the marriage plot in the realm of sexuality rather than economics. In *Rebecca* the rich woman is vilified by being associated with sexual perversion or degeneration rather than the crassness of the vulgar uses of wealth. Her inward turning, what we might call her endogamy, is associated with the body rather than with money. In the novel's revelatory climax, Rebecca de Winter turns out to have had a sexual relation with her cousin and, as her maid Mrs. Danvers reveals, to have "despised all men. She was above all that" (340). These images of perversion are prefigured in the novel's opening dream vision of an overgrown Manderley, where "the beeches with white, naked limbs leant close to one another, their branches intermingled in a strange embrace" (1). The rhododendrons had "entered into alien marriage with a host of nameless shrubs, poor bastard things that clung about their roots as though conscious of their spurious origin" (2). These images suggest incest more explicitly than the ones we have seen haunting the nineteenth-century novel, and they are images of sexual rather than social incest. This concern with sexuality is apt given that concerns with perversion were part of general discourse at the time. (Radclyffe Hall's *The Well of Loneliness* had been published ten years before *Rebecca*.) These images also reflect the juncture at which the marriage plot ceases to function as a literary structure that reflects immediate social issues and becomes instead something that as it is associated with the natural world begins to seem natural itself. That shift is reflected in the word "vulgar," which, as we move into the twentieth century, comes to be associated with sexual impropriety more than with the crimes of taste, the improper use of money by the *nouveau riche*, that was key to what made it in the nineteenth century one of the most painful words in the English language.

This shift in meaning suggests how the narrative tension that makes the rich woman the demonized antithesis of a poorer counterpart can live on in the twentieth century, like Manderley, a ghost or memory of its former self. No longer directly linked to the historical context from which it arose, that plot allows us to think through, in a variety of different contexts, the relationship that Bourdieu has described in the postscript to *Distinction* as the tension between purity and vulgarity, a tension that requires works of art, and the individuals who consume them, to posit a way of distancing themselves from the vulgarity of a number of things (of money, of sexuality, of commonness itself) in order to insist on the purity of the aesthetic. Badiou has argued that

> the saturation of a configuration . . . in no way signifies that said configuration is a finite multiplicity. Nothing from within the configuration itself either delimits it or expresses the principle of its end. . . . there is always a virtually infinite quantity of subject points—minor, ignored, redundant, and so on—that are no less part of the immanent truth whose being is provided by the artistic configuration. (13)

In this book I have delimited the multiplicity of the marriage plot by examining it only in the arena of the novel of manners. Yet I hope that my examination has led readers to sense how that configuration saturates the nineteenth-century novel, appearing in texts not just by Austen, the Trollopes, Oliphant, and James but also by Scott, Dickens, Thackeray, Collins, Meredith, the Brontës, and others. I have charted the process by which novelists use that configuration more and more consciously over the course of latter half of the nineteenth century and into the twentieth. But even as novelists become conscious of and cynical about the marriage plot, they continue to use it. Initiated in the nineteenth century, it proves to be a structure whose possibilities are almost impossible to exhaust, a structure whose antithesis still shapes our thinking about both money and vulgarity, about, what Frances Trollope so aptly called, "the vulgar question of money."

INTRODUCTION: Rich Woman / Poor Woman

1. Reading this story from the point of view of the woman the hero chooses, Clara Tuite describes it as "the marriage-plot of upward female mobility, where a bourgeois female subject is elevated into an aristocratic class which is at once the ultimate object of desire and reward for this exemplary form of bourgeois female subjectivity and desperately in need of reform and renovation through this exemplary female subject" (10).

2. Fredric Jameson seems to do a four-sided reading of the relation between property and desire in *The Political Unconscious* when he uses Greimas's semiotic rectangle to analyze the role of the heiress in Balzac's *La veille fille* (151–69). But in his analysis, the female figure remains a monolithic image of property. It is the male figure that is divided, this time twice, to represent the four corners of the rectangle. Building on Sedgwick, Sharon Marcus argues, as I do, that we need to read the feminine position as doubled rather than singular, hence the title of her book: *Between Women*. See especially 10–11 for Marcus's discussion of *Between Men*.

3. For extensive readings of "The Neurotic's Individual Myth," see John Brenkman's *Straight Male Modern* and John Forester's *Truth Games*.

4. Ngai has also argued that we need to recognize "female twoness or nonsingularity" (155). For her, such splitting involves "the production of 'compound subjects' necessary for group formation" (143). These are the compound subjects Lacan analyzes and the marriage plot makes visible.

5. As Rita Felski has explained, citing Georg Simmel's work on gender, "whereas the masculine is linked to dualism, the feminine is 'the absolute on which the unity of human nature rests in a substantial and static self-contained completeness, in a sense prior to the division into subject and object'" (46). The marriage plot of the nineteenth-century novel consistently represents the objective position associated with femininity as divided rather than whole.

6. Another way to think of this split would be in terms of Matthew Arnold's assertion in *Culture and Anarchy* that "our best self . . . is not manifold, and vulgar, and unstable, and contentious, and ever-varying, but one, and noble, and secure, and peaceful" (136). The rich woman makes visible the vulgar, divided self that will, by the novel's end, be replaced by an image of the noble, unified self that is celebrated in marriage.

7. Characters like Mr. Veneering and Mr. Podsnap in *Our Mutual Friend* are also examples of vulgar masculinity in the sense that they present themselves as if they have

more wealth than they do in the same way that the explicitly vulgar Ferdinand Lopez does in Trollope's *The Prime Minister*.

8. Like Nunokawa, I argue that the nineteenth-century novel uses a doubled feminine position, a position associated with a lack of altruism and an excessive enmeshment with materialism, to deal symbolically with "capitalism's discontents" (3), but for me the economic anxieties encoded in that split inhere in the realm of capitalist accumulation.

9. In rethinking nineteenth-century middle-class identity Dror Wahrman makes a point about myth similar to the one I make here using Lacan and Bourdieu. Wahrman cites Barthes, who argues that "myth does not deny things[;] . . . on the contrary, its function is to talk about them[;] . . . it gives them a natural and eternal justification, it gives them a clarity which is not that of an explanation but that of a statement of fact. . . . In passing from history to nature, myth acts economically: it abolishes the complexity of human acts, it gives them the simplicity of essences" (18).

10. In his reading of Lacan's essay Brenkman explains that "the individual myth is itself the mediating link between one's personal circumstances and relationships and the institutional-symbolic complex" (59).

11. Poovey also cites this passage from Bourdieu to read the relation between literary and economic values as a form of denial. See *Genres*, 437n25.

12. My reading of the relation between the rich and the poor woman would confirm Woloch's observation that "it is often precisely in the interaction between character-spaces (rather than merely in the characters or stories themselves) that novels touch history" (20).

13. As Pocock notes, "In every phase of Western tradition, there is a conception of virtue—Aristotelian, Thomist, neo-Machiavellian or Marxian—to which the spread of exchange relations is seen as presenting a threat" (104).

14. A number of critics explore this relation. In *The Body Economic*, Gallagher discusses Malthusian economics and depictions of the body and desire in the nineteenth-century English novel. Christopher Herbert discusses Smith, Malthus, and Bagehot in terms of anthropological discussions of culture echoed in the novels of Anthony Trollope in *Culture and Anomie*. And Poovey reads political economy and the novel as parallel discourses in "Aesthetics and Political Economy."

15. Michael McKeon has traced the overlap of the two discourses in the era preceding the late eighteenth century, arguing that in those earlier texts "the language of the aesthetic and of exchange, joint products of the ongoing effort to theorize the adjustment of actual particularity to concrete virtuality, have a great deal more in common than in contradiction" (385).

16. For other critics who read Victorian anthropology as articulating narratives that are as much about nineteenth-century gender relations as primitive ones, see George Stocking, *Victorian Anthropology*, especially 197–208, and Marcus, 217–22.

17. McLennan argues similarly that "laws may be said to have first grown round the marital relation, next round the institution of property" (xxx).

18. Maine insists in *Lectures on the Early Histories of Institutions* that "the assertion, then, that there is a relation between civilisation and the proprietary capacities of women is only a form of the truth that every one of those conquests, the sum of which we call civilisation, is the result of curbing some one of the strongest, because

the primary, impulses of human nature" (340). Spencer calls this a "dying out of the mercantile element in marriage" (*Principles* 1.765).

19. Lori Merish notes that these narratives assume that "whereas in barbaric, pre-modern societies, women are physically enslaved or held captive, brutally used, and exploited, commercial societies are characterized by the 'free' social circulation of women and a new respect for women's affectional choices within the heterosexual mar-riage and commodity markets" (41).

20. We might think of the heiress's exceptional position in the system of general exchange as an instance of what Amanda Anderson has called "the project of univer-salism," which "will only become and remain viable if its terms are set by the excluded particular" (143). The rich woman is an excluded particular. Such exclusions typically involve what Slavoj Žižek has described as "a certain fissure, an asymmetry, a cer-tain 'pathological' imbalance which belies the universalism of the bourgeois 'rights and duties'" (21). The heiress makes such fissures visible in both nineteenth-century anthropology and the novel.

21. Though the terms "endogamy" and "exogamy" were, as Corbett notes, not in use until the mid-nineteenth century, English discussions of the failure to exchange the heiress predate Austen's novels. Pollak cites Lord Bolingbroke, who argued that "it is in many cases . . . agreeable . . . to preserve possessions and wealth in the families to which they belong, and not to suffer them to be carried away by any female caprice into others" (51). She also references Jeremy Taylor, who was much read in the nineteenth century and who insisted that "if the woman was an heiress she was to pleasure her own family rather than strangers" (52).

22. In thinking about endogamy and exogamy in relation to property I am follow-ing Corbett, who invites critics "to take up questions of economics and status, thus breaking the stranglehold of an ahistorical conception of the nuclear family and the incestuous paradigm said to govern it" ("Cousins" 243–44).

23. In *Novel Relations*, Perry links the depiction of family relationships in eigh-teenth-century English novels to the intense drive for capital accumulation that domi-nated the period. That drive meant that women were increasingly restricted in what they could possess: "Provisions in common law began limiting women's inheritance of land, and a series of statutes in ecclesiastical law reduced women's rights to reasonable parts from their husbands' or fathers' moveable goods" (47).

24. As Pollak notes, referencing Juliet Mitchell, "In economically advanced socie-ties . . . economic forms of exchange other than kinship exchange dominate" (13).

25. Franco Moretti has argued that these geographical placements spatially incar-nate the social movements of the marriage market: "Austen's plots join together—'marry'—people *who belong to different counties.* Which is new and significant: it means that these novels try to represent what social historians refer to as the 'National Mar-riage Market': a mechanism that crystallized in the course of the eighteenth century, which demands of human beings (and especially of women) a new mobility: physical, and even more so *spiritual* mobility" (14–15, emphasis in the original).

26. As Eileen Cleere asserts, "more flexible models of family are needed to in-terrogate the manner in which endogamy itself becomes an economic strategy" ("Re-investing" 114).

27. The differences between the marriages Lady Catherine and Miss Bingley en-vision reflect the difference Randolph Trumbach has noted of eighteenth-century

marriages centered on property, "the difference between seeing marriage as an act of incorporation that *maintained* a family's standing, since cousin marriage (in which a daughter married the son of her father's brother) prevented the loss of a family's name or land, and seeing it as an alliance that could *improve* a family's social standing" (18–19, emphasis in the original).

28. These novels follow the pattern that Perry notes in the eighteenth-century novel, in which "the heroes of novels never married women wealthier than they" (54).

29. Q. D. Leavis argues that the novel's heroine Lucilla Marjoribanks "belongs in the company of Lady Catherine de Burgh [sic], Lady Bracknell[,] . . . Emma Woodhouse and the rest—all women of ability and presence" (3.157) and, I would argue, most importantly, wealth.

30. Oliphant's emphasis on retaining the family name reflects the biblical passage most cited in Renaissance and anthropological discussions of the heiress, the passage from Numbers where Zelophehad's daughters ask Moses, "Why should the name of our father be done away from among his family, because he hath no son?" (Num. 27:4).

31. *The Elementary Structures of Kinship* is dedicated to Lewis Morgan.

32. This turn to folklore supports David Schneider's argument that, in Lévi-Strauss's writings and in the work of the nineteenth-century anthropologists who preceded him, the models of kinship worked out describe less the mechanisms of non-Western cultures than the cultural thinking of the anthropologists themselves: "European social scientists use their own folk culture as the source of many, if not all, of their ways of formulating and understanding the world around them" (193). Schneider's argument would help explain why Victorian anthropologists and novelists treat the heiress in a similar manner. Both are using familiar folktale patterns to think through anxieties raised by nineteenth-century social developments.

33. *The Woman in White* also confirms my observation about the difference between narratives in which a man is poised between two women and one in which a woman is poised between two men. While it may look as if Laura Fairlie is caught between two men who desire her rather than her wealth, in fact Sir Percival is not wealthy and the entirety of the novel's complex plot revolves around his attempts to hide the fact that he is not the legitimate heir to his own estate.

34. In Brontë's novel as in Eliot's the marriage of a poor man to a rich woman is linked to anthropological images. Louis asks Shirley playfully whether, if he emigrates, "any Indian tribe of Black-feet or Flat-heads, would afford . . . a bride" (576). For a discussion of *Shirley* as a novel about a woman of property, see chapter 1 of Tim Dolin's *The Mistress of the House*.

35. The negative feelings readers are invited to have for the heiress are similar to the feelings triggered by social incest: "The individual repulsion and social reprobation directed against the unilateral consumption of certain goods" (Lévi-Strauss 61).

36. Lévi-Strauss introduces the term "scandal" in the opening pages of *The Elementary Structures of Kinship*, where, as Derrida notes, he "encounters what he calls a *scandal*, that is to say, something which no longer tolerates the nature/culture opposition he has accepted, something which *simultaneously* seems to require the predicates of nature and of culture. This scandal is the *incest prohibition*. The incest prohibition is universal; in this sense one could call it natural. But it is also a prohibition, a system of norms and interdicts; in this sense one could call it cultural" (283, emphasis in the original). In the same way, the rich woman in the novel feels as if she triggers a repulsion that is

natural, but that repulsion turns out to be a key part of the general set of rules governing marital exchange in the text. I am indebted to one of my anonymous *PMLA* readers for suggesting the concept of scandal as a way of capturing the complexity of the rich woman's function in the novel.

37. Armstrong argues similarly in *How Novels Think* that "Victorian fiction portrayed the despicable qualities of ruling-class masculinity as truly despicable *only* when those qualities appear to animate women" (81, emphasis in the original).

38. In *The Ethnography of Manners* Nancy Bentley explains that the discourse of manners "fosters for the writer an enhanced authority over a bounded sphere of culture, an aesthetic and intellectual 'ownership' of manners intended to surpass coarser forms of cultural possession" (1).

39. As Dupin explains in Poe's story, "There is a game of puzzles . . . which is played upon a map. One party playing requires another to find a given word—the name of town, river, state or empire—any word, in short, upon the motley and perplexed surface of the chart. A novice in the game generally seeks to embarrass his opponents by giving them the most minutely lettered names; but the adept selects such words as stretch, in large characters, from one end of the chart to the other. These, like the over-largely lettered signs and placards of the street, escape observation by dint of being excessively obvious; and here the physical oversight is precisely analogous with the moral inapprehension by which the intellect suffers to pass unnoticed those considerations which are too obtrusively and too palpably self-evident" (340–41).

40. See Harth, 130–32, for a discussion of various assessments of the marriage act, which tend to come down on one side or the other, to see either defenders of the act or opponents to it as endorsing marital and economic freedom. See Katherine Sobba Green's *The Courtship Novel*, 69–79, and Kelly Hager's *Dickens and the Rise of Divorce*, 33–43, for a discussion of the act, and marital reform in general, in relation to the evolving form of the novel.

41. That career pattern was successful enough that one of the other best-selling novelists of the latter half of the eighteenth century repeated it. Frances Burney followed *Evelina; or, The History of a Yong Lady's Entrance into the World* (1778), her tale of a heroine who apparently has no wealth, with *Cecilia; or, Memoirs of an Heiress* (1782), the story of one who, like Richardson's Clarissa, is tormented by her possession of property.

42. For a discussion of the relation between women and property in the "uncharted literary terrain of the novel from 1748 to 1818, the *terra incognita* between Samuel Richardson and Jane Austen" (3), see Perry's *Novel Relations*.

43. Arrighi argues that capitalism evolves in cycles of dominance, Genoa being replaced by Holland, Holland by England, and England by America as we move from the 1500s to the twentieth century (see fig. 10, 364). For a discussion of the relevance of Arrighi's theories for readings of early twentieth- as well as nineteenth-century literature, see Frederic Jameson, "Culture and Finance Capital," and Ian Baucom, *Specters of the Atlantic*, 22–31 and 141–45.

44. Though *The Theory of Moral Sentiments* was first written in 1759, Smith revised it in 1789 just prior to his death. It is the pessimistic additions he made to that final version that are most clearly addressed in Austen's novels.

45. For further consideration of these issues, see Pocock's *Virtue, Commerce, and History*.

46. For discussions of this period, see Maxine Berg, *The Machinery Question and the Making of Political Economy, 1815–1848*, and Harold Perkin, *The Origins of Modern English Society*.

47. For discussion of the relation between money and appetite, see Denise Gigante, *Taste*.

48. Frances Trollope helped Anthony Trollope place his earliest novels with her own publisher.

49. For a discussion of the ideological shifts associated with this period, see Martin Wiener, *English Culture and the Decline of the Industrial Spirit*.

50. For a discussion of these figures, see W. D. Rubinstein, *Men of Property*.

51. This remark about anthropology as a new science comes from William James's 1868 review of *The Progress of Anthropology*, which his brother Henry helped edit.

52. In making these comparisons I face the same challenge as others who are attempting to locate the practice of literature within the field of the social sciences, which is "to grasp the unliterary dimensions of literature while preserving a sophisticated appraisal of its literary qualities, to discover the aesthetic or narrative dimensions of the nonliterary, without losing sight of its objective status" (Mizruchi 4).

53. Mizruchi argues that "border texts testify to the engagement of major literary authors with contemporary social theory. They also reveal the outlines of a genuinely interdisciplinary region, one that might be regarded as a precursor to the postmodern literary critical field of cultural studies" (15).

CHAPTER ONE: Social Distinction in Jane Austen

1. See Peter Knox-Shaw, *Jane Austen and the Enlightenment*, 27–72, for an informative discussion of the Austens' general knowledge of Enlightenment thinkers.

2. Jane Austen began writing her juvenilia in 1789. "Love and Freindship," "A History of England," "Lesley Castle," and "A Collection of Letters" were all produced between 1789 and 1791.

3. Knox-Shaw points out that "in successive revisions to the *Theory of Moral Sentiments* (1759–90), Adam Smith worried more openly over the thought that the pursuit of wealth and fame cuts across the path that leads to wisdom and virtue, and that the best possible world may be far from a good one" (63). As Jean-Pierre Dupuy explains, "a major difficulty arises, one that is destined to torment Smith throughout his life, finally causing him to add a key chapter to the sixth edition of *The Theory of Moral Sentiments* (and thus long after the publication of *The Wealth of Nations*). This chapter is entitled 'Of the corruption of our moral sentiments, which is occasioned by this disposition to admire the rich and the great, and to despise or neglect persons of poor and mean condition'" (55).

4. We do not know whether Austen read Smith or not, but *The Theory of Moral Sentiments* might have come her way since it was deemed appropriate reading for women. As Austen's contemporary William Rose commented in the *Monthly Review*, "The whole work, indeed, shews a delicacy of sentiment, and acuteness of understanding, that are seldom to be met with; and what ought particularly to be mentioned, there is the strictest regard preserved, throughout, to the principles of religion, so that the serious reader will find nothing that can give him any just ground of offence" (quoted in Raphael and Macfie 27.) This means that, as another contemporary commented, "this

doctrine of sympathy bids fair for cutting out David Hume's Immaterialism, especially with the ladies" (quoted in Raphael and Macfie 30). Smith's text makes an appearance in Maria Edgeworth's *Belinda* (1801), where, as Knox-Shaw notes, the heroine "keeps a copy of the *Theory* on her dressing table" (7n17).

5. In reading these three novels as a progression, I am agreeing with David Monaghan, who argues that we need to conceive of Austen's novels not as separate texts but as engaging ongoing arguments: "Read in sequence, the six novels reveal an evolving social vision and a continual search for an appropriate form within which to embody that vision. Thus it becomes evident that, ultimately, Jane Austen's greatness is to be found in a consideration of the complete body of her work rather than in any single novel, considerable as some of them are" (15). Woloch also reads Austen's novels as engaged in a sequential commentary on themselves, arguing that "*Mansfield Park* and *Emma* unravel the achieved construction of centrality that has just taken place in *Pride and Prejudice*. . . . These two novels . . . are a remarkable artistic response to the author's own achievement" (346n26).

6. Cardinal Newman's comment that Austen's novels involve "a thinking out into language" (Southam 2.201) seems particularly apt in the context of my argument. She uses the language of fiction to think through the same problems that Hume and Smith address in their prose. For a discussion of wealth as purchasing power, see Edward Copeland, *Women Writing about Money*, 89–114.

7. Deidre Shauna Lynch has argued that in the eighteenth century "caricaturists *flaunted* their excesses"; for them, "conveying the identity of the person was a matter of producing a surplus—producing too much" (58, emphasis in the original). Austen flaunts the excesses of caricatured rich women so that readers see that those characters represent values one should not to choose. As Lynch explains, "characters have supplied readers with the means with which to implement the work of cultural classification and stratification that Bourdieu calls distinction," particularly when "pitted against caricature" (19).

8. Engrossment referred to the uniting of estates, the appropriation and enclosure of what had previously been common or open land, and the consolidation of commercial enterprises. As Jerome Christensen notes, "When Hume comes to talk about monopolism, whether it be Roman, Catholic, or English, he usually tropes the massive absorption of material, power, and profit as 'engrossment,' as when he warns that were it not for intrinsic limits to growth 'commerce . . . would go on perpetually increasing, and one spot of the globe would engross the art and industry of the whole'" (197).

9. The Bingley sisters "were rather handsome, had been educated in one of the first private seminaries in town, had a fortune of twenty thousand pounds, were in the habit of spending more than they ought, and of associating with people of rank; and were therefore in every respect entitled to think well of themselves, and meanly of others" (11). Similarly, Lady Catherine de Bourgh, as Wickham explains, "has the reputation of being remarkably sensible and clever; but I rather believe she derives part of her abilities from her rank and fortune, part from her authoritative manner, and the rest from the pride of her nephew, who chuses that every one connected with him should have an understanding of the first class" (57–58).

10. This problem has been central to the critical reception of *Mansfield Park*; critics have repeatedly asked how one can be attracted to a heroine, who, in the words of Leo Bersani, is "not merely weak" but "almost *is not*" (76, emphasis in the original).

11. For a discussion of the social nature of Smith's argument, see Todorov, "Living Alone Together."

12. When Austen said she worried that in Emma she had created a heroine that no one but herself could like, she may have been thinking about the risk she was taking in transforming the figure that had typically been the heroine's antithesis into the novel's protagonist.

13. J. G. A. Pocock has argued that in Edmund Burke's writing "the expansive power of the monied interest is being expressly brought together with the uncontrollable energy of enthusiasm, the intellect divorced from all natural relations—from manners and subordinations, from the laws of nature and nature's God—feeding on its own fantasies and substituting itself for every other form of power" (204). This sequence marks the shifts Austen makes as she moves from *Pride and Prejudice* to *Mansfield Park* to *Emma*. In Miss Bingley and Lady Catherine de Bourgh, she explores wealth's propensity to corrupt manners and subordinations, in Mary Crawford its ability to pervert relations with nature and with God, and in Emma its tendency to feed fantasies that enable the prosperous individual to substitute herself for every other form of power.

14. Such internalization makes sense if Austen's novels are working through the implications of Smith's thinking in *The Theory of Moral Sentiments*, a text that, as Imraan Coovadia has pointed out, "presents a system of perspectives that cannot so much be argued for as internalized" (831).

15. For a discussion of how virtue is made sexually attractive in the earlier *Tom Jones*, see Paul Kelleher's "'The Glorious Lust of Doing Good.'" Kelleher argues that "Fielding . . . recasts the sublime object of wisdom as something more closely resembling a lovely English girl" (174): "Sex allies itself with virtue and vice becomes the repository of desire or conduct that falls outside the vision of man and woman progressing toward (presumably) the married state" (175).

16. The scenes at Pemberley follow what Christensen calls the "Humean model of progressive refinement, which envisages the rise to politeness of all members of the state" (119n25).

17. Lynch argues that the pervasive images of swelling in eighteenth-century literature convey both unruly sexual desire and a fear "that the nation is unbalanced by the influence of its moneyed interests" (25). Christensen describes Humean engrossment as "a graphically active version of absorption . . . [that] renders the monopoly as voracious and repellently swollen" (197). In *Emma*, Emma comments of the wealthy and tyrannical Mrs. Churchill that "where little minds belong to rich people in authority . . . they have a knack of swelling out, till they are quite as unmanageable as great ones" (96). As I show in chapter 2, this association of the wealthy woman with swelling is intensified in the novels of Frances Trollope.

18. These negatively depicted fictional figures allow Austen to define the stance that was so difficult for Hume to identify. As Christensen has argued, "If luxury is itself excess, defining what is too much excess, that excess which takes us beyond the economic toward individual and social ruin is extremely difficult" (116).

19. In *The Theory of Moral Sentiments* Smith argues that we admire the rich in part because "their dress is the fashionable dress; the language of their conversation, the fashionable style; their air and deportment, the fashionable behaviour" (64).

20. As Joyce Appleby explains, "Under the sway of new tastes, people had spent more, and in spending more the elasticity of demand had become apparent. In this

elasticity, the defenders of domestic spending discovered the propulsive power of envy, emulation, love of luxury, vanity, and vaulting ambition" (169).

21. Austen's reference to elegance echoes the seventeenth issue of the *Loiterer* in which the author argues, satirically, that refinement "has taught us to live elegantly, while our fortune lasts, and fashionably, when it is gone" (11).

22. This openness makes the marriage plot relatively easy for Bingley; like a good consumer he meets Jane Bennet and knows immediately what he likes. Austen's positive portrait of Bingley, who derives his wealth from trade, reflects the position taken in the *Loiterer*, which argues that once the society has been freed from its illiberal prejudice against the new wealth, then "the only blot that disgraces the annals of Trade shall at length be erased, and the BENEVOLENCE of Commerce be equalled only by its Utility" (24).

23. Poovey has argued that "the logic of fashion gradually began to expose . . . the persistence of aesthetic concerns within economic exchanges, and the persistence of a market logic in the domain of beauty or art" ("Aesthetics" 94). Guillory makes a similar point, explaining that "the internal division of the commodity into its aspect of beauty and its aspect of use . . . preemptively assimilated the distinction between the work of art and the commodity into the definition of the latter" (312).

24. I have made a claim elsewhere for the significance of this mixture for the form of the novel as a whole, explaining that as the novel works to disentangle the language of political economy from aesthetics, or commerce from the arts, "it inevitably invokes the dangerous mixing of the two in order to represent the mélange from which aesthetic difference, and even aesthetic superiority, can emerge" ("'Rich Woman / Poor Woman'" 432). The rich woman's association with the mixture of elements the novel otherwise attempts to keep separate marks her as a scandal in the Lévi-Straussian sense.

25. Austen's depictions of Miss Bingley can be seen as participating in "the controversy between 'virtue' and 'corruption' and . . . the associated debate between 'landed interests' and 'monied interests'" (Pocock 109). Her insistence on the similarities between Miss Bingley's and Lady Catherine's attitudes reflects social history. In the late eighteenth century, as Williams points out, "an acquisitive, high bourgeois society [was] at the point of its most evident interlocking with an agrarian capitalism that is itself mediated by inherited titles and by the making of family names" (*Country* 115). Jules Lubbock also notes the link rather than the opposition between the two classes, explaining that "*The Spectator* envisaged the monied interest as the 'heir' to the landed interest, both as Britain's ruling class and as the source of her wealth" (109–10).

26. In thinking about the similarities between Austen's portrait of Lady Catherine and that of Miss Bingley, it is helpful to keep in mind Spring's assertion that estate owners were "a businesslike, capitalist class. This last, perhaps, is central to the removal of misunderstandings among Jane Austen interpreters. Although English landowners were not commercial or industrial capitalists, they were agrarian capitalists" (64). The landed classes "sought for productivity, and in the form of increased rents for an increase in their profits. They were not, however, as single-minded as a merchant or manufacturer in the pursuit of profit, inasmuch as they wanted other things as much or more, notably the exercise of political power. . . . Still, theirs was a capitalist money culture. Well before Jane Austen's lifetime, they had ingeniously turned a variety of landed resources into money. . . . In the eighteenth century their money incomes grew markedly, as did their borrowing" (65). Christopher Lasch argues similarly that "the eigh-

teenth century was in many ways a period of aristocratic revival in England. . . . But it is important to understand that the resurgence of aristocratic power was based on an agrarian revolution that was eradicating feudal traditions, abolishing feudal tenures, and commercializing agriculture, in the course of which the landed gentry and even the nobility had to acquire a thoroughly 'middle-class' out-look on the management of their estates, on child-raising and education, and on marriage" (102–3).

27. The equation of talent with wealth that Lady Catherine assumes is presented in literal form and with mock seriousness when the authors of the *Loiterer* ask whether, for a person who lacks talents, it is "not natural that he should endeavour to purchase, by an elegant profusion of wealth, that honour and respect which he can no other way procure" (17).

28. We might think of Lady Catherine's response as a form of prejudice in the sense that Hume uses that term when he asserts that "a person influenced by prejudice . . . obstinately maintains his natural position, without placing himself in that point of view which the performance supposes" (145). Miss Bingley's reactions to Elizabeth Bennet might also be read as a form of prejudice in the sense that the *Loiterer* uses that term. Miss Bingley's disparagement of Elizabeth for having relatives in trade even though her own fortune derives from commercial sources reflects the *Loiterer*'s insistence that those who have been enriched by trade are the most likely to condemn the commercial activities of others. The author deems them "censurable, for censuring," insisting that their behavior, far from being "genteel," is "illiberal, and ungentlemanlike" (24). James Austen characterizes the automatic condemnation of everything associated with commerce as "the habit of Prejudice" (*Loiterer* 24).

29. The difference between Lady Catherine and Elizabeth in this scene is marked by their views on the necessity of work to nurturing a skill. Lady Catherine assumes that she would not need to work at it. She would automatically have been an excellent player if only she had learned. Elizabeth too believes her fingers are as "capable as any other woman's of superior execution" (117) but acknowledges that she has not practiced enough to reach such a state of excellence.

30. D. A. Miller also argues in a different context that "what Elizabeth calls her 'impertinence,' and we her wit, draws the chief of its energies from a plainly visible psychic process of denial" (*Jane Austen* 43). Miller is interested in the way that Elizabeth defines herself by differentiating herself from "her vulgar, dysfunctional family and its imperiled economic position" (43). I am suggesting that Austen's heroine walks a tightrope that depends on her being differentiated both from those home influences and from the differently vulgar pomposity of the women whose economic position is not just secure but comfortable.

31. The poor women of the later novels, Fanny Price, Harriet Smith, Jane Fairfax, and Miss Bates, are more indigent than Elizabeth Bennet. Fanny is a dependent relation, the poverty and disorder of whose parental home are emphasized in the Portsmouth scenes. Harriet Smith is a bastard who must marry to obtain clear social status. Jane Fairfax's birth family lacks financial means, and she is brought to the verge of going to work as a governess. Miss Bates is the most needy of all these characters, since there is no possibility of her marrying to establish herself.

32. In *Pride and Prejudice*, the privileging of wealth is a localized phenomenon, displayed most visibly at the estates of the wealthy, but in *Mansfield Park* we see commercial values expressed and enacted everywhere. In watching the amateur theatricals, for

example, Fanny Price perceives that "selfishness . . . more or less disguised, seemed to govern them all" (93), virtually echoing eighteenth-century descriptions of the market-place, with its dominant motivation of self-interest. Wealth and exchange are implicitly referred to, as Tatiana Holway has argued, in the game of speculation, during which Henry Crawford attempts to "sharpen [Fanny's] avarice, and harden her heart" (164). These tropes recur in the descriptions of Fanny who is told "you must really begin to harden yourself to the idea of being worth looking at" (136) and to immerse herself in "the trade of *coming out*" (183, emphasis in the original).

33. Copeland argues that "consumer desire fuels the moral action of *Mansfield Park*, and sexual desire is inextricably intertwined in the struggle" (102).

34. As Katie Trumpener explains, "Accustomed to getting her own way and being able to buy anyone whose services she needs, Mary is openly irritated at the 'sturdy independence' of the local farmers" (181). While Trumpener goes on to associate this attitude with slaveholders and French aristocrats, I would argue that it speaks to gen-eral fears about the increasing power of mobile wealth.

35. Trumpener argues that "Austen's novel aligns both Crawfords—with their French connections, open disrespect for organized religion, and private willingness to flout moral rules—with the false allures of Jacobinism" (181). Their associations with foreignness would also have linked them to contemporary anxieties about consump-tion. Barker-Benfield cites Henry Mackenzie, who had argued in a 1786 essay that "the influx of foreign riches, and of foreign luxury, which this country has of late experi-enced, has almost leveled every distinction but that of money among us" (146).

36. Lubbock cites this passage in *The Tyranny of Taste*, arguing that "the power of the greater nobility, which even the feudal system had failed to diminish, was now undermined not by force but by the imported luxuries of these great trading cities. The glitter of these luxuries attracted the vanity of the nobles and tempted them to send their 'rude produce' to market in exchange for such toys and baubles instead of sharing their produce with their servants and dependants through bounty and hospi-tality" (140). Such anxieties about frivolity were articulated throughout the literature of the period. The Smith passage is virtually echoed in the *Loiterer*, which notes that "we frequently hear of whole fortunes expended in one single entertainment, estates lavished on an equipage, and even several acres of good land converted into a pair of buckles" (17).

37. The other term that Austen uses to talk about this state that is deeper than manners is "character." Edmund refers to values of a different character and temper. At the end of the novel Sir Thomas Bertram will recognize that "with all the cost and care of an anxious and expensive education, he had brought up his daughters, without their understanding their first duties, or his being acquainted with their character and temper" (314).

38. In representing the differences between Fanny Price and Mary Crawford Austen also alludes to contemporary discussions of Stoic versus Epicurean philosophy. Hume paired an essay on the Stoic with one on the Epicurean. Austen describes the Crawfords as brought up in the "school of luxury and epicurism" (277).

39. Fanny Price is drawn to see Mary Crawford "every two or three days; it seemed a kind of fascination; she could not be easy without going, and yet it was without loving her, without ever thinking like her" (143).

40. Anna Despotopoulou uses Smith to read this same passage in her discussion

of *Mansfield Park* (572). She argues that Fanny's control of the moral gaze allows her
an independence that Mary Crawford lacks because she is defined by the social, by the
love of praise. I do not see Austen fully engaging with Smith's theory of the impartial
spectator until she gets to *Emma*.

41. The contrast between health and sickness will be reiterated in both *Emma* and
Persuasion, in which wealthy women are, as the narrator comments of Emma, the picture of health, while their poorer rivals (Harriet Smith, Jane Fairfax, Anne Elliott) are
prone to headaches, cold, and toothaches. Both *Mansfield Park* and *Persuasion* emphasize that this excessive health can be a negative trait if a woman refuses to be constrained by boundaries, as, for example, when Julia Bertram climbs over the ha-ha and
Louisa Musgrove insists on being jumped down the stile. If we read the rich woman as
associated with the economy in these scenes, then Louisa's fall and Julia's inappropriate behavior reflect anxieties about the possibility that England's prosperity was too
healthy. The rich woman's propensity to break through proper boundaries reflects fears
about "vicious luxury," which "is what erases the bounds between a restricted economy
and one generalized beyond any measure" (Christensen 116).

42. Christensen notes how easily anxieties about social engrossment transfer to
both the body and writing. Hume writes in a letter to a friend that "I am really so much
ashamed of myself when I see my Bulk on a shelf, as well as when I see it in a Glass, that
I would fain prevent my growing more corpulent either way" (quoted in Christensen
198). Obviously Austen's reputation works in the opposite direction: the small canon
of her works and their apparently limited subject matter is associated with smallness
of the body and fineness of taste.

43. The movement of Austen's narrative at this juncture perfectly reflects the tension that I discuss in my introduction in referencing Lacan's essay "The Neurotic's
Individual Myth." Lacan argues that "each time the subject succeeds, or approaches
success in assuming his own role, each time he becomes, as it were, identical with himself and confident that his functioning in his specific social context is well-founded, the
object, the sexual partner, is split—here in the form *rich woman or poor woman*" (417,
emphasis in the original). So, in *Mansfield Park* Edmund's confusion between Fanny
Price and Mary Crawford becomes most intense as he is preparing to be ordained:
"Edmund was at this time particularly full of cares; his mind being deeply occupied
in the consideration of two important events now at hand, which were to fix his fate
in life—ordination and matrimony" (175). Austen's assertion that the novel's subject is
ordination makes sense once we think of the confusion between Mary and Fanny as
circling around the issue of Edmund's career choice.

44. As Richard Teichgraeber argues, Smith "always made it clear that he could fashion no unambiguous moral defense of that particular aspect of self-interest that drives
men to pursue riches: vanity. . . . For while vanity may be the crucial motive of economic activity, it also caused many men to mistake wealth and greatness for virtue and
wisdom" (136–37). Austen's novel shows how even a character like Edmund, who is not
obviously vain, can still mistake wealth for virtue as he imagines Mary Crawford to be
the same as Fanny Price.

45. Passages like this appear throughout the middle section of the novel, as Edmund's courtship is reaching a climax. He tells Fanny that "a friendship between two so
very dear to him was exactly what he could have wished" (145). He is no longer attracted
to other women because "you and Miss Crawford have made me too nice" (241). Ironi-

cally, given the novel's insistence on the physical difference between the two women, they even begin to look the same to him. This becomes clear when, seeing Fanny in a certain dress, he asks, in a fit of abstraction, "Has not Miss Crawford a gown something the same?" (153).

46. "According to the famous story told by Socrates, Hercules, 'the greatest of all Stoic heroes,' at a crossroads faced the choice between the hard, uphill road to Virtue and the soft, easy path to Pleasure. The case for each was made to him by the appropriate goddess-personifications of Virtue and Pleasure" (Barker-Benfield 109), which is how one might read Fanny Price and Mary Crawford.

47. Here, as Edmund finally comes to disparage the woman he previously loved, we see confirmation of Smith's argument that wealth and greatness "may, no doubt be completely degraded by vice and folly. But the vice and folly must be very great, before they can operate this complete degradation" (*Theory of Moral Sentiments* 63).

48. Smith's concerns about the excessive admiration of wealth were part of the climate of the period. They are reiterated in *Spectator* 294, where we hear that "the consideration of fortune has taken up all our minds and, as I have often complained, poverty and riches stand in the places of guilt and innocence."

49. Noting "the sense of revulsion" (133) Austen's description of the Prices' home in Portsmouth manifests, Ruth Yeazell argues that Fanny "sees her family home as stained and polluted" (133) and that the narrative seems almost to revel in "the intensity of this consciousness of dirt" (133).

50. Smith is not the only contemporary of Austen's to emphasize the unhealthy imaginative appeal of wealth. Addison argued in the *Guardian* that "it is evident that a Desire terminated in Money is fantastical; so is the Desire of outward Distinctions, which bring no Delight of Sense, nor recommend us as useful to Mankind" (quoted in Lubbock 189).

51. Susan Fraiman has noted the delusiveness of these recollections. Fanny has not actually experienced Mansfield as an environment of order. She only sees it this way in "idealizing retrospection" (809), a detail that underscores the sense that Fanny, too, is caught up in the delusive imaginative appeal of wealth. This fantastical looking back from Portsmouth to Mansfield also confirms Moretti's assertion that in Austen's novels, "cities . . . are all real, whereas those homes were all fictional: an asymmetry of the real and the imaginary—of geography and literature" (18). Knox-Shaw notes of Austen that "she was aware too, if only in a general way, of the new field of city studies, first made statistical through the actuarial research of Richard Price, but going back to Hume and Smith, and to the philanthropist whom she called the 'famous Dr. Percival of Manchester.' Her brother James, who particularly praised the Portsmouth scenes of *Mansfield Park*, and wrote about urban poverty himself, seems also to have been familiar with such work" (175).

52. Hume makes a similar assertion that seems applicable to Austen's novel. As Adela Pinch comments, he argues in the *Treatise* that "our pleasure consists 'in our sympathizing with the proprietor of the lodging,'" perhaps because he feels, "like Elizabeth Bennet visiting Pemberley, that the proprietor of such a house deserves more of our sympathy" (38).

53. *Emma* confirms Adam Smith's assertion that "our imagination, which in pain and sorrow seems to be confined and cooped up within our own persons, in times of ease and prosperity expands itself to every thing around us" (*Theory of Moral Senti-*

ments 183). Wealth's tendency to feed imaginative desires had been noted from early on in the writings of those concerned with the troubling effects of the rise of commerce. Lubbock notes that Nicholas Barbon, who wrote *A Discourse of Trade* in 1690, "believed that . . . whereas the 'Necessitys of the Body,' for basic food and shelter, were finite, once they had been satisfied 'those wants, most of them proceeding from imagination' which he described as 'the Wants of the Mind' were infinite" (97).

54. Austen's portrayal of the virtues of the middle ranks may remind us of Edmund Bertram's assertion to Mary Crawford that "poverty is exactly what I have determined against. Honesty, in the something between, in the middle state of worldly circumstances, is all that I am anxious for your not looking down on" (147).

55. Such passages confirm Smith's assertion that "in the middling and inferior stations of life, the road to virtue and that to fortune, to such fortune, at least, as men in such situations can reasonably expect to acquire, are, happily, in most cases, very nearly the same" (*Theory of Moral Sentiments* 63).

56. We might think of the relation between the rich and the poor woman in terms of Ngai's discussion of envy. Ngai explains that the commonplace approach to envy treats it as "a term describing a *subject* who lacks, rather than the subject's affective *response* to perceived inequality" (126, emphasis in the original). In Austen's novels the rich woman needs the poor woman to be defined as lacking in order for her own status to be reinforced as enviable. Such situations can, as Ngai argues, lead to "'unhappy self-assertion,' including a negative relationship to property we might call 'unhappy possessiveness'" (130). She is thinking here of the envier's relation to possessions, but Austen's novels brilliantly show the instability of envy. They insist that women who are wealthy, in imagining themselves the object of the envy of others, enter into an unhappy relation with their own possessions.

57. As Smith writes of the individual, "When he looks back upon it, and views it in the light in which the impartial spectator would view it, he finds that he can enter into none of the motives which influenced it. He is abashed and confounded at the thoughts of it, and necessarily feels a very high degree of that shame which he would be exposed to, if his actions should ever come to be generally known" (*Theory of Moral Sentiments* 118).

58. Here I am echoing Williams's assertion that Austen "provided the emphasis which had only to be taken outside the park walls, into a different social experience, to become not a moral but a social criticism" (*Country* 117).

59. Oliphant argues that "in one case only, so far as we can recollect, in the character of Miss Bates in *Emma*, does she . . . touch the region of higher feeling by comprehension of the natural excellence that lies under a ludicrous exterior" (Southam 1.217).

60. Emma feels literally approved of by a spectator when she looks across the room at Mr. Knightley and feels "as if his eyes received the truth from her's, and all that had passed of good in her feelings were at once caught and honoured" (253).

61. Smith conceives of the internalization of the impartial spectator as involving a splitting of the self: "When I endeavor to examine my own conduct, when I endeavor to pass sentence upon it, and either to approve or condemn it, it is evident that, in all such cases, I divide myself, as it were, into two persons; and that I, the examiner and judge, represent a different character from that other I, the person whose character is examined into and judged of" (*Theory of Moral Sentiments* 113). Here Smith sounds like

Lacan in "The Neurotic's Individual Myth" describing the "internal division that makes the subject the alienated witness of the acts of his own self" (416).

62. Knox-Shaw also comments that "so highly does Emma come to value Mr. Knightley's approval that he figures for her as the nearest thing to an 'impartial spectator,' as when she imagines him seeing into her heart and fining no blemish in her dealings with Jane Fairfax" (204). Austen anticipates this moment in the scene in *Pride and Prejudice* where Elizabeth Bennet's "thoughts were all fixed on that one spot of Pemberley House, whichever it might be, where Mr. Darcy then was. She longed to know what at that moment was passing in his mind; in what manner he thought of her, and whether in defiance of every thing, she was still dear to him" (164).

63. It is because sympathy drives us to acknowledge the equality of others that it functions, at a psychological level, in a manner analogous to the way the famous invisible hand functions economically. As Smith argues in *The Theory of Moral Sentiments*, "The rich only select from the heap what is most precious and agreeable. They consume little more than the poor, and in spite of their natural selfishness and rapacity, . . . though the sole end which they propose from the labours of all the thousands whom they employ, be the gratification of their own vain and insatiable desires, they divide with the poor the produce of all their improvements. They are led by an invisible hand to make nearly the same distribution of the necessaries of life, which would have been made, had the earth been divided into equal portions among all its inhabitants" (184–85).

64. Dupuy has argued that "this is a remarkable passage because in a certain sense it suggests that the only way to overcome self-love is through even more self-love. The full complexity of Smith's thought is summed up in this conflict and combination of self-love with itself" (48). Audrey Jaffe has also noted the self-reflexive nature of sympathy as Smith represents it, arguing that "the other's experience . . . may be apprehended only through the mediation of the spectator's self-image, and the sympathetic object is, in effect, a projection or fantasy of the spectator's identity" (*Scenes* 10). For a discussion of sympathy and the genesis of the Victorian novel, see the introduction to Rachel Ablow's *The Marriage of Minds*. Rae Greiner has also written extensively on both Adam Smith and the relation of *The Theory of Moral Sentiments* to Austen in "Sympathetic Realism and the Nineteenth-Century Novel."

65. Note the language of calling here as well as watching. Vivienne Brown uses this moment to read Smith's *The Theory of Moral Sentiments* as dialogic in the Bakhtinian sense as opposed to the more monologic *Wealth of Nations*.

66. As Woloch notes, there is a "disturbing recession of equality to the invisible horizon of Austen's narrative" (124).

67. Both Anne Ruderman and Sara Emsley have linked the concept of virtue in Austen to classical antecedents. Reading her novels in relation to Aristotle and Aquinas, Emsley argues that "Jane Austen represents a union of the classical and the theological virtues" (10). Ruderman, too, associates Austen with Aristotle but also connects those representations of virtue to that of eighteenth-century authors like Burke. She argues that "Austen's novels show that attention to self-interest is not the way to happiness— many of them point out that virtue requires a capacity for self-denial" (8). In *After Virtue*, Alasdair Macintyre likewise joins Austen to Aristotle, arguing that "she praises the virtues of being socially agreeable, as Aristotle does" (241). He sees her as marking the threshold after which virtue will become utilitarian and finds the emblem of this

position in Fanny Price, who "pursues virtue for the sake of a certain kind of happiness and not for its utility" (242). All of these assessments tend to read Austen voicing virtue in an absolute sense rather than as exploring the contingent and problematic relation of virtue to commercial values that makes her so much a part of her age.

68. Hume goes on to argue that "a good palate is not tried by strong flavours, but by a mixture of small ingredients, where we are still sensible of each part, notwithstanding its minuteness and its confusion with the rest" (142).

CHAPTER TWO: Frances Trollope and the Problem of Appetite

1. As Pamela Neville-Sington notes, "To imagine the world in which Fanny Trollope, née Milton, grew up, one need go no further than the novels of Jane Austen. Jane was only four years Fanny's senior; their fathers, George Austen and William Milton, were the rectors of Steventon and Heckfield, respectively, both situated in the same Hampshire deanery of Basingstoke. Jane and Fanny would have admired the same red coats of the local militia, visited the same milliners' shops, worn the same fashions, subscribed to the same circulating libraries, and danced in the same assembly rooms above Basingstoke's town hall. They enjoyed the same pastimes: dancing, country walks, amateur theatricals, and reading. There was, however, one important, if subtle, distinction between the two girls: Fanny's grandfather was a Bristol tradesman; Jane came from more genteel stock" ("Jane Austen," 45).

2. While we might associate Frances Trollope with the early Victorian period, since her novels began to appear in the 1830s, she was in her fifties when she published her first novel, having been born in 1780. She came to maturity during the Romantic era. Many of the critics who have been most useful to me in thinking through the patterns implied by her work—Colin Campbell, Philip Connell, and Donald Winch—write about Romanticism's complex engagement with political economy.

3. As Boyd Hilton has argued, the gold standard period, from 1797 to 1821, "coincided with the most hectic and most visible stages of economic growth, a period in which it seemed to commentators that mushroom fortunes and satanic towns and cities were developing almost overnight" (*Age of Atonement* 126). This was also the period when the public's interest in political economy reached its ascendancy: "Looking back from the late 1870s, Walter Bagehot wrote that 'Political Economy was, indeed, the favourite subject in England from about 1810 to about 1840, and this to an extent which the present generation can scarcely comprehend'" (Connell 6). Maxine Berg similarly notes that in the 1830s "it was economic growth and its now limitless prospects created by technological advance which became the new centre, not just of the analysis of the economy, but of the analysis of politics and society as well. The economy was no longer conceived as subordinate to broader social and political ideals" (10).

4. The extraordinary fecundity of the economy had not been predicted by Smith, who "thought that the natural goal towards which this and other advancing countries were moving was 'the stationary state,' in which the existing methods of production had been carried as far as they could be made to go, and economic growth ceased" (Perkin *Origins* 99). Austen's novels too suggest a movement toward stasis. In contrast, Frances Trollope's novels deal with potential limitlessness.

5. Denise Gigante argues that "by the turn of the nineteenth century, the dialectical

counterpart to taste was not only bodily appetite but also the wider sphere of material desires fed by consumer culture" (3).

6. Trollope's contemporaries were fully aware of this process, which George Combe's brother Andrew described in his 1846 book *The Physiologies of Digestion* as "the confounding of appetite with taste*, and continuing to eat from the gratification of the latter after the former is satisfied. In fact, the whole science of a skilful cook is expended in producing this *willing* mistake on our part" (43, emphasis in the original).

7. Though Malthus published the first edition of *An Essay on the Principle of Population* in 1798, his work was in the public eye in the years when Trollope was writing. As Hilton explains, "the Malthusian perspective retained a hold over 'Christian economists' and over the 'official mind' until the 1850s" (*Age of Atonement* 65). Trollope's *One Fault* (1840) includes a feminist who reads Malthus and Harriet Martineau. In her anti-Poor Law novel *Jessie Phillips: A Tale of the Present Day* (1843), the manufacturer who sits on the board of the local workhouse "is clearly echoing Malthusian fears about population growth in light of what was perceived to be a growing competition for resources" (Graff 59).

8. As Hilton explains, "Chalmers's most daring insight was in perceiving an analogy between Malthus's theories of population and capital" (*Mad* 338).

9. Combe's book was extraordinarily popular, selling 350,000 copies; "only the Bible, *Pilgrim's Progress*, and *Robinson Crusoe*, icons all of middle-class literacy, outsold Combe's treatise" (Dames *Amnesiac* 81). Combe was noted during his time as a phrenologist. Trollope references phrenology in *The Three Cousins* (1847), where she describes it satirically as "one of the *avant couriers* of human knowledge" (20). Her scatterbrained intellectual heroine consults "one of the most celebrated phrenologists in Great Britain" (27).

10. Malthus became for both Coleridge and Southey "a compendium term designed to cover an impoverished way of thinking about society that was materialistic, utilitarian, unpatriotic, and a potent source of dissension between classes in an already dangerously divided nation" (Winch 289).

11. Trollope understood that her descriptions of America commented on English commercial society. She concludes her observation about money by explaining that "this unity of purpose, backed by the spirit of enterprise, and joined with an acuteness and *total* absence of probity, where interest is concerned, which might set canny Yorkshire at defiance" (38, emphasis in the original).

12. These novels were quite popular when they appeared. *The Widow Barnaby* was so successful that Trollope wrote two sequels: *The Widow Married* (1840) and *The Barnabys in America; or, The Adventures of the Widow Wedded* (1843). Like *The Widow Barnaby*, which went through a number of editions and remained in print till 1885, *The Ward of Thorpe-Combe* and *The Life and Adventures of a Clever Woman* remained in print until 1895 and 1879 respectively. Both *The Widow Barnaby* and *The Ward of Thorpe-Combe* were translated into French and appeared in a Gagliani European edition.

13. The reviewer for the *Athenaeum* similarly commented that the "gifts and graces" of the niece are less interesting than the "more prominent airs and absurdities of her tawdry aunt" ("*The Widow Barnaby*" 9).

14. In *The Widow Barnaby*, the virtuous Agnes Willoughby becomes the ward of her aunt Martha Barnaby. In *The Ward of Thorpe-Combe*, the spiritual Florence Heathcote

must live under the aegis of her cousin Sophia Martin-Thorpe when Florence's uncle chooses Sophia to be his heir. In *The Life and Adventures of a Clever Woman*, Zelah Richards, the impoverished daughter of an artist, is virtually adopted by the novel's title character, the daughter of a wealthy retired banker.

15. The political economists who were Trollope's contemporaries understood that the Protestant ethic emerged out of such pleasurable desires. As J. R. McCulloch argued in 1836, "To make men industrious . . . they must be inspired with a taste for comforts, luxuries, and enjoyments. . . . Whenever a taste for comforts and conveniences is generally diffused, the desires of man become altogether illimitable" (quoted in Gallagher 55).

16. Chandra Mukerji makes a similar argument about the early modern period, insisting on the importance of "the role played by Europe's hedonistic culture of mass consumption," which "contradicts the usual image of the sixteenth century as the birthplace of that ascetic rationality (the 'Protestant Ethic') that Max Weber describes as the source for the spirit of modern capitalism" (1–2).

17. Consideration of the relative merits of saving and spending were in the air in the years before Trollope began her writing career. In a series of articles published in *Blackwood's* from 1829 to 1830, David Robinson emphasized that in order "to keep wages and profits at their proper height it was essential not only to keep up manufactures but continually to extend them; and the self-defeating tendency of the propensity to save" (Perkin *Origins* 248).

18. For another critic who reads the literature of Trollope's period as engaging in Malthusian debates, see Silvana Colella. The plots Colella describes, which involve characters not having children in an echo of Malthus's arguments about population, are common in Trollope's novels. Gallagher's *The Body Economic* provides an extended discussion of the impact Malthusian thinking had on the evolution of nineteenth-century literature.

19. Trollope's narrator states explicitly that Aunt Betsy and Martha Barnaby represent "two modes of education which lead the mind in after life into very erroneous estimates respecting [the value of money]. The one is being brought up to spend exactly as much money as you please, and the other having it deeply impressed on your mind that you are to spend none at all" (66). The two embody the contrast between "the pure ascetic rationalist of Weberian theory [who] accumulates capital goods" and "the hedonist consumer [who] revels in amassing consumer goods" (Mukerji 4).

20. Trollope may be deliberately echoing Malthus, who praised the spinster because she "exalted others by depressing herself. Her self-denial has made room for another marriage, without any additional distress. . . . Like the truly benevolent man in an irremediable scarcity, she has diminished her own consumption, instead of raising up a few particular people by pressing down the rest" (1992 271–72). He also approved of people who keep their own cows, which Betsy Compton also does: "It should be observed also, that one of the reasons why the labourers who at present keep cows are so comfortable is that they are able to make a considerable profit of the milk which they do not use themselves" (1992 314).

21. The emphasis on the widow's size, energy, bustle, and monstrosity all suggest that she is a perfect emblem for more general negative emotional responses to England's economic expansion. Matthew Bramble, in Smollett's *Humphry Clinker*, describes Bath, the city where the widow Barnaby's journey concludes, in the following way:

The rage of building has laid hold on such a number of adventurers, that one sees new houses starting up in every out-let and every corner of Bath; contrived without judgment, executed without solidity, and stuck together with so little regard to plan and propriety, that the different lines of the new rows and buildings interfere with, and intersect one another in every different angle of conjunction. They look like the wreck of streets and squares disjointed by an earthquake, which hath broken the ground into a variety of holes and hillocks; or as if some Gothic devil had stuffed them altogether in a bag, and left them to stand higgledy piggledy, just as chance directed. What sort of a monster Bath will become in a few years, with those growing excrescences, may be easily conceived. . . . All these absurdities arise from the general tide of luxury, which hath overspread the nation, and swept away all, even the very dregs of the people. Every upstart of fortune, harnessed in the trappings of the mode, presents himself at Bath, as in the very focus of observation. (65)

22. This reaction to her niece's body/sexuality almost immediately shades over into concerns about the propensity to spend, as she thinks "while I am saving hundreds of pounds, may she not be acquiring thousands of vulgar habits that may again quench all my hopes?" (88).

23. Blushing signifies both sexuality and is associated the lower classes throughout Trollope's novels. In *The Vicar of Wrexhill*, when the widow of a village squire receives letters from a seductive evangelical vicar, "her delicately pale face became as red as a milkmaid's" (216). In *Jessie Phillips* there is a virtual contagion of blushing as the upper-class Ellen Dalton and middle-class Martha Maxwell realize that Ellen's brother has seduced the working-class heroine of the novel. "Ellen colour[s] violently" (137) when Jessie asks to see her; "the idea that her brother had, perhaps, already been guilty of the wild imprudence of making her his wife. This thought caused the bright carnation of a sudden agitation to dye her cheeks" (138). When Martha comes to ask Ellen about her brother's delinquency, "It was now Miss Maxwell's turn to blush, which she did violently" (145). When Ellen finally puts Jessie's shame into words, describing the birth of the illegitimate baby, both she and Martha Maxwell "coloured violently" (178).

24. See also Gaskell's comments about boys who, "at an age when they should have been sedulously kept apart from opportunities of indulging their nascent sexual propensities, were thrust into a very hot-bed of lust" (98–99).

25. In her reading of Trollope's novel Kay Heath notes that "Victorians thought rouging improper (though it became increasingly popular and more accepted over the course of the century), because it was considered not only vanity, but a visual lie. Mrs. Merrifield writes in 1854, 'We violate the laws of nature when we seek to repair the ravages of time on our complexions by paint[;] . . . it is not only bad taste, but it is a positive breach of sincerity'" (97). In 1828 Edward Irving described figures like the widow Barnaby as "old women who affect the girl all their life" (419).

26. The arguments about sexuality in *An Essay on the Principal of Population* imply that "the woman's bloom of youth is both the prized thing one wants to 'arrest,' in the sense of fixing forever, and the culprit whose 'arrest' would be necessary to stop the enfeebling process of reproduction" (Gallagher 39).

27. Malthus "is one of the first modern thinkers to insist that sexual intercourse is both ineradicable and essential to human happiness. Malthus strengthened the side of

British radicalism that emphasized the motivating force of bodily pleasure and made the needs of desiring bodies the basis of economic thought" (Gallagher 10). But in the 1830s, such desires were also associated with the intense distaste that Trollope depicts in Betsy Compton. That distaste was perhaps expressed most powerfully by Robert Southey, who argued that "a morbid change has been wrought in the great body of population" (77). For Southey, Malthus's philosophies exalted "the shallow, the selfish, the sensual, and the vain" (79).

28. The full expansion of women's sexual and commercial desires into the public sphere was associated with pleasure centers like Bath. See Barker-Benfield, 29–31, 180–90, and 198–201, for discussions of women's relation to spas.

29. It is almost impossible for a modern critic to read this passage without thinking about the famous moment in Freud's case history of Dora, when she comes to his office wearing "at her waist—a thing she never did on any other occasion before or after—a small reticule of a shape which had just come into fashion; and, as she lay on the sofa and talked, she kept playing with it—opening it, putting a finger into it, shutting it again, and so on" (94). Freud concludes that "Dora's reticule . . . was nothing but a representation of the genitals, and her playing with it . . . was an entirely unembarrassed yet unmistakable pantomimic announcement of what she would like to do with them—namely, to masturbate" (95). The overlap between Freud and Trollope suggests that episodes like the playing with the reticule are, as Lacan argued in his analysis of the Ratman, less individualistic acts than one might expect. They are instead, as I argue in my introduction, myths, in this case one that overlaps economic and sexual drives in the image of the eroticized purse.

30. With her reference to Lord Muckleberry's wardrobe, Trollope makes fun of the prince regent. As Gigante notes, "Biographers like to describe how George 'designed shoe buckles and lavishly frogged surtouts for himself'" (167). The prince regent functioned as an emblem for the excessive consumption (sexual, gastronomic, and sartorial) in the early decades of the nineteenth century and was associated with resorts like Brighton.

31. In describing the prurient effects of *The Vicar of Wrexhill*, Chorley the critic for the *London and Westminster Review* asserts that novel "is essentially *convulsionnaire* in its power" (115).

32. This whole section of the novel involves a satiric reworking of the end of Dickens's *The Pickwick Papers*. The widow Barnaby attempts to sue Lord Muckleberry for breach of promise using the same lawyer that Mrs. Bardell uses in Dickens's novel. But in *The Widow Barnaby*, institutional evils—the grasping practitioners of the law in *The Pickwick Papers*, for example—are not the cause of the heroine's confinement to debtors' prison. Rather, Mrs. Barnaby goes to jail because she spends too much and cannot pay her bills. Trollope's matter-of-fact realism makes one realize that in Dickens's novel almost no one is actually imprisoned for expenditure.

33. Contemporary reviewers recognized the novel's use of fairy-tale patterns. As the critic for the *Athenaeum* comments of Betsy Compton's function, "She it is, who, like a benevolent fairy, peeps out, ever and anon, through the mazes of the story, to assure us that Affection, and Good-fortune, and Justice, have not utterly forsaken the Cinderella of the tale; but are, ultimately, to bring to confusion Selfishness and vulgar Pretension" ("*The Widow Barnaby*" 9).

34. In linking sexuality to expenditure Trollope's novel reiterates the logic of Chal-

mers's arguments. He had insisted "that the quintessential sin of the middle classes—the 'desire to be rich'—led inexorably to an 'oversurplus' of capital, just as sexual incontinence among the lower orders led to overpopulation. And, just as wars, famine, and pestilence got rid of 'excrescent population,' so cycles of national bankruptcy, occurring roughly every six or seven years, could get rid of speculation" (Hilton *Mad* 338).

35. Trollope had already suggested that a Puritan exterior could hide secret pleasures in *The Widow Barnaby*. Aunt Betsy "had no confidant but her broker. This mystery, this profound secrecy, in the silent rolling up of her wealth, was perhaps the principal source of her enjoyment from it" (26).

36. For novelists that followed Trollope, neatness of dress, elegance, and cleanliness typically identify the heroine as possessing the middle-class virtues of care and self-control. One needs only to think of Charlotte Brontë's Jane Eyre and Lucy Snowe with their obsessive concern for the neatness of their dress and the cleanliness of their houses. As a radical Tory Trollope is relentlessly critical of the middle-class values that Brontë will endorse. We hear that critique in the narrator of *The Ward of Thorpe-Combe*'s snide comment that Sophia Martin-Thorpe exhibits "the neatness of a young lady behind a counter" (1.249).

37. In her portrait of this oddly unappealing heroine, Trollope captures the characteristics of the period that Mill was to deplore when he looked back on it in his autobiography: his fear that "the signs of riches, were almost the only things really respected" and that "the life of the people was mainly devoted to the pursuit of them" (136) and his culture's propensity to "dwell upon the physical relation and its adjuncts, and swell this into one of the principal objects of life" (95).

38. Trollope understands these are values her heroine could have learned from novels. In both *The Widow Barnaby* and *The Life and Adventures of a Clever Woman*, Trollope comments on the effect of novel reading. In the former, she notes of Aunt Betsy that "Miss Compton, as she sat in her secluded bower, had for years been looking out upon the fashionable world through the powerful, though somewhat distorting *lunette d'approche*, furnished by modern novels" (87). In the latter, she comments that "novel-reading, if it teaches nothing else, must decidedly teach something more of the manners of the world, and the age in which we live, than any other study whatever" (1.57).

39. Such considerations were in the air at the time that Trollope was writing. Irving had argued in 1828 that "of all pleasures, the most seductive, and subtle, and flattering, and likewise, as I think, the most prevalent, is the pleasure of pleasing" (331).

40. As Combe also explained of the human mind, "Every faculty stands in a definite relation to certain external objects;—when it is internally active it desires these objects;—when they are presented to it they excite it to activity, and delight it with agreeable sensations" (54).

41. Trollope was cynical about what Patrick Brantlinger characterizes as Dickens's "sentimental radicalism" (13). She insistently mocks the sentimentality that Dickens incarnates in benevolent middle-class figures. In *The Life and Adventures of Michael Armstrong, the Factory Boy*, for example, she makes fun of the scenes in *Oliver Twist* where Mr. Brownlow takes pleasure in dressing Oliver in the clothes of a gentleman and discarding the clothes he wore as a pauper. Trollope's novel contains a similar scene, in which the virtuous mill hand, who is clearly modeled on Oliver Twist, is given a new suit of clothes by the mill owner, Sir Matthew Dowling. But in Trollope's novel the boy

resents this gesture, which he understands to be motivated by the mill owner's desire to aggrandize his reputation through public acts of apparent charity.

42. Trollope's portrait of her savvy heroine anticipates the arguments of modern theorists that "within consumer culture, which approximately coincides with the culture of narcissism, the new conception of self which has emerged, which we shall refer to as the 'performing self,' places greater emphasis upon appearance, display and the management of impressions" (Featherstone 163): "Behind the emphasis upon performance, it can be argued, lies a deeper interest in manipulating the feelings of others" (164).

43. As Campbell notes, Puritanism takes "a position of . . . outright hostility to the 'natural' expression of emotion" (74).

44. Like the Protestant entrepreneur of Weber's *The Spirit of Capitalism*, Sophia is successful because she exercises systematic self-control or what Trollope calls "the habitual weighing of words to which [she] had for years drilled herself, whenever she thought her interest concerned" (3.143–44).

45. These scenes of private enjoyment provide an extraordinarily clear image of what Merish has called one of liberalism's unspoken agendas: "an emotional and sentimental, as well as a rational and utilitarian, justification for private property, in which the protection of one's economic assets is underwritten not so much by a right to self-interested and rational profit-making as by an imperative to enjoy one's intimate belongings at length with the confidence of secure proprietorship" (17).

46. Such practices show how "Puritanism might lead to . . . hypocrisy and self-love" (Campbell 213).

47. With the advance of consumer society, "individuals do not so much seek satisfaction from products, as pleasure from the self-illusory experiences which they construct from associated meanings. The essential activity of consumption is thus not the actual selection, purchase or use of products, but the imaginative pleasure-seeking to which the product image lends itself, 'real' consumption being largely a resultant of this 'mentalistic' hedonism" (Campbell 89).

48. The association of Sophia Martin with comfort and the description of her as "the *douce* Sophia" (1.273) would have identified her, for Trollope's readers, with what was known, in the eighteenth and nineteenth centuries, as *doux commerce*. This was the idea that commerce, in widening horizons and opening up consumption to a whole new range of goods would, in fact, refine individuals and societies, making them more civilized. Albert O. Hirschman discusses the French origins of *doux commerce* in *The Passions and the Interests*, 56–63. Joseph Childers has argued of its persistence into the early nineteenth century that "whether in Carlyle and his acolytes or the evangelicalism of the low Church movement and dissenting sects such as the Primitive Methodists or the Baptists, the residue of *doux commerce* remained to inform both moral and fiduciary activities" (53).

49. This description is also accurate in terms of real developments taking place in Trollope's time; the middle classes "almost alone enjoyed the increase in coffee from one ounce per head in 1801 to one pound seven and a half ounces in 1841" (Perkin *Origins* 142). When Sophia worries that she may not be able to afford to serve such an expensive delicacy and wonders idly whether she should purchase an island in the West Indies to offset the price, she marks contemporary awareness of the relation between new patterns of consumption and the British Empire. The specialized foods Sophia

enjoys—coffee, crystallized ginger, and sherry—reflect the consumers' propensity to let "their appetites . . . run riot" and to "pamper themselves with delicacies for which east and west are ransacked" (Lamb 132).

50. "One gets the impression from the growing obsession with French chefs, gargantuan feasts, and exotic foods, and from the spate of cookery books, that in the early nineteenth century the rich were spending much more on the variety and elaboration of their food than formerly, and that in this they were increasingly emulated by the middle class" (Perkin *Origins* 142). Stephen Mennell argues that "gastronomic theorizing as a genre . . . burgeoned fully during the nineteenth century" (145). In *The Life and Adventures of a Clever Woman* (1854), one of the novel's aristocratic characters comments that "the character of a man's cook is often, I believe, considered as being of more importance . . . than his own" (1.204).

51. Trollope was long interested in caricaturists. She depicts another in her novel *The Lottery of Marriage* (1849). These figures are, I would argue, a nod to Trollope's conception of herself as a novelist, which was as someone who produced exaggerated portraits of characters that embodied contemporary ills. Like Dickens, Trollope conceived of her novels as being similar to the satiric etchings that William Hogarth produced in series like *The Rake's Progress* or *Wealth and Idleness*. Reviewers also noted that "as a caricaturist, we are perfectly willing to recognize Mrs. Trollope" ("*Hargrave; or, The Adventures of a Man of Fashion*" 333).

52. Interestingly, the novel's antimaterialist romantic heroine's personal identity is as linked to possessions as is that of its main character. Agnes Willoughby is defined as intellectual by the case of books she carries with her; "her aunt had suffered [it] to accompany her unchallenged, because she presumed it to be the treasury of all 'her best things'; a species of female property for which the widow had never-failing respect, even when it did not belong to herself" (109). While such a comment clearly underscores the difference between aunt and niece, it also identifies the books as the property or object that Agnes carries with her that allows her to define herself. See John Plotz, *Portable Property*, for a discussion of how in the Victorian era "as never before or since, trinkets and ornaments became the metonymic placeholders for geographically disaggregated social networks" (xiii).

53. Mirah Lapidoth in George Eliot's *Daniel Deronda*, with her musical talent, diminutive stature, and gambling father, seems to be modeled on Zelah.

54. Like *The Widow Barnaby* and *The Ward of Thorpe-Combe*, *The Life and Adventures of a Clever Woman* has a rushed ending. The novel's heroine finally marries, not because she is in love but because she has outspent her budget, needs more money from her father, and knows he will provide that wealth to finance her wedding. Her husband proves to be a wastrel, a gambler, and an abuser. After Charlotte's father dies and she receives her inheritance, her husband imprisons her in the house in order to gain access to it. She is rescued at the eleventh hour—her husband is starving her to death—by Zelah's husband, the novel's romantic hero, after which she turns evangelical and retires to a watering place.

55. There are less heavily emphasized utilitarian strains apparent in Trollope's earlier novels. In *The Widow Barnaby* the widow chastises her niece by saying "what earthly use are you of to any body?" (140). In *The Ward of Thorpe-Combe* a servant describes Sophia as "her dry, hard calculating, avaricious young mistress" (3.66). The statement

that "it was a principle with her never to deprive herself of anything pleasant" (3.83) might be read as an echo of Bentham's philosophies.

56. There are hints of the mechanistic aspect of materialist desires in *The Ward of Thorpe-Combe* when Sophia Martin is described as "put[ting] forth two fingers of her stiff little hand to each of the family in succession, with the air of a machine, which could make one movement but no other" (2.137), and when we hear of her eating habits that "the operations . . . were performed with a steady regularity, which, if it did not, in its fragrant detail, resemble clock-work, was at least in most perfect accordance with it" (3.16).

57. See, for example, the *Athenaeum*'s review of *The Widow Barnaby*, which argues, that "the account of [the widow's] earliest exploits, as Miss Martha Compton, is almost worthy of the authoress of 'Pride and Prejudice': higher praise we scarcely know how to give" (*"The Widow Barnaby"* 9).

58. See Monique Frazee, *Mrs. Trollope and America*, 45ff., for a series of contemporary descriptions of Trollope as vulgar. Eliza Lynn Linton, for one, described her as a "vulgar, brisk, and good-natured kind of well-bred hen-wife, fond of a joke and not troubled with squeamishness"; Elizabeth Barrett Browning, for another, remarked that she had "neither the delicacy nor the candour which constitute true nobility of mind'" (45). Reviewers insisted that "she treats her subject cleverly, no doubt, but coarsely, literally, and vulgarly—not so much with vulgarity of manner, but by an appeal to the vulgar prejudices and vulgar cant which animate the ignorant and narrow-minded of every grade" (quoted in Heineman 217).

59. Anthony may be more ambivalent about his mother because, as biographers have noted, his relation to her was more fraught than his brother's was. Frances was extraordinarily close with her son Tom, who ended up living with her and managing her villa in Florence, a villa whose expenses were partially covered by Tom's wife's inheritance. In contrast, Anthony felt himself to be the son who did not interest her. When the family went to America, Anthony was the one who was left behind. Anthony believed that his mother was completely unaware of the sufferings he went through both in school and in his early years at the post office.

60. Both Lamb and his contemporary and Hazlitt sought to rescue the word "gusto" and make it a term of critical approval rather than opprobrium. See especially Hazlitt's "On Gusto."

61. Writing of *Macbeth*, Miller notes that "the witches' brew, a grossly comic indulgence in the horror of disgust and the uncanny, mixes up a recipe for the disgusting that needs little translation to trigger the sentiments in us that it was meant to trigger back then" (164).

62. The rhetoric of food is so powerfully associated with Trollope that even modern critics attempting to recuperate her from critical opprobrium tend to resort to it, as when she is described as "savoring extravagance" (Harsh 134).

CHAPTER THREE: Anthony Trollope's "Subtle Materialism"

1. For readings of *The Way We Live Now* and *The Prime Minister* in relation to finance capital see Paul Delany, *Literature, Money, and the Market*, 19–31, Tara McGann and Audrey Jaffe, "Trollope in the Stock Market," and Nathan K. Hensley, "Mister Trollope."

2. As Asa Briggs argues, "For Trollope the world of wealth was associated not with the creation of valuable real capital . . . but with senseless speculation, dangerous bubbles and 'the infamous trade of stock-jobbing'" (331).

3. Because Trollope uses his heiresses to trace the large-scale historical movements that were changing the shape of his culture, he describes their impact not in single novels, as Austen and Frances Trollope do, but through movements that take place across the sequence of texts. The story of Miss Dunstable runs through three of the five Barsetshire novels. Lady Glencora's story is introduced in the fifth of the Barsetshire novels and runs through all of the Palliser novels until her death at the opening of *The Duke's Children*. Madame Max is introduced in *Phineas Finn* (1867) and appears until the end of the series. All of these heiresses' stories take more than ten years of Trollope's writing life and at least three volumes to be fully developed.

4. Peter Mathias notes, discussing the period following 1870, that "in much light industry and food processing—from pharmaceutical firms . . . to distilling and brewing—British enterprise, in scale of production and vigorous expansion, had an enviable record. Beecham, Lever in soap making, Cadbury and Frye in chocolates, Guinness and Bass, became household names on the strength of such expansion in exactly these decades" (372–73). Perkin cites an even longer list, explaining that

> the non-landed wealth holders who now claimed their place in London and county "society" were an extraordinary mixed group. Some represented traditional industrial and commercial wealth, like Beatrice Webb's father, Richard Potter, son of a cotton merchant and the first Lord Mayor of Manchester—the son recouped his dwindling inheritance by becoming a timber merchant, Chairman of the Great Western Railway and President of the Canadian Pacific Railroad; the Guest family Lords Wimborne, ironmasters and landowners; Samuel Cunliffe-Lister, Lord Masham of wool-combing fame; Lord Armstrong of Cragside, pioneer engineer and armaments king; John Hubbard, Lord Addington, Russia merchant and Governor of the Bank of England; the rival brewers Henry Allsop, Lord Hindlip and Michael Bass, Lord Burton and the Guinness peers, Lords Ardilaun and Iveagh; and, to include some of the rare "new women," Lady Hambledon, widow of W. H. Smith the bookseller, and Margot Asquith, the sharp-tongued society hostess and daughter of the Tennant family, chemical manufacturers of Glasgow. Others represented brand new wealth, some of it not very appealing to the old: the South African diamond and gold millionaires Beit, Barnato, Rhodes and Wernher; the new yellow press Lords Northcliffe and his brother Rothermere, the soap manufacturer Lord Leverhulme, Baron de Stern the merchant banker, and so on. (*Rise* 72)

5. "The majority of landowners who had no other rents from mines or urban property found themselves overtaken in income—and still more in wealth as the capital value of rural land declined even further than rents—by their industrial and commercial rivals, and they were left standing by the great urban and mine-owning aristocrats who alone could keep up with the new millionaires" (Perkin *Rise* 38). Glencora's Scots' ancestry reflects "another noteworthy feature of the period," namely, "the increased importance of Scotland as a centre of wealth-production. In 1855–7 only six Scottish estates of £100,000 or more had been probated, but in 1859 and 1861 this figure rose to seven each year, and in the 1870s to about 12 per annum. This period coincided with the

emergence of Clydesdale as a national centre of commerce, engineering, and shipping" (Rubinstein *Men* 39).

6. Trollope was a friend of Baron Meyer Rothschild, who "had lived as a country gentleman for some thirty years, taking no direct part in the family bank. In January, February, and March of 1873, Trollope regularly hunted with him at his lavish Berkshire estate, Mentmore" (Delany 26). This was two years before Trollope wrote the two novels that deal most extensively with the social power of money, *The Prime Minister* and *The Way We Live Now*.

7. The fact that Madame Max's dark looks make the Duke of Omnium "remember to have seen, somewhere in Greece, such a houri as was this Madame Goesler" *(Phineas Finn* 2.199) might also be linked to international finance. The Greeks, like the Jews, "profited from their international connections, often with links . . . within the Levant and Middle East" (Rubinstein *Men* 94). The description of Madame Max, "tucking her feet up under her as though she were seated somewhere in the East" (2.202), reinforces her association with the Middle East, the region most identified with the financiers who "engaged exclusively or almost exclusively in foreign or government loans" (Rubinstein *Men* 91).

8. While we might assume that such scientific thinking was far from the world of the novel, Maxwell's theories were so popularized and the link between them and money so accepted that Margaret Oliphant is able to reference them directly in her 1883 banking novel, *Hester*. Her narrator comments that "it is astonishing how money grows when it is in the way of growing—when it had got the genuine impulse and rolls every kindred atom near it, according to some occult law of attraction, into itself" (7) and later notes "the electricity of the contact" (9) between rumors that leads to the failure of the bank.

9. Trollope's novel *The Belton Estate* was appearing in the *Fortnightly Review*, a journal he helped found, at the same time as Bagehot's *English Constitution*. See Briggs, "Trollope, Bagehot, and the English Constitution," for a discussion of the relation between the two men.

10. Despite Ruskin's dramatic emphasis on the worship of gold, he seems to understand that what is at stake is not the material presence of money but something more akin to an absence. As he posits in haranguing consumers, "But it is not gold you want to gather! What is it? greenbacks? No; not those neither. What is it then—is it ciphers after the capital I? Cannot you practice writing ciphers and write as many as you want! Write ciphers an hour every morning, in a big book, and say every evening, I am worth all those noughts more than I was yesterday. Won't that do?" ("Traffic" 245).

11. This identification of the Jews with the worship of wealth, which we also find in Trollope's Palliser series, is in some sense ironic. As Jean-Joseph Goux has pointed out, "an exhortation to leave behind tangible forms in order to accede to a supersensible reality" (141) accompanies Moses' descent from the mountain with the Ten Commandments and their "prohibition against figuring the deity."

12. Such plain speaking was particularly associated with financial dealings. In Oliphant's *Phoebe Junior*, when a bank refuses to renew a bill of exchange, the language of that refusal is characterized as "downright Dunstable" (183).

13. Trollope virtually echoes the words he puts in the mouth of Miss Dunstable when, in his autobiography, he excoriates "clergymen who preach sermons against the love of money, but who know that the love of money is so distinctive a characteristic of

humanity that such sermons are mere platitudes called for by customary but unintelligent piety" (*Autobiography* 105–6).

14. Dr. Thorne is defined as "knowing neither in the ways of the share market, nor in the prices of land" (*Framley Parsonage* 335).

15. Thorne's marriage to Miss Dunstable reflects the movement Cannadine describes in which "the increasingly prosperous and assertive middle class shaded imperceptibly into the new and fabulously rich international plutocracy" (26). For a discussion of the evolving relationship between professionalism and the new wealth, see my analysis of Oliphant in chapter 4. For discussions of Trollope and professionalism, see Nicholas Dames, "Trollope and the Career," Jennifer Ruth, *Novel Professions*, and Lauren Goodlad, *Victorian Literature and the Victorian State*.

16. As Andrew Miller has argued, "the representation of material culture [in Trollope's novels] is extraordinarily thin" (160).

17. Laurie Langbauer notes another figurative reference to economics when "in *Framley Parsonage*, Trollope has one of his impecunious aristocrats who is vying for the hand of the incredibly rich quack-medicine (Ointment of Lebanon) heiress, Miss Dunstable, teach her 'to blow soap-bubbles on scientific principles'" (110n72). That image evokes without specifically naming the commercial bubbles that threatened to destroy consumer confidence in the speculative economy.

18. Trollope likes this figurative reference to joint-stock banks enough that he uses it again in *Can You Forgive Her?* He describes the wealthy widow Greenow as having "created a little joint-stock fund of merriment between the whole party, which was very much needed. The absence of such joint-stock fund is always felt when a small party is thrown together" (680).

19. "[T]he Companies Act of 1884 legalized joint-stock companies," and "the concept of limited liability [was] established by the Parliamentary Act [of 1855] and the Joint Stock Companies Act of 1856" (Reed, 184, 185). Poovey adds that "the Joint Stock Companies Act and the more sweeping act of 1862 also helped facilitate company flotations by enabling as few as seven persons to incorporate a company merely by registering a memorandum of association; each shareholder, moreover, only had to subscribe to one share, with no minimum value and on which no money need have been paid. As a consequence of this legislation, by 1862 England had the most permissive company law in the world" (*Making* 157).

20. One contemporary review noted that readers "may think they recognize traits in . . . the great heiress Miss Dunstable" (Smalley 73). There were several patent medicine barons of the period. "Each . . . was notable or colourful in his way: Thomas Holloway (1800–83), the celebrated proprietor of 'Holloway's Pills' who endowed Holloway College for Women with £700,000, erected a sanatorium for 'the mentally afflicted of the lower-middle class,' and left £596,000; James C. Eno (1828–1910), the millionaire vender of 'Eno's Fruit Salts,' whose birthplace and ancestry are completely unknown, and whose granddaughter, implausible as it may seem, is Lady Cripps, widow of Sir Stafford; Sir Joseph Beecham, 1ˢᵗ Bt. (1848–1916), of 'Beecham's Pills' fame, whose son was Sir Thomas, the great conductor; Sir Henry Wellimore (1854–1936), who was born on the American frontier, made his £3 million by manufacturing the 'tabloid' form of drugs . . . and founded the Wellcome medical mission" (Rubinstein *Men* 79–80). The only one who fits Miss Dunstable in terms of timeframe and in terms of the product manufactured is Holloway.

21. Since these endorsements were written by Holloway and his product was designed largely to have nothing harmful in it, Holloway's business would have been an instance of what Ruskin calls "lying label, title, pretence, or advertisement" (190). For an overview of nineteenth-century attitudes toward advertising see Regenia Gagnier, *Idylls of the Marketplace*, 52–56. Trollope himself references Holloway in his send-up of advertising in *The Struggles of Brown, Jones, and Robinson*.

22. For a discussion of patent medicine advertising in the period following Holloway's success, see Thomas Richards, *The Commodity Culture*, 168–204.

23. For a further discussion of Victorian response to Holloway and their links to Trollope's portrait of Miss Dunstable see my "A Woman of Money."

24. Posters for Holloway's pills and ointments were plastered beside the Great Pyramids of Egypt and Niagara Falls. "It was reported . . . that when a young lieutenant was asked what had struck him most about on first landing in the Fiji islands he replied, 'Why, the placard posted on a pile of stones at the entrance of the harbour announcing the arrival of a hogshead of Holloway's Pills'" (Harrison-Barbet 31).

25. These representations were not limited to non-English-speaking peoples. "During the Civil War in the United States, wounded Union soldiers could be seen on posters stretching out imploring hands for Holloway's Ointment" ("The Victorians and the Pill" 43).

26. The series of passages about the worship of wealth I cite here all appeared in the period around the time the second Reform Act was passed. Bagehot's *The English Constitution* was serialized beginning in 1865. Ruskin's "Traffic" was published in 1866. Arnold's *Culture and Anarchy* came out in 1867. In *The Vulgarization of Art*, Linda Dowling discusses Arnold's essay as a panicked response to reform and the riots in Hyde Park.

27. The merchant Laurence Oliphant insisted in "The Autobiography of a Joint Stock Company (Limited)," published in *Blackwood's Edinburgh Magazine* in 1876, the same year that *The Prime Minister* appeared, that "I may yet hope that a process of natural selection is in progress, and that joint-stock companies, like the human race, are to rise into new and better conditions through the 'survival of the fittest'" (96).

28. For a discussion of midcentury thinking about variation in the social and biological realms, see Corbett, *Family Likeness*, 116–18, 120, and 134–40. She notes that Darwin annotated the essays that make up *Physics and Politics* when they first appeared in the *Fortnightly Review* in 1868 (134).

29. In representing such a marriage as positive, Trollope was, as he seems to have been aware, violating the basic tenet of the marriage plot, which demands that purely mercenary marriages be condemned. He indicates his retrospective uneasiness about Glencora's marriage in *An Autobiography* where he comments that "to save a girl from wasting herself, and an heiress from wasting her property on such a scamp, was certainly the duty of the girl's friends. But it must ever be wrong to force a girl into a marriage with a man she does not love,—and certainly the more so when there is another man whom she does love. In my endeavor to teach this lesson I subjected the young wife to the terrible dangers of overtures from the man to whom her heart had been given. I was walking no doubt on ticklish ground" (182).

30. Several different models have been suggested for Lady Glencora Palliser: Lady Palmerston, Lady Frances Waldegrave, Ann Maria Elliot (Lord John Russell's second wife), and the wife of Edward John Strachey, Second Baron of Alderley. (See William

Amos, *The Originals*, and John Halperin, *Trollope and Politics*.) The closest fit is Lady Frances. As K. D. Reynolds notes, Trollope's "accounts of [Lady Glencora's] parties, especially in *The Prime Minister*," held "in Carlton Terrace and Richmond" are "a clear reference to Lady Waldegrave's house in neighbouring Twickenham" (165).

31. Ironically, given that Lady Glencora is, at least briefly, a prime minister's wife, Lord Granville is also reported to have told Lady Frances, "You ought to be a Prime Minister's wife[;] . . . you would have kept the Whig party together" (quoted in Hewett *Strawberry* 97). Comments such as these circulated as political gossip in the clubs we know Trollope frequented. See Halperin, *Trollope and Politics*, for a discussion of Trollope's avid interest in politics.

32. "Frances never exactly knew how much she had spent on the building of Strawberry Hill but when the calculations reached £100,000, she decided she must have made a mistake in her mathematics!" (Carroll 21). She was one of the first people to install gas lighting in her home. When she felt the rooms of the house were not high enough to give visitors a good view of the grounds she had the lawns excavated to lower them. Like Glencora, who is described as spending "thousands of pounds . . . in a very conspicuous way" (*Prime Minister* 1.159), Lady Frances was reported as having committed extravagances like ordering two thousand peacock feathers to decorate one corner for sitting out at one of the famous balls she held there (Hewett *Strawberry* 254). For a discussion of the political impact of Lady Frances's various entertainments, see Reynolds, *Aristocratic Women*, 163–78.

33. In Trollope's characterizations of his heiresses this problem of mixture is also represented as a problem of a confusion of gender roles. Mary Thorne knows that Miss Dunstable is "womanly in her feelings" but finds that "she could not quite say ladylike" (*Framley Parsonage* 342). Trollope's narrator asserts of Lady Glencora that "there were many things about this woman that were not altogether what a husband might wish. She was not softly delicate in all her ways; but in disposition and temper she was altogether generous. I do not know that she was at all points a lady, but had Fate so willed it she would have been a thorough gentleman" (*Can You Forgive Her?* 523–24). Though Madame Max is the most feminine of the three characters, traces of gender mixture are apparent in the fact that she is almost never referred to as Maria. Lady Frances Waldegrave was also called Lady Frank by her friends. As Hewett notes, Lord Granville wrote "that 'Frank Waldegrave is the great political woman of the day'" (*Strawberry* 137).

34. The narratives in which Alice Vavasor and Emily Wharton figure mark the divisions between political parties as well as money/families. The two suitors are split between Liberal (George Vavasor, Ferdinand Lopez) and Conservative (John Grey, John Fletcher), and there is no meeting ground between them. Indeed in *The Prime Minister*, besides being rivals in love, Lopez and Fletcher are opposing candidates for the same seat in Parliament.

35. Again Trollope's fictional representations of the politics of the Pallisers is in tune with the real life story of Lady Frances who was particularly adept at forming and maintaining unions of opposing political factions. She was the only hostess to bring Disraeli and Gladstone together in a social arena.

36. Miss Dunstable's worries about whether the reporter Tom Towers will attend her parties also reflect changes of the period as the press began to be incorporated into political entertainments. As Reynolds notes, "Both Lady Palmerston and Lady Waldegrave recognized the importance of the press for demonstrating the success of their

endeavors and as a vital tool in the cultivation of political and popular opinion. . . . Lady Waldegrave improved on Lady Palmerston's contacts with the press" (176–77). Writing to Lady Clarendon in 1857, Lady Frances commented that "Lady Palmerston and I are two Delilahs. She has cut the hair of the *Times* and I of the *Saturday*" (quoted in Hewett *Strawberry* 132). For Queen Victoria's negative response to the increasing political power of newspaper reporters, see Reynolds, *Aristocratic Women*, 178.

37. Sir William Gregory, for example, recorded in his diary "that he was dissuaded by Lady Waldegrave from his intention to move an amendment to the bill disestablishing the Irish Church" (Reynolds 154). Lady Frances was conscious of her power. After a successful negotiation in which a parliamentary decision went the way she wished, she wrote to a friend, asking "Do you remember the *Times* saying the *Salons* had *no* influence now? That *put my back up* & I am *very* glad we came to town in time to be of use" (quoted in Reynolds 173, emphasis in the original).

38. The encounter between Plantagenet Palliser and Lady Glencora stands on a cusp marked by the changing meaning of the word "snob." As Davidoff explains, "In the terminology of the 1860s a 'snob' was a businessman trying to become a gentleman. Those who tried hardest were called 'vulgar' and the ultimate in vulgarity was a 'cad.' Within two generations the meaning of 'snob' was completely inverted. A 'snob' was now any social superior who on a 'false' basis of wealth *or* breeding rather than achievement or inherent human qualities, held himself to be better than those socially below him" (60, emphasis in the original). In *The Prime Minister* Ferdinand Lopez is such a cad, and Lady Glencora, through her backing of him, is also tarred with the brush of vulgarity. Yet as Plantagenet Palliser looks down his aristocratic nose at his wife's vulgar improvements he could easily be read, as he himself is aware, as being a snob in its second meaning, feeling his superiority on the basis of class—he is better than a haberdasher—rather than of achievement.

39. Davidoff argues that "new forms of wealth as well as newly wealthy groups produced a flood of applicants that threatened to overwhelm the life-style itself" (15).

40. Simmel refers to "naked acquisitiveness" (*Philosophy* 222), which he argues is associated with socially ostracized peoples like the Jews.

41. As Joseph Litvak has noted, this imagery of the smearing of wealth is also evoked in Victorian images of greasy Jews. He describes "the vulgarity with which other Jews, preeminently Disraeli, would soil Christian space" ("Jewish Geographies" 127), thinking here of Trollope's references in the autobiography to Disraeli exuding a "smell of hair oil" (*Autobiography* 259) and of his depiction of Lizzie Eustace's greasy suitor, the Reverend Joseph Emilius, and of Jewish Ferdinand Lopez in *The Prime Minister* whom John Fletcher describes as "a greasy, black foreigner" (*Prime Minister* 1.153).

42. Contemporary reviewers described Madame Max as "one of Mr. Trollope's most graceful and carefully studied characters" (Smalley 379). In contrast, the same reviewer argued that Trollope "gives a generally too 'loud' tone to the characters of his women, and that he succeeds best with those women who, like Lady Glencora, are distinguished by a preference for brusque and piquant rattle" (Smalley 378).

43. She is "dying to handle her money" (*Eustace Diamonds* 1.12) and grasps nothing of its abstract workings; "she had learned to draw cheques, but she had no other correct notion as to business. She knew nothing as to spending money, saving it, or investing it" (1.15). "For so clever a woman she was infinitely ignorant as to the possession and value of money and land and income" (1.11). A number of critics have explored

this objectification of wealth as it is identified with the diamonds of the novel's title. Andrew Miller reads them in relation to possessive individualism, John Plotz as a form of portable property, Bill Cohen and Christopher Linder in relation to fetishism in its Freudian and Marxist/Žižekian form. For me, *The Eustace Diamonds* is a throwback in Trollope's career. It exaggerates the contrast between a negatively depicted rich woman and positively depicted poor one, which is familiar from novels like Austen's, rather than using the more ambiguous Trollopean formulation in which the heiress is a positive figure.

44. These sentiments are echoed by Plantagenet Palliser in the last of the Palliser novels, *The Duke's Children*, when he argues that "money is the reward of labour . . . or rather, in the shape it reaches you, it is your representation of that reward. You may earn it yourself, or, as is, I am afraid, more likely to be the case with you, you may possess it honestly as prepared for you by the labour of others who have stored it up for you. But it is a commodity of which you are bound to see that the source is not only clean but noble" (517). I would argue that Palliser is able to make such an argument in part because wealth has in *The Duke's Children* taken on a foreign incarnation in the person of the American heiress Isabel Boncassen. She is a member of what Cannadine calls "a new and even richer élite [that] had come into being across the Atlantic, appropriately dubbed by Berenson, 'the squillionaires'" (112), who will be the subjects of Henry James's novels.

45. The narrator opens this description by commenting that "my pen may not dare to describe the traceries" (*Phineas Finn* 2.26). Here, as in his reference to Miss Dunstable and figurative language, Trollope is marking how difficult it is to talk about economic instruments directly. All he can do is give an image that suggests them.

46. The echo of racial mixture was always present in the term Bagehot used to talk about the possibility of mixture, "commingling." Arnold used the same word to refer to racial crossing in his essay *On the Study of Celtic Literature*, which seems to reiterate the narrative Bagehot tells about the separation of nations and races and their mixture. While Arnold's father insisted that "the Celt [was] separated by an impassable gulf from the Teuton," Arnold saw instead the possibility of mixture: "Here, then, if commingling there is in our race are two very unlike elements to commingle; the steady-going Saxon temperament and the sentimental Celtic temperament" (quoted in Corbett *Allegories* 156, 164). But he also saw the dangers of mixture: "So long as this mixed constitution of our nature possesses us, we pay it tribute and serve it; so soon as we possess it, it pays us tribute and serves us" (quoted in Corbett *Allegories* 164).

47. As a cultured Jew, Madame Max seems to represent the movement Goux describes when he argues that "more than any other, modern society has divorced economic practices from their diffuse symbolic valences. This divorce is even what has made possible the autonomy of the economic, establishing it as an independent agency" (122). She is without any of the symbolic tags we saw associated with money in the hands of Miss Dunstable or Lizzie Eustace or Lady Glencora, but as a Jew, she is also established as separate from and independent of the mainstream of English society.

48. Polanyi argues of the Rothschilds that "in the last resort, their independence sprang from the needs of the time which demanded a sovereign agent commanding the confidence of national statesmen and of the international investor alike; it was to this vital need that the metaphysical extraterritoriality of a Jewish bankers' dynasty domiciled in the capitals of Europe provided an almost perfect solution" (10). Cheyette dis-

cusses this issue in terms of nationalism, arguing that "the urgency and frequency with which Jews after the 1870s were positioned as 'other' to the 'English nation' reflects the extent to which they came to symbolize the fruits of a universalizing State as opposed to a supposedly indigenous national community" (53). See also Ragussis, *Figures of Conversion*, and Freedman, *Temple of Culture*, for discussions of the exclusion of the Jews.

49. Such ethnically or racially excluded communities mark the presence of endogamy within highly evolved cultures that otherwise seem to promise full freedom of choice in marital exchange. Lévi-Strauss notes that "modern American society" (by which he presumably means the society of the 1940s) "combines a family exogamy, which is rigid in the first degree but flexible for the second or third degrees onwards, with a racial endogamy, which is rigid or flexible according to the particular State" (46). See Adam Kuper's "Fraternity and Endogamy" for a discussion of the way the Rothschild family consciously practiced endogamy in order to keep money within the family and the various international branches of the bank interconnected.

50. Trollope explicitly suggests a parallel between Glencora's anxieties about the duke marrying Madame Max and the question of England's relation to Ireland, which is also represented as a marriage: "It was at any rate necessary to England's character that the bride thus bound in a compulsory wedlock should be endowed with all the best privileges that a wife can enjoy. Let her at least not be a kept mistress" (*Phineas Finn* 2.180). See Trumpener's *Bardic Nationalism*, Corbett's *Allegories of Union*, and Patrick Lonergan's "The Representation of Phineas Finn" for discussions of marriage as both an image and plot device in the course of the nineteenth-century novel's thinking about the relation between England and Ireland. See Jane Elizabeth Dougherty's "An Angel in the House" for a discussion of social contract, the relation between England and Ireland and the way "marrying exogenously, is, in the Palliser novels generally, portrayed as disastrous" (142).

51. Corbett argues that "Trollope makes some strategic choices, and one of them lies in departing from the explicit stereotypes of Irishness in his central character and his plot(s) while projecting them on other characters" ("'Two Identities'" 120).

52. Litvak, Cheyette, and Langbauer all note that Madame Max purifies herself and saves Phineas Finn by exposing the guilt of another Jewish figure, the Reverend Emilius, allowing him to function as the essence of anti-Semitic representations. Litvak argues that "a certain ethnic cleansing" (127) is apparent in Trollope's treatment of Madame Max.

53. As Cheyette has argued, "Jews were at the center of European metropolitan society and, at the same time, banished from its privileged sphere by a semitic discourse" (12). Polanyi describes the position of the Jews as a "metaphysical extraterritoriality" (10).

54. Cosmopolitanism has a complex history that predates the Victorian period and has been associated with arenas other than politics. For useful synopses of the development of the idea of cosmopolitanism from Kant through the nineteenth century see Peng Cheah, "The Cosmopolitical," and Amanda Anderson, *Powers of Distance*, 63–66. Trollope's creation of a figure like Madame Max shows that the idea of cosmopolitanism and its association with distance that has been traced by Anderson was particularly useful in launching defenses against fears of commercial engrossment and social commingling.

55. Reynolds argues that all the great nineteenth-century political hostesses were in

one way or another social outsiders: "The one characteristic that the successful Victorian political hostesses seem to have shared was unorthodox social position. The Canningite Palmerston, it has been noted, 'had never been really liked or accepted by the Whigs: he was not one of themselves,' while his wife belonged to a family new to the peerage, with distinctly impeachable moral credentials. Lady Jersey's money came from banking; Lady Holland had been divorced; Lady Molesworth took care to disguise her antecedents, but had been a professional singer for a number of seasons; Lady Waldegrave had bourgeois, theatrical Jewish parents, and four husbands" (158).

56. Her ethnic background triggered anti-Semitic comments like the one Lady Laura Kennedy makes when she describes Madame Max as "this Moabitish woman[,] . . . this half-foreigner, this German Jewess, this intriguing unfeminine upstart" (*Phineas Redux* 2.225). When Frances was about to marry William Harcourt, her third husband, his mother is said to have exclaimed, "To think that all of this will go to the Jewess!" (Carroll 13). Lady Frances refused to hide her race. As her fourth husband notes in his journal of 1852, "*Nov. 18*. The duke of Wellington's funeral. Lady W. was & looked delightful. She talked of Dizzy & the Jews, said she was proud of being a Jew" (Hewett *Diaries* 36).

57. The lives of the Waldegrave brothers were so publicly scandalous that they were parodied in 1844 in John Mills's book *D'Horsay; or, The Follies of the Day*.

58. Her second marriage would have been incestuous because of the 1835 act that forbade a wife to marry her deceased husband's brother. But the law was moot in her case "since the first husband was illegitimate. The Attorney-General himself took a hand in making the second marriage legally admissible" (Hewett *Diaries* 4). However, Lady Frances remained sensitive to these issues. Fortescue notes in his journal of 1860 that "she had been provoked by a charge of the Bishop of Oxford's, in which he denounces marriage with a deceased wife's sister as 'incest,' and she asked me 'as a favour' to write a letter to some paper in answer to it" (Hewett *Diaries* 174). See Corbett, *Family*, for a discussion of the Deceased Wife's Sister's Act and its relation to depictions of familial ties in the nineteenth-century novel.

59. Lady Frances married her second husband twice, once in England and once in Scotland. Scotland had no law forbidding a wife's marriage to her deceased husband's brother.

60. As Hewett comments in his annotations to Fortescue's journals, "The irregularity with which Fortescue kept his diary during 1862 reflects the anxiety that tormented him from the moment of Mr. Harcourt's death. His chief at the Colonial Office, the Duke of Newcastle, had been notoriously devoted to Lady Waldegrave since he had divorced his wife in 1850. Two widowers, Lord St. Germans and Lord Granville, were other rivals whom Chichester Fortescue feared" (190).

61. Fortescue, Lord Carlingford, was a minister in two of Gladstone's cabinets, held the position of chief secretary for Ireland, worked in the Colonial Office, lobbied for Irish tenant rights, and was instrumental in writing the bill that led to the disestablishment of the Irish Church. Like Phineas, he was handsome and charming but somewhat wooden in his public manner. As he put it after a session in Parliament, "speech didactic and flat. I couldn't make it *tell*" (Hewett *Diaries* 10, emphasis in the original). He was, as is Phineas in Trollope's novels, extremely well liked; his friend Edward Lear said he had "never known anyone with more good qualities to ensure happiness in his companions." But he never became famous; as the editors of his journals note, "he did nothing badly, he did several things very well: but, unforgivably, he somehow did not

seem to matter" (3). He was a member of "the Cosmopolitan Club, started by Robert Morier as a Sunday evening gathering of his friends, of which membership was later to become a much coveted honour. As 'The Universe' it plays a prominent part in Trollope's 'Phineas Redux' of which Fortescue is largely the hero" (Rintoul 326).

62. The transcendence of crass material interest was doubly associated with the Jews, who typically represented what was being transcended, as in Karl Marx's famous assertion that "emancipation from haggling and from money, that is practical real Judaism, would be the same as the self-emancipation of our age" (quoted in Cheyette 97). But "acculturated Jews," like Madame Max, could also, as Cheyette argues, "represent a potent transcendence of an empty materialism" (54). For further discussions of these issues, see Freedman, *Temple of Culture*, especially 43–88, and Ragussis, *Figures of Conversion*.

63. Lady Frances married Chichester Fortescue in 1863, immediately before Trollope began writing the Palliser series. It was in 1865, with the death of Lord Palmerston, that she gained her full preeminence as a hostess. Lady Frances was also actively engaged in Irish politics (Trollope does not hint at such a possibility for Madame Max, however). She went with Fortescue when he was appointed lieutenant governor of Ireland, and "*The Times*, which reported on the brilliance of the 1866 season in Dublin, ascrib[ed] it to the influence of Lady Waldegrave, who 'has reminded the older citizens of Dublin of what the Viceregal Court once was. She has shown them what it should be'" (Reynolds 176).

64. "World" was a code word the Victorians used to condemn the improper influence of money, as when Trollope asserts, with the same logic of denial we find in the discussion of Lady Frances, that Miss Dunstable was "not worldly, though it was possible that her present style of life might make her so" (*Framley Parsonage* 293).

65. Though they sound Darwinian, Simmel's comments do not, in fact, echo Darwin's position on marriage for money. Darwin argued in *Descent of Man and Selection in Relation to Sex* that "civilized men are largely attracted by the mental charms of women, by their wealth, and especially by their social position" (530). Taking the same position that Lévi-Strauss does, he claimed that "men rarely marry into much lower rank. . . . With respect to the opposite form of selection, namely, of the more attractive man by the women, although in civilized nations women have free or almost free choice[,] . . . yet their choice is largely influenced by the social position and wealth of men" (530–31).

66. This view was so powerfully constructed at the time that it persists to the modern day. Cannadine, for example, asserts of Lady Frances and her circle that "in its heyday, [it] was confined to 'a very definite and very limited class,' which was almost exclusively aristocratic. It was a self-confident, self-perpetuating social élite, and it was extremely difficult for ambitious parvenus to get in" (*Decline and Fall* 344). Clearly Lady Frances was anything but exclusively aristocratic. Yet the mixed nature of her origins simply vanishes in this evocation of English society as able to exclude those who threatened to broach its borders.

67. James's reviews of both *Can You Forgive Her?* and *Miss Mackenzie*, which both appeared in 1865, played a key role in tipping Trollope's image as a writer from that of qualifiedly vulgar to absolutely vulgar. James insisted that Trollope "deliberately selected vulgar illustrations" (Smalley 235) and that "they vulgarize experience and all

the other heavenly gifts" (Smalley 237). For discussions of the relation between Trollope and James see Sarah Blair, "'Preparation for Culture,'" and Michie, "Odd Couple."

68. Connell has similarly argued that the split I explore in chapter 2 between Romantic or intellectual impulses and sensual self-interest persists in modern critical thinking: "Both left-culturalism and the academic innovations which it inspired, involved, to a greater or lesser extent, 'the critique of a certain reductionism and economism,' identified within Marxism" (280).

CHAPTER FOUR: Margaret Oliphant and the Professional Ideal

1. Oliphant and Trollope cannot be said to have been writing in different economic eras. The two were almost contemporaries. Oliphant was thirteen years younger than Trollope and continued to publish until 1895, twelve years after his death. But both began their careers at about the same time. Oliphant's first novel was published in 1849, Trollope's in 1847. Nevertheless, a key conceptual shift takes place in the period between his novels and hers, a shift I associate with the coming to prominence of the writings of John Stuart Mill.

2. In reviewing *Phoebe Junior*, the critic for the *Saturday Review* noted that its heroine was similar to the title character of *Miss Marjoribanks*: "Both are characterized by the same superhuman self-reliance, the same personal aims, the same absence of high motives, the same heroic courage in carrying out with unshrinking resolution the motives that actuate, the same good nature and good will, so far as these do not interfere with the career steadily kept in view" ("*Phoebe Junior*" 112). For a discussion of the history and various meanings of the word "career" see Burton Bledstein, *The Culture of Professionalism*, 171.

3. This is a period when, as John Morley argued, all intellectuals "bear traces of [Mill's] influence, whether they are avowed disciples or avowed opponents. If they did not accept his method of thinking, at least he determined the questions which they should think about" (3.39).

4. Tulloch wrote that "it is a great pleasure to me to be allowed to associate your name with these Lectures. Slight as they are, I have been reminded more than once, during their preparation, of a large subject which used to engage our discussion many years ago, and in the treatment of which you were to bear what would have proved by far the most interesting part" (iii).

5. Such ideological oppositions had material consequences. As Rick Rylance notes, "In 1860 [Bain] failed to gain a chair at St. Andrews because of his 'desolating' philosophy and lack of religious orthodoxy. The Principal at St. Andrews was John Tulloch, whose hostility to both Comtists and the Utilitarian liberals spread over decades. Especially hostile to Mill, Tulloch was also sharply opposed to Bain. His summative *Movements of Religious Thought in Britain During the Nineteenth Century* (1885) contains a chapter-long attack on 'John Stuart Mill and his School' (including Bain)" (165).

6. When in the ghost story "Old Lady Mary," Oliphant criticizes a character who asserts that "everybody will tell you, my dear, that the mind is so dependent upon the body" (216), she echoes Tulloch, who insisted, in contradistinction to Mill, that "man is more than matter—that mind is more than any combination of matter" (240). In one of the Little Pilgrim tales, "The Land of Darkness," Oliphant's narrator comments of human existence that "the messages are less of pleasure than of pain. They report to

the brain the stroke of injury far more often than the thrill of pleasure: though sometimes that too, no doubt, or life could scarcely be maintained. The powers that be have
found it necessary to mingle a little sweet of pleasurable sensation, else our miserable
race would certainly have found some means of procuring annihilation. I do not for a
moment pretend to say that the pleasure is sufficient to offer a just counterbalance to
the other" (247–48). Such statements implicitly counter the emphasis on pleasure that
was central to the arguments of both Mill and his precursor Bentham.

7. Even Tulloch acknowledged that "*On Liberty* was probably the most popular of
all his books, as it is the most charming to read. There are few minds of a liberal turn
who can have perused it for the first time without a thrill of delight, even if the continual advance of liberal thought has now made some of its eloquence relatively commonplace" (229). In a footnote he explains more anecdotally that "Charles Kingsley,
when he first took up the volume in Parker's shop, became so entranced with it that he
sat down and read it through without stopping. As he left the shop he said it had 'made
him a clearer-headed, braver-minded man on the spot.' I read it first on the railway
between Oxford and London with something of the same ennobling effect" (229n1).

8. Leavis argues that "Bentham and Coleridge are not only, in actual history, the key
and complementary powers by reference to which we can organize into significance
so much of the field to be charted; even if they had had no great influence they would
still have been the classical examples they are of two great opposing types of mind"
(introduction 7)

9. Perkin describes this as "the transition in John Stuart Mill, Bentham's godson,
from Benthamite individualism to Benthamite collectivism" (*Rise* 121–22).

10. See Perkin's *The Rise of Professional Society* for a full discussion of these decades.
Jennifer Ruth argues that "at mid-century . . . the Victorians began to conceptualize an
emergent professional class. The late 1840s and the 1850s . . . established the cultural
conditions for the class's explosion in both numbers and power in the 1860s, 1870s, and
1880s" (3). Bledstein charts a similar process in America: "By the 1860s it was evident to
an observer that ambitious middle-class persons were seeking a professional basis for
an institutional order, a basis in universal and predictable rules to provide for a formal
context for the competitive spirit of individual egos" (31).

11. Oliphant too understands that "ministers and women . . . were intent on claim-
ing culture as their peculiar property" (Douglas 10).

12. For a discussion of the professionalization of the home, see both Monica Cohen, *Professional Domesticity in the Victorian Novel*, and Elizabeth Langland, *Nobody's
Angels*.

13. In "The Rector," the story of an inept clergyman in need of better training who
retires from active clerical duties to return to the scholarly seclusion of Oxford, Oliphant addresses the need for educational reform that was part of a general move to
higher professional standards. As Perkin explains, "the average Oxford and Cambridge
don was transformed during the late Victorian age from a celibate clergyman awaiting
a college living in the church on which he could marry to a career-oriented, and usually married, teacher and scholar or scientist" (*Rise* 87). Both *Salem Chapel* and *The
Perpetual Curate* also address the individual's relation to a church that is conceived of
as a professional group. In *Salem Chapel*, Oliphant focuses on a Dissenting clergyman
who, unlike his Anglican counterpart, is hired and can be fired by his congregation.
This allows her to explore the question central to professional ethics of how much

the individual should be beholden to those who pay him. Describing in *The Perpetual Curate* tensions between High and Low Church practices and conversion to Catholicism, Oliphant asks how far the individual should follow his own conscience and how far he must conform to the standards his profession expects of him.

14. The gender difference between the two halves of the series—the fact that male professionals dedicate themselves to higher goals, while the female protagonists exhibit pragmatic self-interest—reflects the distinction Bourdieu notes in *An Outline of a Theory of Practice* between men's association with symbolic profits and women's with the economics of exchange. The entrepreneur Copperhead voices this distinction when he tells the heroine of *Phoebe Junior*, "Honour! That's for men[,] . . . but for women there's no such thing" (410). As Bourdieu argues, "Lending between women is regarded as the antithesis of the exchange of honour" (*Outline* 62).

15. As individuals who never marry and become most successful in middle age, Catherine Vernon and Kirsteen Douglas are examples of the women Oliphant argues in her critique of *The Subjection of Women* do merit equal social rights: "the class of highly cultivated, able, mature, unmarried women who have never undergone the natural experiences of their sex, and really feel themselves in the position to compete with men" (590). They are "at the height of life and health, superior to other women by their exemption from all the disabling consequences of marriage, superior to men by their more perfect temperance and self-restraint. . . . They know themselves full of power to work and act as men do, and can perceive no reason why they should be limited to those arts of domestic management and industry which are the natural accompaniments of a life interrupted by childbirth and absorbed in family cares" (590–91). For a reading of the heroines of *Phoebe Junior*, *Hester*, and *Kirsteen* in relation to Oliphant's reaction to *The Subjection of Women*, see Wendy Jones, *Consensual Fictions*, 155–81.

16. This passage creates a literal image of the professional as someone who, as Bledstein has argued, "penetrated beyond the rich confusion of ordinary experience, as he isolated and controlled the factors, hidden to the untrained eye, which made an elaborate system workable or impracticable, successful or unattainable" (89).

17. As Mill argued in *On Liberty*, "Persons of genius are, *ex vi termini, more* individual than other people—less capable, consequently of fitting themselves, without hurtful compression, into any of the small number of molds which society provides in order to save its members the trouble of forming their own character" (74, emphasis in the original).

18. Oliphant goes on to explain of her heroine that she "was not perhaps, very intellectual, but she was independent and original, little trained in other people's ideas and full of fancies of her own, which, to my thinking, is the most delightful of characteristics" (164). Her thinking here dovetails with that of Mill, who insisted that as society becomes increasingly routinized, "originality is the one thing which unoriginal minds cannot feel the use of. They cannot see what it is to do for them" (*On Liberty* 74).

19. Ruth uses this passage from Herrnstein Smith to address the tensions inherent in professional self-definition, asking, "What do you do when the very terms with which you have traditionally defined yourself are in direct opposition to the terms that now enjoy, well, purchase?" (108). Pausing before she introduces the monetary term "purchase," Ruth refers again to Victorians' uneasiness with the explicitly economic side of professionalism, an uneasiness that Anthony Trollope underscores when he has Miss Dunstable note the clergy's unwillingness to be paid a salary. Stefan Collini

likewise mentions this uneasiness. As he is about to raise the question of professional intellectuals' salaries, he announces that "we must turn . . . to the traditionally ungenteel question of money" (35). Ruth argues that "the double discourse of value remained relatively intact . . . from the late eighteenth century until about the last quarter-century" (108). Oliphant's novels suggest that the breach between the two opened in the 1860s as contemporaries began to think through the implications of Mill's arguments.

20. Mill cites Coleridge to argue in a similar vein "that a gentleman should regard his estate as a merchant his cargo, or a shopkeeper his stock" (*Dissertations and Discussions* 374).

21. The figure Žižek dwells on is the Jew, who represents "capitalism's . . . hatred of its own innermost, essential feature" (206). I have been arguing throughout this book that the rich woman has a similar function in the nineteenth-century novel of manners.

22. Penelope Fitzgerald describes what she calls "the Mrs. Oliphant effect. In part it is the 'uncomprehended, unexplainable impulse to take the side of the opposition' that she recognized in herself and in Jane Carlyle. It is the form her wit takes, a sympathetic relish for contradictions" (37).

23. For Maine's thinking on gender and property, see note 18 in the introduction to this book. For a critic who draws on Maine to think through marital exchange in the Victorian novel, see Marcus, *Between Women*, 227–56. Marcus analyzes *Can You Forgive Her?* in light of Maine's arguments about status and contract.

24. Tulloch called Mill "the Apostle of Circumstance, as opposed alike to Free will in human conduct and the freedom of Divine Action in Nature" (231). Oliphant returns to the question of circumstances and the rich woman in *Hester*, in which one character tells another, "You are mixing up circumstances and principles. . . . It is circumstances which make Aunt Catherine powerful; chiefly because she is rich" (50). Oliphant makes it explicit here that the rich woman represents not an absolute moral state but a differing set of circumstances.

25. These comments, which are dotted throughout Oliphant's fiction, act as a version of the "*ironic* detachment" Amanda Anderson finds in Oscar Wilde that "pulls back and comments upon a topic, a prior response, a set of conditions" (158, emphasis in the original). Anderson locates this detachment in the epigram, a stylistic device common also in Oliphant, whom one might read as a precursor of Wilde. For a sampling of Oliphant epigrams, see the Brainy Quote website, which lists the following Wildean-sounding quotations: "As for pictures and museums, that don't trouble me. The worst of going abroad is that you've always got to look at things of that sort. To have to do it at home would be beyond a joke"; "For everybody knows that it requires very little to satisfy the gentleman, if a woman would only give her mind to it"; "It has been my fate in a long life of production to be credited chiefly with the equivocal virtue of industry, a quality so excellent in morals, so little satisfactory in art"; "Oh, never mind the fashion. When one has a style of one's own, it is always twenty times better"; "Temptations come, as a general rule, when they are sought"; "To have a man who can flirt is the next thing to indispensable to a leader of society"; "What happiness is there which is not purchased with more or less of pain?" (http://www.brainyquote.com/quotes/authors/m/margaret_oliphant.html).

26. In critiquing sentiment Oliphant again looks forward to Wilde, who seeks "to move away from any sentimental or moral rhetoric without ceding the ethical sphere

entirely to those social and political reformers who employ such rhetoric" (Anderson 150).

27. Douglas insists that "sentimentalism is a complex phenomenon. It asserts that the values a society's activity denies are precisely the ones it cherishes; it attempts to deal with the phenomenon of cultural bifurcation by the manipulation of nostalgia" (12). She could be describing the bifurcation of the marriage plot, which, with its choice between wealth and virtue, allows nineteenth-century readers to imagine transcending the pursuit of wealth at the same time that their culture is obsessed with it. The tone of Oliphant's novels suggests that it is not until the later half of the nineteenth century that that narrative logic begins to be perceived as sentimental. To define or perceive it in that way is, in some sense, to begin to move beyond it.

28. Mill introduces these three qualities in order to argue that Bentham addresses only the last, the rational category. The problem Mill sought to solve in his own writings was how to infuse the rational stance of utilitarianism with elements that made it appeal also to the emotions. Coming from the opposite direction, Oliphant sought to infuse the rationality of Mill's arguments into a literary genre, the novel, which is typically experienced as appealing to the emotions.

29. With such imagery, Oliphant marks her awareness of the patterns of novels like *Jane Eyre* in which the smallness of the heroine's body is contrasted with the large size of her wealthier rivals, Bertha and Blanche. We hear hints of this mocking tone in Anthony Trollope's *Framley Parsonage* when Lord Lufton and his mother disagree over whether he should marry the relatively poor Lucy Robarts, who is "little, brown, plain, and unimportant" (160) and lacks "social weight" (417), or Griselda Grantley, whom Lord Lufton characterizes as "some bouncing Amazon, some pink and white goddess of fashion who would frighten the little people into their proprieties" (506).

30. Maine describes "the trifling inconsistency of praising a man for being disinterested in the first place, and paying him 300,000*l.* for his disinterested conduct immediately afterwards" (77).

31. She commented to her publisher, in submitting installments of *Miss Marjoribanks*, "I meant it to be only four or five numbers, but I have already put in too many details to make that possible, and it seems to suit my demon best to let it have its own way," noting later that "I feel a little too *fluent*, as if I had all run to words" (Colby and Colby, 63).

32. When William Blackwood suggested that she give her main character a more sympathetic or softer aura, she replied, "As for what you say of hardness of tone, I am afraid it was scarcely to be avoided. . . . I have a weakness for Lucilla, and to bring a sudden change upon her character and break her down into tenderness would be like one of Dickens's maudlin repentances. . . . Miss M[arjoribanks] must be one and indivisible" (quoted in Langland 152).

33. Citing the opening line of Mill's essay on Bain—"The scepter of psychology has decidedly returned to this island" (72)—Margaret Schabas argues that "during the Victorian era, the conception of the economy and its salient features underwent a significant transformation. One critical factor in this process was an unprecedented but relatively short-lived enthusiasm by economists for the science of psychology, starting with Mill's declaration of 1859 . . . and ending more or less with Marshall" (77). Mill's essay on Bain was reprinted in *Dissertations and Discussions*, the book Phoebe Beecham is reading in *Phoebe Junior*.

34. Barbara represents a specific example of the general problem Lucilla confronts in Carlingford, where there is "a great deal of capital material . . . without . . . a single individual capable of making anything out of it" (21). In *Miss Marjoribanks*, as in Mill's writings, the capital material the extraordinary individual works with is human; it consists of the people out of whom one can forge an active and vital social whole.

35. As Bain argues, "if we find a person exceedingly deficient in the command of his feelings, being under all the ordinary motives that would inspire restraint, we must represent the fact by saying either that the emotional wave is unusually vehement, or that the volitional link is naturally or habitually feeble" (367). Barbara's propensity to stage public scenes suggests she is such a person.

36. In the same way Lucilla's "cultivated" soprano voice rises above but is also fueled by the more powerful notes of Barbara's swelling yet less controlled contralto.

37. Bain also "frequently uses images, metaphors, and illustrations drawn from combat and battle" (Rylance 197).

38. Mill's arguments invariably involved highlighting the difference between a higher and a lower position. He contrasted "the consistency of his own position and the purity of his own motives with the logical confusions and self-interested prejudices of others" (Collini 131).

39. The difference between self-interest and selfishness became key to professional self-definition: "Self-interest, a powerful human motive for industry, could be an enlightened source of benevolent action for every productive man who identified his particular interest with the general. Selfishness, on the other had, released by unrestrained competition, exploitation, and a strictly economic view of work, was a social vice that destroyed both public prosperity and public tranquility" (Bledstein 10).

40. For Ruskin sacrifice takes "two distinct forms: the first, the wish to exercise self-denial for the sake of self-discipline merely, a wish acted upon in the abandonment of things loved or desired . . . ; and the second, the desire to honour or please someone else by the costliness of the sacrifice. . . . In the latter case, the act is commonly, and with greatest advantage, public" (9). By abandoning what she loves in a visible fashion, Lucilla publicly demonstrates her commitment to the social good.

41. As Hadley has explained, "a commitment to formalized cognitive practices of disinterestedness and capaciousness of vision are a crafted response to the unpredictable circumstances of human temperament at play in the actual world" ("'On a Darkling Plain'" 96).

42. Bain argued that "whenever consciousness changes, there is the fact of discrimination, whether or not we make any account of it" (552).

43. Cavendish is such an individual, "a man habitually prone to run off after everything that attracted him" (109). He displays the attributes Bain describes—"intemperance, indolence, prodigality, neglect of opportunities, giving offence to those that would assist us, and all sorts of reckless behaviour . . . simply because the sense of our lasting interests does not move the will with the same energy as the relish for stimulants, for ease, for indulgence of emotions, and such like" (463–64).

44. This would mean that society as a whole was as fallible as Cavendish proves to be when he cannot distinguish between Lucilla and Barbara. As the narrator comments, "The best judges had not been able to discriminate between the false and true" (153).

45. Michelle Mouton argues that "Lucilla's self-assurance, the rapid growth of her

power and influence, her self-interest . . . , and the narrator's mock-heroic tone toward her prepare readers for certain conventions of the female bildungsroman—namely, some exposure of Lucilla's interference as misguided, her interpretations of people and situations as inaccurate, and her motivations as selfish—all part of the heroine's process of maturity. However, Lucilla's reading of the situation proves accurate" (223). Mouton concludes that "such validation by the narrative outcome stresses the efficacy of her social intuition, administrative competence, and rhetoric" (223). But while Mouton goes on to argue that the scene shows that *Miss Marjorbanks* can be read as Oliphant's defense of women's superior social readings of people and situations" (224), I argue that it also uses a woman to explore the possibilities (and liabilities) of Mill's gender-neutral category of the liberal subject.

46. As Mill acknowledged, "Capacity for the nobler feelings is in most natures a very tender plant, easily killed, not only by hostile influences, but by mere want of sustenance. . . . Men lose their high aspirations as they lose their intellectual tastes, because they have not time or opportunity for indulging them; and they addict themselves to inferior pleasures, not because they deliberately prefer them, but because they are either the only ones to which they have access, or the only ones which they are any longer capable of enjoying" (*Utilitarianism* 281–82).

47. This was, as Collini has noted, the aspect of Mill's argument that was least appealing to Victorians: "The feature of *On Liberty* to which contemporary critics took strongest exception was its perceived glorification of individual caprice and selfish indulgence at the expense of the stern demands of duty" (102).

48. This passage echoes the rhetoric of numerous essays of the period, in which "the characterization of the alternative to performing one's duty stressed giving in to temptation or being seduced by one's inclinations," inclinations that "were regarded as inherently selfish" (*Public* 63).

49. Mouton argues that Lucilla's support of Ashburton as "the man for Carlingford" (340) "echoes, with levity, John Stuart Mill" (225). Both in his own bid for election and his writings in *Essays on Representative Government*, "Mill wanted to ensure the election of meritorious candidates who would make decisions for the common good without having to pander to their (eventually working-class) constituencies' desires, and so he was reluctant to assert that issues be part of campaigns. Such politicians, probably members of the professional classes and intellectual elite, would 'take the lead in a general way,' . . . influencing constituencies rather than being influenced by them" (225).

50. This choice is described in terms that make it sound like Matthew Arnold's "Dover Beach," a poem published a year after *Miss Marjoribanks*. Lucilla's "mind was like a country held by two armies, one of which by turns swept the other into a corner, but only to be driven back in its turn" (465). Hadley has argued that "Dover Beach" may deliver "the very loveliest version of the Victorian fantasy of liberal agency" ("'On a Darkling Plain'" 93). The end of *Miss Marjoribanks* shows how such fantasies creep into the writing of even the most sardonic critics.

51. Oliphant consciously intervenes in the Victorian literary tradition as she chooses to make grocers and entrepreneurs key figures in her novel. The fact that Phoebe has read Anthony Trollope and Charlotte Yonge means, as she tells Reginald May, the son of an Anglican vicar, that "I know you as well as if I had known you all my life; a great

deal better than I know Clarence Copperhead; but then, no person of genius has taken any trouble about him" (234).

52. Phoebe puts these subliminal prejudices into words when she tells Mr. May that Anglicans treat Dissenters "as if we were some strange kind of creatures, from the heart of Africa perhaps. They don't think we are just like themselves: as well educated; meaning as well; with as much right to our own ideas" (213). May reacts with an interior laugh at the idea that Dissenters might consider themselves, in George Eliot's famous phrase, as having equivalent centers of self to Anglicans. However, the novel works to make Dissenters and Anglicans confront one another as individuals rather than stereotypes, thereby representing the processes that undermine "those prejudices and superstitions which made mankind hate each other for things not really odious; to make them take a juster measure of the tendencies of actions, and weigh more correctly the evidence on which they condemn or applaud their fellow-creatures" (Mill *Dissertations and Discussions* 147).

53. With such a description Oliphant is deliberately going against the view of art as a touchstone that makes possible an absolute distinction between intellectual and material property. In discussing the importance of this distinction to professional identity, Ruth cites H. Byerly Thompson's 1857 *The Choice of a Profession*, in which he argues that "the test by which an operation belongs to intellectual, or to bodily labour, or to barter is by observing what is the *principal object* of the exertion. Thus an artist sells to his client a certain quantity of canvas, covered in a thick coat of paint, the whole surrounded by a gilt frame; but he is not therefore a merchant, the principal object and real consideration of the purchase being the intellectual and imaginative design expressed by the picture, to which point canvas and frame are subordinate accessories" (25). In her portrait of Copperhead Oliphant makes visible a position Thompson does not address in which the merchant recognizes that imaginative or intellectual capital can be a material value.

54. Bourdieu provides further discussion of the connoisseur (*Distinction* 66, 279–80). Freedman notes that "aestheticism's valorizing of aesthetic connoisseurship led to the creation of the profession, both within the academy and without, of the art expert, the person whose job it was to search out and authenticate great works of art for clients and to advise those clients as to which art they should and should not purchase" (*Professions* 54).

55. Asa Briggs has argued of Oliphant's period that "if there was fear in society, it was not fear of the machine-breaker or of the demagogue, but of the grocer and the merchant" (327). Oliphant introduced the grocer Tozer in *Salem Chapel*, which narrates the story of his dealings with the Dissenting minister Mr. Vincent. She returns to those earlier characters in *Phoebe Junior* by way, as she typically does, of a minor character who is almost a wholly negative figure in that earlier novel. Tozer's daughter Phoebe relentlessly pursues the intellectual Vincent, who is disgusted by her red face and propensity for bringing him puddings from the grocery. That novel ends with Phoebe marrying Vincent's successor, Beecham, a much less educated and more vulgar avatar of the Dissenting minister. Tozer calls the heroine of Oliphant's later novel Phoebe Junior because that character is a reiteration of the Phoebe from Oliphant's earlier novel.

56. Oliphant's story of an educated individual returning to a lower-class background out of which she has emerged is characteristic of narratives that address the

complexities of professional self-identification. As Bruce Robbins argues, intellectuals, particularly those with working or lower-middle-class origins, typically experience their life as "an exemplary tale of upward mobility and ethnic assimilation" (26).

57. As Freedman notes, in the late nineteenth century cultivation was "defined for the Anglo-American audience by the likes of German idealist philosophers and romantic poets" (*Professions* xix). Mill praised Beethoven in *Dissertations and Discussions*, arguing that "the poetry of music seems to have attained its consummation in Beethoven's Overture to Egmont, so wonderful in its mixed expression of grandeur and melancholy" (60).

58. Mill argues that most individuals' perceptions are limited because they "have never thrown themselves into the mental position of those who think differently from them" (quoted in Anderson 17).

59. The professional "shows the provinces to be, also, a metropolis" (Robbins 127).

60. The cultivated individual brings groups of diverse people together, "proposing to themselves a collective, not an individual interest, as the aim . . . of their actions. So long as they are co-operating, their ends are identified with those of others; there is at least a temporary feeling that the interests of others are their own interests" (Mill *Utilitarianism* 304).

61. These scenes have a peculiar halcyon quality; they make readers feel what Hadley has described as a "belief in the liberal subject's ability to seek out a private space of thoughtful emotion, of human intimacy, where subjects alienated in mind or body can become fully authentic and intentional in relation to themselves and to each other, in spite of the chaotic world without" ("'On the Darkling Plain'" 93).

62. When Ursula and Phoebe initially meet at the Copperhead's ball, it looks as if Phoebe will be the wealthy antithesis to Ursula's genteel poverty. As Ursula asks, "Why should one girl have so much and another girl so little?" (61). The parameters of this contrast are, however, undercut: Ursula and Phoebe become friends rather than rivals, Phoebe rather than Ursula turns out to be the intellectual, and the apparent financial difference between the two proves insignificant. From Clarence's point of view, "they haven't a penny, either the one or the other" (124).

63. The terms with which Oliphant characterizes Phoebe's decision resonate with Schabas's description of the key intellectual change that took place among Mill and his fellow materialist thinkers. They "cut themselves free of the Enlightenment association with physical nature that once saw the production and distribution of wealth as part of a providential order. The economy was now depicted in terms of man-made social institutions. To put it most emphatically, the economy went from a natural entity to a social one" (78). Oliphant's novel demonstrates that this shift in thinking virtually necessitates a revision of the marriage plot, which, in its typical form, implies a natural or providential force that comes into play as characters learn to make a moral distinction between wealth and virtue. Phoebe's marital choice is guided by a social rather than a natural distinction.

64. Mill makes a similar about-face in defending Bain's psychology. After acknowledging that Bain's "mode of interpreting the phenomena of the mind is not unfrequently stigmatised as materialistic," he goes on to insist that "with materialism in the obnoxious sense, this view of the mind has no necessary connexion," after which he redefines the term, explaining that "if it be materialism to endeavor to ascertain the

material conditions of our mental operations, all theories of the mind which have any pretension to comprehensiveness must be materialistic" ("Bain's Psychology" 348).

65. In Anthony Trollope's *The Warden* the Reverend Mr. Harding is publicly lambasted for possessing a religious preferment that is described in terms that make it almost identical to the one evoked in Oliphant's novel. In Trollope's world, Victorian readers' desire for the choice of virtue over wealth is satisfied when Mr. Harding resigns his post and becomes one of Trollope's most beloved and unworldly characters. See Joseph O'Mealy's "Rewriting Trollope and Yonge" for a discussion of Oliphant's use of *The Warden*.

66. When he inherits his father's curacy after Mr. May dies, Reginald is described as a "pluralist, and almost rich" (418). "Sinecure" and "pluralist" were terms the Victorians typically used to mark their uneasiness about religious practices that seemed too mercenary. Those terms carried over to professionalism. As Collini notes, Sir Henry Maine's "contemporaries were on occasion a little scandalized by his pluralism" (46). Maine himself described his mastership as "a sinecure of £600 a year and a good house" (quoted in Collini 48). Oliphant was particularly sensitive to these issues, since she repeatedly sought a post at *Blackwood's* that would give her a regular salary. She was never able to achieve such professional independence and continued to live on what she thought of as piecework, providing a review here and there, a biography, an essay, a novel in parts. For a discussion of Oliphant and work, see Deirdre d'Albertis's "The Domestic Drone."

67. Monica Cohen argues that Reginald performs "paid unpaid work" (6).

68. In both scenes, the heroine confronts a male combatant who is "speechless with rage" (*Miss Marjoribanks* 322), while she "alone stood calm" (*Phoebe Junior* 399). Both novels represent that stance as the apotheosis of the heroine's power: "Lucilla rose to the height of the position" (296); Phoebe's "self-confidence reached the heroic point" (378).

69. Mill argued that "the distinction between moral and immoral acts is not a peculiar and inscrutable property in the acts themselves. . . . The particular property in actions, which constitutes them moral or immoral, in the opinion of those who hold this theory . . . is the influence of those actions, and of the disposition from which they emanate, upon human happiness" (*Dissertations and Discussions* 100). Phoebe can assess May's forgery as an act that is not immoral, because she can see that it need not harm the happiness or well-being of the community. The money can be repaid to Tozer, and the forgery will then only impact May (who indeed ends up dying of the mental stress of fearing discovery and punishment).

70. Langland has argued that *Miss Marjoribanks* can be read as a narrative of class relations: "In the attraction he feels for Barbara, Cavendish finally betrays his lower-middle-class origins, elucidating how desire seems to be articulated within particular class formulas" in being drawn to "Barbara's similarly class-inscribed body" (168–69). However, in *Phoebe Junior*, the transgression that threatens social union is committed not by a member of the lower-middle classes but by an Oxford-educated clergyman who is related to a land-owning gentry family. The movement from *Miss Marjoribanks* to *Phoebe Junior* reiterates the movement from Miss Bingley to Lady Catherine de Bourgh in *Pride and Prejudice*, a shift in emphasis in the plot from class to wealth.

71. Contemporary reviewers harped on the vulgarity of the senior Mr. Copperhead. The critic for the *Spectator* called him "an atrociously vulgar father, who has made a

grand fortune in contracts," and argued that "Mrs. Oliphant is like Mr. Disraeli, she hates a rich vulgarian till she will not trouble herself to analyse him" ("*Phoebe Junior*" 769, 770). The *Pall Mall Gazette* described him as "large, rich, and costly, swelling with pride and self-complacency," and argued that "his vulgarity is in a measure redeemed by his humour" ("*Phoebe Junior*" 12). The *Saturday Review* asserted that his manners "are impossible in the rude insolence of their boast of wealth. A man may talk of his money; but one inclines to think that such talk as Mr. Copperhead's should be separated from modern society by long centuries and the interposition of the dark ages" ("*Phoebe Junior*"113).

72. When Copperhead comes to visit Clarence while his son is being tutored by May, the sight of the reverend's books "made the millionaire's soul shrink within him" (334). Tozer is similarly awed and fascinated by the educated ministers who come to serve in the Dissenting chapel in both *Salem Chapel* and *Phoebe Junior*, a fascination he abjures at the end of the *Phoebe Junior*, asserting, "I'm cured of clever men and those as is thought superior. They ain't to be calculated upon. If any more o' them young intellectuals turns up in Carlingford, I'll tell him right out, 'You ain't the man for my money'" (417).

73. Perkin notes that "some London clergy . . . including a few dissenting ministers, could earn up to £1,500 a year" (*Rise* 91). Phoebe's parents live in the Regent's Park area and are "in no want of money to buy what pleased them" (120).

74. In contrast, "the Conservative who has had any idea of the meaning of the name which he carries, wishes, I suppose, to maintain the differences and the distances which separate the highly placed from their lower brethren. He thinks that God has divided the world as he finds it divided, and that he may best do his duty by making the inferior man happy and contented in his position, teaching him that place which he holds is his by God's ordinance" (*Prime Minister* 2.264). Trollope is typically read as divided between the two positions; as Gagnier has argued, "while his liberalism is . . . rational . . . , his conservatism is affective" ("Gender" 239).

75. This upward mobility involves the expansion of property as well as of intellect: "We must leave to history to unfold the gradual rise of the trading and manufacturing classes, the gradual emancipation of the agricultural. . . . We need only ask the reader to form a conception of all that is implied in the words, growth of a middle class; and then to reflect on the immense increase of the numbers and property of that class throughout Great Britain, France, Germany, and other countries" (*Dissertations and Discussions* 133).

76. *Phoebe Junior* is not in the Oliphant works Woolf lists, which include "*The Duke's Daughter, Diana Trelawny, Harry Jocelyn*[,] . . . the lives of Sheridan and Cervantes[,] . . . the *Makers of Florence and Rome* . . . and the innumerable faded articles, reviews, sketches of one kind and another which she contributed to literary papers" (139).

77. Ironically, Phoebe represents what Woolf's uncle James Fitzjames Stephen described as "the circle—not distinguished by any definite label but yet recognized among each other by a spontaneous free-masonry—which forms the higher intellectual stratum of London society" (quoted in Collini 13). Outrageously, Oliphant identifies that circle with what she calls in *Hester* "the business people, the professional classes, and those who considered themselves to be acquainted with the world" (5).

CHAPTER FIVE: Henry James and the End(s) of the Marriage Plot

1. For a detailed reading of the preface to *The Golden Bowl*, see J. Hillis Miller, *The Ethics of Reading*.

2. *The Spoils of Poynton* has typically been read as marking the shift into the late phase of James's career. It is "a turning point in the fiction of Henry James" (Leon Edel quoted in Gargano 67), "the pivotal novel in his artistic career" (*Notebooks* xi). I read *The Wings of the Dove* and *The Golden Bowl* as sequential. They were written one after the other: "*The Wings of the Dove*, though published before *The Ambassadors*, was in fact written after it" (Cameron 153).

3. As Rahv explains, "There is no ignoring the consideration, however, that in the case of the heiress, as in the case of most of James's rich Americans, money is in a sense but the prerequisite of moral delicacy" (230). In contrast to the wealthy and angelic Milly Theale, the poor but ambitious Kate Croy seemed "the arch-vampire, the supreme harpy and anti-heroine of the plot" (Gargano 46). The reversal of the two positions is so complete that in his notes for the novel James describes Milly as "the poor (that is the rich) girl" (*Notebooks* 105). Within the novel, she conceives of herself as being "reduced . . . to her ultimate state, which was that of a poor girl—with her rent to pay for example—staring before her in a great city" (175). Michael Martin argues that, Milly "remains able to experience her relationship to the poor around her as characterized by similarity" (112).

4. Such a perception is key to the way that twentieth-century anthropologists would come to understand kinship and marital exchange. As Lévi-Strauss explains in *The Elementary Structures of Kinship*, the definition of one woman as an acceptable spouse, the other as unacceptable is arbitrary: "If there is a prohibition it is not because there is some feature of the object which excludes it from the number of possibilities. It acquires these features only in so far as it is incorporated in a certain system of antithetical relationships, the rôle of which is to establish inclusions by means of exclusions, and vice versa" (113–14).

5. Jameson defines this as the moment of high-finance capitalism, when "capital itself becomes free-floating. It separates from the concrete context of its productive geography. Money becomes in a second sense and to a second degree abstract" ("Culture" 251). As Baucom explains, "The decades spanning the end of the nineteenth and the beginning of the twentieth century . . . define themselves as the highest moments of finance capital, moments in which capital seems to turn its back entirely on the thingly world, sets itself free from the material constraints of production and distribution, and revels in its pure capacity to breed money from money—as if by a sublime trick of the imagination" (*Specters* 27).

6. Simmel's essay "The Psychology of Money" appeared in America in 1889, when Henry James's own work was just beginning to take off. James might have known Simmel's work through his brother William. As Ross Posnock notes, "William James thought [Simmel] an ally, and with good reason" (98).

7. At the end of *The Philosophy of Money* Simmel uses several analogies to convey money's fluidity: "Like money, the ocean is a mediator, it is the geographical version of the means of exchange" (391); "Money can be compared to the bloodstream whose continuous circulation permeates all the intricacies of the body's organs and unifies their functions by feeding them all to an equal extent. Thus money, as an intermedi-

ate link between man and thing, enables man to have, as it were, an abstract existence, a freedom from direct concern with things and from a direct relationship to them" (469).

8. Collin Meissner makes a similar point about James and Simmel in his discussion of *The American Scene*, arguing that, "the prose style of the late phase shares a good deal of similarity with Simmel's explanation of money as 'nothing but the vehicle for a movement in which everything else that is not in motion is completely extinguished.' Like Simmel's money, James's late prose deploys itself 'in continuous self-alienation from any given point and thus forms the counterpoint and direct negation of all being itself'" (248).

9. I am thinking here particularly of Bill Brown's *A Sense of Things* and Thomas Otten's *A Superficial Reading of Henry James*.

10. James's insistence on the enormous size of the fortunes possessed by the heiresses in his late novels confirms Simmel's assertion that "in the case of extraordinarily large sums of money the purely quantitative character of money actually provides a place for a nuance of qualitative distinctiveness. The indifference, the refinement and banality that are peculiar to money that is constantly circulating do not affect, to the same extent, these rare and spectacular concentrations of immense fortunes in a single hand" (*Philosophy of Money* 308).

11. Economic readings of Henry James have tended to conflate money and objects by stressing the importance of consumption and the commodity in his work. See, for example, Jean-Christophe Agnew, "The Consuming Vision of Henry James" and Mark Seltzer, "Physical Capital." The work of both Brown and Otten complicates these readings by separating things out from the category of commodities. But their work does not explore the way the concreteness of things is counterbalanced by an abstraction that is itself associated with money. Carolyn Porter, who uses the Marxist cycle in which commodities are transformed into money and money into the abstraction of capital to read *The Golden Bowl*, comes closest to acknowledging this tension. See *Seeing and Being*, especially 143–49.

12. Brown links these comments to William James, who asks, "What do you call one's self? Where does it begin? It overflows into everything that belongs to us—and then it flows back again. . . . I have a great respect for *things*" (quoted in Brown *Sense* 140). One could as easily cite Simmel who argued that "the Ego is surrounded by all its possessions as by a sphere in which its tendencies and character traits gain visible reality. Possessions form an extension of the Ego which is only the centre from which impulses extend into things" (*Philosophy of Money* 322).

13. Giddens distinguishes "two types of disembedding mechanisms intrinsically involved in the development of modern social institutions. The first of these I refer to as the creation of *symbolic tokens*. . . . By symbolic tokens I mean media of interchange which can be 'passed around' without regard to the specific characteristics of individuals or groups that handle them at any particular juncture. Various kinds of symbolic tokens can be distinguished, such as media of political legitimacy; I shall concentrate here upon the token of *money*" (22, emphasis in the original).

14. We might think of the difference between fashion and art or between the rich and the poor woman in terms of the distinction Wilhelm Worringer made between abstraction and empathy. A colleague of Simmel's, Worringer argued that while empathy (which he associated with naturalism) responds to "organically beautiful vitality"

(14), "abstraction finds its beauty in the life-denying inorganic, or in the crystalline, or, in general terms, in all abstract law and necessity" (4). These descriptions capture the tension between Kate, with her organic and sexual vitality, and Milly, with her literally life-denying aesthetic purity. Worringer's references seem particularly apt given the emphasis in *The Golden Bowl* on the bowl's crystalline structure. For further discussion of theories of empathy that identify it with the individuals' relation to objects, see Otten, "Slashing Henry James," 313–14.

15. In this scene Charlotte is also imaged as a curio cabinet: "The bits and pieces of her body . . . strike Amerigo as 'a cluster of possessions of his own'" (Otten *Superficial* 16). For Otten, the appeal of objects is linked to Charotte's appeal as a material, that is, sensual/sexual object: "In James's late fiction, a suppressed account of adultery reappears as an account of the material world" (*Superficial* 112). Though neither Kate Croy nor Merton Densher are married, James does refer to the sexual liaison that takes place between them as adultery (*Notebooks* 103). In *The Wings of the Dove* (as well as in *The Golden Bowl*), "the missing accounts of sexual liaisons work their way into the novel's representations of the concrete world as material things" (Otten *Superficial* 112).

16. In the preface to *The Golden Bowl*, James describes "a shop of the mind, of the author's projected world, in which objects are primarily related to each other" (xii).

17. Bentley has read *The Spoils of Poynton* "as a significant departure from the domesticity of the earlier Victorian novel" (124) in its linkage of kinship and property to the story of courtship and marriage. I argue that James's novel makes visible the strains that have been implicit in the structure of the marriage plot since Austen's *Pride and Prejudice*.

18. My reading of *The Spoils of Poynton* could be critiqued on the same grounds I have been critiquing readings of the novel of manners, namely, for not paying enough attention to the rich woman. As Stephanie Foote has argued, "Mona is the most undercritiqued and undervalued character in the novel, perhaps because she seems so obvious" (44). I would, nevertheless, suggest that in this novel, James is more interested in using the rich woman to lay out the configuration of the marriage plot than in developing her as a full locus of value.

19. Here James refers to the crassness of new wealth in terms that might remind us of the scene where Plantagenet Palliser condemns Lady Glencora as vulgar in Anthony Trollope's *The Prime Minister*. Her expenditures at Gatherum Castle are crass because they involve "sheer display," "an assumed and preposterous grandeur that was as much within the reach of some rich swindler or of some preposterous haberdasher as of himself" (1.174, 175). James's reference to the grocer might also remind us of Oliphant's use of that figure in her Carlingford novels.

20. James was quite familiar with Trollope's novel, having reviewed it for the *Nation* (Smalley 249–53).

21. Interestingly, this plot is so compelling that it drives the actions not just of characters within the novel but also of the writer. In his notes for the novel James commented that he had not planned to have Owen fall in love with Fleda: "I had not intended to represent a feeling of that kind on Owen's part. . . . [I]t inevitably took that turn and I must accept the idea and work it out" (*Notebooks* 132).

22. We might think of Owen's role in *The Spoils of Poynton* in terms of the case history of the Ratman. In Freud's case history, as in James's novel, the valuing of love

over wealth is learned rather naturally. The Ratman learns to think that life should follow the pattern of a nineteenth-century novel when his mother mocks his father for having married her for her money instead of the poor woman he loved. So, too, in James's novel, Owen learns to disparage Mona and to value Fleda after his mother intrudes, mocking the materialist values of the Brigstocks and celebrating those of her penniless protégée.

23. In his notes to the novel, James refers to these issues in legal terms, asserting that in the historical episode that lay behind *Spoils*, "the son married—married promptly and young—and went down with his wife to take possession—possession *exclusive*, of course—according to English custom" (*Notebooks* 79, emphasis in the original).

24. As Jan Van Baal points out, "a son's marriage with a woman of a lower social status shields the family from intervention by the new wife's relatives" (91).

25. Brown notes that "the 'things' at Poynton are not so much objects as they are congealed actions, passionate acts of seeking, selecting, and situating" (*Sense* 146). Otten identifies the link between the things and writing, observing that "Poynton is thus said to be 'written in great syllables of colour and form' by 'the hands of rare artists'—as if it possesses not only the individuality of literary style but also the idiosyncrasies of handwriting" (*Superficial* 42).

26. Brown reads the moment as "the conflagration in which realism as such is consumed" (*Sense* 150). I read it as symbolic of the destruction of a novelistic tradition of the marriage plot that Mrs. Gereth has tried so desperately and futilely to impose.

27. Brown argues that, in contrast to the vaguely evoked spoils, "highly particularized objects appear elsewhere in the novel's decorative landscape—in Fleda's sister's and her father's house, and, above all, at Waterbath. . . . But as though such individualizing description were to be preserved for the elements of bad taste alone" (*Sense* 147).

28. Otten reads this description as establishing a keynote for the novels that follow: "The objects of the last novels are both 'slippery' and 'sticky' like Lionel Croy's repulsive sofa . . . ; they are full of 'duplicity' . . . ; they are 'promiscuous properties'" (*Superficial* 112).

29. These bits of food seem to be an instantiation of what James described in the preface to *The Golden Bowl* as the "patches of crude surface, the poor morsels of consciously-decent matter that catch one's eye with their rueful reproach" (xxi). He is here referencing Balzac. So one might argue that scenes like the one where Fleda looks at the biscuit represent an intrusion of French realism into the familiar but very different structure of the English novel of manners. For a discussion of James's relation to Balzac, see Peter Brooks, *Henry James Goes to Paris*.

30. In the preface to the novel, James characterizes its opening chapters as "saturated with her presence, her 'personality'"; he "felt all her weight in the scale" (10–11). Maud Lowder is too materially present to allow the distance needed for refinement: "She stood there too close . . . and too solidly" (*Wings of a Dove* 43). As Bourdieu argues in the concluding section of *Distinction*, vulgarity is a function of excessive closeness rather than of the distancing effects of art.

31. The characterization of her as "Britannia of the Market Place" (*Wings of a Dove* 21) links Maud to the mid-Victorian writers who fear their society's propensity to worship wealth. The phrase comes from Ruskin's *The Crown of Wild Olive*, in which he characterizes commercial England as obsessed with "the ruling goddess[,] . . . the

'Goddess of Getting-on,' or 'Britannia of the Market'" (242). For an extended discussion of James's relation to Ruskin, see Jonathan Freedman's *Professions of Taste*.

32. The contrast between Maud and Milly is a new version of the contrast evoked in *The Spoils of Poynton* between Waterbath and Poynton. Like the Brigstocks, Aunt Maud is associated with the "florid philistinism" (*Wings of a Dove* 21) of nouveau-riche taste. But she is much more sympathetically depicted than her precursors, as if James has been brought to accept the presence and possible value of such taste in modern English culture. She is opposed to Milly, who is, like the objects at Poynton, associated with an aesthetic taste that has its fullest expression in her enjoyment of the history represented by the rented palace in Venice. But Milly is more detached than Mrs. Gereth because she possesses such an enormous amount of wealth that she is beyond being identified with objects as possessions or spoils.

33. James is not alone in associating the new perception of money with America. Simmel also argued that "the growing Americanism of the times, has obviously been nourished on this power and this result of money" ("The Problem of Style" 251).

34. James marks the abstractness of his heiress's wealth in contrast to the wealth depicted by his precursor Anthony Trollope when Kate comments that Milly "won't smell, as it were, of drugs" (*Wings of a Dove* 247). This comment echoes the description of Miss Dunstable in Trollope's novels as someone whose vulgar wealth could smell of the drugs that produced it.

35. One way to read the novel's fascination with Milly's dying state is as an emblem of her dying out of the novel as a center of consciousness. After her failing health leads her to go to Venice, the novel turns away from her perspective and voice to present her only from the perspective of others, preventing us even from having access to her last letter to Densher when Kate burns it unopened.

36. Simmel argues of jewelry in his essay "Adornment" that "by virtue of this brilliance, its wearer appears as the centre of a circle of radiation in which every close-by person, every seeing eye, is caught. As the flash of the precious stone seems to be directed at the others—like the lightning of the glance the eye addresses to him—it carries the social meaning of jewels, the being-for-the-other, which returns to the subject as the enlargement of his own sphere of significance. The radii of this sphere mark the distance which jewelry creates between men— 'have something which you do not have.' But, on the other hand, these radii not only let the other participate: they shine in *his* direction; in fact, they exist only for his sake. By virtue of their material, jewels signify, in one and the same act, an increase in distance and a favour" (209, emphasis in the original).

37. In the preface, he notes "the building-up of Kate Croy's consciousness to the capacity for the load little by little to be laid on it" (9).

38. James could easily have come in contact with the work of Bachofen through his friendship with the classicist and anthropologist Jane Ellen Harrison, who used Bachofen's theory of mother right in her own work. Both Bentley and Mizruchi have commented on James's interest in anthropology and the fact that he owned a copy of *Primitive Marriage*. Both also read his novels in light of anthropology, Bentley in terms of the exchange of symbolic goods, Mizruchi of sacrifice.

39. James uses similar imagery in the preface to *The Wings of the Dove* when he talks about Milly's impact, explaining that "our young friend's existence would create rather, all round her, very much that whirlpool movement of the waters produced by the sink-

ing of a big vessel" (6). The author invokes the imagery circulation around a still point to describe his own relation to the heiress, noting that he must approach her "circuitously, deal with her at second hand, as an unspotted princess is ever dealt with" (16). James will abandon this circuitous approach in the second half of *The Golden Bowl*.

40. James's library included a copy of Taylor's *The Rule and Exercises of Holy Living* as well as McLennan's book.

41. The novel's linking of familial relations (of father and daughter and husband and wife) with property issues (of banking and finance) reflects the persistent nineteenth-century anthropological insistence that the evolutions of marital and property relations were linked. Morgan's *Ancient Society* charts the evolution of marriage in its first three sections only to turn to the growth of the idea of property in part 4. In *The Origin of the Family, Private Property and the State*, Engels sets out to chart "the relationship between the emergence of private property and the monogamous family form" (7). Spencer insists that "the development of the conception of property in general, has had much to do with the development of the marital relation" (*Principles* 645).

42. Though I concentrate here on Maggie's role in this failure of exchange, it would be possible also to look at Amerigo's. Two figures, Lévi-Strauss argues, mark the limits of systems of marital exchange, the poor man and the rich woman. For a critical reading that focuses on Prince Amerigo and the problem he represents in terms of assimilation, see Thomas Peyser's "The Imperial Museum" in *Utopia and Cosmopolis*. There he reads James in relation to early twentieth-century anxieties about immigration, arguing that "in an important sense, *The Golden Bowl* echoes . . . concerns about the assimilation of the foreigner, the stranger, the survivor from a previous age" (138). Through Amerigo, the novel asks, "To what extent could immigrants be assimilated to American life?" (142).

43. Maggie's desire, as an heiress, to be connected to others without participating in an exogamous system of exchange is curiously echoed by the comments of a real heiress, Genevieve Vaughan, documented in Margaret Randall's *The Price You Pay*. Vaughan observes that "these anthropologists talked a lot about reciprocity. But couldn't the bonds be created without reciprocity, simply by knowing someone else had satisfied your need, or by becoming aware of someone else's need and satisfying it?" (117). As she goes on to explain, "When I read about Lévi-Strauss's ideas on the exogamic exchange of women between groups of men . . . it occurred to me that what these men were exchanging were free givers, gift-sources" (117).

44. One way to think of the Ververs would be in terms of what Lévi-Strauss calls the "omnipresent danger but irresistible attraction of a 'social incest,' more dangerous to the group, even, than biological incest" (454). As Adam Verver tells his daughter of the four principal characters of *The Golden Bowl*, "We're selfish together—we move as a selfish mass. You see we want always the same thing . . . and that holds us, that binds us, together" (367).

45. James's decision to use an untranslated French word rather than an English word to convey this idea of reciprocity might remind us of moments in Anthony Trollope's novels and Walter Bagehot's economic writings in which the prose turns to French when the author wants to convey the explicitness of economic motives without those motives seeming vulgar.

46. James concludes the preface to *The Wings of the Dove* by noting that "in 'The Wings of the Dove,' I had become conscious of overstepping my space without having

brought the full quantity to light. The failure leaves me with a burden of residuary comment of which I yet boldly hope elsewhere to discharge myself" (16). I read *The Golden Bowl* as the space where he discharges himself of the material he was not able to bring to light in *The Wings of the Dove.*

47. Amy Ling notes that the pagoda is associated with Maggie's "circulation" (387).

48. Holland argues of the pagoda that "the 'tall tower of ivory'—a 'structure plated with hard, bright porcelain' and ominously remote—is a figure for the pair of marriages which leave the four principal characters interlocked" (336)

49. Peter Brooks has described the bridge-playing episode as "the true climax of the novel" (191).

50. As Cameron notes, "The novel's most prolific referrers are the Assinghams, whose name puns on (spoken) assignments/assignations of meaning" (fn. 118).

51. Mizruchi discusses the thirteen-year-old James's fascination with Henry Holman Hunt's painting *The Scapegoat* (189).

52. As Simmel explains, "Moral merit always signifies that opposing impulses and desires had to be conquered and sacrificed in favour of the morally desirable act" (*Philosophy of Money* 88).

53. The two scenes that seem to be allegorically about the structure of novels, both this scene and Maggie's contemplation of the imaginary pagoda, are associated with gardens. In the preface to *The Golden Bowl*, James identifies novels with gardens, arguing that the novelist's "own garden, however, remains one thing, and the garden he has prompted the cultivation of at other hands becomes quite another; which means that the frame of one's own work no more provides place for such a plot than we expect flesh and fish to be served on the same platter" (x).

AFTERWORD: From Pemberley to Manderley

1. One could think, for example, of the film *Arthur* with its valorization of the poor Liza Minnelli character as the proper match for its wealthy title character.

2. For a discussion of the association of the country house with history of empire, see chapter 5 of Ian Baucom's *Out of Place*. Baucom has argued that "the patent inventedness of a phenomenon does not prevent it from having a very real affective appeal, from seducing, from convincing its beholder to forget that it is a piece of counterfeit, or to worship it regardless" (188). See also Raymond Williams's *The Country and the City* for a discussion of such houses in relation to class differences.

3. With its marriage between a heroine who is herself already wealthy and a hero whose estate is less an image of aesthetic achievement than of the workaday world of raising apples, leasing farms, and maintaining strawberry beds, *Emma* also provides readers with less of an erotic charge than *Pride and Prejudice*. We get, I would argue, the closest approximation to the pleasure of that early novel in the scene in *Persuasion* where Wentworth finally proposes again to Anne Elliott. That pleasure is, however, itself written as a repetition or recouping of a time long gone. Also, interestingly, the union is no longer that between landed wealth and an impoverished heroine but between a naval fortune and a heroine whose father has wasted his estate.

4. For a discussion of the implication of Brontë's description of these rooms, see Nancy Armstrong's *Desire and Domestic Fiction*, 205–13. Armstrong argues that "some of the mystery of the old aristocracy clings onto the cultural debris one finds in the

rooms of Thornfield Hall and makes the objects of the past appear all the more mysterious because they cannot be reproduced in a middle-class world" (211).

5. Like Armstrong, Baucom associates Thornfield with memory. Working from Jean Rhys's *Wide Sargasso Sea*, he argues that Rochester realizes that he can put Caribbean rum and sugar to work, using their proceeds "to build an 'English' country house in which to imprison Antoinette, in which to contain the imperial excesses she embodies. That mansion will be a sort of memory house. . . . This, finally, is where the text leaves us, . . . in the prison house of memory" (*Place* 172). Rhys's novel allows us to read the country house "as a carceral space, as a reformatory of English identity, as a monument to the cultivated remembrances and willed amnesias of empire" (172).

6. The series of estates that follow Pemberley is also interesting because all of them are financed in part by women's as well as men's wealth. Rochester has absorbed Bertha's estate when he returns to Thornfield. Satis House is in the possession of Miss Havisham. Poynton is occupied by the married Mona Brigstock. This movement suggests an awareness of the impossibility of maintaining landed estates without the incursion of nonlanded wealth. Yet that incursion also seems to taint the estate such that it can no longer represent the values that are embodied in Pemberley. The persistence of fires in these texts suggests a form of cleansing. It also implies that these estates that are funded by women are, in some sense, abominations that must be fully destroyed, burned away until there is nothing left.

Ablow, Rachel. *The Marriage of Minds: Reading Sympathy in the Victorian Marriage Plot*. Stanford: Stanford University Press, 2007.

Addison, Joseph. *Spectator*. London: Macmillan, 1896.

Agnew, Jean-Christophe. "The Consuming Vision of Henry James." In *The Culture of Consumption*. Ed. Richard Wightman Fox and T. J. Jackson Lears. New York: Pantheon, 1983. 65–100.

———. *Worlds Apart: The Market and the Theater in Anglo-American Thought, 1550–1750*. Cambridge: Cambridge University Press, 1986.

Amos, William. *The Originals: An A-Z of Fiction's Real-Life Characters*. Boston: Little Brown, 1980.

Anderson, Amanda. *The Powers of Distance: Cosmopolitanism and the Cultivation of Detachment*. Princeton: Princeton University Press, 2001.

Appadurai, Arjun. *The Social Life of Things: Commodities in Social Perspective*. Cambridge: Cambridge University Press, 1986.

Appleby, Joyce. *Economic Thought and Ideology in Seventeenth-Century England*. Princeton: Princeton University Press, 1978.

Armstrong, Nancy. *Desire and Domestic Fiction: A Political History of the Novel*. New York: Oxford University Press, 1987.

———. *How Novels Think: The Limits of Individualism from 1719–1900*. New York: Columbia University Press, 2005.

Arnold, Matthew. *Culture and Anarchy*. Ed. Samuel Lipman. New Haven: Yale University Press, 1994.

Arrighi, Giovanni. *The Long Twentieth Century: Money, Power, and the Origin of Our Times*. London: Verso, 1994.

Auden, W. H. "Letter to Lord Byron." In *Letters from Iceland*. New York: Random House, 1937. 17–24.

Austen, James, ed. *The Loiterer*. www.theloiterer.org.

Austen, Jane. *Emma*. Ed. Stephen M. Parrish. New York: Norton, 2000.

———. *Mansfield Park*. Ed. Claudia L. Johnson. New York: Norton, 1998.

———. *Persuasion*. Ed. Patricia Meyer Spacks. New York: Norton, 1995.

———. *Pride and Prejudice*. Ed. Donald Gray. New York: Norton, 2001.

———. *Sense and Sensibility*. Ed. Claudia L. Johnson. New York: Norton, 2002.

Austen-Leigh, J. E. *A Memoir of Jane Austen*. Gloucester, UK: Dodo Press, 2009.

Ayres, Brenda, ed. *Frances Trollope and the Novel of Social Change*. Westport, CT: Greenwood Press, 2002.

Baal, Jan Van. *Reciprocity and the Position of Women: Anthropological Papers*. Amsterdam: Van Gorem, 1975.

Badiou, Alain. *Handbook of Inaesthetics*. Stanford: Stanford University Press, 2004.

Bagehot, Walter. *Economic Studies*. London: Longman's, 1911.

———. *The English Constitution*. Cambridge: Cambridge University Press, 2001.

———. *Lombard Street: A Description of the Money Market*. New York: Wiley, 1999.

———. *Physics and Politics*. Chicago: Ivan R. Dee, 1999.

Bain, Alexander. *The Emotions and the Will*. New York: Cosimo, 2006.

Balfour, Stewart. *The Conservation of Energy*. New York: Appleton, 1876.

Barker, Juliet. *The Brontës: A Life in Letters*. Woodstock, NY: Overlook Press, 1997.

Barker-Benfield, G. J. *The Culture of Sensibility: Sex and Society in Eighteenth-Century Britain*. Chicago: University of Chicago Press, 1992.

Barrie, J. M. Introductory note. *A Widow's Tale and Other Stories*. By Margaret Oliphant. Edinburgh: Blackwood and Sons, 1898. v–viii.

Bartrum, Barry A. *The Parliament Within: A Study of Anthony Trollope's Palliser Novels*. Ph.D. diss., Princeton University, 1976.

Baucom, Ian. *Out of Place: Englishness, Empire, and the Locations of Identity*. Princeton: Princeton University Press, 1999.

———. *Specters of the Atlantic: Finance Capital, Slavery, and the Philosophy of History*. Durham: Duke University Press, 2005.

Bell, Millicent. "James, the Audience of the Nineties, and *The Spoils of Poynton*." *Henry James Review* 20.3 (1999): 217–26.

Bentley, Nancy. *The Ethnography of Manners: Hawthorne, James, Wharton*. Cambridge: Cambridge University Press, 1993.

Berg, Maxine. *The Machinery Question and the Making of Political Economy, 1815–1848*. Cambridge: Cambridge University Press, 1980.

Bersani, Leo. *A Future for Astyanax: Character and Desire in Literature*. Boston: Little Brown, 1969.

Bingham, Caroline. *The History of Royal Holloway College, 1886–1986*. London: Constable, 1987.

Blair, Sara. "'Preparation for Culture': Anthony Trollope, the American *Century*, and the Fiction of Freedom." In *Henry James and the Writing of Race and Nation*. Cambridge: Cambridge University Press, 1996. 60–89.

Bledstein, Burton J. *The Culture of Professionalism: The Middle Class and the Development of Higher Education*. New York: Norton, 1976.

Bodenheimer, Rosemarie. *The Politics of Story in Victorian Social Fiction*. Ithaca: Cornell University Press, 1988.

Bourdieu, Pierre. *Distinction: A Social Critique of the Judgment of Taste*. Trans. Richard Nice. Cambridge, MA: Harvard University Press, 1984.

———. *Outline of a Theory of Practice*. Trans. Richard Nice. Cambridge: Cambridge University Press, 1977.

Brantlinger, Patrick. *The Spirit of Reform: British Literature and Politics, 1832–1867*. Cambridge, MA: Harvard University Press, 1977.

Brenkman, John. *Straight Male Modern: A Cultural Critique of Psychoanalysis*. New York: Routledge, 1993.

Briggs, Asa. "Trollope, Bagehot, and the English Constitution." *Cambridge Journal* (1951–52): 327–38.

Brontë, Anne. *The Tenant of Wildfeld Hall.* Ed. Stevie Davies. London: Penguin, 1996.

Brontë, Charlotte. *Shirley.* Ed. Jessica Cox. London: Penguin, 2006.

Brooks, Peter. *Henry James Goes to Paris.* Princeton: Princeton University Press, 2007.

Brown, Bill. *A Sense of Things: The Object Matter of American Literature.* Chicago: University of Chicago Press, 2003.

———, ed. *Things.* Chicago: University of Chicago Press, 2004.

Brown, Vivienne. "Dialogism, the Gaze, and the Emergence of Economic Discourse." *New Literary History* 28.4 (1997): 697–710.

Brydges, Egerton. *The Autobiography, Times, Opinions, and Contemporaries of Sir Egerton Brydges.* 2 vols. London: Cochrane and M'Crone, 1834.

Butler, Marilyn. *Jane Austen and the War of Ideas.* London: Clarendon, 1975.

Cameron, Sharon. *Thinking in Henry James.* Chicago: University of Chicago Press, 1989.

Campbell, Colin. *The Romantic Ethic and the Spirit of Modern Consumerism.* London: Blackwell, 1987.

Cannadine, David. *The Decline and Fall of the Aristocracy.* New Haven: Yale University Press, 1990.

Carlyle, Thomas. *Chartism.* New York: Wiley and Putnam, 1847.

———. "Occasional Discourse on the Negro Question." 1849. *Collected Works of Thomas Carlyle.* Ed. H. D. Traill. Vol. 29. London: Chapman, 1899. 348–83.

Carroll, Kathleen. *Lady Frances Waldegrave: Political Hostess at Strawberry Hill, 1856–1879.* Twickenham, UK: Twickenham Local History Society, 1998.

Cecil, David. *Jane Austen.* Cambridge: Cambridge University Press, 1935.

Cheah, Peng. "The Cosmopolitical—Today." In *Cosmopolitics: Thinking and Feeling beyond the Nation.* Ed. Peng Cheah and Bruce Robbins. Minneapolis: University of Minnesota Press, 1998. 20–41.

Cheyette, Bryan. *Constructions of "the Jew" in English Literature and Society, 1875–1945.* Cambridge: Cambridge University Press, 1992.

Childers, Joseph. "*Nicholas Nickleby's* Problem of *Doux Commerce.*" *Dickens Studies Annual: Essays in Victorian Fiction* 25 (1996): 49–65.

Chorley, Henry Fothergill. "*The Vicar of Wrexhill.*" *London and Westminster Review,* 28 Oct. 1837, 112–31.

Christensen, Jerome. *Practicing Enlightenment: Hume and the Formation of a Literary Career.* Madison: University of Wisconsin Press, 1987.

Cleere, Eileen. *Avuncularism: Capitalism, Patriarchy, and Nineteenth-Century English Culture.* Stanford: Stanford University Press, 2004.

———. "Reinvesting Nieces: *Mansfield Park* and the Economics of Endogamy." *Novel* 28.2 (1995): 113–20.

Cohen, Deborah. *Household Gods: The British and Their Possessions.* New Haven: Yale University Press, 2006.

Cohen, Monica J. *Professional Domesticity in the Victorian Novel: Women, Work and Home.* Cambridge: Cambridge University Press, 1999.

Cohen, William A. "Trollope's Trollop." In *Sexscandal: The Private Parts of Victorian Fiction.* Durham: Duke University Press, 1996. 159–90.

Colby, Robert, and Vineta Colby. *The Equivocal Virtue: Mrs. Oliphant and the Victorian Literary Marketplace.* Hamden, CT: Archon Books, 1968.

Colella, Silvana. "Intimations of Mortality: The Malthusian Plot in Early Nineteenth-Century Popular Fiction." *Nineteenth-Century Contexts* 24.1 (2002): 17–32.

Collini, Stefan. *Public Moralists: Political Thought and Intellectual Life in Britain, 1850–1930.* Oxford: Clarendon, 1991.

Colquhuon, Patrick. *A Treatise on the Wealth, Power, and Resources of the British Empire.* London: Mawman, 1814.

Combe, Andrew. *The Physiology of Digestion Considered with Relation to the Principles of Dietetics.* Boston: Marsh, Capen and Lyon, 1836.

Combe, George. *The Constitution of Man Considered in Relation to External Objects.* Boston: William D. Ticknor, 1838.

Connell, Philip. *Romanticism, Economics and the Question of "Culture."* Oxford: Oxford University Press, 2001.

Coovadia, Imraan. "George Eliot's Realism and Adam Smith." *Studies in English Literature* 42.4 (2002): 819–35.

Copeland, Edward. *Women Writing about Money: Women's Fiction in England, 1790–1820.* Cambridge: Cambridge University Press, 1995.

Corbett, Mary Jean. *Allegories of Union in Irish and English Writing, 1790–1870.* Cambridge: Cambridge University Press, 2000.

———. "'Cousins in Love, &c.' in Jane Austen." *Tulsa Studies in Women's Literature* 23.2 (2004): 237–59.

———. *Family Likeness: Sex, Marriage, and Incest from Jane Austen to Virginia Woolf.* Ithaca: Cornell University Press, 2008.

———. "'Two Identities': Gender, Ethnicity, and Phineas Finn." In Markwick et al., 117–30.

Cotugno, Clare. "'Stay Away from Paris!': Frances Trollope Rewrites America," *Victorian Periodicals Review* 38.2 (2005): 240–57.

D'Albertis, Deirdre. "The Domestic Drone: Margaret Oliphant and a Political History of the Novel." *Studies in English Literature* 37 (1997): 805–29.

Dames, Nicholas. *Amnesiac Selves: Nostalgia, Forgetting, and British Fiction, 1810–1870.* Oxford: Oxford University Press, 2001.

———. "Trollope and the Career: Vocational Trajectories and the Management of Ambition." *Victorian Studies* 45.3 (2003): 247–78.

Darwin, Charles. *Descent of Man and Selection in Relation to Sex.* New York: Barnes and Noble Books, 2004.

Davidoff, Leonore. *The Best Circles: Women and Society in Victorian England.* Totowa, NJ: Rowman and Littlefield, 1973.

Delany, Paul. *Literature, Money and the Market: From Trollope to Amis.* London: Palgrave Macmillan, 2002.

Deleuze, Gilles, and Félix Guattari. *Anti-Oedipus: Capitalism and Schizophrenia.* Minneapolis: University of Minnesota Press, 1986.

Derrida, Jacques. "Structure, Sign, and Play in the Discourse of the Human Sciences." In *Writing and Difference.* Chicago: University of Chicago Press, 1978. 278–93.

Despotopoulou, Anna. "Fanny's Gaze and the Construction of Feminine Space in *Mansfield Park.*" *Modern Language Review* 99 (2004): 569–83.

Dolin, Tim. *Mistress of the House: Women of Property in the Victorian Novel.* Farnham, UK: Ashgate, 1997.

Dougherty, Jane Elizabeth. "An Angel in the House: The Act of Union and Anthony Trollope's Irish Hero." *Victorian Literature and Culture* 32.1 (2004): 133–45.

Douglas, Ann. *The Feminization of American Culture*. New York: Knopf, 1977.

Dowling, Linda. *The Vulgarization of Art: The Victorians and Aesthetic Democracy*. Charlottesville: University Press of Virginia, 1996.

du Maurier, Daphne. *Rebecca*. New York: Avon, 1971.

Dupuy, Jean-Pierre. "A Reconsideration of *Das Adam Smith Problem*." *Stanford French Review* 17 (1993): 45–57.

Durkheim, Emile. *The Division of Labor in Society*. New York: Free Press, 1984.

Elias, Norbert. "On Human Beings and Their Emotions: A Process-Sociological Essay." In Featherstone et al., 103–25.

Eliot George. *Daniel Deronda*. London: Penguin, 2003.

Elliott, John. *Palaces, Patronage and Pills: Thomas Holloway: His Sanatorium, College and Picture Gallery*. London: Royal Holloway, University of London, 1996.

Emsley, Sara Baxter. *Jane Austen's Philosophy of the Virtues*. London: Palgrave Macmillan, 2005.

Engels, Friedrich. *The Origin of the Family, Private Property and the State*. Harmondsworth, UK: Penguin, 1985.

Featherstone, Mike. "The Body in Consumer Culture." In *The Consumption Reader*. Ed. David B. Clarke, Marcus A. Doel, and Kate M. J. Housiaux. New York: Routledge, 2003. 163–67.

Featherstone, Mike, Mike Hepworth, and Bryan S. Turner, eds. *The Body: Social Process and Cultural Theory*. London: Sage, 1991.

Felski, Rita. *The Gender of Modernity*. Cambridge, MA: Harvard University Press, 1995.

Fitzgerald, Penelope. *The Afterlife*. New York: Counterpoint, 2003.

Foote, Stephanie. "Henry James and the Parvenus: Reading Taste in *The Spoils of Poynton*." *Henry James Review* 27.1 (2006): 42–60.

Forrester, John. *Truth Games: Lies, Money, and Psychoanalysis*. Cambridge, MA: Harvard University Press, 1998.

Fraiman, Susan. "Jane Austen and Edward Said: Gender, Culture and Imperialism." *Critical Inquiry* 21.4 (1995): 805–21.

Frazee, Monique Parent. *Mrs. Trollope and America*. Caen: Faculté des lettres et sciences humaines de l'Université de Caen, 1969.

Freedgood, Eileen. *The Ideas in Things: Fugitive Meaning in the Victorian Novel*. Chicago: University of Chicago Press, 2000.

Freedman, Jonathan. *Professions of Taste: Henry James, British Aestheticism, and Commodity Culture*. Stanford: Stanford University Press, 1990.

———. *The Temple of Culture: Assimilation and Anti-Semitism in Literary Anglo-America*. Oxford: Oxford University Press, 2000.

Freud, Sigmund. *Dora: An Analysis of a Case of Hysteria*. New York: Collier, 1963.

Gagnier, Regenia. "Gender, Liberalism, and Resentment." In Markwick et al., 235–48.

———. *Idylls of the Marketplace: Oscar Wilde and the Victorian Public*. Stanford: Stanford University Press, 1986.

———. *The Insatiability of Human Wants: Economics and Aesthetics in Market Society*. Chicago: University of Chicago Press, 2000.

Gallagher, Catherine. *The Body Economic: Life, Death, and Sensation in Political Economy and the Victorian Novel*. Princeton: Princeton University Press, 2005.

Gard, Roger, ed. *Henry James: The Critical Heritage*. London: Routledge and Kegan Paul, 1968.

Gargano, James W. *Critical Essays on Henry James: The Late Novels*. Boston: G. K. Hall, 1987.

Gaskell, Peter. *Artisans and Machinery*. New York: Augustus M. Kelley, 1968.

Giddens, Anthony. *The Consequences of Modernity*. Stanford: Stanford University Press, 1990.

Gigante, Denise. *Taste: A Literary History*. New Haven: Yale University Press, 2005.

Goodlad, Lauren M. E. *Victorian Literature and the Victorian State: Character and Governance in Liberal Society*. Baltimore: Johns Hopkins University Press, 2000.

Goux, Jean-Joseph. *Symbolic Economies: After Marx and Freud*. Trans. Jennifer Curtiss Gage. Ithaca: Cornell University Press, 1990.

Graff, Ann-Barbara. "'Fair, Fat, and Forty': Social Redress and Fanny Trollope's Literary Activism." In Ayres, 53–70.

Green, Katherine Sobba. *The Courtship Novel, 1740–1820: A Feminized Genre*. Lexington: University of Kentucky Press, 1991.

Greenblatt, Stephen. *Renaissance Self-Fashioning: From More to Shakespeare*. Chicago: University of Chicago Press, 1980.

Greiner, Rae. "Sympathetic Realism and the Nineteenth-Century Novel." Manuscript.

Guillory, John. *Cultural Capital: The Problem of Literary Canon Formation*. Chicago: University of Chicago Press, 1993.

Hadley, Elaine. "'On a Darkling Plain': Victorian Liberalism and the Fantasy of Agency." *Victorian Studies* 48.1 (2005): 92–102.

———. "The Past Is a Foreign Country: The Neo-Conservative Romance with Victorian Liberalism." *Yale Journal of Criticism* 10.1 (1997): 7–38.

Hager, Kelley. *Dickens and the Rise of Divorce: The Failed-Marriage Plot and the Novel Tradition*. Farnham, UK: Ashgate, 2010.

Halperin, John. *Trollope and Politics: A Study of the Pallisers and Others*. New York: Barnes and Noble Books, 1977.

Hardy, Thomas. *Far from the Madding Crowd*. New York: Barnes and Noble, 2005.

"*Hargrave; or, The Adventures of a Man of Fashion*." *Athenaeum*, 8 Apr. 1843, 333–34.

Harrison-Barbet, Anthony. *Thomas Holloway: Victorian Philanthropist*. London: Royal Holloway, University of London, 1994.

Harsh, Constance. "Putting Idiosyncrasy in Its Place: *Michael Armstrong* in Light of Trollope's Early Fiction." In Ayres, 119–36.

Harth, Erica. "The Virtue of Love: Lord Hardwicke's Marriage Act." *Cultural Critique* 9 (1988): 123–54.

Hazlitt, William. "On Fashion." In *Selected Writings*. Oxford: Oxford University Press, 1991. 148–54.

Heath, Kay. "Marriageable at Midlife: The Remarrying Widows of France Trollope and Anthony Trollope." In Ayres, 85–102.

Heineman, Helen. *Mrs. Trollope: The Triumphant Feminine in the Nineteenth Century*. Athens: Ohio University Press, 1979.

Hensley, Nathan K. "Mister Trollope, Lady Credit, and *The Way We Live Now*." In Markwick et al., 147–60.

Herbert, Christopher. *Culture and Anomie: Ethnographic Imagination in the Nineteenth Century*. Chicago: University of Chicago Press, 1991.

———. "Filthy Lucre: Victorian Ideas about Money."*Victorian Studies* 44.2 (2002): 185–213.

Hewett, Osbert Wyndham, ed. *"And Mr. Fortescue": A Selection from the Diaries from 1851 to 1862 of Chichester Fortescue, Lord Carlingford, K. P.* London: John Murray, 1958.

———. *Strawberry Fair: A Biography of Frances, Countess Waldegrave, 1821–1879.* London: John Murray, 1956.

Hilton, Boyd. *The Age of Atonement: The Influence of Evangelicalism on Social and Economic Thought.* Oxford: Clarendon, 1988.

———. *A Mad, Bad, and Dangerous People?* Oxford: Clarendon, 2006.

Hirschman, Albert O. *The Passions and the Interests: Political Arguments for Capitalism before Its Triumph.* Princeton: Princeton University Press, 1997.

Holland, Lawrence Bedwell. *The Expense of Vision: Essays on the Craft of Henry James.* Princeton: Princeton University Press, 1964.

Holway, Tatiana. "The Game of Speculation: Economics and Representation." *Dickens Quarterly* 9.3 (1992): 103–14.

Hont, Istvan, and Michael Ignatieff. *Wealth and Virtue: The Shaping of Political Economy in the Scottish Enlightenment.* Cambridge: Cambridge University Press, 1983.

Hume, David. *Selected Essays.* Ed. Stephen Copley and Andrew Edgar. Oxford: Oxford University Press, 1993.

Irving, Edward. *The Last Days: A Discourse on the Evil Character of These Our Last Times Proving Them to Be the "Perilous Times" of the Last Days.* London: James Nisbet, 1850.

Jaffe, Audrey. *Scenes of Sympathy: Identity and Representation in Victorian Fiction.* Ithaca: Cornell University Press, 2000.

———. "Trollope in the Stock Market: Irrational Exuberance and *The Prime Minister.*" *Victorian Studies* 45.1 (2002): 43–64.

James, Henry. *The Complete Notebooks of Henry James.* Ed. Leon Edel and Lyall H. Powers. Oxford: Oxford University Press, 1987.

———. *The Golden Bowl.* New York: Barnes and Noble Books, 2000.

———. *The Portrait of a Lady.* New York: Bantam Books, 1983.

———. Preface. *The Golden Bowl.* New York: Scribner's, 1937. v–xxv.

———. Preface to the New York edition. *The Wings of the Dove.* New York: Norton, 1978. 3–16.

———. *The Spoils of Poynton.* Ed. Bernard Richards. Oxford: Oxford University Press, 2000.

———. *The Wings of the Dove.* New York: Signet, 1999.

James, William. "The Progress of Anthropology." *The Nation,* 6 Feb. 1868, 113–15.

Jameson, Fredric. "Culture and Finance Capital." *Critical Inquiry* 24.1 (1997): 246–65.

———. *The Political Unconscious: Narrative as a Socially Symbolic Act.* Ithaca: Cornell University Press, 1981.

"Jane Austen." *St. Paul's Magazine,* Mar. 1870, 631–43. Rptd. in Southam, 226–40.

Jevons, William Stanley. "John Stuart Mill's Philosophy Tested." Part 4. *Contemporary Review,* Nov. 1879, 521–38.

———. *The Theory of Political Economy.* London: Macmillan, 1888.

Jones, Wendy. *Consensual Fictions: Women, Liberalism, and the Novel.* Toronto: University of Toronto Press, 2005.

Joshi, Priti. "*Michael Armstrong:* Rereading the Industrial Plot." In Ayres, 35–51.

Kay-Shuttleworth, James. *The Moral and Physical Condition of the Working Classes Employed in the Cotton Manufacture in Manchester.* New York: Augustus M. Kelley, 1970.

Kelleher, Paul. "'The Glorious Lust of Doing Good': *Tom Jones* and the Virtues of Sexuality." *Novel* 38.2–3 (2005): 165–92.

Kent, Christopher. "'Real Solemn History' and Social History." *Jane Austen in a Social Context.* Ed. David Monaghan. London: Macmillan, 1980. 86–104.

Keynes, John Maynard. *Essays in Biography.* London: Macmillan, 1933.

Kissel, Susan S. *In Common Cause: The "Conservative" Frances Trollope and the "Radical" Frances Wright.* Bowling Green: Bowling Green State University Press, 1993.

Knox-Shaw, Peter. *Jane Austen and the Enlightenment.* Cambridge: Cambridge University Press, 2004.

Kristeva, Julia. *Powers of Horror: An Essay in Abjection.* New York: Columbia University Press, 1982.

Kucich, John. *The Power of Lies: Transgression in Victorian Fiction.* Ithaca: Cornell University Press, 1994.

Kuper, Adam. "Fraternity and Endogamy: The House of Rothschild." *Social Anthropology* 9 (2001): 273–87.

Lacan, Jacques. "The Neurotic's Individual Myth." *Psychoanalytic Quarterly* 48.3 (1979): 386–425.

Lamb, Charles. "Grace before Meat." In *Selected Prose.* New York: Appleton, 1912. 129–39.

Langbauer, Laurie. *Novels of Everyday Life: The Series in English Fiction, 1850–1930.* Ithaca: Cornell University Press, 1999.

Langland, Elizabeth. *Nobody's Angels: Middle-Class Women and Domestic Ideology in Victorian Culture.* Ithaca: Cornell University Press, 1995.

Laqueur, Thomas W. "Sex and Desire in the Industrial Revolution." In *The Industrial Revolution and British Society.* Ed. Patrick O'Brien and Roland Quinault. Cambridge: Cambridge University Press, 1993. 100–123.

———. *Solitary Sex: A Cultural History of Masturbation.* New York: Zone Books, 2003.

Larson, Magali Sarfatti. *The Rise of Professionalism: A Sociological Analysis.* Berkeley: University of California Press, 1977.

Lasch, Christopher. "The Suppression of Clandestine Marriage in England: The Marriage Act of 1753." *Salmagundi* 26 (1974): 90–109.

Leavis, F. R. Introduction. *Mill on Bentham and Coleridge.* New York: Harper and Brothers, 1950. 1–38.

Leavis, Q. D. *Collected Essays.* 3 vols. Cambridge: Cambridge University Press, 1983.

Lévi-Strauss, Claude. *The Elementary Structures of Kinship.* Boston: Beacon Press, 1969.

"*The Life and Adventures of Michael Armstrong, the Factory Boy.*" *Athenaeum*, 10 Aug. 1839, 587–90.

Linder, Christopher. "Trollope's Material Girl." *Yearbook of English Studies* 22 (2002): 30–54.

Ling, Amy. "The Pagoda Image in Henry James's *The Golden Bowl.*" *American Literature* 46.3 (1974): 383–88.

Litvak, Joseph. "Jewish Geographies: Trollope and the Question of Style." In *Nine-*

teenth-Century Geographies: The Transformation of Space in the Victorian Age and the American Century. Ed. Helena Michie and Ronald R. Thomas. New Brunswick: Rutgers University Press, 2002. 123–37.

———. *Strange Gourmets: Sophistication, Theory, and the Novel*. Durham: Duke University Press, 1997.

Lonergan, Patrick. "The Representation of Phineas Finn: Anthony Trollope's Palliser Series and Victorian Ireland." *Victorian Literature and Culture* 32.1 (2004): 147–58.

Lubbock, Jules. *The Tyranny of Taste: The Politics of Architecture and Design in Britain, 1550–1960*. New Haven: Yale University Press, 1995.

Lukács, Georg. *History and Class Consciousness*. Cambridge, MA: MIT Press, 1971.

Lynch, Deidre Shauna. *The Economy of Character: Novels, Market Culture, and the Business of Inner Meaning*. Chicago: University of Chicago Press, 1998.

MacIntyre, Alasdair C. *After Virtue: A Study in Moral History*. South Bend: University of Notre Dame Press, 1987.

Maine, Sir Henry Sumner. *Lectures on the Early Histories of Institutions*. London: John Murray, 1905.

Malthus, Thomas Robert. *An Essay on the Principle of Population*. Ed. Donald Winch. Cambridge: Cambridge University Press, 1992.

———. *An Essay on the Principle of Population*. Ed. Philip Appleman. New York: Norton, 2004.

Marcus, Sharon. *Between Women: Friendship, Desire, and Marriage in Victorian England*. Princeton: Princeton University Press, 2007.

Markwick, Margaret, Deborah Denenholz Morse, and Regenia Gagnier, eds. *The Politics of Gender in Anthony Trollope's Novels: New Readings for the Twenty-First Century*. Farnham, UK: Ashgate, 2009.

Martin, Michael R. "Branding Milly Theale: The Capital Case of *The Wings of the Dove*." *Henry James Review* 24.2 (2003): 103–32.

Marx, Karl. *Karl Marx: Selected Writings*. Ed. David McLellan. Oxford: Oxford University Press, 1977.

Mathias, Peter. *The First Industrial Nation: An Economic History of Britain, 1700–1914*. London: Methuen, 1969.

McGann, Tara. "Literary Realism in the Wake of Business Cycle Theory: *The Way We Live Now*." In *Victorian Literature and Finance*. Ed. Frances O'Gorman. Oxford: Oxford University Press, 2007. 133–56.

McKendrick, Neil. "The Consumer Revolution of Eighteenth-Century England." In *The Birth of a Consumer Society: The Commercialization of Eighteenth-Century England*. Ed. Neil McKendrick, John Brewer, and J. H. Plumb. Bloomington: Indiana University Press, 1982. 9–33.

———. "Josiah Wedgwood and the Commercialization of the Potteries." In *The Birth of a Consumer Society: The Commercialization of Eighteenth-Century England*. Ed. Neil McKendrick, John Brewer, and J. H. Plumb. Bloomington: Indiana University Press, 1982. 99–144.

McKeon, Michael. *The Secret History of Domesticity: Public, Private, and the Division of Knowledge*. Baltimore: Johns Hopkins University Press, 2006.

McLennan, John. *Primitive Marriage: An Inquiry into the Form of Capture in Marriage Ceremonies*. Chicago: University of Chicago Press, 1970.

Meissner, Collin. "'What Ghosts Will Be Left to Walk': Mercantile Culture and the Language of Art." *Henry James Review* 21.3 (2000): 242–52.

Mennell, Stephen. "On the Civilizing of Appetite." In Featherstone et al., 126–56.

Merish, Lori. *Sentimental Materialism: Gender, Commodity Culture, and Nineteenth-Century American Literature.* Durham: Duke University Press, 2000.

Michaels, Walter Benn. "Romance and Real Estate." *Raritan* 2.3 (1983): 66–87.

Michie, Elsie B. "Buying Brains: Trollope, Oliphant, and Vulgar Victorian Commerce." *Victorian Studies* 44.1 (2001): 77–97.

———. "The Odd Couple: Anthony Trollope and Henry James." *Henry James Review* 27.1 (2006): 10–23.

———. "Rich Woman / Poor Woman: Toward an Anthropology of the Nineteenth-Century Marriage Plot." *PMLA* 124.2 (2009): 421–36.

———. "A Woman of Money: Miss Dunstable and Vulgar Victorian Commerce." In Markwick et al., 161–76.

Mill, John Stuart. *Autobiography.* Ed. John M. Robson. London: Penguin, 1989.

———. "Bain's Psychology." In *Collected Works of John Stuart Mill.* Ed. J. M. Robson. Vol. 11. Toronto: University of Toronto and Routledge and Kegan Paul, 1978. 341–73.

———. *Dissertations and Discussions.* London: G. M. Routledge, 1905.

———. *On Liberty* and *The Subjection of Women.* Ed. Alan Ryan. London: Penguin, 2006.

Mill, John Stuart, and Jeremy Bentham. *Utilitarianism and Other Essays.* Ed. Alan Ryan. London: Penguin, 2004.

Miller, Andrew H. *Novels behind Glass: Commodity Culture and Victorian Narrative.* Cambridge: Cambridge University Press, 1995.

Miller, D. A. *Jane Austen; or, The Secret of Style.* Princeton: Princeton University Press, 2003.

———. "The Late Jane Austen." *Raritan* 10.1 (1990): 55–79.

Miller, J. Hillis. *The Ethics of Reading: Kant, de Man, Eliot, Trollope, James, and Benjamin.* New York: Columbia University Press, 1986.

———. *Literature as Conduct: Speech Acts in Henry James.* New York: Fordham University Press, 2005.

Miller, William Ian. *The Anatomy of Disgust.* Cambridge, MA: Harvard University Press, 1997.

Mirowski, Philip. *More Heat Than Light: Economics as Social Physics, Physics as Nature's Economics.* Cambridge: Cambridge University Press, 1989.

Mizruchi, Susan L. *The Science of Sacrifice: American Literature and Modern Social Theory.* Princeton: Princeton University Press, 1998.

"Modern English Novels." *Dublin Review,* Aug./Nov. 1839, 225–49.

Monaghan, David. *Jane Austen: Structure and Social Vision.* London: Macmillan, 1980.

Moretti, Franco. *Atlas of the European Novel, 1800–1900.* London: Verso, 1998.

———. *The Way of the World: The Bildungsroman in European Culture.* London: Verso, 1987.

Morgan, Lewis H. *Ancient Society.* Boston: Belknap Press of Harvard University Press, 1964.

Morley, John. *Critical Miscellanies.* 4 vols. London: Macmillan, 1892–93.

Mouton, Michelle J. "Margaret Oliphant and John Stuart Mill: Disinterested Politics and the 1865 General Election." *Dickens Studies Annual* 35 (2005): 209–40.

Mukerji, Chandra. *From Graven Images: Patterns of Modern Materialism.* New York: Columbia University Press, 1983.

Mullan, John. *Sentiment and Sociability: The Language of Feeling in the Eighteenth Century.* Oxford: Clarendon, 1988.

Neville-Sington, Pamela. *Fanny Trollope: The Life and Adventures of a Clever Woman.* New York: Viking, 1998.

———. "Jane Austen and the Trollopes." *Persuasions: The Jane Austen Journal* 20 (1998): 44–49.

Newman, John Henry. "The Danger of Riches." In *The Works of Cardinal Newman in Eight Volumes. Parochial and Plain Sermons.* Vol. 2. London: Longman, Green, 1902. 343–57.

Ngai, Sianne. *Ugly Feelings.* Cambridge, MA: Harvard University Press, 2005.

Nunokawa, Jeff. *The Afterlife of Property: Domestic Security and the Victorian Novel.* Princeton: Princeton University Press, 1996.

Oliphant, Laurence. "The Autobiography of a Joint-Stock Company (Limited)." *Blackwood's Edinburgh Magazine*, July 1876, 96–122.

Oliphant, Margaret. "The Doctor's Family" In *The Doctor's Family and Other Stories.* Ed. Merryn Williams. Oxford: Oxford University Press, 1986. 67–205.

———. "The Executor." *The Doctor's Family and Other Stories.* Ed. Merryn Williams. Oxford: Oxford University Press, 1986. 1–33.

———. "The Great Unrepresented." *Blackwood's Edinburgh Magazine*, Sept. 1866, 367–79.

———. *Hester.* Ed. Philip Davis and Brian Nellist. Oxford: Oxford University Press, 2003.

———. *Kirsteen: The Story of a Scotch Family Seventy Years Ago.* London: Dent, 1984.

———. "The Land of Darkness." In *A Beleaguered City and Other Stories.* Ed. Merryn Williams. Oxford: Oxford University Press, 1988. 232–85.

———. "Miss Austen and Miss Mitford." *Blackwood's Edinburgh Magazine*, Mar. 1870, 294–305. Rptd. in Southam, 215–25.

———. *Miss Marjoribanks.* Ed. Elisabeth Jay. London: Penguin, 1998.

———. "Old Lady Mary." In *A Beleaguered City and Other Stories.* Ed. Merryn Williams. Oxford: Oxford University Press, 1988. 163–229.

———. *Phoebe Junior: A Last Chronicle of Carlingford.* Ed. Elizabeth Langland. Peterborough, ON: Broadview, 2002.

———. "The Subjection of Women." *Edinburgh Review*, Oct. 1869, 572–602.

O'Mealy, Joseph H. "Rewriting Trollope and Yonge: Mrs. Oliphant's *Phoebe Junior* and the Realism Wars." *Texas Studies in Literature and Language* 39.2 (1997): 125–38.

Orel, Harold. *Victorian Literary Critics.* London: Macmillan, 1984.

Otten, Thomas. "Slashing Henry James (On Painting and Political Economy, circa 1900)." *Yale Journal of Criticism* 13.2 (2000): 293–320.

———. *A Superficial Reading of Henry James: Preoccupations with the Material World.* Columbus: Ohio State University Press, 2006.

Parker, Patricia A. *Literary Fat Ladies: Rhetoric, Gender, Property.* London: Methuen, 1987.

Perkin, Harold. *Origins of Modern English Society.* London: Routledge, 1972.

———. *The Rise of Professional Society: England since 1880.* London: Routledge, 1989.

Perry, Ruth. *Novel Relations: The Transformation of Kinship in English Literature and Culture, 1748–1818.* Cambridge: Cambridge University Press, 2004.

Peyser, Thomas. *Utopia and Cosmopolis: Globalization in the Era of American Literary Realism.* Durham: Duke University Press, 1998.

Phillipson, Nicholas. "Adam Smith as Civic Moralist." In Hont and Ignatieff, 179–202.

"*Phoebe Junior.*" *Athenaeum,* 24 June 1876, 851–52.

"*Phoebe Junior.*" *Pall Mall Gazette,* 5 July 1876, 12.

"*Phoebe Junior.*" *Saturday Review,* 22 July 1876, 112–13.

"*Phoebe Junior.*" *Spectator,* 17 June 1876, 769–70.

Pinch, Adela. *Strange Fits of Passion: Epistemologies of Emotion, Hume to Austen.* Stanford: Stanford University Press, 1996.

Plotz, John. *Portable Property: Victorian Culture on the Move.* Princeton: Princeton University Press, 2008.

Pocock, J. G. A. *Virtue, Commerce, and History: Essays in Political Thought and History, Chiefly in the Eighteenth Century.* Cambridge: Cambridge University Press, 1983.

Poe, Edgar Allan, "The Purloined Letter." In *The Portable Edgar Allan Poe.* Ed. J. Gerald Kennedy. New York: Penguin, 2006. 327–44.

Polanyi, Karl. *The Great Transformation.* New York: Farrar and Rinehart, 1944.

Pollak, Ellen. *Incest and the English Novel, 1684–1814.* Baltimore: Johns Hopkins University Press, 2003.

Poovey, Mary. "Aesthetics and Political Economy in the Eighteenth Century: The Place of Gender in the Social Constitution of Knowledge." In *Aesthetics and Ideology.* Ed. George Levine. New Brunswick: Rutgers University Press, 1994. 79–105.

———. *Genres of the Credit Economy: Mediating Value in Eighteenth- and Nineteenth-Century Britain.* Chicago: University of Chicago Press, 2008.

———. *Making a Social Body: British Cultural Formation, 1830–1864.* Chicago: University of Chicago Press, 1995.

Porter, Carolyn. *Seeing and Being: The Plight of the Participant Observer in Emerson, James, Adams, and Faulkner.* Middletown: Wesleyan University Press, 1981.

Posnock, Ross. *The Trial of Curiosity: Henry James, William James, and the Challenge of Modernity.* New York: Oxford University Press, 1991.

Psomiades, Kathy. "Heterosexual Exchange and Other Victorian Fictions: *The Eustace Diamonds* and Victorian Anthropology." *Novel* 33.1 (1999): 93–118.

Ragussis, Michael. *Figures of Conversion: "The Jewish Question" and English National Identity.* Durham: Duke University Press, 1995.

Rahv, Philip. "The Heiress of All the Ages." *Partisan Review* 10.3 (1943): 227–47.

Randall, Margaret. *The Price You Pay: The Hidden Cost of Women's Relation to Money.* New York: Routledge, 1990.

Raphael, David D., and Alec L. Macfie. Introduction. In Adam Smith, *The Theory of Moral Sentiments.* Oxford: Clarendon, 1976. 1–52.

Reed, J. R. "A Friend to Mammon: Speculation in Victorian Literature." *Victorian Studies* 27.2 (1984): 179–202.

Reynolds, K. D. *Aristocratic Women and Political Society in Victorian Britain.* Oxford: Clarendon Press, 1993.

Richards, Thomas. *The Commodity Culture of Victorian England: Advertising and Spectacle, 1851–1914.* Stanford: Stanford University Press, 1990.

Rintoul, M. C. *A Dictionary of Real People and Places in Fiction*. London: Routledge, 1993.

Robbins, Bruce. *Secular Vocations: Intellectuals, Professionalism, Culture*. London: Verso, 1990.

Rubin, Gayle, "The Traffic in Women: Notes on the 'Political Economy' of Sex." In *Toward an Anthropology of Women*. Ed. Rayna Reiter. New York: Monthly Review Press, 1975. 157–210.

Rubinstein, W. D. *Capitalism, Culture, and Decline in Britain, 1750–1990*. London: Routledge, 1993.

———. *Men of Property: The Very Wealthy in Britain since the Industrial Revolution*. New Brunswick: Rutgers University Press, 1981.

Ruderman, Anne. *The Pleasures of Virtue: Political Thought in the Novels of Austen*. Lanham, MD: Rowman and Littlefield, 1998.

Ruskin, John. *The Seven Lamps of Architecture*. New York: Wiley and Halsted, 1857.

———. "Traffic." In *Unto This Last and Other Writings*. Harmondsworth, UK: Penguin, 1997. 233–49.

Ruth, Jennifer. *Novel Professions: Interested Disinterest and the Making of the Professional in the Victorian Novel*. Columbus: Ohio State University Press, 2006.

Rylance, Rick. *Victorian Psychology and British Culture, 1850–1880*. Oxford: Oxford University Press, 2000.

Sadleir, Michael. *Trollope: A Commentary*. New York: Farrar, Straus and Company, 1947.

Said, Edward. *Culture and Imperialism*. New York: Knopf, 1993.

Schabas, Margaret. "Victorian Economics and the Science of the Mind." In *Victorian Science in Context*. Ed. Bernard Lightman. Chicago: Chicago University Press, 1997. 72–93.

Schaub, Melissa. "Queen of the Air or Constitutional Monarch? Idealism, Irony, and Narrative Power in *Miss Marjoribanks*." *Nineteenth-Century Literature* 55.2 (2000): 195–225.

Schneider, David Murray. *A Critique of the Study of Kinship*. Ann Arbor: University of Michigan Press, 1989.

Sedgwick, Eve. *Between Men: English Literature and Male Homosocial Desire*. New York: Columbia University Press, 1985.

———. "Jane Austen and the Masturbating Girl." *Critical Inquiry* 17 (1991): 818–37.

Seltzer, Mark. "Physical Capital: The Romance of the Market in Machine Culture." In *Bodies and Machines*. London: Routledge, 1992. 47–90.

Shairp, J. C. "Moral Theories and Christian Ethics." *North British Review*, Sept. 1867, 1–46.

Shelley, Percy Bysshe. *Shelley's Poetry and Prose*. Ed. Donald H. Reiman and Neil Fraistat. New York: Norton, 2002.

Simmel, Georg. "Adornment." In Simmel, *Simmel on Culture*, 206–11.

———. "Fashion." *American Journal of Sociology* 62.6 (1957): 541–58.

———. *The Philosophy of Money*. Trans. Tom Bottomore and David Frisby. London: Routledge and Kegan Paul, 1978.

———. "The Problem of Style." In Simmel, *Simmel on Culture*, 211–17.

———. *Simmel on Culture: Selected Writings*. Ed. David Frisby and Mike Featherstone. London: Sage, 1997.

Simpson, Richard. "*A Memoir of Jane Austen.*" *North British Review*, Apr. 1870, 129–52. Rptd. in Southam, 241–65.

———. "The Morals and Politics of Materialism." *Rambler* 6 (1856): 445–54.

Smalley, Donald, ed. *Anthony Trollope: The Critical Heritage.* London: Routledge and Kegan Paul, 1969.

Smith, Adam. *The Theory of Moral Sentiments.* Ed. David D. Raphael and Alec L. Macfie. Oxford: Clarendon, 1976.

———. *The Wealth of Nations.* 2 vols. London: Dent, 1957.

Smith, Barbara Herrnstein. *Contingencies of Value: Alternate Perspectives for Critical Theory.* Cambridge, MA: Harvard University Press, 1988.

Smollett, Tobias. *Humphry Clinker.* London: Penguin, 1985.

Southam, B. C. *Jane Austen: The Critical Heritage.* 2 vols. London: Routledge and Kegan Paul, 1987.

Southey, Robert. "On the State of the Poor, the Principle of Mr. Malthus's Essay on Population, and the Manufacturing System." In *Essays Moral and Political.* Vol. 1. London: John Murray, 1832. 73–155.

Spencer, Herbert. *The Evolution of Society: Selections from Herbert Spencer's Principles of Sociology.* Ed. Robert L. Carneiro. Chicago: University of Chicago Press, 1967.

———. *The Principles of Sociology.* 3 vols. New York: Applegate, 1910.

"*The Spoils of Poynton*: Fine Spun Work." *New York Times*, 20 Feb. 1897, 1. Rptd. in Gargano 29–30.

Spring, David. "Interpreters of Jane Austen: Literary Critics and Historians." In *Jane Austen: New Perspectives.* Ed. Janet Todd. New York: Homes and Meier, 1983. 53–72.

Stocking, George. *Victorian Anthropology.* New York: Free Press, 1987.

Teichgraeber, Richard F. *"Free Trade" and Moral Philosophy: Rethinking the Sources of Adam Smith's* Wealth of Nations. Durham: Duke University Press, 1986.

Thackeray, William Makepeace. "Our Batch of Novels for Christmas, 1837." *Fraser's Magazine*, Jan. 1838, 79–85.

Thompson, F. M. L. "Business and Landed Elites in the Nineteenth Century." In *Landowners, Capitalists, and Entrepreneurs: Essays for Sir John Habakkuk.* Oxford: Clarendon, 1994. 139–70.

———. *English Landed Society in the Nineteenth Century.* London: Routledge, 1963.

Thompson, James. *Between Self and World: The Novels of Jane Austen.* University Park: Pennsylvania State University Press, 1988.

———. *Models of Value: Eighteenth-Century Political Economy and the Novel.* Durham: Duke University Press, 1996.

Todorov, Tsvetan. "Living Alone Together." *New Literary History* 27.1 (1996): 1–14.

Trilling, Lionel. "Manners, Morals, and the Novel." In *The Liberal Imagination: Essays on Literature and Society.* New York: Charles Scribner's and Sons, 1976. 205–22.

Trollope, Anthony. *An Autobiography.* Ed. Michael Sadleir and Frederick Page. Oxford: Oxford University Press, 1992.

———. *Can You Forgive Her?* Ed. Stephen Wall. Harmondsworth: Penguin, 1972.

———. *Doctor Thorne.* Harmondsworth: Penguin, 1991.

———. *The Duke's Children.* Oxford: Oxford University Press, 1977.

———. *The Eustace Diamonds.* Oxford: Oxford University Press, 1977.

———. *Framley Parsonage.* Ed. David Skilton and Peter Miles. London: Penguin, 1986.

———. *The Last Chronicle of Barset*. Ed. Stephen Gill. Oxford: Oxford University Press, 1980.

———. *Phineas Finn*. Oxford: Oxford University Press, 1977.

———. *Phineas Redux*. Oxford: Oxford University Press, 1977.

———. *The Prime Minister*. Ed. Jennifer Uglow. New York: Oxford University Press, 1983.

———. *The Small House at Allington*. London: Penguin, 1993.

———. *The Struggles of Brown, Jones, and Robinson*. Ed. N. John Hall. Oxford: Oxford University Press, 1992.

Trollope, Frances. *Domestic Manners of the Americans*. Ed. Pamela Neville-Sington. London: Penguin, 1997.

———. *Jessie Phillips: A Tale of the Present Day*. London: Henry Colburn, 1844.

———. *The Life and Adventures of a Clever Woman: With Occasional Extracts from Her Diary*. London: Hurst and Blackett, 1854.

———. *The Life and Adventures of Michael Armstrong, the Factory Boy*. London: Henry Colburn, 1840.

———. *The Three Cousins*. Phoenix Mill: Sutton Publishing, 1997.

———. *The Ward of Thorpe-Combe*. 3 vols. London: Richard Bentley, 1842.

———. *The Widow Barnaby*. London: Richard Bentley, 1840.

Trollope, Thomas Adolphus. *What I Remember*. New York: Harper and Brothers, 1888.

Trotter, David. *Cooking with Mud: The Idea of Mess in Nineteenth-Century Art and Fiction*. Oxford: Oxford University Press, 2000.

Trumbach, Randolph. *The Rise of the Egalitarian Family: Aristocratic Kinship and Domestic Relations in Eighteenth-Century England*. New York: Academic Press, 1978.

Trumpener, Katie. *Bardic Nationalism: The Romantic Novel and the British Empire*. Princeton: Princeton University Press, 1997.

Tuite, Clara. *Romantic Austen: Sexual Politics and the Literary Canon*. Cambridge: Cambridge University Press, 2002.

Tulloch, John. *Movements of Religious Thought in Britain during the Nineteenth Century*. New York: Charles Scribner's Sons, 1886.

Twain, Mark. *Life on the Mississippi*. New York: Heritage Press, 1944.

Vernon, John. *Money and Fiction: Literary Realism in the Nineteenth and Early Twentieth Centuries*. Ithaca: Cornell University Press, 1984.

"*The Vicar of Wrexhill*." *The Literary Examiner* (Oct. 1837): 628–29.

"*The Vicar of Wrexhill*." *The London and Westminster Review* 28 (Oct. 1837): 112–31.

"*The Vicar of Wrexhill*." *Times* 25 Oct. 1837, 2.

"The Victorians and the Pill." *Sunday Times Magazine*, 18 February 1968, 43–44.

Wahrman, Dror. *Imagining the Middle Class: The Political Representation of Class in Britain, c. 1780–1840*. Cambridge: Cambridge University Press, 1993.

Weber, Max. "Class, Status, Party." In *From Max Weber: Essays in Sociology*. Oxford: Oxford University Press, 1958. 180–95.

———. *The Protestant Ethic and the Spirit of Capitalism*. New York: Routledge, 1992.

Wharton, Edith. *A Backward Glance: An Autobiography*. New York: Appleton-Century, 1934.

"*The Widow Barnaby*." *Athenaeum* 584 (1839): 9–10.

"*The Widow Barnaby*." *Times*, 24 Jan. 1839, 5.

Wiener, Martin J. *English Culture and the Decline of the Industrial Spirit, 1850–1980.* Cambridge: Cambridge University Press, 1982.

Williams, Raymond. *The Country and the City.* New York: Oxford University Press, 1975.

———. *Culture and Society, 1780–1850.* New York: Columbia University Press, 1983.

Winch, Donald. *Riches and Poverty: An Intellectual History of Political Economy in Britain 1750–1834.* Cambridge: Cambridge University Press, 1996.

"*The Wings of the Dove*: Society as Organized Cannibalism." *Spectator*, 4 Oct. 1902, 498–99. Rptd. in Gargano, 26–27.

Woloch, Alex. *The One vs. the Many: Minor Characters and the Space of the Protagonist in the Novel.* Princeton: Princeton University Press, 2003.

Woolf, Virginia. *Three Guineas.* New York: Harcourt, Brace, 1938.

Worringer, Wilhelm. *Abstraction and Empathy: A Contribution to the Psychology of Style.* Chicago: Ivan R. Dee, 1997.

Yeazell, Ruth Bernard. "The Boundaries of *Mansfield Park.*" *Representations* 7 (1984): 133–52.

Žižek, Slavoj. *The Sublime Object of Ideology.* London: Verso, 1989.

———. *Tarrying with the Negative: Kant, Hegel, and the Critique of Ideology.* Durham: Duke University Press, 1993.

Zlotnick, Susan. *Women, Writing, and the Industrial Revolution.* Baltimore: Johns Hopkins University Press, 1998.

Trollope, Frances Milton, 1, 14–15, 21–22, 23, 24, 64, 65–102, 103, 105, 108, 110, 138–39, 197, 221, 222; appetite and, 65–70, 73–80, 83–87, 95–96, 228n.47, 238n.5, 239n.6, 244n.49; Protestant ethic and, 71, 88–92, 95–96, 240n.15, 240n.16; saving and, 67, 72–73, 83–84, 90–91, 240n.17, 241n.22 (see also spending). Works: *The Barnabys in America; or, The Adventures of the Widow* Wedded, 239n.12; *Domestic Manners of the Americans*, 65, 68, 101; *Hargrave; or, The Adventures of a Man of* Fashion, 245n.51; Jessie *Phillips: A Tale of the Present* Day, 239n.7, 241n.23; The *Life and Adventures of a Clever Woman. Illustrated with Occasional Extracts from her Diary*, 1, 23, 68, 71, 87, 88–97, 101–2, 239n.12, 239n.14, 243n.38, 245n.50, 245n.54; *The Life and Adventures of Michael Armstrong, the Factory Boy*, 14–15, 22, 101, 243n.41; *The Lottery of Marriage*, 245n.51; *One* Fault, 239n.7; *The Three* Cousins, 239n.9; *The Vicar of Wrexhill*, 68, 99–101, 241n.23, 242n.31; *The Ward of Thorpe Combe*, 23, 68, 70–71, 74–75, 79–88, 93–97, 100, 239n.12, 239n.14, 243n.36, 245n.54, 245n.55, 246n.56; *The Widow Barnaby*, 23–24, 66, 68–81, 83–84, 86–87, 93–96, 99, 100, 197, 239n.12, 239n.13, 239n.14, 240n.21, 241n.25, 242n.32, 242n.33, 243n.35, 243n.38, 245n.54, 245n.55, 246n.57; *The Widow Married*, 239n.12

Trollope, Thomas Adolphus, 98–99, 246n.59

Trotter, David, 65

Trumbach, Randolph, 225n.27

Trump, Donald, xi

Trumpener, Katie, 233n.34, 233n.35, 254n.50

Tuite, Clara, 223n.1

Tulloch, John, 143–44, 257n.4, 257n.5, 257n.6, 258n.7, 260n.24

Twain, Mark, 101

Tylor, Edward, 119

unworldly, 80, 87, 92, 170, 266n.65. *See also* worldliness

utilitarian, 94, 144, 169, 237n.67, 239n.10, 244n.45, 245n.55, 257n.5, 261n.28

"Utilitarianism." *See* Mill, John Stuart

Vaughan, Genevieve, 273n.43

The Vicar of Wrexhill. See Trollope, Frances Milton

Villette. See Brontë, Charlotte

vulgarity, 5, 66, 98, 125, 137–40, 142, 169, 175, 192, 196–97, 199, 203, 211, 214, 221, 223n.6, 246n.58, 252n.41, 256n.67; Bourdieu on, xii–xiii, 2–3, 98–102, 221, 271n.30; class and, x, 51, 69, 74–75, 78, 112, 127–28, 132, 140, 165, 173–74, 177, 252n.38, 265n.55, 266n.71; distinction and, x, 2–3, 26, 100, 102, 187; money and, ix–x, xiii, 1, 3, 5, 8, 41, 63, 66, 68–69, 78, 97–98, 114, 119, 127–29, 131–32, 136, 138, 140–41, 148, 165, 169–70, 182, 185–58, 198, 203, 208, 314, 217–18, 220, 222, 223n.7, 241n.22, 270n.19, 272n.34, 273n.45; rich women and, xi–xiii, 1–2, 4–5, 23–24, 63, 68–70, 72–74, 76, 78–79, 86–88, 98, 125–29, 131–32, 134, 137, 139–40, 169, 182, 189, 191, 193, 197–98, 208, 223n.6, 232n.30, 242n.33. *See also* engrossment; materialism

Wahrman, Dror, 46, 224n.9

Waldegrave, Lady Frances (née Braham), 123–27, 134–38, 141, 169, 175, 250n.30, 251n.33, 251n.36, 252n.37, 254n.55, 255n.57, 255n.60, 256n.63

The Warden. See Trollope, Anthony

The Ward of Thorpe Combe. See Trollope, Frances Milton

Waterloo, Battle of, 85, 87

The Way We Live Now. See Trollope, Anthony

The Wealth of Nations. See Smith, Adam

Webb, Beatrice, 110, 247n.4

Weber, Max, x, 71, 88, 90–92, 96, 112, 127–28, 132, 240n.16, 240n.19, 244n.44; *The Protestant Ethic and the Spirit of Capitalism*, x, 71, 244n.44

Wedgwood, 36, 166

Wehner, Julius, 110

Wharton, Edith, 209

The Widow Barnaby. See Trollope, Frances Milton

The Widow Married. See Trollope, Frances Milton

Wiener, Martin, 104, 106, 133, 228n.49